BOOK
AND
DAGGER

ALSO BY ELYSE GRAHAM

You Talkin' to Me?

A Unified Theory of Cats on the Internet

The Republic of Games

BOOK

AND

DAGGER

HOW SCHOLARS AND LIBRARIANS BECAME THE UNLIKELY SPIES OF WORLD WAR II

ELYSE GRAHAM

ecco

An Imprint of HarperCollins*Publishers*

HarperCollins books may be purchased for educational, business, or sales promotional use. For information, please email the Special Markets Department at SPsales@harpercollins.com.

Ecco® and HarperCollins® are trademarks of HarperCollins Publishers.

FIRST EDITION

Designed by Alison Bloomer

Library of Congress Cataloging-in-Publication Data

Names: Graham, Elyse, 1985- author.
Title: Book and dagger: how scholars and librarians became the unlikely
    spies of World War II / Elyse Graham.
Identifiers: LCCN 2024013142 | ISBN 9780063280847 (hardcover) | ISBN
    9780063280861 (ebook)
Subjects: LCSH: United States. Office of Strategic Services--Officials and
    employees--Biography. | Spies--Recruiting--United States--History--20th
    century. | World War, 1939–1945--Secret service--United States. | World
    War, 1939–1945--Secret service--Europe. | Espionage,
    American--History--20th century. | College teachers--United
    States--Biography. | Librarians--United States--Biography. | Curtiss,
    Joseph T., 1901-1992. | Kibre, Adele. | Kent, Sherman
Classification: LCC D810.S7 G68 2024 | DDC 940.54/8673--
    dc23/eng/20240418
LC record available at https://lccn.loc.gov/2024013142

24 25 26 27 28 LBC 5 4 3 2 1

To Catherine, for listening

Then, Baldock, you must cast the scholar off,
And learn to court it like a gentleman. . . .
You must be proud, bold, pleasant, resolute,
And now and then stab, as occasion serves.
—CHRISTOPHER MARLOWE, *EDWARD THE SECOND*

What if all those PhDs stop just defending and
actually start attacking?!?
—WOLFGANG VIECHTBAUER

CONTENTS

INTRODUCTION

In the late summer of 1941, Mr. Roosevelt called me to Washington and asked me to draft a plan for a new intelligence service cut to fit a global war. "You will have to begin with nothing," he said, in effect. "We have no intelligence service."
—General William Donovan[1]

ONE DAY IN AUGUST 1942, JOSEPH CURTISS, A YOUNG PRO-fessor of English at Yale, received a visit from Wallace Notestein, the head of his department. Curtiss lived in a faculty apartment in a residential college at the school: a book-lined suite surrounded by moody corridors and Gothic stone towers. This, a more private space than his office, is where Notestein came for a talk.

It was an unusual occurrence. Notestein was a silver-haired eminence who awed faculty into respectful silence when he spoke during meetings, and the holder of a Sterling professorship, the highest honor that Yale gives to professors. Such a discreet visit may well have made Curtiss nervous, since it might mean that the department felt his work wasn't up to par. Perhaps Notestein would shake his head, indicate that Curtiss wasn't among the junior faculty members the department wished to encourage, and murmur that it was time for Curtiss to move on.

But Notestein didn't do that.

Instead, he shut the windows, looked around to make sure the room was safe from possible eavesdroppers, and then asked Curtiss to visit the Yale Club in New York City the next day. Curtiss must wear "a blue suit and a purple tie." He would see a man sitting in the lounge who would light, then quickly put out, a cigarette; this man had a proposition for him.

Curtiss agreed. He could hardly turn down a Sterling professor's request, and besides—what a strange set of instructions; there was only one way to find out fully what they meant. The trip to New York and back would take a full day, and Curtiss was busy teaching classes in an emergency summer term that Yale had set up so that students could graduate as quickly as possible and join the fight against Hitler.

The Yale Club in midtown Manhattan is a stern limestone tower that, if you can get through the door, greets visitors with discreetly spaced tables and high art-deco ceilings that drown the noise of conversation in a meaningless hum: very ornate, very private. The man Curtiss met there had a lined and sun-hardened face that gave him the look of someone in his forties—a decade older than his true age. His name was Donald Downes. He explained that he worked for the Office of Strategic Services, the new intelligence service that President Franklin Roosevelt created on America's entry into the war. The OSS had concocted a plan for the Yale Library to serve as a cover for a secret agent: a Yale professor would go abroad ostensibly to acquire books for the library, but actually to gather intelligence. The OSS needed a real Yale professor, in part because the cover would need to be performed as competently as the spycraft. Was Curtiss willing to do the job?

He was.

TINKER, TAILOR, SCHOLAR, SPY

The story that follows is not going to sound like it really happened, but it did. The OSS—the predecessor to today's Central Intelligence Agency—really did recruit Joseph Curtiss to become a secret agent in a dangerous undercover mission abroad. It was a mission that required his knowledge (and love) of books, just as a fighter pilot's mission requires a knowledge of planes. And the OSS recruited hundreds of others like him: mild-mannered professors and oddball archivists and restless librarians. Because America had no standing intelligence agency at the start of the war and needed to build up an instant bank of expertise on every subject in the library, the OSS simply raided the library for recruits. These bookish types were pulled into the "cloak-and-dagger brigade" and trained, in the words of one contemporary, "in all the black arts of mystery, deception and mayhem."[2]

Their adventures took them—and the saboteurs, swindlers, and human smugglers they found themselves suddenly collaborating with—to the covered bazaars of Istanbul. A legation in Stockholm. A salt mine in Austria. A seedy café in Marseilles. A deception training camp outside of Los Angeles that might as well have been a studio lot. A power plant hidden in the snowy mountains of Norway that the Nazis were using in a scheme to develop a secret weapon.

But above all, their adventures took them through the world of books.

At the start of the war, the United States was utterly outmatched by every other country in terms of intelligence experience. For centuries, the rest of the world had been playing the game of spycraft. The English sent poets in doublets and ruffs to spy on rival courts. The French court of Louis XIV maintained a paper database of reports from throughout the empire that was so meticulous it would make an Excel specialist weep. The Japanese developed, over centuries, tactics of spycraft in the secret world of the ninja that informed their spy school in Nakano during World War II. The Germans had spies on their own streets; after all, they ran a police state.[3]

In July 1941, President Roosevelt appointed a man named William Donovan to take charge of starting up a new intelligence service. Donovan was a lawyer by training. He had been a war hero during World War I, and in 1940, a Warner Brothers film about his heroics appeared in theaters, portraying Donovan as a natural leader, someone of high ideals and authoritative command. (*The Fighting 69th*, starring James Cagney. George Brent portrayed Donovan.[4]) Perhaps the film influenced Roosevelt's decision. Whatever the case, appointing Donovan to lead the new service—which was called the Office of the Coordinator of Information (COI) before changing its name, in June 1942, to the Office of Strategic Services (OSS)—was a decision that had a profound effect on the war.

There was no way that Donovan and his crew could catch up with their intelligence rivals in terms of experience. So instead, they re-invented intelligence. They looked around for an intelligence resource that the other players in the war were underestimating, and they found an answer that would not only turn the war around, but also reshape the global system of espionage: scholars, and the wonders they could work in the world of books and paper.

The very first branch that Donovan built in his new intelligence agency was called Research and Analysis (R&A).[5] It represented something new in the world of spycraft. The Research and Development branch of the OSS, which employed researchers in the applied sciences—chemistry, engineering, fields that prepared one to build weapons and spy gear—was a long-established type of institution in other countries. But R&A, which pulled researchers from university departments in the humanities and social sciences, had no equivalent in other spy agencies.

Donovan sought out these humble drudges of the archive, as no spymaster had done before, because Donovan was accustomed, as a law-yer, to reading the literature before he made decisions—to studying and gathering insights from all the information in print.[6] His R&A agents did this—and more. The historians, philologists, psychologists, econo-mists, and other humanists of R&A examined materials that ranged from ordinary books to classified documents, trash, enemy newspapers, phone books, railway rate schedules, and "Aunt Min photos," or vaca-tion photos from ordinary Americans that showed a loved one ("Aunt Min") waving cheerfully in front of some building in Europe that the OSS wanted to burgle or demolish.[7] Working first in the Annex Build-ing of the Library of Congress, the branch ultimately grew to more than nine hundred members, located in bases across the United States and Europe.[8] Agents called R&A the "Chairborne Division"—but as we will see, R&A's work depended on, and produced, hair-raising adventures in the field.

And so: imagine, please, the world of bookshelves, the smell of old paper, and the sense of expectation that haunts any labyrinth of texts—as if, just by wandering among the stacks, you might chance upon a secret that has eluded everyone else. As magical as it is, this is a world that we often think of as a kind of back room: a place to read about history, not a place where history happens. But it is, and it was. The war may have been fought on battlefields, but it was won in libraries.

PAPER PLANES

The Nazis didn't entirely grasp how books would be used as weapons against them. But they knew that books were dangerous to their cause. Books remind us of the brutal follies of tyrants, big and small. They teach us that knowledge is an ongoing process, not a fixed set of givens. They show us the remarkable variety of humanity: how wonderfully different people were and are from each other, despite our persistent efforts to cram each other into the boxes of familiar categories.

But more than that, a book is—to quote the poet John Milton—a human spirit treasured up for a life beyond life. If the Nazis were to succeed in utterly wiping a people from the Earth, they would have to destroy their books as well. Which is why, as the librarian Richard Ovenden later said, "The persecution of the Jews of Europe under the Nazi regime fell with terrifying force not just on the People of the Book (as Jews have self-identified for thousands of years) but also on their books."[9]

Over the course of the Holocaust, the Nazis demolished more than one hundred million books, scholars estimate.[10] On May 10, 1933, crowds of students gathered outside German universities and piled together Jewish books to make bonfires. The event was reportedly a bit of a farce, since books don't actually burn very well; the fires took an embarrassingly long time to get going and, afterward, books were retrieved from the piles barely charred.[11] But people around the world recognized the threat for what it was, and they protested vehemently against the conflagration. Helen Keller, whose books were in the bonfires because her disabilities refuted the Nazi ideal of physical perfection, wrote an open letter to the students of Germany: "You can burn my books and the books of the best minds in Europe, but the ideas in them have seeped through a million channels and will continue to quicken other minds."[12]

But the fire continued to spread. Already, German students, carrying guns and wearing Nazi insignia, were raiding public and university libraries and removing "un-German literature," tens of thousands of books at a time. The police helped.[13] As Germany annexed Austria and then started to seize more territory across Europe, the Nazis extended their purge to private libraries, state libraries, bookstores, and religious houses. (A prominent Nazi librarian called unpurged libraries "literary bordellos.")[14]

The Jewish poet Heinrich Heine was right to say, "Those who burn books will, in the end, burn people." In 1933, Hitler gave the order to burn books. In 1941, he gave the order to burn people.

POWER FROM BELOW

This book is, in part, a lesson in the ability of ordinary people to make great changes. Even to help win wars. The will of Hitler's victims and opponents to fight back, even when their weapons were as frail as paper, is indisputable, and they performed remarkable feats using the materials available to them, whether they fought from an Allied place of refuge or Occupied Europe.

We can find a small but mighty expression of that will—to choose one of countless examples—in the Lithuanian city of Vilna, where the Nazis ordered a group of scholars in the Jewish ghetto to sort through the books in the city's synagogues and Jewish libraries, identify the most valuable books—which the Nazis would keep as treasure—and leave the rest to be pulped. Inhabitants of the ghetto gave this group the nickname "the Paper Brigade." Recognizing that the Nazis saw bibliocide as integral to their genocide, the scholars smuggled books home to the ghetto, concealing the bulk under their shirts and trousers. By the fall of 1943, Ovenden writes, "thousands of printed books, and tens of thousands of manuscript documents, made their way back to the

Vilna Ghetto thanks to the astonishing, risky, and dangerous biblio-smuggling of the Paper Brigade."[15]

The Paper Brigade not only put their lives on the line to rescue as many books as they could, but also kept many of those books in an underground bunker that their fellow prisoners used to store weapons for the ghetto resistance. They smuggled other books to underground schools. Still others they stole for tactical purposes: for example, a book that gave instructions for making Molotov cocktails.[16]

The victory that the Allies achieved in World War II wouldn't have been possible without the heroic work of refugees and *résistants*, like those in the Paper Brigade. The scholars who worked for the OSS included a huge number of refugees from Hitler's Europe, and both the OSS and the Allies at large relied on underground agents to do things that whole fleets of bomber planes could not. Donovan's new intelligence service understood what Hitler never did: the power of power from below.

This book is also a lesson in innovation. Not just the innovation of *résistants* who fought back by using cleverness to counter strength, by making use of the very fact that they were easy to overlook—but, more especially, the innovation of scholars who, having suddenly and astonishingly become intelligence agents, found they could help the war effort in crucial and unsuspected ways.

The experience of being an outsider can lead to extraordinary achievements, but merely being an outsider in a field isn't enough. The library rats of the OSS were able to do brilliant work in intelligence because they had expertise in fields that their enemy counterparts didn't. They approached problems differently. They saw military intel in newspaper society columns, maps to unfamiliar cities in phone books, potentially devastating enemy vulnerabilities in humble items like ball bearings. They turned out to be excellent at what intelligence actually entails: innovation.

In other words, Donovan's agency didn't gain an unexpected advantage just by throwing outsiders at the problem; they gained that advantage by realizing the value of experts in the arts, the social sciences, and the humanities.* Expertise in these fields entailed expertise in working with messy data, hunting down evidence in unsuspected places, and, above all, finding clues in the types of papers that others overlooked. And Donovan's agency welcomed refugees from Europe—many of whom were also experts in those fields, and all of whom were determined to fight back against Hitler and win—to contribute to the cause.

Finally, this is a book about the power of stories. During the war, books were weapons, and it was through books that stories often found their way into the target's hands. But a story could travel in other ways, from lips to ears, and burrow into hearts and minds. Stories were the gunpowder and the flame.

Compelling stories were at the center of many of the Allies' most successful operations. The Battle of Normandy relied on using actors and theater workers to tell a story that placed the central arena of the fight hundreds of miles from where it really was. And the most famous deception operation of the war, the British-run Operation Mincemeat, convinced the Germans to believe in a coincidence that was, on its face, ridiculous, simply because it was a compelling story. Members of the counterespionage unit of the OSS, which Joseph Curtiss eventually joined, learned the tricks of contriving compelling stories that enemy civilians *wanted* to spread. On the grand scale, stories helped win this war.

On a smaller scale, stories helped its fighters too. Many of the people in this book, having no intelligence experience, only had stories *about* spies to guide their earliest forays into spycraft. They watched Hollywood movies or they read spy novels. Some of these agents used spy stories to their advantage: to give themselves courage, for instance, or to persuade a witness to forget what he just saw. Others got caught up in the mystique of the role: they made everyone play parts in their

---

* Scholars who study expertise say that experts and novices—whether in the fields of chess, physics, or anything else—behave differently when they tackle the same problems. Experts work faster, because they can more easily see the common patterns of different problems, which gives them useful experience in areas that might, at first glance, seem unrelated. They know how to work directly with the data, in contrast to novices, who impose the goal upon the data. While working on problems, they tend to focus on core principles, while novices often focus on superficial details and therefore get distracted by irrelevancies. Fernand Gober, *Understanding Expertise: A Multi-Disciplinary Approach* (New York: Palgrave, 2016), 73–74.

spy movie, and in the process, revealed to everyone that they were a spy. Even on the most humble, day-to-day level, the stories that spies used for their covers were judged so important that they often gave up weapons so they could cloak themselves with more plausible fictions.

Today, in the story we tell ourselves about the war, the library rats have been forgotten. It suited the United States to make physicists the heroes of the war, for reasons that we shall see. To be sure, the physicists of the Manhattan Project did astonishing and frightening work: in the words of one onlooker, they played with materials that God never invited into nature. But the idea that the Manhattan Project was solely a triumph of physicists was itself the very last strike in the war: a misinformation campaign designed to draw the attention of America's enemies away from the actual tactics that brought America to victory, so that those enemies couldn't replicate them.

That misinformation campaign worked so well that it's the story that Americans tell themselves about the war even still. But now, more than ever, we need to recover this hidden history.

In the United States, fascism is on the rise. Libraries are under attack. Some pundits ask why universities bother with departments that don't just teach students to write computer code. Violent bigotry is fashionable again, and for many people, the appeal of politics is the opportunity to impose cruelty on others. The admonition to remember has never seemed so important.

Almost eight decades have passed since the end of the war. It's time, at last, for this story to be told. It's time to remember the scholars and bookworms who helped to win the war, and who fought to give future generations a better world than the one they lived in.

PAPER TRAILS

Researching this story took me all over the world. I visited the Old Book Bazaar in Istanbul, rare-book dealers in Stockholm, the British Library, the Library of Congress, the New York Public Library, and university archives from Ann Arbor to Austin to New Haven to Princeton. I tasted, against my tour guide's advice, the clay underfoot in a salt mine in Austria (it tasted like salt) and peered in the windows of a condemned building where the Allies once interrogated high-ranking Nazis. I filed Freedom of Information Act requests and received, in return, packages from the CIA, which I hope made me look very mysterious to my mail carrier. I regret having learned such intimate details as the fact that Carleton Coon, the anthropologist and racist whose career in the OSS appears in later chapters, had folliculitis of the buttocks, but nothing is irrelevant to the dedicated researcher. Call it a warts-and-all history.

I also spoke with intelligence experts. Some of the former intelligence officers who talked with me declined to let me print their names, on the rationale that "something can be known, but it doesn't have to be shouted." (Meaning: it's possible to find out they have intelligence connections, but they don't want to make it easy.) The rest appear in the acknowledgments section. My heartfelt thanks go to everyone who shared their time and expertise over the course of this project.

For the sake of continuity, I have included occasional imagined scenes in this book, which are always clearly indicated. The historical record often neglects certain kinds of stories. For example, in the Library of Congress, OSS veterans helped to catalogue the OSS records; this was a good service to history, but they often catalogued the names of men and not the names of women. In memoirs that men wrote about the war years, the names of women are, likewise, often absent—they're "a shapely analyst," say, or "a woman from Harvard." I'm grateful to have a way to fill in the stories of figures who, despite their importance, don't receive their due space in the archives.

And I'm grateful to have a way to ask, now and then, what details might have been lost in the gaps in the historical record. As a historian, I sometimes think about that purple tie—the tie that Joseph Curtiss's visitor asked him to wear to the Yale Club, the tie that would signal him as the right man for his mysterious contact to approach. Because what the hell, who has a purple tie?

I imagine Curtiss closing his front door after his visitor left, murmuring to himself, "A blue suit and a purple tie," and then startling and saying, louder, *"A purple tie?"* I imagine him running over to J. Press, a gentleman's clothier across the street from his apartment in Yale's Jonathan Edwards College, and quietly asking the salesman whether they had any purple ties. Of course, they wouldn't have any. I imagine him visiting colleagues at their homes on some flimsy pretext—returning borrowed books, say—and, while there, asking to use the toilet, ducking into their bedrooms, and paging desperately through their necktie collections. No purple ties there either. And I imagine him, as evening purples the sky above him, running to a grocery store—not much time left—and buying, let's say, grape gelatin powder or dehydrated grape juice. At home, he mixes the powder with water in a glass, stirs one of his nice J. Press neckties into the purple mixture, and then lays out the necktie to dry overnight.

None of this is in the historical record. But we tell stories in the interstices of the facts that history leaves to us.

BOOK
AND
DAGGER

THE SPY WHO CAME IN FROM THE CARREL

THE CALL TO ADVENTURE CAME IN LIBRARIES, IN FACULTY offices, at campus football games. Few of those called were remotely prepared for this moment. So far, the genre of their lives had been the campus novel: dreaming gray spires; velvet nights on the quad; dark library corridors; the rustling whisper of rare-books rooms; scholars laundering gossip into the historical record by writing books with juicy hints; scholars furiously extracting that gossip from the record by visiting the library regularly to misshelve the offending book so readers can't find it; grudges; betrayal; rivalries; discoveries; generations of students sprouting, growing, scattering; treetops turning to gold, tan, and red.

To those with a certain taste—a taste for creature comforts and drawing-room dramas—this can be the whole world. Intrigue doesn't need to be globe spanning; stories don't need to occupy a large frame. But the thing about stories is that you don't always get to choose the one you're in.

The year following the attack on Pearl Harbor, which came on December 7, 1941, was a year of painful reality checks for America. The country, which had done its best to ignore many of the stories unfolding in Europe—stories about strongmen ascending to power and Nazi student demonstrations and German companies investing in arms production, not to mention the Blitz in Britain and Germany's outright invasion of its neighbors—was now pulled into a world war.[1]

Pearl Harbor was an intelligence failure of devastating magnitude. The most alarming part was that America had no intelligence infrastructure to prevent such an event from happening again. The country had stopped collecting intelligence in any comprehensive sense in 1929, after Henry Stimson, the secretary of state, ordered the closure of a key federal office dedicated to deciphering the messages of foreign powers. "Gentlemen do not read each other's mail," he said.[2] World War I, then called "the War to End All Wars," was long over, and perhaps the hope was that gentlemanly cordiality would be the rule from then on.

Suddenly at war again, and urgently in need of gifted minds, the U.S. government called upon campuses to supply fighters in the shadow war of espionage. And so it was that the nation's professors were plucked from their campus novels and thrown into history's greatest spy thriller.

THE MAN WITH A RED CARNATION

On October 19, 1942, Joseph Curtiss, the mild-mannered English professor from Yale, stepped aboard a train to Baltimore. He knew that he was about to start training at a school for spies. He was told to look out for a man with a red carnation in his buttonhole, but the details beyond that were a mystery to him.

He didn't carry luggage; personal belongings would link him to an identity he was about to shed. Soon Joseph Curtiss would, at least for a while, cease to exist.

When he disembarked in the Baltimore train station—huge, shadowy, filled with Doric columns that a dozen trenchcoated spies might lurk behind—he spotted the man with a red carnation in his buttonhole. Curtiss thought the red carnation business was a bit too much like a pulp paperback. What's next: Swooning heiresses? Martinis laced with poison? Dead men with clues in their pockets? Then again, though Curtiss didn't know it, the people training him might have been getting their ideas from spy fiction. His instructors were new at undercover work, just as he was.[3]

Three other men emerged from the crowd and moved toward the man with a red carnation. Curtiss would have company. No chance to make introductions though; they had all been told in advance that students at the spy school must never talk about their real lives. They weren't even allowed to mention their names.

After a puzzled moment where an introduction should be, the four nameless men followed the man with a red carnation to a car idling outside. They traveled in silence for more than an hour. Perhaps Curtiss peered at the sun through the window and figured out that he was heading west.[4]

THE OWL OF MINERVA

The classics reading room at the University of Chicago was a quiet, eerie space, with high chandeliers throwing dim light suitable for Minerva's owl on readers who sat apart at private desks: "A stern, austere, dignified reading room," the campus newspaper said at the time, "where women in tailored suits answer to the greeting, 'Vale Augusta.'"[5] Elsewhere on campus, students schlepped around in saddle shoes and slouchy sweaters, but the women of the classics department preferred clothes that set a different tone, something a little more "I just arrived from the British Library and how dare you speak to me while I'm working": fitted jackets, tweed skirts, swish and smart.[6]

The library had installed a telephone in the reading room so that people could call and ask the classics librarians questions ("What's the past tense of *ad lib.*?") or get in touch with scholars who were in the room working.[7] But convenient as the reading room phone was, it wasn't exactly a private line. Everyone likes to listen to whispers in the library.

Adele Kibre—dark-haired, wicked-eyed, a classicist by training—might have been in the reading room when a telephone call came for her from Washington. Let's imagine that scene.

"Adele, is that you?"

"Yes. May I ask—"

"Wait. Not a word. This is Eugene Power calling from Washington, D.C. Sorry I haven't been in touch, but the boys have me running in circles with government work. I take it there are other people in the room with you?"

"Yes, of course."

"Hang up and find another telephone to call me back from—a telephone someplace where nobody can listen in on the conversation. My number is National 5399. I promise I'll explain everything. If you understand, thank me and say you're stepping out to meet me for lunch."

"Thank you so much, Ernest. I'd be delighted to meet you for lunch. I'll see you outside the library."

"Aces every time, Adele! Talk to you soon."

Eugene Power ran a company that made microfilm copies of texts for university libraries.[8] He knew Kibre from the Vatican archives, where, in 1939, the two crossed paths while hunting down rare texts. The Vatican archives are famously difficult to navigate: twenty-five miles of shelves hidden out of view without a remotely complete catalogue, you can only ask to see items you already know are there, and when you ask, often the answer is simply "no." The best stuff is buried under a tangle of bureaucratic paper shuffling as baroque as the Vatican's gilded statues of the angelic host guarding the entrance to heaven.*

Kibre, who held a PhD in Latin from the University of Chicago, impressed Power with her nimbleness in that world. She was, in a word, *resourceful*. When they met, she had spent almost a decade hopping from archive to archive across Europe, earning cash by taking photographs of rare texts for scholars back home in the States, who did not have, in those days before the internet, any other way of seeing such texts besides visiting the archives themselves. (One of her clients was the Yale Library.)[9] Power hired her to find and photograph texts for his microfilm company, and soon found that with Kibre on the job, no text was unobtainable.[10]

---

*   And the best stuff is breathtaking: love letters from Henry VIII to Anne Boleyn; manuscripts that date to the lifetime of Christ; Bibles written in letters of real gold; a grimoire, or book of black magic, allegedly written by the Devil himself; court documents attesting to crimes by the Knights Templar, a Church-funded army that fought the Crusades in the twelfth and thirteenth centuries; records from Vatican meetings to vote on whether to canonize people as saints—meetings during which a so-called "devil's advocate" would present, as a sort of opposing attorney, damning details about the would-be saint.

In 1940, for instance, when Kibre asked to see an "especially rare" manuscript in the Vatican archives, an attendant "was horrified," read a Los Angeles newspaper at the time. "He explained that only a certain cardinal could grant such permission. Miss Kibre immediately asked to see the cardinal. This horrified the attendant even more." Unfazed, Kibre, the daughter of movie-set designers, sent a tempting card of introduction up to His Eminence: "Miss Adele Kibre—Hollywood, California."[11]

A moment later, the attendant came down. The cardinal had sent for her, saying, "So you are from Hollywood! Come, let's talk."

Kibre's career in the archive world depended on charming men who considered themselves clever. That day in the Vatican in 1940, she amused the cardinal with an hour and a half of gossip about studio intrigue. (He asked whether it was true, as he had heard, that Hollywood is surrounded, like Vatican City, with a great wall. Her answer isn't recorded, but one likes to think it was something cheeky, like "Yes, that's why it's so hard to break into the film industry.") Ultimately, Kibre got the blessing she needed to see the manuscript.[12]

Soon after Pearl Harbor, Eugene Power—whose company had employed Kibre ever since that chance meeting at the Vatican—joined the OSS (then the COI) at a rank that put him on intimate terms with the office's head, William Donovan, who needed his expertise with the new technology of microfilm. In July 1942, Donovan told Power that an important undercover assignment had opened up in Stockholm. The Norwegian underground had figured out how to intercept mail sacks on their way from Berlin to Oslo—and how to open the envelopes, access the contents, reseal the envelopes, and return the mail sacks with nobody the wiser. It was too much to read all at once, so the Allies needed to put a man in Stockholm who could photograph the stolen mail—and who could, while he was at it, get copies of every other document the Allies needed from that region. Everything had to be done secretly. Could Power think of a man who was up to the job?[13]

He couldn't think of a man. But he could think of a woman.

Through the 1930s, Kibre had—like many people in love with Europe at the time, who didn't fully understand, at first, the seriousness of what was happening in Germany—relinquished her hold on the Continent slowly and reluctantly. Keeping just outside of the spreading Nazi conquests, she moved from Berlin to Oslo to Copenhagen to The Hague to Paris. Finally, no place in Europe was safe.

She wound up at her PhD alma mater, the University of Chicago. The archives there were acceptable. The school aspired to the European sophistication that she loved so much, with its turreted buildings along the Midway Plaisance park designed to look like the towers of Oxford, and she had mentors there who respected her talents, though nobody had much work for her to do.

Then Power called from Washington and asked her to use her talents in a different way. She would have to undergo special training at the British Library—as well as, we can guess, if she had the training of a typical undercover agent, at an undisclosed location abroad where military types taught such agents how to survive. The work would be harder than anything she'd ever done. She would be in terrible danger at every moment.

"She jumped at the assignment," Power said.[14]

Perhaps Kibre surprised herself with her eagerness. Or perhaps she had waited for months for a phone, any phone, to ring. No matter. She was going to England. She was back in the game.

THE JAR OF HEADS

In casting a wide net for scholars, this call to adventure sometimes brought in folks who were eager to join for all the wrong reasons. This was the case for an anthropologist named Carleton Coon, who, sometime before Curtiss's and Kibre's recruitments, was given his own scene from a spy novel: a visit from a well-dressed stranger to his office at Harvard. That day, the usually quiet campus was in an uproar. Undergraduates in ironically worn raccoon coats, navy ensigns in gold braid, middle-aged men in sack suits with boyish looks of glee on their faces: they had come from all over the Northeast, waving blue and crimson flags, to attend the annual Harvard-Yale football game, which Harvard and Yale alumni simply call "the Game."[15]

The stranger who called upon Coon chose an excellent day for his visit. On the day of the Game, who would notice one more outsider walking around campus?

Coon knew the visit was coming. He had every reason to be pleased with himself. As a boy growing up in a wealthy small town in Massachusetts, he fantasized about becoming a gentleman adventurer. "There should be nothing unusual in this," he later wrote; "it is probably the secret ambition of every boy to travel in strange mountains, stir up tribes, and destroy the enemy by secret and unorthodox means."[16]

In those years, boys from upper-class families were among the most devoted readers of spy fiction—and, when they grew up, were certainly the most successful *writers* of spy fiction. Ian Fleming, the creator of James Bond, devoured spy novels throughout his upper-class childhood and then—after serving in British intelligence during World War II—extended the tradition by becoming a spy writer himself. In England, while lower-class boys read stories about elite boarding schools (think Harry Potter without the magic) well into their teen years, boys *at* elite boarding schools had spy novels in their dorm libraries. For readers who expected to inherit the world, these stories promised a future of running international affairs, beating lesser men in combat, and roving around gallantly above the rule of law.[17]

So it was with Coon in America. After graduating from Phillips Academy Andover, he enrolled at Harvard and took classes— Egyptology, Arabic—that he hoped would set him up for his own colonial adventures: "Most of all I wanted to learn to pray flawlessly so that when I became an explorer I might pass as a proper Muslim, like my fabled heroes, Sir Richard Burton and Charles Doughty."[18]

Majoring in anthropology was a natural next step: anthropology promised travel, and the field was congenial, at the time, to the sort of people who believed, as Coon did, that different ethnic groups should be treated as different species. Coon studied the skulls of Indigenous people from the Canary Islands, which his adviser kept in a personal collection. (The same adviser owned a jar that contained, soaked in alcohol, three human heads: one Native American, one South Asian, and one Chinese.)[19] He wrote scholarly texts arguing that we can see racial "types" in the skull, and that the European racial type is superior—which explains, he said, why Europeans have been so good at dispatching other groups. In 1935, when he got the chance to write a blurb about himself in *The Atlantic Monthly*, he wrote: "Carleton S. Coon is happiest when measuring skulls."[20]

This way of treating ethnic groups as species vying for dominance was bad science even by the standards of the time. But Coon's preoccupation with measuring skulls was quite common in his chosen discipline. By his measure, anthropology's central project was to show that racism is scientific. In this, he had much in common with his peers in Germany, where professors at the University of Strasbourg asked Heinrich Himmler, the head of the Gestapo and overseer of the system of concentration camps, to give them the heads of murdered Jewish prisoners so they could use the skulls in their research.[21]

"Skull science," the practice of taking measurements from skulls in order to argue for the inferiority of whole ethnic groups, was discredited by Darwin's time in the nineteenth century—smarter people don't have bigger skulls—but it became vogue in the early twentieth century precisely because people who wanted to commit horrific acts against other ethnic groups thought skull science gave them a veneer of scientific objectivity.

After the war, the discipline of anthropology would undertake a serious examination of its complicity in the Holocaust and other crimes against humanity. For now, however, the jar of heads in Coon's department was just another pedagogical tool, and the department's denizens saw themselves as rather grand figures—as students of mankind who held in their hands the *destiny* of mankind, and as well-bred Harvard men who could pull off a turn, should the opportunity arise, as another Lawrence of Arabia.

For a time, it looked like all of Coon's work preparing to be a gentleman adventurer was for nothing. He got stuck, as one does, in the amber of academic life, becoming a graduate student, still at Harvard, and then an instructor. He sat through dull classes and made fun of his professors' speech impediments. He married a woman who was a

junior in college and had her drop out so she could join him as a research assistant on a trip to Morocco to do fieldwork for his dissertation.
He never mentioned her in his work.[22]

He attended tedious meetings. He did committee work. He watched
class after class of seniors graduate, always the same age, always young
and fresh and full of promise. He grew older. He got fat.

When war erupted in Europe, Coon, now in his late thirties, saw a
chance to finally fulfill his boyhood fantasies. He let it be known among
his colleagues, guessing that some must have government connections,
that he would not turn down an assignment in intelligence. When a
friend spoke to Army Intelligence on his behalf, they rejected Coon right
away, probably on account of his age and sedentary profession. Then word
came that a man belonging to a new outfit, the Office of the Coordinator
of Information, was willing to talk to Coon on Game Day.[23]

A knock at the door revealed a silver-haired gentleman in a blue
serge suit: Wallace Phillips, United States Navy, who reported directly
to William Donovan. Coon recounted in his memoir the scene that
followed:

> First he swore me to utter secrecy, then he told me more about
> myself than I had dreamed anyone else could know. He asked
> me if I wanted to serve my country. I told him that I was
> already in the Massachusetts State Guard at Sudbury, but that
> was not enough. He then informed me that I had been chosen
> to be the Lawrence of Morocco.[24]

Since Coon usually wrote dialogue from memory in his memoir, we
may assume that he put a bit of paraphrase into this exchange. Based
on other memoirs by OSS agents, Phillips probably said something like
"We have interests in Morocco that must be looked after with the ut-
most care. You are the man we want for the job." But Coon was the sort of
man to believe his story must be the center of the drama. The dialogue,
as written, leaves no doubt about the desired message: that history
recognized he was destined for great things.

The founding years of a powerful institution are years of moral peril. The people who join during these years have a special opportunity to shape the institution's values. Consider, for instance, some of the ethical concerns that arise in the spy business: Do we spy on allies? Do we help tyrants abroad because doing so will serve our interests? How do we feel about using academic fields, like anthropology, that seek to understand (for instance) people's foodways in order to deplete their food sources?

In the years to come, Coon would do his best to shape the values of the intelligence agency that had recruited him. But Harvard's anthropology department, with its penchant for collecting human heads, did not prepare him to tackle these issues with much in the way of humility or compassion.

THE DON WITH DAGGERS

All education—whether it's tailored for scholars, slackers, spies, or saboteurs—is really an education in the signs of belonging. We learn to wear the right clothes, say the right things, know the right codes— sometimes for a cover identity, sometimes for an identity we're determined to make our own. Coon, in his bid to craft his own legend, wrote of a spy agency seeing the promise in a big man on campus to become a big man in the war: a perfect fit for his role. But sometimes a spy reveals himself as a natural because he *doesn't* fit his role. Such was the case for another scholar in this story.

On a cold day in November 1942 in Washington, D.C., Sherman Kent, a history professor from Yale, stood on the sidewalk on Constitution Avenue outside one of the temporary wooden buildings that the U.S. government built, soon after the country entered the war, to hold the employees of its swelling intelligence services. A black car pulled up beside him. He paused to memorize the car's identifying features— Chevrolet, black paint, Maryland plates, license number 208-566— and then got inside. He had no idea where he was going.[25]

Kent was one of the very first professors to leave campus to work for U.S. intelligence. He joined Donovan's Office of the Coordinator of Information in the fall of 1941, before the Japanese bombed Pearl Harbor. His job there was to help build a "war information section" in Donovan's agency, which would organize the wartime information flowing in unsteady torrents around every sector of government.[26] His qualifications to do this included the fact that he was the curator of the Yale Library's war collection, an assembly of publications that documented historically significant military conflicts. As it happened, this was the same collection that Joseph Curtiss soon afterward used as his book-collecting cover.[27]

Kent and Curtiss were friends; they belonged to a little group of young Yale professors that called itself "the Guild of St. Golias." As Kent later explained, "St. Golias, in medieval Europe, particularly in medieval France, was the patron saint of students, and the Guild of St. Golias was a group of young Yale College teachers who endeavored to follow after the high-flying antics of the fourteenth-century young men." Of course, the Guild's idea of high-flying antics was limited by the fact that they were humanist nerds: "A typical evening of the Guild would take place in one of the member's rooms, and after a bounteous amount of firewater of one sort or another, and some sort of a meal, the crowd would fall into putting on plays which they would almost improvise on the spot, and act out, to their own great delectation."[28]

It was a cozy little world. But though Kent lived in this world, he wasn't suited for it. He should have been a drill sergeant instead of a professor.

A deceptively sweet-looking man, Kent looked the part of a kindly campus professor. He could play that part, too, modeling easy gentility while addressing the students, as all Ivy League professors did, as "gentlemen." But in private, Kent swore like a sailor who had been thrown off the ship for indecent language. He reasoned like a devil who had been kicked upstairs because downstairs couldn't trust him. If a situation was fraught, he called it "hot as a pregnant pig." If someone irritated him, he'd share his displeasure in terms expertly garnished with the word *fuck*. Even when giving a definition of *semantics*, he tipped into glib obscenity: "A husband says, 'Darling, I've got my semi-annual hard-on.' His wife replies, 'George, you always get mixed up in your English. You mean that you've got your annual semi-hard-on.'"[29]

Some people channel their aggression by grousing or gossiping or writing snide letters. Kent played around with turning unlikely objects into weapons. In his classes, he developed a habit of disposing of used-up pieces of chalk by throwing them out a window he left open at the back of the classroom. Whenever anyone fell asleep in class, he wrote in an unpublished memoir, "I would very frequently fire a piece of chalk at him. This practice was much appreciated by the others in the class, but not all of them always laughed at me or smiled." Once he was so annoyed by a student's constant yawning that he fired a piece of chalk right into the student's open mouth.[30] After he trained with the OSS, Kent became famous for being able to "throw a knife better than a Sicilian."[31]

Years after the war, an acquaintance recalled seeing Kent stand up mid conversation to show how he could fold a newspaper "into a hard concentrated weapon with sharp creased corners that, in a pinch, could be used to injure or maim."[32] (He learned this trick at his first spy training camp in 1942.)[33]

Perhaps Sherman Kent felt, at Yale, like a knife too sharp for its sheath.

In Kent's memoir, one of his complaints about his life as a young professor is that academic work piled so high around him that he scarcely noticed events in the outside world. When a hurricane upended New Haven in 1938, he didn't even notice: he spent the day working in the basement of an administrative building, nipping out at noon to grab lunch from home, and only realized later that a hurricane had raged through the city all day, knocking down trees and blowing off roofs. He had unwittingly walked home and back in the eye of the storm. "It was almost as if I had been sitting in a bomb-proof shelter at the time that the first nuclear bomb had gone off, and that I was unaware of anything that had happened until I came out to take a firsthand glimpse at the wreckage," he said.[34]

In September 1939, he was in the same basement, working on the same interminable administrative tasks, when he learned of another figurative bombshell going off: "One of our colleagues cheerfully came into the room to announce the German attack on Poland, which all of us were quick to realize was almost certainly the beginning of a World War . . . the real World War II that we had been hoping and praying against for the last three or four anxious years."[35]

So when Donovan's outfit in Washington invited Kent to work with them, he went. Here was a chance to stand in the wind instead of hiding underground.

Kent started his work in Washington as the head of R&A's North Africa division. After about a year, the OSS sent him to a training camp so that he could better understand the methods of agents in the field.

Just beforehand, when Joseph Curtiss was preparing to embark on his spy mission using the war collection as a cover, he called Kent and told him his cover story: that he would be traveling abroad to gather books for the collection.[36] Why not? Kent had been the curator of that collection for a long time, and the occasion gave Curtiss an excuse to talk to his friend.

But Kent was sharp. Guessing, as none of Curtiss's other colleagues did, that something was afoot, he asked his friend whether he was up to more than book collecting. Curtiss panicked, hung up, and didn't talk to Kent again before leaving New Haven for espionage training.[37] It must have been awkward when they first spotted each other at the same training camp.

A SCHOOL FOR SCANDAL

The U.S. government, new to espionage on a national scale, had only the broadest idea of what it was doing when it recruited professors and archivists out of their carrels to become its first full-scale network of professional spies. The idea was this: at the start of the war, America had only one standing army of experts who were trained to dig relentlessly for hidden information. These were the humble drudges in the nation's universities who hunted in the stacks for forgotten histories and weaseled their way into closed archives and scoured old correspondence for gossip. Gentlemen may not read other people's letters, but scholars do. They're good at it.

More than this: the real reason that Japan's attack on Pearl Harbor took the United States by surprise was that, although the U.S. government *had* the necessary intelligence—it had, thanks to a project called Magic, copies of most of the diplomatic messages that Japan was sending around the world, together with a key for decoding those messages—it did not have the expertise necessary to *understand* those messages. (Decoding messages just means translating them from a cipher text to a plain text: from IFMMP to HELLO. Understanding messages means figuring out what is actually being said: does HELLO mean *hello* as in "Greetings," or does it mean *hello* as in "Hello? Is anybody there?")

Before Pearl Harbor, the U.S. government simply sent the decoded Japanese diplomatic traffic straight to a top echelon of government officials, who could not tell, for instance, that Japan was leaving its diplomats in Washington out of the loop on a planned attack but was still warning them in roundabout ways that a crisis between Japan and the United States was "imminent."[38]

Raw intelligence has little value without experts who can make meaning of the intelligence. The United States needed a central intelligence service staffed by experts in every field, from history to economics to linguistics to textual studies.

The professors were experts by definition: they had staggered to the top of mountain after mountain of secondary literature, worked at primary sources like a dog chewing a bone, written thick books about "strangely neglected" subfields within their fields of expertise, and spent afternoons trying to explain it all to ungrateful undergraduates. Sure, their knowledge was book knowledge, but times were desperate: in urgent need of expertise on every subject in the library, Donovan and his new intelligence agency raided the library for recruits. The world's least glamorous people for the world's most glamorous profession.

The problem now was to train them. How do you teach men and women who hold ordinary jobs—not just professor, but teacher or librarian or secretary or hospital technician—to suddenly become saboteurs, prisoner interrogators, undercover agents, resistance cell liaisons, or even *pigeoneers*? Following the guidance of the British intelligence services, which had more experience in these matters, the OSS hastily built secret training camps around the country in national parks and other remote locales.

The staff had little more experience with cloak-and-dagger business than the students did. Had they admitted this inexperience to their trainees, it might have amused the professors among them, since professors often learn class material by teaching it.[39]

No matter. Even for someone who is very good at learning in school, the usefulness of classroom skills has a clear limit. The training camps were a world beyond that limit. It was time for the professors to learn in a different kind of school.

A LONG WAY FROM NOWHERE

After more than an hour of riding in a silent car, the man once known as Joseph Curtiss emerged in—well, to him, a place off the map. The training camp was on a muddy, hilly, forested estate, one hundred acres in size, that the War Department took over from the National Parks Service early in the war. It was known as Area B—which stood, one alumnus wrote grimly, for "By God, it's a long way from nowhere." (Today, the location is known as Catoctin Mountain Park in Maryland.)[40]

OSS training camps sought to strip the students of their identities as quickly as possible, in part to protect them from each other should anyone be captured. Even though he already knew he would operate under his real name when he went abroad, Curtiss received a fake name and background story to use during his training.[41] Curtiss, who came from an old New England family, thereby lost, in one stroke, everything that gave him status: his family name, his WASP trappings, his Yale affiliation. Whatever self he built in the camp would be solely his own. He rankled at the loss of his name and secretly consoled himself, he later said, by pretending that his old name still held and that his new one was only a nickname.[42]

Curtiss didn't leave a record of his time in Area B, but based on camp reports, it's likely he would have been handed a kit bag and a set of fatigues as soon as he arrived and told to change out of his civilian clothes *right away*. Some camps were even stricter and required their students to change into fatigues in town (after arriving by train or elsewise from their hometowns) before they got a ride to camp. The idea was to keep the staff and other students from glimpsing in anyone's clothes even the briefest clue to his real identity. But humans are as relentless at scenting gossip as sharks are at scenting blood, and the staffers at those camps found themselves paying particular attention, though they weren't supposed to, to the socks and shoes of any students who kept their civilian footwear for that first trip—imagining a whole backstory from these items "as sole indicators of taste and social status," as one camp report later said.[43]

WE HAVE WAYS OF MAKING YOU TALK

The students were at the camp to learn, yes, but the staff were not just there to teach. They were tasked with determining, in quite a short amount of time—for Curtiss's cohort, training lasted three weeks—whether a given student could be trusted with a secret, with someone's life, with intelligence that could tip the scales of the war.

In one test, staffers brought one student at a time into a mocked-up hotel room where someone had apparently left his belongings. After examining the room, the student had to answer questions about the owner of the belongings: "For example, questions concerning his age, marital status, weight, occupation, color of hair and eyes, residence, for some of which there was clear evidence, for others doubtful evidence, and for still others no evidence at all." How good a detective was the student? Was he capable of refraining from making up answers when there was no evidence?[44]

Students also had to show they could withstand interrogation. Staffers dressed as guards and other officials threw the students one by one into a dark room, shone a bright light in their faces, and shouted questions at them. They made the students stand in a stress position with their hands over their heads. As the interrogation progressed, it became even more hostile, with the staffers screaming insults and forcing the students into increasingly excruciating positions. Demonstrating the seriousness of this exercise was very, very important. In real life, OSS operatives whom the enemy captured had to hold out under interrogation for forty-eight hours. Not because it would take that long to rescue them; they weren't getting rescued. Forty-eight hours was how long it would take for their allies to go underground.

The student's mission during the interrogation was to create, and stick to, a cover story to explain a suspicious activity that he was caught doing. Donald Downes—Curtiss's contact at the Yale Club, who went through a similar training course in Canada shortly after America entered the war—later described, in a novel based on his experiences, a version of this exercise in which two students came up with a cover story together and then underwent separate interrogations:

"Silence! I will ask, and you will answer. Where were you this afternoon?"

"Bournemouth. I spent a couple of hours there with Lars Krog."

"I did not ask you who you were with. What were you doing in Bournemouth?"

"We followed some girls for a couple of hours."

"Fifty girls, or three girls? Be specific, please."

"Two girls."

"Did you follow two girls for two hours, or one girl for part of the time and one girl for the rest of the time, and how much time?"

"Well, one girl first."

"And how long did you and Lars follow this first girl?"

"About twenty minutes."

"What was she wearing?"

"I don't remember, sir."

"I assume she was wearing clothes?"

"Oh, yes, sir."

"What clothes?"

"A coat."

"A coat. An overcoat?"

"Yes, sir. It's been a very cold day."

"So it has. And it's going to be a very cold night. What color was the overcoat?"

"I can't remember, sir."

"Well then, shall we try raising our hands over our head until we do remember?"[45]

The student in Downes's novel fails the interrogation—but, the staffers tell him later, everyone fails his first interrogation. They advise him, next time, to keep the story simpler, closer to truth: you and your friend went for a walk—no imaginary girls to make you look ridiculous. Talk slowly the whole time; don't give some answers quickly and some answers slowly, or you'll be handing your interrogators a cheat sheet to detect when you're lying.[46]

The hardest part of this exercise was still to come. The first room, the room with bright lights and screaming interrogators, was enough to undo many of the candidates. No one could blame them. Some of the students were refugees from Europe who had already endured great violence; by this time, November 1942, scholars in Nazi-occupied countries were trying desperately to find paths to the United States, with a few heroic colleagues banding together to bring as many people as possible—too few, far too few—past immigration barriers designed to keep out Eastern Europeans, Southern Europeans, and Jews.[47] Some of these scholarly refugees provided valuable information to the OSS about wartime research under way in those countries; others became researchers in the United States on secret projects like the atomic bomb; others turned right around and trained as interrogators and undercover operatives at intelligence training camps like Area B and Camp Ritchie, determined to return to the terrors of Europe, this time with an army behind them.

But for at least one such student, as a report later disclosed, the interrogation in the first room was enough to set off what today we would call PTSD:

One refugee from Europe, who had had a brush with the Gestapo and had so skillfully come through the questioning to which they had subjected him that he was allowed to go free, became very much disturbed in the Stress Interview. In Post-Stress he asked to be released from . . . any commitments to the OSS. Attempts to keep him quiet were of no avail. The emotion stirred in him by Stress kept him awake that night; and the next morning his anxiety reached the point where, in another situational test, he fainted. It was clear that it would be unwise to force him to finish the assessment program since he was completely unfit to operate in Europe under cover.[48]

There was no torture in the second room, no imitation of what the students most feared from the Gestapo. Instead, the staffers told each student that they had failed—watching their faces carefully as they did so—and then brought them one by one into a room set up for debriefing. A well-loved staffer, someone who had been kind to everyone since the start of training, was there; he gave the student a cigarette, gestured to an armchair, and said, "Sit down and make yourself comfortable." Then he leaned back in his own chair and asked, "Well, how have things been going?" The student usually gave an unhappy reply, and the staffer sympathized. After some chitchat about the student's cover story and why it hadn't held up under interrogation, the staffer asked, with the idle intentness of a practical man, "Just what events did you use from your real life and how did you alter them? I'm interested in the technique you used."

And this was the hardest part of the exercise to pass. Here, with a trusted listener, thinking the interrogation was over, many students blew their cover. They talked about their real lives, which they were never, ever supposed to do. That was the biggest lesson. If, after you've been captured, you see a friendly smile or a face you recognize, don't trust them.[49]

KICK TO THE FORK

Curtiss was clever and imaginative, and he was prepared to sift through endless pages in an archive to find exactly the reference that he needed, but he wasn't exactly used to callusing his hands. He'd always had comfort, always had funds. The historian Robin Winks seems to suggest that Curtiss didn't even bother to draw a paycheck from Yale; though his salary was set at a specific amount, $4,250, he didn't accept the funds, instead waiving his salary in an act of noblesse oblige from the son of a good family. Before he joined the OSS, he didn't have a social security number.[50]

So Curtiss wasn't likely, at the start of his training, to win any street fights. But street fights were precisely the specialty of William Ewart Fairbairn, who wrote the manuals that the OSS used to train its personnel in close combat. Fairbairn wore horn-rimmed glasses and looked like an accountant—one whose nose had been broken twenty times. He was a British Royal Marine who had worked for three decades with the municipal police in Shanghai, where he developed a system of crippling close combat. This was what the OSS wanted: a fighting system that would put one's opponent on the sidelines or in the ground, fair play be damned. One student called Fairbairn's training course "the Fairbairn method of assault and murder"—a perfectly accurate, if terrifying, phrase.[51]

As it happens, Fairbairn was teaching at Area B while Curtiss's cohort was there. He was a striking presence at the camp. As one of his fellow instructors later recalled, "Fairbairn went around in British battle dress with his knife on his leg and would pull it out to make his points. . . . He frequently, and unexpectedly, would draw the knife from its concealed location and place the point at either the throat or stomach of various OSS personnel whom he was meeting for the first time. Needless to say, he got their attention and left more than a lingering impression."[52]

When he met a group of students for the first time, Fairbairn— fifty-seven years old, five foot ten, and about 170 pounds—would select one of the biggest students in the group, call him up to the front, and challenge him to a fight.[53] If the student turned him down, either from prudence or reluctance to hurt a man nearing retirement age, Fairbairn would kick the student in "the fork" (to use Fairbairn's phrase) until the student gave in and attacked. Fairbairn always beat the student handily—and sometimes sent him flying.[54] The point was to show that his close-combat methods worked even against an opponent who was bigger and stronger and younger.

Kick to the fork: that was Fairbairn's constant advice to students training in close combat. Has your opponent grabbed hold of you? Break the hold and then kick to the fork. Do you want to blind your opponent? Put your fingers in his eyes and then kick to the fork. One of his students, Richard Helms—who went on to become the director of Central Intelligence—recalled of Fairbairn's training, "Within fifteen seconds I came to realize my private parts were in constant jeopardy." Attacking the fork was ungentlemanly, but in war, Fairbairn reminded his students, "gentlemanly combatants tended to end up dead."[55]

It was good advice.

The students at Area B nicknamed Fairbairn "Major Foul-Blow." One explained, "All of us who were taught by Major Fairbairn soon realized that he had an honest dislike for anything that smacked of decency in fighting."[56]

For many of the students, the hard part was not the fighting itself, but learning to ignore the decency that told them not to do this to another human being. "Students will have noted that no holds or locks on the ground are demonstrated," Fairbairn says in one of his combat manuals. "*This is war:* your object is to kill or dispose of your opponent as quickly as possible and go to the assistance of your comrades."[57]

And they'd need that training soon enough.

THE BAKER STREET IRREGULARS

Across the Atlantic Ocean, the British were going about the business of spycraft with a rather more polished facade of gentility.

Baker Street in London is a smart little district lined with tall houses built in the Queen Anne style, with redbrick facades and narrow windows trimmed with lacelike woodwork. In the time of Sir Arthur Conan Doyle's Sherlock Holmes, who lived at the fictitious address 221B Baker Street, it was a respectable address—which also meant it was not a posh address of the kind Londoners favor when they are so wealthy as to be *above* respectability.[58] But by 1942, Baker Street was exceedingly posh, and the Special Operations Executive (SOE), the newest civilian branch of Britain's intelligence service, had its head-quarters there.

Above respectability or beneath it: those were the only two options for English strategy now that the nation was at war with the Nazis. In 1940, just before Winston Churchill stepped into the role of prime minister, the politician Robert Bower warned him, referring to the Queensberry rules of fair play in boxing, that he must abandon all notions of gentlemanly conduct: "When you are fighting for your life against a ruthless opponent you cannot be governed by Queensberry rules. This government"—the government of the departing prime minister, Neville Chamberlain—"would rather lose the war under Queensberry rules than do anything unbecoming to an absolutely perfect gentleman. That kind of thing will not do."[59]

Agents sometimes called the SOE "the Baker Street Irregulars," in reference to the nickname Sherlock Holmes gave to a group of street urchins whom he recruited to gather information for him in secret. But the spy agency on Baker Street in the 1940s needed grown men and women to carry out most of its operations, and so it assigned Selwyn Jepson, an upper-class mystery writer and screenwriter, to evaluate potential agents.[60]

Jepson had joined the war effort as soon as war broke out in Europe, quickly landing in the SOE, and was in charge of interviewing potential agents who were women. The women he sent into training came from Britain, France, the United States, and further abroad. It's not impossible that Jepsen was the one to interview Adele Kibre before her training as an undercover agent. Though no records of her time in Britain survive, it seems likely she would have gone to a training school; after all, the job she thought she would be doing—working undercover in neutral territory to acquire documents for the Allies—was the same as the job Joseph Curtiss thought he would be doing. (As we will see, however, they wound up doing very different things.)

Jepson had an office on Baker Street, but he kept other offices for meeting candidates; that way, none of the candidates he met would walk away with the location of the SOE's headquarters. One office was in a hotel on Northumberland Avenue; that room was completely empty save for two folding chairs: a bare and slightly menacing setup designed to rebuff prying eyes.[61] Another was in the War Office building on Whitehall, an infinitely grand neo-Baroque building that was seven floors high and a full city block wide.[62]

Let's suppose that this is where he chose to meet, on a cloudy day in November 1942, an American woman named Adele Kibre. The Americans had been at war for less than a year, they were scrambling to build an intelligence agency from absolutely nothing, and they needed to know just with whom they were dealing. The scene that follows is pure conjecture.

Jepson had received a good deal of information about Kibre in advance: she knew the film industry, as he did, and she had a classicist's handful of languages together with a historian's appetite for gossip. She was a professor—or close enough to it—as all of these Americans seemed to be. She was also a woman, which for him was a plus. "In my view, women were very much better than men for the work," he later said of the candidates he sent into the field. "Women, as you must know, have a far greater capacity for cool and lonely courage than men. Men usually want a mate with them."[63] All Kibre knew was that the OSS had sent her to London as a potential liaison operative.

The room that she entered was imposing, with plush carpets, ornately carved wooden chairs, and an immense mahogany desk piled neatly with file folders. The man who sat waiting in one of the chairs was aggressively nondescript, with a smooth-shaved face that he seemed to wear like a mask.[64] Upon walking in, Kibre looked immediately at the books on a shelf behind him. He marked her glance, wrote something in her file, and then looked her up and down.

"You're wearing your makeup like a Hollywood actress," he said. "I can tell that you've got on different shades of"—he gestured disdainfully—"rouge and lipstick to shape your lips and face. We don't do that here in England. If you're going to be an undercover operative, you must learn to be inconspicuous. You must seem like an absolutely average woman from whatever place you happen to be in. That includes copying the local styles of makeup."[65]

"Noted. What shade of lipstick do *you* usually use?" she asked, sitting down. A good way to find out whether a man hates women, she had found, is to make a joke that implies he does something feminine;

many men react to such a suggestion with vicious anger. She wanted to know this information about a man who might have something to do with whether she lived or died.

"Scarlet," he replied with a straight face. "Everyone knows that Hitler hates scarlet lipstick. He has forbidden German women from wearing it in public. He thinks it looks cheap. Naturally, English-women welcome the opportunity to annoy the Führer."

"Will I be stationed in England, then?"

"Wouldn't you rather be stationed in England? Agents who go abroad take on terrible risks. For instance, if you went to work for us in France, your odds of getting killed would be fifty-fifty."[66]

"When Hitler attacked Europe, he attacked my home. I'm far more interested in my odds of getting even."

He wrote something else in her file, then fixed her with a cool eye. "We don't yet know whether you'll be stationed at all. You'll have to pass our training first. If you pass—well, then we have an idea of where you'll be stationed, and it is not England. You will work for the American Office of Strategic Studies, and liaise with our Special Operations Executive, in an undisclosed country abroad."[67]

"It's the Office of Strategic Services. So I'm going to be sent to a training camp?"

"The *Americans* have training camps. I imagine that your agents-in-training live in tents and wrestle bears. That kind of thing simply will not do in England. Our intelligence services date back to before the time of Sir Francis Walsingham and Christopher Marlowe. We have had time to build an institution that does things properly.

"You will pass through a training course at our Special Training Schools. These are in discreet but well-equipped locations around the country. Some agents call our training 'the tour of the Stately 'Omes of England.' Because you are to be a photography specialist, your training will include a stint at Special Training School 37a. I believe that one is a castle. And you will complete your training, as all our agents do, at a finishing school."

"Your spies go to finishing school? Do they learn the right fork to use at supper?"

"Yes, but they also learn the right word to finish that sentence. A well-bred Englishwoman would call it *dinner*, and a lower-class Englishwoman would call it *tea*."

"What happens if I don't pass the training?"

"We dispose of agents at a site called the Cooler." He paused and reflected. "It's probably best not to ask about that one."

She sighed. "Well, this is all wonderful, in a frightful sort of way. If you're telling me all this, I guess I passed whatever kind of evaluation this is. Where do I report next for training?"

"Your training starts at the British Museum's library. I understand that you know your way around a library, so this should start you on familiar ground. We'll start with things you know well, like books, and move on to more difficult things, like forks."

She stood to leave.

"One more thing," he said. He rummaged through his desk drawer and pulled out a small black cylinder. He held it out to her.

"Your lipstick," he said.

2

A GIRL'S GUIDE TO BURGLARY

If I cannot bend the heavens,
then I shall move the powers of hell.
—VIRGIL[1]

AREA B, THE MARYLAND SCHOOL FOR OSS AGENTS, WAS A school for devilry that had a curriculum right out of hell. Curtiss and his fellow students, who just days before had been living modest lives as professors, lawyers, salesmen, and the like, crawled through the woods, practiced disarming guards and garroting sentries, and learned to shoot like gunslingers. (The instructors favored live ammunition, to teach "battle conditions."[2]) The training camp's syllabus covered every aspect of spycraft: how to withstand interrogation; how to memorize someone's appearance without resorting to useless descriptors like "normal height" or "average face"; how to write in code; how to steal and alter identity documents; how to fight; how to kill *quietly*.

Every student received a kit bag full of weapons.[3] What appeared to be a black wand was actually a cosh, or a weighted baton to be used for bludgeoning opponents. A fighting dagger was included, in a sheath that made it look like a spatula. And then there was a huge knife called a "smatchet," a term that Fairbairn, the combat instructor at Area B, had invented together with the weapon itself.[4] *Smatchet* was short for "smashing hatchet": the blade and bulky handle could be used, variously, for hacking at limbs, breaking jaws, and intimidating opponents.[5]

Fairbairn had also invented the fighting dagger that the students used, together with an associate in Britain named E. A. Sykes.[6] The dagger had two sharp edges rather than one, which made the weapon ideal for slashing, Fairbairn explained, and also kept opponents from grabbing the weapon away.[7]

Knife fighting turned out to be a keystone of the curriculum. "The knife is a silent and deadly weapon that is easily concealed," an OSS training syllabus advised, "and against which, in the hands of an expert, there is no sure defense, except firearms or by running like hell."[8] The knife is the weapon of the fugitive, the assassin, the secret courier, the turncoat—in short, the spy. Because the students would be expected, as agents, to carry as few weapons as possible, the instructors taught them to make precise knife attacks with one hand while using the other hand to make backup weapons from any ordinary items within reach. With the blade, aim for the gut, the hand, the forearm; with your free hand, do something that tricks your opponent into uncovering those tender spots. Scoop up dirt and throw it in the other man's eyes. Or throw your hat in the other man's eyes. Or throw your hanky in the other man's eyes. Get creative.[9]

Fairbairn himself wore the knife he'd invented in a sheath sewn directly into his trousers. One of his fellow instructors later recalled how, after a boozy evening at the Army and Navy Club near OSS headquarters, Fairbairn "stuck himself in the thigh while sheathing the knife. What the British call a 'bloody mess' ensued."[10]

Fairbairn had the students practice holding their knives correctly. He had them pair off and practice the style of knife attack you'd use against a sentry. Crawl up from the rear, quietly. When you get five feet away from the sentry, slip your knife from its sheath and spring up, using one hand to cover his mouth and nose and the other to drive your knife up into the small of his back, piercing his kidneys. Use the hand over his mouth to yank his body back onto the knife, then pull the knife free and cut his throat. For the students taking a turn as attackers, live practice forced them to learn habits that didn't come naturally, the foremost of which was: you must start the attack *the instant* you get five feet from the sentry, without taking time to gather yourself for a leap, because otherwise his prey instinct that tells him he's being watched will alert him. For the students taking a turn as sentries, the lesson was simpler: *Always protect your rear.*[11]

The students also practiced, in pairs, what their instructors called "the assassin's trick." Let's say you're on a bustling city street. Walk toward your target face-on, as though you're an ordinary passerby who's going to pass him on the street. You should carry your knife in your sleeve, like a magician. At the moment you're passing your target, flick the knife free and stick it up behind you into his lower back. (His kidneys again; in Fairbairn's pedagogy, the kidneys were in nearly as much danger as the testicles.) After that, you can disappear into the bustle unnoticed; whether you leave the knife in your target or remove it is your choice.[12]

TROUSER AND COAT TACTICS

Fairbairn showed the students how to search each other for hidden blades. Agents might conceal knives in side sheaths, in front sheaths, in thigh sheaths, in their boots, tucked under their belts, on cords dangling down their backs, behind their lapels, in their sleeves, in their hats.[13] They might conceal razors in their clothes lining, taped to the undersides of their feet, and even taped to their scrotums.[14]

In case the students had to take someone prisoner without using handcuffs or rope, he showed them a quick, dirty way to restrain them, which another instructor called "trouser and coat tactics." Pull off the target's suspenders or belt; maybe pull off a few of his trouser buttons too. Then you can choose, depending on how completely you want to restrain him, to pull his trousers down to his feet or just leave them hanging loose, so that he must occupy one of his hands with desperately keeping his trousers up. In either case, you should also yank the target's coat halfway down to hold his arms at his sides. Now you can search him without fearing that he'll make a break for it. Or you can stand and keep watch over, perhaps, a whole *team* of enemy agents you've pantsed;

in their makeshift restraints, they're less likely to overwhelm you. (And the *psychology* of this tactic, no doubt, was marvelous. No man feels brave with his trousers down.)[15]

The students practiced these moves again and again. Soon they seemed to have no secrets from each other. Well, except for their real names. The students used cover identities at the camp partly so they couldn't give each other away in the field, but also so they could practice, under every kind of pressure, *sticking to* their cover identities. Roger Hall, who wrote a memoir of his own intelligence training at Area B, later said the students there and at similar OSS camps were constantly trying to trick each other into revealing their identities: "The prime object at most OSS schools and areas catering to 'special bodies' was to break the other fellow's 'cover.'"[16]

STUDYING FOR SURVIVAL

The professors may have been out of their element when they were learning to fight, but they doubtless felt more comfortable during the training camp's long hours of classroom work. At about fifteen students to a cohort, the students at Area B fit with their classmates in a single classroom. They sat at wooden desks and listened to lectures on how to interrogate civilians, how to interrogate prisoners of war, and how to liaise with members of underground resistance groups. They memorized the whole hierarchy of the German and Italian armies, the insignia on their uniforms down through every branch, the look and capabilities of their cars and tanks and guns. They learned how to read aerial photographs, how to do reconnaissance in the field, and how to make sense of documents that had been captured from the front. They learned Morse code.

But the lectures on cover stories were particularly thorough and rigorous.[17] Everything, *everything*, depended on maintaining a good cover. It's incredibly easy to carry, unawares, some receipt or piece of trash that disproves your cover, and for that reason, you must keep on your person an absolute minimum number of pieces of paper, and make sure these agree with your cover. The Nazis once captured an agent whose cover story required him to insist that he hadn't visited Brussels, but who had, in his pocket, a Brussels streetcar ticket.[18]

You must keep track of two types of cover: *general cover*, or the pretense that you're a nun, not an underground courier, and *particular cover*, or the pretense that you're on the street at night because you're returning from Vespers. You'll have an easier time surviving police checks and interrogations if your cover aligns with what you already are and know. Your particular cover should have two layers: an innocent layer ("I'm returning from Vespers, officer, God be with you") and a guilty layer that a civilian would wish to hide ("Enough, enough, I confess: I'm not returning from Vespers at all, I'm carrying on a secret affair with a man in town, and I'm sneaking back to the nunnery after meeting him in his apartment").[19]

For your general cover, you might choose (depending on your assignment) your real identity, or the identity of someone who has fled or died, or the identity of someone who doesn't exist. The latter is the most common, but also the most dangerous, because a fictional character's papers won't correspond with the records in an actual government's archives. You might try to get around this problem by choosing a hometown where the government's archives were bombed to rubble.[20]

If you adopt a new name, you must drill yourself on it until you look up unconsciously when someone says that name—and until you *sign* that name unconsciously when someone hands you a piece of paper. One OSS agent working in occupied Europe, when checking in to a hotel at night, was too tired to think carefully when writing his information in the paperwork that the police made hotels keep on their guests. As a lecture packet for intelligence instructors recounts: "Just before going to sleep, he suddenly became aware that, although he had printed his assumed name in block capitals at the end of the form, he had inadvertently signed his real signature at the foot." Luckily, he already knew the habits of the local police, including the time of day they picked up guests' papers from hotels, so he skedaddled before they could catch his mistake.[21]

On that last point: to help protect your cover, you must know everything you can about the local police, about local police informants, about local collaborators. You must know the local customs that govern whether, for instance, civilians salute men in German uniform, and you must know the latest adjustments to the regulations that dictate what papers civilians should carry, what places they can't enter, when they can move about. In short, you must know all the little details that help the police and the Gestapo identify suspicious characters.[22] Even if you're working in a neutral country, even if you're working under your own name, this kind of preparation is essential. The best way to survive an interrogation is not to get picked up in the first place.

The papers you carry on your person should look haphazard and incidental, but actually be deliberate—again, without a spare scrap. They should include, exactly and exclusively, official papers (identity documents, ration booklet), unofficial papers (club memberships), and personal papers (receipts). You must ensure that your ration booklet looks spent up to the current date, even if you just arrived in town and received the booklet as a prop.[23]

Just as you should carefully prune the papers on your person to support your cover, so you should carefully prune the papers in your room. In addition, you *must* keep your room clean; that's the easiest way to tell, by little signs of disturbance, whether the authorities have searched your room while you were out. You can plant an "indicator" by the entrance to your room, like a tissue dropped where an intruder's feet would disturb it, but don't drape a thread on the doorknob; everyone knows that one.[24]

Don't keep dangerous papers in your room. If you *must* keep dangerous papers in your room, store them with sheets of cellophane inserted among the pages, or with lumps of paraffin wax ready to spread across the whole; that will let you burn them *fast* in an emergency. Don't stash papers near the fireplace; everyone knows about the fireplace. Stash them behind a strip of wall molding, or between the panels that make up the top of a cabinet.[25]

Your clothes and belongings should affirm your cover in every stitch. The label from the tailor, the cut of the jacket, the make of your eyeglasses, the titles of the books you're reading, even the marks that laundries put on clothes to set apart one patron's order from another must match your ostensible identity. Your clothes and accessories should always be a little old.[26] (American universities hosted a program called "I Cash Clothes" that asked refugee scholars who arrived on campus to give up their old clothes. Supposedly, a charity gave them to desperate civilians in Occupied Europe; the clothes had to be European so the Gestapo wouldn't bother the poor downcast recipients. Actually, the OSS gave the clothes to spies.[27])

Cover is so important that if carrying out a subversive mission would harm your cover, you must protect the cover and ditch the mission.[28]

The local police might stop you for a random check on the street, or even take you down to the station to ask you a few questions. Your cover will likely be safe in these situations, as the police don't usually imagine the civilians they interrogate are subversives. If you're in Axis territory, though, and the Gestapo catches you up, you're in trouble. But you may be able to rely on proven methods to survive an interrogation with your secrets—and perhaps even your cover—intact.[29]

The Gestapo will catch you up in a sudden blow; you won't know it's coming. Before they start breaking your fingers, they'll try to break you emotionally. They'll take away your clothes, or make you put on a bra and panties while a woman watches, or ask you questions while you stand raising your hands in a stress position, or ask you questions while you sit on a chair with a missing leg and try to keep from falling over. They'll let silence drag out after you give an answer: a psychologist's wait, meant to make you so uncomfortable that you fill the space with more details. They might withhold food and give you only alcohol to drink, in the hope of eliciting a drunken confession. They might tell you, at length, that you're free to go, then put you in a holding cell while they process your release. Some of your associates will be in the holding cell; you might be so relieved that you share with them all you know. The holding cell will be bugged.

They might do worse than this—beat you with a bludgeon, partially drown you, whip you, pull out your fingernails.[30] In that case, all you can do is try to keep them distracted for forty-eight hours.[31] Not because rescue is coming in forty-eight hours; rescue isn't coming. Forty-eight hours, recall, is the amount of time it will take for your associates to go to ground.

While you answer their questions, remember: you're slow witted, not very observant, and not much of a political thinker. "Create the impression of the average bewildered, frightened, and stupid citizen," advises the SOE training material that the American training camps drew on. Take your time when you talk and pause to think before you give every answer; that way, any pauses you need to take when you invent lies will seem natural. (That said, invent as few lies as possible. The stressful conditions of an interrogation are not a good setting in which to devise clever new details for a cover story. What you devise won't be as clever as you think.) Simulate a poor memory even for true events, and keep everything as simple as possible: "'I went to the cinema,' *not* 'I went to the cinema with x.'"[32]

The Gestapo might question you and your associates at the same time. You should all have corresponding cover stories committed to memory, of course, but they may think of details to question you on that you didn't think of beforehand. Before any of you are captured, you should all agree that any question about a detail that isn't in the agreed-upon narrative will have an answer in the negative. (*When you were at the cinema, did you see a Mademoiselle Dubois? No, I didn't. That's funny, because she says she saw you. Oh, that can't possibly be true, sir—she must be mistaken, or you must be mistaken that she said that.*)

If your tricks work and the Gestapo let you go, assume afterward that they will secretly follow you everywhere. They might be hoping you'll drop your guard. *Then*, among friends, in the glad open spaces of freedom, maintaining your cover is more important than ever.[33]

This is the kind of information relayed in the lectures at Allied intelligence training camps, including Area B. So much of being a successful spy comes down not to fighting daggers or cool gadgets or ingenious stunts, but to classroom skills like paying attention, pattern-finding, puzzle-solving, and memorization. It's the kind of job a professor can excel at.

Perhaps the professors in the audience, as they sat at their wooden desks and took in these lectures, reflected—having been, just weeks ago, at the *front* of the classroom—on education. Or perhaps they watched each other to see what the return to the classroom revealed about their old selves. Sometimes those who find themselves playing the role of student again will revert to who they were as students. An old loafer, in the slang of the time, becomes a loafer again. An old sport becomes a sport; an old grind becomes a grind. One reason the instructors impressed so forcefully on the students that a cover identity should draw upon the truth is that, no matter how many new stages in life we graduate through, we can never quite get away from ourselves.

THE FINISHING SCHOOL FOR SPIES

Like Curtiss, Kibre, too, must have had intelligence training before she went out in the field, where she would be doing undercover work gathering documents and squeezing informants. Beyond this, she was expected to liaise with the Norwegian underground. The OSS wouldn't have sent her in cold; she would have endangered every Allied agent she met, and might even have become an unwitting informant for the other side. Eugene Power, who recruited Kibre to the OSS, says in a memoir that her training started in England, with an orientation at the British Museum.[34] After that, the record is silent—but then the record is silent on almost everybody's training. We only know Curtiss and Kent trained at Area B because they mentioned it to a historian they knew at Yale; those details don't appear in official records.

Lacking other information, I'll place her where every agent-in-training in Britain ended up: a "finishing school" in a well-groomed forest south of London, where agents put a final perfecting gloss on any training they might have received in other SOE schools.[35] All American agents who operated under SOE direction, including those working for joint OSS-SOE operations, studied in SOE schools, and Kibre was about to embark on a joint OSS-SOE operation.[36]

Let's say, then, that Kibre, like every student at the finishing school who wrote a memoir about their experiences, traveled to the school by rail or truck, without knowing the name of the place she was headed. A train from London to the village of Brockenhurst, which was deliberately *not* the train station closest to her destination, and from there a chauffeured ride in a car. Or a longer ride in the back of a four-by-four staff truck that had the canvas flap across the back closed so she couldn't see where she was going.[37] If she listened, she might have heard, under the roar of the engine, the layered, rustling quiet of the woods.[38]

A staffer, a young woman, might have walked her down a long gravel road to what looked like a storybook cottage blown up to the dimensions of a manor house. If it was the house that women students usually stayed in, it had a redbrick front, four chimneys, and seven bedrooms; the front was as broad as four ordinary houses set side by side. Wisteria and other flowering plants climbed the brick. Someone would open the front door, and Kibre would walk through it—into a new world.

BIRDS SINGING IN MORSE CODE

For the students, this finishing school had no name. The SOE called it by the name of the place where it was run: *Beaulieu*, pronounced *Bewley*, the original name before some ancestral landowner decided the French spelling was more elegant.[39]

It was a grand estate beside a royal forest, the New Forest, about a hundred miles southeast of London. It was also the kind of rustic that only city wealth can afford. There were birds singing, sheltered paths, rivers bending beneath alder and birch.[40] A student who trained in wireless telegraphy at Beaulieu later recalled: "We learned Morse code by listening to recordings of such classics as 'The Wedding March,' *da-da-di-da*, and Beethoven's Fifth, *di-di-di-da*. We even dreamt in Morse, and when we woke in the morning, the birds outside the bedroom window were singing in Morse."[41]

For the SOE, this kind of rustic was strategic. The forest provided cover from above; enemy planes on reconnaissance missions would be able to see little, if anything, of the campus below.[42] The school's field-craft instructor, who in civilian life was a gamekeeper at the royal estate at Sandringham, dug pits in the forest that he stocked with weapons and then camouflaged with nets and leaf litter. If the Germans invaded England from France, Beaulieu might be one of the first places they hit; the mouth of the Beaulieu River was right across the English Channel from Normandy. In such an event, "stay-behind parties" of school instructors and staffers would hide in the forest pits, wait for the Germans to pass by, and then attack them from behind with the weapons stashed there.[43]

The finishing school at Beaulieu comprised more than a dozen country houses that one Baron Montagu, who owned the estate, had invited his friends to build on his land in 1905, so they could all enjoy the countryside together. In 1941, the newly founded SOE requisitioned the houses and turned them into schoolhouses for spies. In civilian life, the houses had names, as posh country houses do—Boarmans, the House in the Wood, Saltmarsh, Vineyards—but the SOE referred to each house by the initials STS (for Special Training School) and a number.

Over the course of the war, more than three thousand students passed through Beaulieu; they represented more than a dozen countries, including Canada and the United States.[44] Many students were refugees from occupied countries who were training to return home as secret agents.[45] The students were sorted into different houses according to their nationalities, with the exception of women students, who had their own house, and the students being trained as wireless telegraphy (W/T) operators, who also lived separately.[*]

The atmosphere at Beaulieu was decidedly more genteel than that of the OSS camps, with their muddy tents and endlessly blaring loudspeakers and ad hoc classrooms filled with folding chairs.[46] In the student dormitories, servants attended to students' every need: each dormitory had, at a minimum, a clerk, two cooks, an automobile driver, a motorcycle driver, two orderlies, and three batmen, or military valets.[47] Each also had a housemaster who looked after the students with the eccentric fussiness of a private-school headmaster. The houses were grand, the furniture polished, the gardens well-groomed, the cooking and cleaning and laundry taken care of by servants as discreet as mice.

---

[*] Operating a radio was the most dangerous job in espionage; the SOE estimated that anyone doing the job would be caught within six months, so their preferred practice was to have a W/T operator training as an understudy to replace any W/T operator currently working. The other students at Beaulieu, when they passed W/T students in the road, cautioned each other not to look them in the eye, lest the W/T students remember them later under interrogation. The W/T students were dead men walking. Cyril Cunningham, *Beaulieu: The Finishing School for Secret Agents* (Barnsley, South Yorkshire: Pen & Sword, 2005), 32.

The English conviction: if we can find the traditions that will save us nowhere else, we can find them in polite dress, polite manners, polite styles of living.

But while the atmosphere differed, the truth is that when the war began, the British, despite their bluster, were nearly as unprepared for serious spycraft as the Americans.[48] So when, in 1940, Winston Churchill hastily established the SOE—uniting three other government bodies specializing in ungentlemanly warfare, all of which had *also* been hastily established just before the start of the war in 1939— the new agency had to train students in espionage without much institutional memory of the skills it taught. One historian says of the SOE agents who ran Beaulieu, "They had to learn virtually from scratch how to organize, train, and control secret agents, and the arts of secret communications, clandestine operating methods, and methods of infiltrating agents into enemy territory and recovering them."[49]

When Britain joined the war, its primary intelligence agency was the Secret Intelligence Service (SIS), a nonmilitary agency that focused on diplomatic espionage in foreign territories. Run by the Foreign Office, it was crumbling from neglect at the start of the war. Nonetheless, the SIS regarded the SOE as shabby and inferior. The Foreign Office reserved special disapproval for the fact that the SOE had, of necessity, to train civilian novices as agents, calling them a "scratch collection of amateurs."[50] The SIS even refused to share most of its institutional knowledge with the SOE, convinced that SOE agents would get captured and give everything away.[51]

No matter. The SOE would start with the traditions it could—and would build its own institutional knowledge from there.

FACT FOLLOWS FICTION

Soon after any new student arrived, her housemaster summoned her to a private meeting and gave her a strict talk about security. In the outside world, she must never mention either Beaulieu or the finishing school there. While at Beaulieu, she must never leave the school grounds.

And although she could keep notebooks for studying, she must give the notebooks to the school before she left.[52]

A typical course of study took three weeks to finish, although students might stay for a longer or shorter duration depending on what they would be doing in the field. To limit the students' exposure to the students in other houses, which would heighten everyone's security risk in the field, the students stayed in place and the instructors moved from house to house to give lectures. Usually, the students would see four instructors per day.[53]

The courses fell into five categories: cryptology, criminal skills like burglary and sabotage, psychological warfare, recognizing enemy police officers and intelligence agents, and secrecy.[54] The instructors supplemented the lectures by assigning the students regular practical exercises, which they called "schemes." A student might have to tail someone in a nearby village without letting that person know they were being tailed. Or they might have to lose someone who was tailing *them*, or give a written message to a fellow agent while in a public place, without alerting any passersby to the handoff.[55]

The students took courses together in subjects that, in the field, they would practice as separate specialties: some students would become couriers, others saboteurs, others recruiters, others propagandists. Some agents would have the job of spreading propaganda, which they would do in their own cells, along their own radial paths; other subspecialists, called "whisperers," whose job required special training in whispering, would work in solitude to set rumors quivering through select populations.[56] (More about them in the next chapter.)

The loneliest lesson that the students at Beaulieu learned was this: in a fundamental sense, a spy works alone. You might be working in an underground cell of three agents, or with a whole office full of agents who are pretending to be an entirely different kind of office, but when you're given an objective, you can't ask why it's necessary or pass it to someone else. You just have to do it, trusting that it's the right thing to do—and even if it *is* the right thing to do, you'll find that often the tactics you use to do the job aren't *nice*. You'll have to sabotage a train track. Or sink a ferry that has civilians aboard. You'll have to lie, to cheat, to secure secrets through every kind of swindling and stealth. The one consolation of this loneliness is that, if a mission is done right, often you and you alone are the one taking the risk.

But the paradox of spycraft is that, even though a spy's work encompasses all manner of moral issues, the real moral issue comes before any of that, during training. Because that's when you make the big decision that leads to all the rest: whether to become a spy at all, knowing full well that you may have to deceive and even kill people. And that's a choice you must make alone: the first, and hardest, lesson in the solitude of spycraft.

INNOCENT LETTERS

Some of the instructors were burned agents who had returned from the field; others had never been agents themselves, but had expertise in other fields that turned out to be remarkably useful for spycraft.[57] The school's first explosives instructor was Bill Cumper, a boisterous character who walked around with his pockets full of bomb parts and "a detonator behind his ear as if it were a cigarette."[58] Cumper was an army engineer who knew, as all army engineers do, that the world has two kinds of engineering journals: civil engineering journals, which explain how to build bridges, and military engineering journals, which explain how to blow up those same bridges.

Paul Dehn, who taught propaganda, worked in civilian life as a reporter and movie critic. After the war, he wrote the screenplays for the movies *Goldfinger*, *The Spy Who Came In from the Cold*, and *Murder on the Orient Express*.[59] Ralph Vibert, a lawyer, used his courtroom experience to teach students how to hold up under interrogation.[60] Peter Folis, an actor, taught cover stories and disguises. And Nobby Clark, that wilderness survival instructor who tended game on the king's estate, used his experience with fighting poachers when he taught students how to become poachers themselves. A good poacher must know a variety of ways to set snares for rabbits, to stalk birds, to knock out fish, to hide his tracks so the authorities can't find him. Clark threw in instruction on how to set traps big enough to catch human beings, which was reportedly one way he fended off poachers at Sandringham.[61]

SOE schools often had shelves of selected spy fiction available for students to read in their free time. The message seemed to be that, in the absence of a more established form of schooling, students could pick up tips on how to be spies by reading spy novels. SOE-approved titles included Helen MacInnes's *Assignment in Brittany* (1942), about an intrepid English spy who goes undercover in France; Geoffrey Household's *Rogue Male* (1939), about an intrepid English hunter who finds himself hunted by, and who then hunts down, a Hitler expy; and John Buchan's *The Thirty-Nine Steps* (1915), then England's most famous spy story, about an intrepid English amateur detective who foils a German invasion of England.[62]

These novels favored high romance over the low practicalities of spycraft; yet they also managed to understate its dangers. As the students who moved through Beaulieu would come to learn in the field, the reality was far deadlier. Nora Inayat Khan, who at one point was the only uncaptured radio operator in all of Paris, was shot, together with three other women agents, in the Dachau concentration camp.[63] Vera Leigh, who was a couture garment maker in civilian life, and whose instructors praised how nimble her fingers were when she wired up explosives, died a horrible death in the Natzweiler concentration camp, where a camp official injected her with a paralyzing agent and then threw her, alive, into a furnace.[64] Andrée Borrel and Diana Rowden, two other SOE agents, died in the same way. One staffer estimated that half of the women who infiltrated France for the SOE died in action, and their deaths were often so cruel and degraded that no novelist would use the stories.[65]

As a result, agents often carried suicide pills—so-called L pills, made from potassium cyanide—to give themselves an easier death than the Nazis would. As a general rule, you could have either a weapon or a cover, but not both; being caught with a gun or a knife, to say nothing of some hybrid shoe-dagger-radio from a spy novel, would give the lie to whatever innocent cover story an agent might give her interrogators.[66] But you could carry a newspaper and keep in your head the knowledge of how to fold it into a weapon. You could carry a matchbox and hope that your combat instructor was right about being able to use it to disarm a gunman.[67] And you could carry a little rubber-coated pill in the lining of your handkerchief—and hope that, when the moment came, you had time to take it.

It might seem like a self-evident fact: spies don't act like spies; they act like normal people. But in novels and movies, which had furnished the students with all they knew about spycraft, spies *don't* act like normal people; they act in ways designed precisely to satisfy the expectations that an audience brings to a spy story. Perhaps that's why, again and again, the training at Allied spy schools stressed the difference between spycraft in fiction and in real life.

If you're a spy, and you want to use a secret passphrase to identify yourself to someone you're meeting in a park or on a street corner, you shouldn't choose a passphrase like "The black falcon flies at midnight," because everyone who overhears you will know you're a spy. They've all been to the movies. Instead, you should choose something belligerent, because then the call-and-response will seem like some loser picking a fight on a bad day. A real password exchange between spies might go:

"Nice hat, chump."

"What the hell's your problem?"[68]

This was just one of many lessons on the real lives of spies that filled the curriculum at Beaulieu, which was designed to be dense, specific, and relentlessly practical. Instructors would have to counter popular ideas about spy behavior at every turn while training these spycraft novices, setting out guidelines from their first moments under cover—to potentially their last.

An agent, regardless of whether she is working in a neutral or an occupied country, should set about assembling a network of informants from the day she enters the field, the instructors at Beaulieu told their students. Most informants don't *know* they're informants, so the network should appear, even to its members, to be an innocent scandal society of people who like to gossip and are in a position to hear the latest stories: for example, bankers, café staff, clergymen, doctors, dressmakers, hairdressers, hotel staff, launderers, mail carriers, railroad employees, shopkeepers, or telephone operators. If the agent is *very* bold, she might make an informant of a police officer.[69]

The agent's method should not be to drill her informants with questions about sensitive topics—how gauche, how obvious—but rather to encourage "careless talk." Trifling gossip over cups of *café national*, the famously terrible rationed coffee of Occupied France. If she wants to know something specific, but doesn't want people to notice her asking questions, she should simply make incorrect statements while in the company of experts. Her companions will correct her, especially if they're men.[70]

The scoops she gets from her informants will help her to survive, help her fellow agents to survive, and help the Baker Street Irregulars back home figure out exactly how to wage their irregular warfare.[71] If the Germans roll out new planes or guns, what's new in the design? (No detail is unimportant. The British were able to distinguish different enemy air squadrons by counting the blades in the propellers.) Have more trains been moving through town recently? Have the police suddenly suspended the civilian use of some roads? Are lots of new soldiers in town? Are soldiers in town complaining about their leave being canceled? (Those last details might indicate preparations for a military strike.)[72]

Women had a reputation for performing well as couriers, so the SOE and the OSS often reserved this role for women agents. Women didn't need to explain to the Gestapo why they weren't off fighting; women faced no danger of getting caught in a *rafle*, one of the periodic raids in which the Gestapo seized the local men who happened to be out on the street and put them on a train to work in some German factory; and women could carry around bulky baskets, big enough to hold, say, a twenty-pound radio transmitter, since a layer of vegetables atop their real cargo was enough to show they were simply out shopping. (Once, a courier in France named Maureen O'Sullivan, while she was moving the radio to a new location on her bicycle, was standing at an intersection when a Gestapo agent leaned out of the window of a nearby car, gestured at the weekend suitcase leashed to her bicycle, and demanded to know what was in it. She gave him a dazzling smile and replied, "I've got a radio transmitter and I'm going to contact London and tell them all about you." He scolded her for joking—"You're far too pretty to risk your neck with such stupidities"—and went on his way.[73])

Radio operators would give coded messages to couriers, and the couriers would deliver them to their associates. The women at Beaulieu learned how to write messages in code and invisible ink, so that they could leave letters in a "letter box" in a library or a bookstore or the forest for associates to find. They learned how write "Innocent Letters" that appeared to be innocent *billets-doux* or picture postcards or reminders to do the shopping. They learned more about paper and ink than many archivists do in a lifetime. If you want to write with invisible ink, you should use plain matte paper and a dip pen, making sure the nib never scrapes the page. You can make good invisible inks from alum powder (tell a pharmacist you have aching feet), lead acetate (you have swollen joints), or ammonia (you want to clean jewelry); or, in a pinch, you can spread Vaseline on a page, let it dry, set the page on top of the Innocent Letter with the Vaseline facing down, and apply your pen to the page on top.[74]

Boffins at Liverpool University worked on devising ever more elaborate invisible inks, but here, as in most other aspects of spycraft, simplicity and shrewdness beat spy-fiction science.[75] The enemy can't find a secret message on a page they don't look at, so crumple up a "blank" sheet with invisible ink on it and throw it next to some tree in the woods like an old food wrapper. Use handwriting instead of a typewriter, since a motivated sleuth can track down a specific typewriter. No need for a color-changing microdot to tell you whether an envelope's been opened; just tip in some cigarette ashes, as if you were smoking as you wrote.[76]

If you encrypt your message with a cipher, you don't need a personal Enigma machine; you just need a book. Include in the letter a five-digit number—37016, for instance—that will tell your correspondent (who has agreed in advance on what book to use) the page (61), line (7), and first *n* number of words (3) to read as the secret message. If you don't have two copies of the same book, you can just commit the same poem to memory, then use a more complicated system involving keywords from the poem to encrypt your message.[77]

Once again, even the classic spy tropes, like invisible ink and secret codes, had to take the most prosaic of forms. The easiest forms to overlook.

TO DANCE AT THE FOLIES BERGÈRE

Those students at Beaulieu who became couriers never knew the names of their fellow couriers in the field, even those who worked in the same town. Spies and resistance agents worked in independent cells of as few as three members apiece, which protected those cells from giving each other up during interrogation. And yet those couriers built, strand by strand, a web along which a whole world of information traveled.

In Paris, Josephine Baker, a famous American dancer at the Folies Bergère, used her star power to schmooze at diplomatic parties and passed back to the Allies all the Nazi military information she overheard. In Oslo, postal workers eased open the envelopes of letters written by German soldiers. In Istanbul, whisperers whispered. And in London and Washington, war planners in the SOE and OSS tried mightily to scrape together facts, *any* facts, about conditions in Occupied Europe—and to convert those facts into plans for cracking the Nazi shield.

What could possibly connect all these people? Only information—only good intel could be the basis for coordinating missions from across great gulfs. Without good information, the whole web would shred.

The SOE and the OSS didn't yet know it, but the very weaknesses that made their own governments look down on them—they had to pull recruits out of *libraries*, for heaven's sake—would force them to introduce methods of information gathering and analysis that were so good they forever transformed the world of spycraft. And in that realm, Adele Kibre was to become, quite quietly and unexpectedly, the Allies' greatest agent.

To be sure, the Allies had *all kinds* of secret systems for gathering intelligence. Today, the most famous of these is Ultra: the code name that the British used for intelligence that came from codebreaking. The British valued this knowledge highly; Winston Churchill would ask for the latest decodes from Bletchley Park, a highly secret facility for codebreaking Axis radio traffic, by saying, "Where are my eggs?"—because, as he used to explain, the cryptologists of Bletchley Park, who gave so much and said so little, were "the geese who laid the golden eggs but never cackled."*

And yet there was much that Ultra intelligence couldn't shed light on. Ultra could tell the Allies—when the cryptologists succeeded in breaking the ever-changing codes—where the Axis was moving troops, or when they planned to make a strike, or whether they believed some piece of disinformation that the Allies were throwing at them. But it couldn't tell the Allies things that the Axis military personnel on the radio didn't know or weren't talking about. Engineering information about some target's vulnerabilities, scientific discoveries that might help with building weapons, industrial information about war manufacturing, the kind of crucial local knowledge that you'd find in small newspapers—none of this was a topic of discussion among the Kriegsmarine or the Luftwaffe, and so the brains at Bletchley couldn't deliver it.

In fact, even Bletchley might have started laying golden eggs sooner with the help of the kind of archival work that Kibre specialized in. The greatest feat of Bletchley's cryptographers was breaking Enigma, a nastily complicated cipher machine that the German military used. The story of how the British cracked Enigma is full of twists and turns, including the temporary theft of an Enigma machine from a railway station in Warsaw, which allowed Polish spies to photograph the machine without the Germans realizing it was missing, and the smuggling of an Enigma replica from Paris to London in a playwright's luggage. But if they'd thought to look, the British could simply have visited the archives of the Patent Office in London and found a full technical dossier of the Enigma machine, in English and with accompanying diagrams, which the machine's inventors had filed there in 1927. They appear not to have thought of it.[78]

---

* How secret was Bletchley? After the war, when the British Crown awarded a knighthood to Edward Travis, who had been in charge of running the facility, Travis's wife asked him, "What for?" Ronald Lewin, *Ultra Goes to War: The Secret History* (London: Hutchinson & Co., 1978), 17, 183.

As one of the Beaulieu training booklets asked, "Why is information indispensable to an agent? . . . Where and how does he get this information?"[79] The agents were trained to understand that if you weren't good at getting information, you died. Luckily for Kibre, she would turn out to have a first-rate skill set when it came to information gathering. For an experienced archive hunter, anything could be a resource: Newspapers. Magazines. Letters on tables. Bookstores. Libraries. Librarians. If you make friends with a bookstore owner, they'll tell you if anyone bought the same book twice, which will tell you who's writing in code. If you make friends with a librarian, they'll let you into the secret catalogue for uncatalogued items—items that are still waiting, maybe for years, to be properly processed. If you make friends with the editor of an academic journal, they can show you the articles they haven't yet published. That's called gray literature. And the articles they haven't read yet. That's called the slush pile.[80]

And as it would turn out, Kibre's methods of information gathering could bring something to the world of intelligence that the most conventional forms of spycraft—stealing military secrets, intercepting military chatter, deciphering codes—couldn't.

A THIEF IN THE NIGHT

The real lives of spies entail less high living and more low crime than you might think. The first instructor in the course on burglary and safecracking at Beaulieu, Johnny Ramensky, was a Scottish safecracker who spent his time dipping in and out of prison—not always through the front door, since jailbreaking was another one of his hobbies. After England entered the war, the British government realized that his talents could be put in the service of national interests. While many of his fellow instructors looked and sounded like they should be sitting in leather armchairs in a Pall Mall club, Ramensky dished out street philosophy and an ever-present wiseacre smile: exactly the man you'd want to teach the low craft of burglary.[81]

As Ramensky explained to his students, they needed to know burglary in case they had to get new identity papers in a hurry—for instance, if they were outed as spies and needed to flee using new identities, the best way to get those papers was to steal them. Another way that spycraft in real life differed from spycraft in fiction: a spy whose cover had been blown didn't need to find a disguise specialist and an eccentric master forger; she just needed to break into someone's house.

The training in burglary culminated in a hands-on exercise: the students, in pairs or small teams, were to creep through the forest and rob one of the other manors while the staff and students who lived there slept or ate a meal. Ramensky told the students that nobody in the house they were targeting knew, on the night in question, that they were coming.[82] Ramensky was lying.

The exercise had two parts: reconnaissance and then the deed itself.[83] One team member would visit the target house, offering a cover story for the visit that an ordinary civilian would accept. During the visit, another team member might sneak around the outside of the house unseen, making note of lines of sight, entryways, paths for escape. (This team member, too, needed to have a cover story ready in case she was caught sneaking around.) Then the team would reassemble and plan the break-in.[84] Based on their reconnaissance, the students could choose what time of the day or night to do the job, though they had to let Ramensky know what time they chose in advance.[85] At the chosen hour, an important item, such as papers or weapons, would be waiting somewhere in the house for them to steal. They would recognize the item when they saw it.[86]

True to Ramensky's word, the students in the target house didn't know they were about to be robbed. But he told two staffers when to expect the burglary: the target house's housemaster and a random member of the staff, who, though the burglars didn't know this, was assigned to pretend to be asleep in the house. Given the slightest excuse, this staffer was to rouse the whole house to alarm.[87]

So, let's imagine a final scene: Kibre and her roommate stumbling through the forest, on a cold night in March, as shouts rise from the target house, a redbrick manor about thirty minutes by foot from where they're staying in the women's house on campus.[88] Kibre's roommate is clutching a sheaf of identity papers; Kibre is carrying a bottle of vintage red Bordeaux. (We'll say the manor's owners left the wine cellar well stocked, and the government of Britain did promise to reimburse any losses—even those from American banditry.)

That night, the women's house drinks to victory.

REPORT CARDS FOR KILLING

If British spy schools resembled posh boarding schools, American spy schools resembled cowboy ranches. In Maryland, the students at Area B spent rather more time working with guns than one would expect in the training of agents who likely wouldn't be allowed to carry weapons on the job.[89]

The explanation that the OSS gave for why they put so much focus on firearms was that an agent might find himself cornered by the enemy in circumstances where he could grab a gun and shoot his way out. As Colonel Rex Applegate, who taught firearms at Area B, explained, an intelligence agent on the run had to shoot up close and to fire without taking any time to use the sights—unlike soldiers, who carried rifles so they could shoot over long distances, and who had time to aim carefully. So, cowboy calculus—what one writer called "triggernometry"—ruled the lesson plans in ballistic weaponry.[90]

The U.S. government did indeed send researchers to consult the papers of Wild Bill Hickok and other Old West sharpshooters, the better to train agents in a quick draw and a sharp eye. A major difference between cowboys in the movies and real Old West gunfighters like Hickok is that movie cowboys fire with the gun at the hip, whereas Hickok fired with the arm held straight out at the height of his eyes.[91] Applegate taught his students to do the same. Standing in arenas with floors of packed dirt and ceilings of trembling winter branches, the students of Area B practiced drawing on each other, and practiced again.[92]

"Do unto others as they would do unto you," he advised in a training manual, "*but do it first.*"[93]

He would also put the students in pairs and make them practice holding each other at gunpoint, with the gun at the small of the back. The gunman was to pull the trigger as soon as he sensed the victim was making a funny move, and the victim was to keep practicing until he could disarm the gunman reliably without getting "shot." (Mercifully, the guns were unloaded for this exercise.)[94]

Applegate, like Fairbairn, agreed that a good fight should be unfair.

The staffers at OSS training camps evaluated their students with report cards. Most of these records don't survive, but the ones that do show that students headed for desk jobs were expected to master the same skills as students going into the field. Even though Sherman Kent, for example, was committed to a position in the Chairborne Division in Washington, he learned to quick draw like a cowboy and stab like an assassin along with everyone else. (He never used the firearms knowledge again, as far as the record shows, but he seems to have cherished the lessons on knives.) Or though Joseph Curtiss expected to be working under his own name, and to be working with books, he still learned how to run a secret organization, together with Morse code, lock picking, and the other spy essentials on the syllabus. As it turned out, he was lucky that his coursework was so comprehensive, because he became, rather accidentally, a *much* bigger boss in the spy world than anyone expected—least of all him.

Curtiss's and Kent's report cards from Area B have disappeared in the midden of history, but surviving report cards indicate that the staffers who evaluated them would likely have recorded each man's performance in general skills (e.g., close combat, cover, demolitions, handling others, mapping, security, weapons), communications skills (e.g., basic procedure, compass and map, cryptography, maintenance, military drill), and further skills with code (e.g., accuracy, code: transmitting, code: receiving, security-cover). They might have added another report card that recorded each man's future mission (e.g., desk field, desk Washington, group leader, interpreter, radioman, undercover), his future cover identity (e.g., businessman, government official, military, professional, scientific), and his personality strengths and weaknesses (e.g., adaptability, cooperation, courage, intelligence, leadership, need for supervision, physical condition, sociability).[95]

Lectures. Blackboards. Classmates. Homework. Tests. Report cards. For the professors who were sitting, for the first time in years, at the back of the classroom, this strange new world must have seemed utterly familiar, though pulled inside out. But maybe the apparatus of schooling served as a support to make up for the strangeness of spycraft; after all, they all knew what to do in a classroom. It was all familiar enough, *for now.* In the field it would be a different story.

GRADUATION

At last, training ended, and the students parted ways to walk into dangerous and uncertain futures.[96]

The lecture materials for the SOE's spy schools, which the SOE shared with the OSS for use in American spy schools, gave strict instructions for the "final arrangements" of students who were about to depart on missions.[97]

Once your superiors give you your assignment, your cover story, your documents, and your clothes, the lectures said, you must carefully study your new belongings and make sure the finest details in each one match your cover. Then, just as carefully, study yourself: "Strip naked and examine yourself *from head to toe*, to ensure that there is not the *slightest mark*—even a bruise—which is not 'covered,' and that all semipermanent features are correct. Special attention to *hands, feet, nails, teeth, nicotine stains*—e.g., if your immediate cover is that you have walked a long way, your feet must be red and blistered."[98]

If you're going undercover as a researcher, for example, you might be expected to have a scholar's stoop, dents on the bridge of the nose from wearing glasses, newsprint rubbed off on the hands. If you're heading to France, you should know that French skirts are short and the jackets long, whereas American skirts are long and the jackets short.[99] And so on.

Try on your clothes; see how everything fits. Feel around in the pockets. Try loading them up with your new accessories. Everything you carry, from matches to money to ticket stubs to makeup compacts, must come from the country you're heading to and must seem to be worn with handling. You should try to carry something expensive—maybe a gold-plated cigarette case—in case you need to bribe someone unexpectedly. Don't leave any tobacco grains in your pockets; if you do, the tobacco should be a brand available in the place you're going.[100]

If you plan to carry a weapon when you drop into the field, remember that its existence demolishes your cover. Don't forget that general rule: you can have a weapon or a cover, but you can't have both. One exception is weapons in the form of drugs; in theory, they're also incompatible with a cover, but you can hide them more easily, and if you need them, you'll be glad you have them. L pills will kill you. Amphetamine pills will keep you up. Ptomaine pills will make an enemy sick enough to keep him out of your way while you're up to mischief, K.O. drops will knock him out, and E pills will knock him out so deeply that you can stage an elaborate death scene for him ("An excellent method of staging a murder as suicide"). But remember that E pills are bitter, so you should put them in a bitter drink, like coffee.[101]

On the morning of your departure, you should do your toilette only with soap, razors, skin cream, and tooth powder that match your cover. Don't let the smell of an unfamiliar soap be the one little piece out of place in the world that makes a police officer notice you as he walks by.[102]

Good luck. Or, as the French say, *Merde*.[103]

3

THROUGH THE LOOKING GLASS

I am listening to Istanbul, intent, my eyes closed.
—ORHAN VELI KANIK[1]

SLINGING A BOOKBAG OVER HIS SHOULDER, PROFESSOR Joseph Curtiss went to Istanbul—which was, in the 1940s, the spy capital of the world.[2]

Turkey, like Sweden, was neutral territory, though each country sustained neutrality in the war by following opposite policies on espionage. The Turkish government asked the Axis and the Allies how Turkey could stay out of the war, and the reply was that Turkey could remain neutral if it let everybody's spies operate in its territory. Turkey agreed. The Swedish government asked the Axis and the Allies how Sweden could stay out of the war, and the reply was that Sweden could remain neutral if it let *nobody's* spies operate in its territory.[3]

And so, although spies were (of course) running around in both countries, the spies in Stockholm had to work totally underground, whereas the spies in Istanbul—well. They were still in the business of keeping secrets, but they occupied a world that presumed *everyone* was a spy. Seventeen different intelligence agencies worked in Istanbul. Their agents often sat at adjoining restaurant tables, trying to eavesdrop on each other's conversation while the waiter eavesdropped on them both.[4]

Imagine arriving in wartime Istanbul. The receptionist who checked you in at the İpek Palas Hotel, a luxury hotel near the Grand Bazaar, was an agent of the Turkish Intelligence Service. The cook at the Yeni Spor café who made your special order of *café Viennois* worked for the Turkish police and the British too. The barmaid who served you raki at the Lux-Bar was an informer for the British, and the nurse at the hospital who treated your hangover was a German agent. Even church wasn't sacrosanct: if you went to a priest the next morning to absolve the night's sins, he might be a spy too; one Father Eilers was a double agent who gave secrets to both the British and the Turkish intelligence services.[5]

Istanbul wasn't new to global drama. It had been the capital city of four empires. It was a city *and* a crossroads. And the Grand Bazaar—one of the oldest and largest covered markets in the world—was the place where everyone met, and everything, including information, was for sale.

As for the Grand Bazaar itself, one might call it, as it was in the 1940s, "the bazaar at the end of empires." The Grand Bazaar boasted treasures of all kinds: Russian heirlooms from the aristocrats who fled upon the fall of the Romanovs; painted manuscripts from the Ottoman dynasty; coins from ancient Greece; bracelets from ancient Egypt; glassware from the Roman Empire. It also held a lot of smoke and mirrors. Tourists often paid treasure prices for worthless trinkets, inflamed by what many called "bazaar fever."[6]

This was the place to practice bargaining—"making bazaar." Shopkeepers would leap out, saying, "Where are you from?" or "One question!" or "Lady, you dropped something—my heart!" and the shopper, pulled into conversation, would have to figure out what was true, what was a trap, what was a beautiful lie, what was a cultural distinction, what was posturing, what was politesse—and what kind of performance would help in bargaining.[7]

In the 1970s, the anthropologist Clifford Geertz would use bazaars as a model for understanding environments filled with unreliable information: "To start with a dictum: in the bazaar, information is poor, scarce, maldistributed, inefficiently communicated, and intensely valued."[8] So it was with intelligence in wartime Istanbul. Civilians ran "truth bourses" or "news exchanges," offering to whoever bid the highest price—journalists, diplomats, espionage agents—whatever news they could scratch together. Refugees sold news about the conditions in the countries they fled: from them, a journalist commented, "a good 'inside story' is worth from twenty-five dollars up"—almost four hundred fifty dollars in today's money.[9]

Not all information was true. But true information was a treasure worth the arduous hunt the bazaar demanded. And this made the bazaar the perfect training ground for a spy fresh from the OSS training camps.

Curtiss reached Istanbul in July 1943. His orders were to set up his cover and wait to be contacted. (How would he be contacted? He'd know when it happened.)[10] Five foot nine and lean to the point of underweight, with brown hair, a solemn round face, and what he described on his draft card as a "sallow" complexion, Curtiss wasn't the kind of man you'd look at twice, either to admire him or to size him up as an opponent. Hell, he wasn't the kind of man you'd look at *once.* The forty-two-year-old bachelor was supposed to wear his own identity as a cover, so he probably dressed at the posher end of professorial. He dug in diligently, setting himself up as a young professor who was in town to collect books for Yale University's library.

This was a readily believable cover—first, because Curtiss was supposed to include, in the finds he sent back to Yale, interesting wartime texts for the use of later historians, which meant he *should* be in a hub like Istanbul; and second, because, in addition to the Grand Bazaar, Istanbul also had beautiful book markets. The Sahaflar Çarşisi, or Old Book Bazaar, was a zigzagging corridor of shops near the Fesçiler Gate of the Grand Bazaar. In the shadows of its high walls, the shop doors glowed. Inside, pleasantly chaotic tables showed off the wares: calligraphy brushes, cut-reed calligraphy pens, and porcupine quills for stirring ink; Ottoman manuscript pages and well-made fakes; framed verses from the Koran; books in modern Turkish, books in old Turkish with Arabic letters, books in English, shipped from overstock inventories in Europe. Forgotten books, books never known enough to be forgotten, and bestsellers to read on the train. Cats slept among the wares on the display tables and inside the bookshops, on bookshelves and reading chairs, in every possible attitude of repose. (Istanbul, sometimes called "Catstanbul" or "the City of Cats," had an enormous population of well-fed street cats.)

Like any innocent newcomer in a storied city, Curtiss went around to see the sights. One imagines he saw the Blue Mosque, lined with more than twenty thousand tiles bearing traceries in the shapes of words and flowers—like a book you can walk around in, written all over with the calligraphy of devotion. The Bosporus by ferry, which offered a panoramic view of the city's domes and minarets. The Topkapı Palace, where the sultan's children once took their schooling in a marble mansion, stocked with a world-class library, on the palace grounds.[11] Istanbul University, right around the corner from the Old Book Bazaar. And of course, the Old Book Bazaar and the Grand Bazaar itself.

Curtiss also connected with Yalies who lived in the city, as anyone would expect a Yale man to do; he shared an apartment with one of them and "filled their quarters with books, partly because it would support his cover, more because he had little else to do."[12]

Then he waited.

And waited.

As days, then weeks, passed, his anxiety mounted. Everyone on every street corner, in every shop in the Grand Bazaar, might be his OSS contact. Where were his allies?

A spy is a man who lives apart, John le Carré said, but surely there's no worse way of living apart than being left out in the cold.

SOMEWHAT LIKE A SPIDER

What sort of man was Joseph Curtiss? Or, since we know who he was in civilian life—a mild-mannered bookworm; somebody who, given that his students never recorded any memories of him, not even tributes when he retired, probably couldn't even get the attention of a waiter— a better way to phrase that question is: what sort of man is a good spy, and was Joseph Curtiss liable to be, or become, that sort of man?

We often think of spies as suave, magnetic, good at capturing the confidence of a room. Maybe it's because the A-list actors who play these roles can demand that the scripts flatter them, and they often do. Maybe it's because studios think viewers go to the movies for pure fantasy. Whatever the case, spy fiction, in its preoccupation with the James Bonds and Jason Bournes, too often misses what really makes a good spy. Usually, a good spy is someone like Curtiss—not glamorous, but forgettable.

Spies aren't charismatic people, *by design*. That remark about not getting the attention of a waiter? It's from the director of the CIA in the 1970s, William Colby, who once said that an ideal spy is someone "who has a hard time catching the eye of a waiter in a restaurant."* Joseph Curtiss had this quality, which may be why Wallace Notestein, the senior professor who called on Curtiss on that fateful day in 1942, chose him as the agent for this mission. Of course he was also an expert on the world of books, which was necessary for this mission, since Allied intelligence leaders made clear that a spy must be competent in the profession that serves as his cover.

But Curtiss, that mild-mannered bookworm, also had adventurous longings that would prove perfect for this mission—a mission that became so much bigger and more consequential than either he or his superiors ever expected.

We can see these longings when examining a work that, while he was still figuring out, as young adults must, the component parts of his personality, he spent three years writing: his dissertation.

A dissertation is an autobiography. That's what scholars always say, and they're right. The idea that a dissertation is, on some level, a confession of the self, an attempt to methodize one's nature, is so commonplace that advisers warn their students not to write dissertations on sexual topics, because no matter what that topic is—sadism in early Puritan sermons, public masturbation in the works of James Joyce, hermaphroditic

---

* He added rather ruefully that even after he himself had risen to one of the highest roles in Washington, "I still have a hard time catching a waiter's eye in a restaurant." Leslie Gelb, "Real Spies Shoot Down Spy Movies," *New York Times*, September 2, 1984.

sex in the works of Shakespeare—hiring committees will assume it's the student's kink.

Of course, when a scholar is still a graduate student, the sources of their fascination with a particular topic are often mysterious to them. (Perhaps the enduring impulse that drives a life of scholarship is like the enduring impulse that drives a life of art: not asking a question that you don't know the answer to, but answering a question that you never figure out how to formulate.) But when that scholar rises through the ranks to become an adviser herself, she'll tell her students the same thing her adviser told her: be careful what you write in your dissertation, because a dissertation is an autobiography.

Joseph Curtiss chose to write his dissertation on the seventeenth-century astrologer William Lilly. It also happens to be a story of the life of a spy.[13]

Curtiss submitted his dissertation in 1926 before joining the literature faculty at Yale as an assistant professor. In the 1920s, the rules for putting together a dissertation in literature were a lot looser. A student could write an *essay*, in the old-fashioned sense of the term: a lyrical, discursive exploration on a subject that probes the writer's own sensibility. And that's what Curtiss did.

The dissertation, about the lives of early modern astrologers, is relentlessly practical in its take on their occult profession. But whenever it talks about their studying, their libraries, the prose becomes a shower of stardust. What fascinated Curtiss about astrologers was that they were a fantastical, through-the-looking-glass version of a scholar. In early modern England, an astrologer wore, like an Oxford professor, "a velvet cap and gown," and he advertised himself to the public as a "professor."[14] He had, of necessity, a scholar's love of books, as Curtiss says repeatedly: "Unless he was an absolute quack, the astrologer was possessed of much deep and curious learning. He was consulted for so many different purposes that he could not neglect his studies." But he used his learning to read the destinies that were written in the stars—or at least he thought so, or at least his clients thought so, since the whole aim of the dissertation is to show why people of Lilly's time believed astrology to be a legitimate science, though we wouldn't call it that now.[15]

Curtiss never loses an opportunity to mention all the time that Lilly spent studying—Lilly's wealth, he says, was "a fact which gave him leisure to read over all his books many times."[16] His astronomers kept, with their books, supernatural items like brazen heads, which were rumored to be able to speak through enchantments. Here is someone who saw romance—intrigue—*literal magic* in the life of learning.

But more than that, this life of learning provided certainty in an uncertain world. Curtiss argues that astrologers probably used their knowledge and cunning to solve many of the problems that clients brought to them. An astrologer was the early modern world's version of a private eye. "Astrologers were expected to serve as the detective bureau of the day," Curtiss wrote in a tone of wistful admiration, adding that, though they must have used earthly cunning rather than celestial signs to get their most important answers, they solved their clients' mysteries "with sufficient success to keep people continually demanding their services."[17] People came to them to ask where to find lost belongings, where to find missing people, when a husband was going to die, whether a wife was plotting to become a widow.[18]

This aspect of the astrologer's work fascinated Curtiss, who wrote about it as if he were writing a detective novel: "Somewhat like a spider he sat in his house, watching the world come in and out with its innumerable petty troubles."[19]

THE DEVIL AND EUCLID

Curtiss took special interest in William Lilly because he was the astrologer who opened up the field from making predictions about small life events to making predictions about events of international import. Lilly, a poised bourgeois with a comb mustache, got deeply into astrology after the death of his older wife left him with a good fortune and time on his hands. He often did detective work in his line as an astrologer, like hunting down malefactors on behalf of their enraged victims.[20]

Before long, he had worked up a whole system for pulling political intelligence out of the stars and publishing it in a series of pamphlets, which nobody in England had ever done before.[21] Oh, sure, astrologers had worked as spies for sovereigns as a *private* matter. Queen Elizabeth I called her court astrologer, John Dee, "my noble intelligencer" and "my ubiquitous eyes," since Dee used his craft to supply the queen with intelligence.[22] But Lilly was doing something new. His pamphlets—with marvelous titles like *The Prophecy of the White King and Dreadfull Dead-Man Explained*—became reliable bestsellers, as the public was desperate for political intelligence during the Civil War.

When he wrote his dissertation, Curtiss had no way of knowing he would be caught up in a wartime revolution of knowledge like the one Lilly worked up. Nor could he know, even after he arrived in Istanbul, that he would soon be a player in an information game of personality and prediction. But he saw in the genteel detective-mystic in scholar's robes an appealing image of the scholar's vocation. Himself through the looking glass: the life he'd like to have if the world was a little more magical.[23]

Espionage and astrology have a few key points in common. An overwhelming drive to control what will happen by gaining total fore-knowledge. A fascination with personalities, and a belief that one can learn enough about someone's personality to predict their actions better than they themselves can. A conviction that one's profession relies on using methods that only initiates must know to uncover information that only initiates *should* know. Like espionage, early modern astrology was a field that concerned itself greatly with ciphers. For example, John Dee corresponded with William Cecil, the head of Elizabeth I's coun-terespionage service, about a book on steganography, a form of cipher that entails hiding one message in another. Dee likely took interest in such ciphers as much to hide the secrets of astrology from nonastrolo-gers as to hide intelligence communications from enemy agents.[24]

And just as Curtiss would in his role as a spy in Istanbul, early modern astrologers used the trappings of university life, in particu-lar, to gain the trust of others. They called themselves professors, wore academic dress, and made much of their master's degrees when they had them—or awarded themselves master's degrees when they didn't.[25] Some spent stints teaching in universities as actual tutors or profes-sors. Likewise, in Istanbul, Curtiss took a teaching job at Robert College, an American university founded by missionaries, which gave him a campus to live on and a handful of students to teach. (His students there, too, didn't seem to remember him later.)[26] In some settings, a tweed jacket and a bookbag can be as useful as a cassock and a collar for quickly signaling to others that you mean no harm.

Curtiss wrote his dissertation as a remarkably novelistic portrait of a scholar-magician who, to use a phrase from one Victorian wag's joke about Lilly and Dee, got his intelligence from "the Devil and Euclid": from mathematics and the mystical alike, the realm of inarguable logic and the realm of unknowable intuition.[27] That was what Curtiss wanted to be when he was twenty-two: a magician; a spider at the center of a world of information; the man who can predict the future.

When Curtiss went to Istanbul in 1943, he didn't have much more life experience than he did at twenty-two. He was smart, but he wasn't slick. If you manage to survive in the world of counterespionage—say, the deceptive information marketplace of wartime Istanbul, which another OSS agent called "a viper's nest of intrigue"—you can't do it by staying that way.[28] The best you can hope for is that when you come out of it, you're slick, but you aren't mean. In the meanwhile, as a novice, he had a few assets on his side: a face that a waiter would forget, a mind that loved information for its own sake, and a heart that believed in the romance of learning.

Not that he could know it yet. Because the days in the Old Book Bazaar piled up, and suddenly two months had gone by since he had arrived in Istanbul—and he still hadn't heard from his OSS contact.

I KNOW THAT'S A SECRET, FOR IT'S WHISPERED EVERYWHERE

Here's the reason nobody came to get Joseph Curtiss. Just as he arrived in Istanbul, the OSS/Istanbul outpost made an absolute shambles of an intelligence-gathering scheme called, after the code name for one of the sources involved, the Dogwood chain. The scheme aimed to use Istanbul's intelligence networks to infiltrate German and Hungarian spy agencies. Instead, one of the drivers who worked for the outpost turned out to be working for the Turkish secret police, and the personal driver for Lanning Macfarland, the outpost's director, turned out to be working for the Russians. By the time Curtiss arrived in the city, the informants who were supposedly supplying OSS/Istanbul with information were expertly *extracting* information from them—giving them, in turn, "chicken feed," or worthless information meant to make them feel like they were eating well. Meanwhile, the British had figured out that OSS/Istanbul was leaking and stopped sharing information with them.[29]

When Washington discovered the scale of the Dogwood screwup, the OSS brass fired almost everyone involved in the operation. Which left the few agents who were still clinging to their jobs at the OSS/Istanbul outpost too worried and distracted to think about the poor book collector who was hanging around the Old Book Bazaar, paging through antique manuscripts and waiting for a hand on the shoulder.

While he waited, Curtiss invested himself in the distraction of his teaching job at Robert College. The work wasn't heavy, just an upper-level English class now and then, but waiting for his OSS contact left him at such loose ends that people were sure to start noticing how much time he spent idle unless he gave himself something to do. The college looked like a Hollywood screenwriter's idea of a grand old Mediterranean college, with a main building fronted by huge white columns and a lush green campus ringed with cypresses. It stood in need of new teachers because most of the permanent faculty had returned to the United States soon after the start of the war. The students found it funny to imagine that the new tweed-clad figures at the front of the classrooms must include some spies—"Trading romantic stories," in the words of one historian, "about which teacher was most likely to have put another body in the Bosporus"—but they didn't extend their suspicion to Curtiss.[30]

Curtiss, though, recognized that students will gladly study the professor if it means they can avoid studying the readings, and that they gossip "as bad as diplomats," as he later told a friend. So he stayed well out of the way of the students when he wasn't in the classroom. He went for walks to gaze from the shoreline across the Bosporus, or to explore Rumelihisarı, a fifteenth-century stone fortress near campus that folds down the hillside in sharp angles, all zigzagging parapet walls and soaring towers. Sometimes he picked out books to donate to the Robert College library.[31]

Eventually, two months into his stay in Istanbul, Curtiss decided he wouldn't wait around anymore. He took the bold step of tracking down Macfarland himself. How he did this the historical record doesn't say, but given how leaky the Istanbul outpost was at the time, perhaps his feat wasn't so remarkable. By that point, the OSS brass had discovered the Dogwood screwup and was hauling most of the agents involved home to the States by the scruffs of their necks. Macfarland was holding on to his own position as director by his fingernails.[32]

Macfarland—perhaps recognizing that he was dealing with a motivated detective, or perhaps deciding to cover his embarrassment at being found by dumping on the finder a huge task that was sure to embarrass *him*, or perhaps just understaffed and desperate—responded to Curtiss's sudden appearance by giving him surprising new orders. As Curtiss later recalled, he was instructed to take "an office in the OSS quarters and set up the basics of an X-2 outfit." To put it plainly, Macfarland asked Curtiss to build a local chapter of the X-2 Counterespionage Section Branch of the OSS, to replace the group of agents who were just fired.[33] (*How? Just do it. You'll figure it out.*) A new director would be coming to take the X-2 branch's helm, but Curtiss would have to get it running before he arrived.

X-2 got its name from the phrase *double-cross*. The purpose of X-2 units in the OSS and the SOE was to track down Axis spies in neutral or Allied territory and turn them into double agents who actually worked for the Allies. More broadly, X-2 units performed counterespionage, which is the art of foiling enemy spycraft—most often by turning enemy agents, making them believe lies, or . . . neutralizing them.[34] Stealing the enemy's secrets won't win you a war unless you also prevent the enemy from stealing yours.

Thus began a remarkable rise for the forgettable, mild-mannered bookworm. Curtiss went to Istanbul expecting that he'd be a low functionary, hunting for intelligence in print under the guise of hunting for books to send back to Yale. Now his superiors were asking him to build and run, without any special training, a whole counterespionage operation. Nor were they finished asking him to push beyond the boundaries of his expertise. He'd soon become the operation's head. In time, as one of his friends later noted, Curtiss's work in Istanbul required him to have not one, not two, but three different roles: a spy, a harmless professor and book collector, and the head of OSS/Istanbul.[35]

AN INFORMATION GAME

So—how do you run a successful counterespionage operation? How do you *build* one? Curtiss's first task was to go over the personality files that the OSS had written up on its sources. He cross-referenced them with any other papers he could find to see whether a source seemed to be working with other intelligence services, or whether they were in the habit of giving the OSS chicken feed instead of useful intelligence, or whether they were lying wholesale. Curtiss did this work in OSS headquarters in the U.S. consulate, a grand old neoclassical building that was thirty minutes to an hour's drive away from the college, depending on whether the city's traffic was impossible or just absurd.[36]

Evaluating the personality files was a huge task, even for someone like Curtiss, who was used to doing similar research in university archives. By the end of the war, OSS/Istanbul had assembled more than two thousand such files, which recorded, wrote its branch director at that time, John Maxson, "all the information available on all the known and doubtful personalities of all enemy services who are operating or who have operated within the country." As part of this job, Curtiss also had to evaluate every single report the OSS had gathered from these sources, using a rating scale that assigned the report's credibility a letter, A to E, and the source's credibility a number, 1 to 5. The results were grim. Often he had to give the reports on his desk a rating off the scale, Z-0: "accounts with no credibility from sources with no credibility."[37]

Assessing the reliability of intelligence sources is particularly complicated because *most sources don't know they're sources*. Agents get information from unwitting informants by using all kinds of tricks, and a favorite trick in Allied intelligence training, as we've seen, was acting loud and ignorant. If you ask questions, people will remember you as someone who asks questions. If instead you make incorrect statements in a loud voice, people will rush to correct you—and they won't remember you at all, except perhaps as an example of how foolish the man on the street can be.

As for sources who know they're sources, the ones who are actively working for you, you need to investigate their backgrounds, maybe follow them around for a while, find out their reputations around the city. What Geertz said about the information marketplace of the bazaar is also true of the information marketplace of spycraft: "Strictly, a bazaar trader or artisan does not have a reputation, good or bad. He has reputations, dozens of them."[38] You might try to cultivate friends in other intelligence agencies, who can supply their own material on the people you're investigating. Perhaps, if British intelligence isn't talking to you, the Turkish police will. (While the Swedish police were aligned with the Gestapo, the Turkish police were sympathetic with the Allies.)[39]

Of course, you need to write dossiers on your sources, and also on *their* sources, called subagents. And you need to assign them a case officer to manage them on an ongoing basis. And assessing the reliability of your sources' accounts is another task still, since what your sources say might not be true even if they believe what they're saying. Because British intelligence didn't trust the OSS/Istanbul outpost, they didn't keep the Americans in the loop of the "whispering," or rumor-spreading, networks they'd planted throughout the city. Some three hundred whisperers who worked for the SOE plied their trade in Turkey.[40] The British were very, very good at formulating whispers that people wanted to share— and wanted to believe. Which meant that Curtiss and his colleagues had to figure out not only what stories were misinformation from the Axis, but also what stories were misinformation from their own allies.

During Curtiss's tenure, OSS Istanbul didn't buy information from the truth bourses in the Grand Bazaar, though the Germans did (which may have been a sign that they were getting desperate).[41] Instead, Curtiss made friends with members of the Turkish police and got hold of—among other things—a collection of police reports on various characters around the city, which he called "the Istanbul notebook."[42]

What Curtiss originally thought he'd be doing in Istanbul was treasure hunting: walk all over the city, slip into the hushed confines of library after library, bookshop after bookshop, and every stall of the Old Book Bazaar, befriend owl-faced librarians and gently mad collectors, and work them up until you've turned their insider book trading into a conspiracy to commit espionage. But what Curtiss wound up doing, when he was assigned to build and run an X-2 branch, was closer to game playing. He was playing an information game.

The sociologist Erving Goffman was among the first to describe information games, but two later scholars developed the concept in ways that are especially useful to understanding Curtiss's assignment: Clifford Geertz, who applied the concept to buying and selling in a bazaar (as we've seen), and Marvin Scott, who applied the concept to horse racing.[43]

OSS agents who worked in Cairo and Istanbul remarked on the way that those cities' bazaar economies—"The playful deceits and negotiations of the bazaar," as a later historian put it, "which became inbred into most social intercourse"—seemed to offer models for their work as agents.[44] The first problem they presented was that of *having too much to know*—the problem of filtering the signal from the noise. The Grand Bazaar, in those years, had some 4,400 shops.[45] The bazaar's shopkeepers acquired their goods from trade routes as far-reaching as the city's imperial past, and so the shops displayed for sale, in a marvelous riot of colors and scents, seemingly anything you could imagine: carpets, clothes, fish, gold, perfumes, prayer rugs, antique sabers, scarves, shoes, spices, tea, Turkish delight, old military uniforms being sold as rags, pestles missing mortars, mortars missing pestles, glass jugs from classical Rome, genuine Neolithic terra-cotta figurines from the excavations at Hacilar, *fake* Neolithic terra-cotta figurines from the excavations at Hacilar, antique flasks that an outsider might think were made to hold gin but were actually made to hold holy water from Mecca, lamps of deep-dyed glass for the lighting of mosques, and much more.[46]

Curtiss, who under his civilian cover would have spent a lot of time around Americans and Europeans who made a whole culture of collecting treasures in the city's bazaars, wouldn't have failed to recognize that the bazaar, like the intelligence arena, was a competition that you could win only by solving the problem of information overload.[47] To buy an item worth bragging about entailed finding it in the chaos. And—more to his purposes in X-2—to *sell* an item entailed persuading a buyer to select it from the chaos.

Better yet is if the seller can make a buyer into a *repeat* buyer. You might think that a counterintelligence service, since it's supposed to oppose the enemy's intelligence services, should try to cut off the enemy from information altogether. Kick out their agents and shut off their resources. But that isn't the case. In fact, the goal of counterintelligence is *to use the enemy's intelligence services to your advantage*, which means you should let those services keep running. The task isn't to cut off information, but rather to control it.[48]

Part of what makes an information game a *game* is that, in order to achieve their ends, the players think about the information that each one has about the others.[49] *I know that you know what I know. I know that you think you know what I know. I know that you think you know that I think I know what you know, but in fact I do know what you know.* And so on.

But for Curtiss, it was: *I know how you know what you know.* In order to build a proper X-2 branch, Curtiss had to know what sources the enemy was using to get information. British counterintelligence experts identified six of these sources to take special note of: pictures taken from the air, telegraph eavesdropping, prisoner-of-war interrogations, diplomats from neutral countries, knowledge that the Germans obtained before the war, and human intelligence (that is, spies and their human sources). A major goal of the X-2 branch that Curtiss set up was to get the Germans to rely on their spies so heavily that they'd stop bothering with their other information sources. If X-2 could turn German spies to the Allied cause and get a steady flow of harmful, but seemingly useful, reports going back to the Germans, then the Germans might well ease up on their other intelligence-gathering systems. From this perspective, letting the Germans run a network of bad spies was more useful than wiping out the German spies altogether. If you wrecked one source properly—that is, while maintaining the enemy's trust in that source—you could wreck, or at least damage, the other sources with the same action.[50]

And double agents could do more than just spread harmful reports. They could also share with their Allied handlers what their Axis employers knew. The Allies were attempting, all over the world, all kinds of deception schemes: whispering, spreading false radio chatter, planting false stories in the newspapers. The question was whether these schemes really were fooling the enemy—and double agents were in a position to answer that question.[51]

Even knowing what questions the Germans were sending their agents to find answers to was useful, since the Allies could infer from that what the Germans were planning. Were they asking about the coastal defenses in the south of England? They likely weren't planning to invade the north. Had they suddenly stopped asking about England's coastal defenses altogether? They'd likely given up on the prospect of invading England.[52]

Moreover, a double agent could tell you how enemy agents trained, what kinds of covers they used, how their cipher systems worked.[53] This made it harder for the enemy to use covering devices (such as concealment, disguises, or other ways of hiding information) in the information game, and it also revealed the hidden constraints (for instance, what situations the enemy could not avoid) that governed the enemy's moves.[54]

There were challenges with using double agents, aside from the very real risk that they were spying *on* you instead of *for* you. The biggest: they wouldn't have a strong enough reputation for the lies they told on your behalf to be believed unless you first spent time giving them true information about your side to pass back to their superiors. "A double agent cannot be summoned from the vasty deep and set upon the stage ready at once to play a leading part," said John Masterman, an architect of the X-2 branch in London. "On the contrary, he must be steadily and cautiously 'built up' in reputation, and that is a process which lasts always for months and often for years. In other words, for the period of his novitiate he is not an asset but a liability." You had to pay for your lies with truths that made you vulnerable. And you could never be absolutely sure which truths were small enough to be safely divulged.[55]

This is one reason why the British placed such emphasis on indirect methods of deception such as whispering. You didn't have to risk truths in the game, as you did when using double agents. Of course, you had to use extreme care in controlling the rumors you whispered into the information game, lest you fall victim to your own machinations. Rumor has a way of getting out of control.

A CITY OF WHISPERS

Cave quid dicis, quando, et cui, goes an old Latin saying: "Beware what you say, when, and to whom." Ironically, this principle was most important in the part of spycraft—spreading rumors—that one might think involves speaking as loudly and widely as possible. As it turns out, the coordination of loose lips had to be as tight as the coordination of special combat forces. Any good counterintelligence chief would have to understand how whispering worked.

The Allies put together rumors at "the Rumor Factory," an internal section of the Political Warfare Executive (PWE). The leader of this section, one John Rayner, had the enviable title "Master Whisperer."[56] Other sections of PWE sent whisper ideas to Rayner, who presented them at a weekly meeting attended by members of the SOE, MI6, and the Ministry of Economic Warfare. The whispers that the attendees approved of, after getting a final go-ahead from the top brass, went out into the world via SOE and OSS outposts in different cities: Bern, Cairo, Istanbul, Lisbon, Santiago, Stockholm, and more. (The OSS branch that created whisper campaigns in collaboration with PWE, called Morale Operations, didn't have an outpost in Istanbul, so the British likely directed more whispering there than the Americans. But as an X-2 agent, Curtiss would have had to understand how whispering worked in order to feed rumors to, and evaluate information from, his sources.)*

---

* Among the Americans, the OSS Morale Operations (MO) Branch and the Office of War Information (OWI), which wasn't part of the OSS, created and disseminated propaganda. OWI focused on overt propaganda, while MO focused on covert propaganda, which included whisper campaigns. Both organizations worked very closely with the British, often directly following the British example. "Propaganda: PWE (Political Warfare Executive)/ SOE co-ordination," manuscript number HS 8/310, National Archives, 187; and Clayton Laurie, *The Propaganda Warriors: America's Crusade Against Nazi Germany* (Lawrence: University Press of Kansas, 1996), 112–40.

In Turkey, the whisper process worked much as it did in other countries. At the top, a so-called "chief whisperer" organized the whispers and managed which agents gave which whispers to which subagents. Many of the subagents didn't even know they *were* subagents. Each of the agents who gave whispers to subagents worked with, and found subagents within, a single category of the Turkish populace: the intelligentsia, the middle class, or the lower class.[57] The agents drew a salary from the OSS, but the subagents didn't; after all, they didn't know they were working for Allied intelligence. Sometimes the agents threw them a present or a tip, to stay on their good side.[58]

The Rumor Factory classified whispers in two categories: "(a) 'Smoke Screen' rumors designed to deceive the enemy about the facts of the British war position or the intentions of the British Government. These rumors should obviously purport to emanate ultimately from this country. (b) Rumors designed to attack the morale, either civilian or military, of the enemy. Such rumors may often purport to emanate from Germany or Italy themselves."[59]

There were rules for whispering, too. The first: "Whispering consists not in talking yourself, but in making other people talk. They will do this only if the whisper interests them and this is more important than that they should believe it." For this reason, it wasn't actually necessary that a whisperer *believe* a whisper in order to spread it. The whisper only had to be *interesting*. A second, related, rule: "A story travels better if it is tied up with topical events—scandal, horrors, or whatever it is people like to talk about."[60] A third rule: a whisper didn't have to be something the subagents *wanted* to happen. "Many people like believing the worst and have a passion for spreading alarmist rumors against their own cause. It does not, therefore, follow that a story which appears to be fantastic, obscene, or anti-German to an intelligent pro-British agent will not travel through certain channels among pro-German people."[61]

How do you start a whisper? First, you can get an agent to share it with subagents, in the hope that they will pass it to others. Second, you can talk loudly in the presence of others who are sure to overhear. ("Talking in front of servants, hairdressers, waiters, etc., is often more effective than direct repetition, because the person overhearing the story imagines 'he is on to a good thing.'") In Istanbul, the SOE got Polish expats who spoke German to hang around the German colony and rehearse the whispers in German. (Not every whisper needs to be a rumor you intend to spread among everyone. In the case of whispers that you want to move to enemy territory from neutral territory, like Istanbul, "it will be far more effective," the SOE's whispering guidelines say, "to get three servants in the chief German hotel repeating the story, than to get the whole of the pro-Allied population telling it to each other." For that reason, agents should choose subagents with an eye to the communities they move in.) Third, you can leave what the SOE called "jetsam," or pieces of trash or other debris, in places where busybodies will find them: "notes left in telephone boxes, letters sent to wrong addresses, wastepaper baskets in hotels, etc." Fourth, you can repeat the whisper on phone lines that you know are tapped.[62]

Finally, you can use the media—but not by doing anything so obvious as straight-up making a newspaper or radio channel into your pipeline for whispers. Instead, you should use the media to launder "evidence" that reinforces whispers into places where people will point to that evidence as proof. Get a small paper, a local paper, to print your whisper—remember, journalists are eager, above all, to print something with the shape of a good story—and then telegraph the local paper's story to a big city, where big papers will quote or reprint the article from the local paper.[63]

Or use another tactic that turns the story's *absence* in the papers into evidence of its truth. In those years, if a news item came into a newsroom after the presses were already rolling on the latest edition, the editors could, if they wished, print the item on a little slip of paper, called a "stop press announcement," that they would insert between the newspaper's pages. X-2 agents sometimes printed up false stop press announcements that announced the whispers as news items. When the actual newspaper didn't follow up on the story in any later editions, the agents would whisper that the item had been "hushed up."[64]

Whispering was a top-down affair. Most whispers could only be circulated by professional whisperers. (An exception was broad rumors that had no purpose but to lower the enemy's morale; any agent was allowed to spread these.) The agents who had been trained as whisperers must not be seen with one another; they should follow the directions of a chief whisperer, whose identity they should never know and whom they should only communicate with using cut-outs.[65] (In the language of espionage, a cut-out is a person who acts as an intermediary between two other parties, so that the two parties are never seen to meet—and perhaps never meet at all.)

And how should you devise a whisper? First, you can't go around repeating the whisper all the time. You should say it only once. "Never speak of the rumor more than once yourself; always make others do the talking for you. The 'whisperer' must be sure that his rumor is intercepted by an inveterate gossip."[66]

You should try to design the whisper so that it's conceivable and also hard to falsify. (The SOE gives the example of a "rumor of typhus in Breslau.") A whisper shouldn't be fuzzy, shouldn't be abstract; you need to talk about real toads in real gardens. "The best way to convey a rumor is to tell it in the form of a story with a point."[67]

One way of telling a story with a point was to fashion it around treasure hunting in the marketplace. In late 1933, the SOE started a whisper that Heinrich Himmler, the head of the SS, had plotted to unseat Hitler in a coup d'état. (And therefore that Hitler's power was weakening, that his friends in foreign governments could not count on him staying in charge.) The hook of the story was that Himmler had been so confident in the success of the coup that he arranged for the German postal service to put out a series of stamps with his picture on them, so that ordinary Germans would get used to seeing him as the face of the Reich. But the postal service released the stamps early by mistake, and when the coup failed, the German government hastily recalled them in order to avoid letting news of the infighting in the Reichstag get out.[68]

As they often did, the British laundered the whisper into the news media. The English newspaper the *Daily Mirror* discussed the stamp rumor, as did the Swedish newspaper *Svenska Dagbladet*, which picked it up in an article with the (translated) headline: IS HIMMLER'S POWER

BROKEN?—RUMORS THAT THE CHIEF OF POLICE PLANNED A COUP D'ÉTAT. Now the German government was in the position of having to deny the rumor, which only gave the rumor legitimacy.[69]

But the real brilliance of the stamp rumor was that the stamps themselves, if any survived the recall, would naturally be very valuable. All over the globe, stamp dealers let it be known that anyone who brought in the Himmler stamps could name their own price. You can imagine how easy it would be to get this rumor going in a new city: just stop by a stamp dealer and ask after the Himmler stamps, or tell your tailor that you're hunting in the bazaar for them, or leave a copy of the relevant issue of the *Daily Mirror* or *Svenska Dagbladet* lying on a public bench. Bazaar fever will take care of the rest. The British actually did create fake Himmler stamps to reinforce the rumor, but the stamps became such a hot commodity that they had to do damage control lest those fake stamps create huge fraud cases in nonenemy countries—for example, in Switzerland, where stamp dealers promised the moon for a single specimen.[70]

In the end, the British steered the stamp whisper away from disaster. But their continued whispers about unrest in Hitler's inner circle would ensnare both them and OSS Istanbul in an actual seditious plot that would have repercussions later.

But that's a story for another chapter.

AND NINETY PERCENT DAGGER

In June 1944, a new agent named Frank Wisner arrived in Istanbul from Cairo. Wisner had the trust of people high up in the OSS, who had given him the mandate to help fix the Istanbul outpost's issues. The outpost was disorganized, inefficient, and—worst of all—leaking like a sinking ship.

On the night of Wisner's arrival, the director of the Istanbul outpost, Lanning Macfarland, invited him to a party in a nightclub. Wisner attended the party with great reluctance; as you can imagine, the worst possible onboarding process for a spy, who will naturally want to keep his face secret, is to bring him to a big public bacchanalia.

Wisner was right to be wary: he quickly learned that Macfarland's cover was so badly blown that every time he walked into one of the city's nightclubs, the band would start playing a song called "Boo-Boo, Baby, I'm a Spy." In fact, during the party, to Wisner's horror, Macfarland climbed onstage in front of everyone and *sang* "Boo-Boo, Baby, I'm a Spy" while the band played! The song is written for over-the-top performance, with a barrage of sexual innuendoes, as the historian George Maior writes:

> I'm so cocky I could swagger,
> The things I know would make you stagger,
> I'm ten percent cloak and ninety percent dagger,
> Boo-boo, baby, I'm a spy![71]

It turned out that Macfarland was sleeping with his sources. *Of course* Macfarland was sleeping with his sources. And of course the two women he was sleeping with were spies working for other agencies— one for the Russians and one for the Nazis.[72]

Wisner immediately saw what the outpost's problem was. He had the agency's higher-ups remove Macfarland and took his place as the outpost's director.[73]

Shortly before all that, another newcomer to the team, John Maxson, had finally arrived to serve as the director of the outpost's X-2 branch. He was impressed when he saw Curtiss's work. By the time he arrived, Maxson later wrote with a hint of gratification, Curtiss—who by then had been in Istanbul for not quite a year—had already torn apart the outpost's old counterintelligence apparatus, found its weaknesses, and made impressive progress on building a new one.[74] Between Maxson, who took over X-2, and Wisner, who took over the whole of OSS Istanbul, the problems that had left Curtiss waiting out in the cold for so long looked to be resolved. Now it was time to see what OSS Istanbul could really do.

Because the consulate building that the OSS worked in was deemed hopelessly insecure, Wisner moved the X-2 branch to new offices in Cihangir, a neighborhood of steep hills and crowded streets lined with brightly colored row houses. At outdoor cafés, artists drank sweet Turkish coffee—"Eat sweet, talk sweet," goes a popular saying in Turkey—and argued bitterly about politics. The OSS gave Curtiss a basement office, where, he found, he could peek out at the Bosporus through a ground-level window.[75]

The outpost was still short staffed from the Dogwood purge, so Curtiss served in three very different X-2 roles: analyst, investigator, and agent handler. As an analyst, he read through reports that OSS agents brought in and figured out what intelligence was credible and important enough to pass up the ladder. As an investigator, he hunted down information and interviewed sources. And as an agent handler, he kept track of double agents and told them what to say and do. This wasn't the strict division of labor that the OSS preferred, but the outpost was in a pinch, so the spy's roles multiplied. By now, Curtiss was important enough to have a code name of his own: Agent 005.

For the young man who once wrote with longing of the life of the scholar-detective-astrologer, somewhat like a spider, pulling on the strands of a web with a thousand radiations, this must have been an astonishing confrontation with his own imagination. He had gone through the looking glass and become the figure of obscure magic he described in his dissertation—because knowledge is, itself, a kind of magic, regardless of whether you get it from the stars or from the sublunary hermeneutics of the human fields of learning.

There was one more role that the OSS wanted Curtiss to take on. One day, his superiors told him to assassinate someone whom he had identified, in his role as an analyst, as a double agent working for the enemy. Spies call this *wetwork*. OSS colleagues later described the "horror" he showed when he received the assignment—though neither he nor they said whether, in the end, he carried it out.[76] His assignments were getting hard to keep track of: book collector, spy, analyst, investigator, handler, and now, assassin.

Let's try, for a moment, to imagine his perspective.

Ever since your boss responded to the news that an informant is a double agent by saying, "You'll have to rub him out"—and then assured you, firmly and repeatedly, that he wasn't joking—you've been wandering through the offices in Cihangir in half a daze, performing your duties while trying to figure out the stages by which your book-collecting job slid into wetwork.

You've been avoiding your assistant, a bright-eyed young man who reminds you of a first-year graduate student: dutiful, eager to please, and entirely out of his depth. He'll do as you say if you tell him to be the one who actually carries out the assassination. You wonder, a little hysterically, whether the etiquette of your occupation as a professor covers this situation. Are you the kind of professor who, busy with Important Research, leaves all the dogsbody work to your graduate students: grading, fetching library books, making mimeograph copies, murder? Or does noblesse oblige—the condescending, in both the old and the new senses, recognition of the fact that your great advantages allow you to be generous to those of lower rank—oblige you to shoulder this burden yourself?

At lunch, you eat *börek* with a fellow analyst while watching the ships from the shore of the Bosporus, far enough away from the men idly casting out fishing lines that you know they can't overhear you. You ask him, as though making casual conversation, "Would you kill someone? If your boss told you to?"

"I don't know," he says. "I don't think I'd be able to. I think that seeing a glimpse of fugitive humanity in his eyes would stop me from doing it. Unless it was Hitler or another, you know, another high-ranking Nazi. Unless I could say he was a murderer himself."

You have the same conversation later that afternoon with Marjorie MacKillop, a secretary from Connecticut College. Like all secretaries, she has probably thought about eliminating people at the office, if doing so would eliminate the inefficiencies and learned helplessness they bring to her desk. She probably has a plan for each of them.

"I would," she says. "Why not?"

"Really?"

"Sure, after I leave the office for the day. But I would plan other things for the evening. I would definitely not want it to be drawn out."

"That's it? No hesitation?"

"Well, I would probably say, 'How am I expected to do it? Am I expected to find this person, or is there intelligence on where he is?'

Then, depending on what he said, I'd get it done, come back the next morning, and tell him, 'It's all taken care of.' Then I'd make my tea."

"You'd make your tea?"

"I like to make my tea first thing in the morning."

You fret over the possible methods. You could follow the man to a bar and, when he isn't looking, crush a cyanide tablet in his drink. But no: this is Istanbul, city of spies, and the bars have all the privacy of a Broadway stage. You'll have to do it the way they taught you at the training camp: walk past him on the street and, as you pass him, stick a dagger behind your back into *his* back, piercing the kidneys. Withdraw the knife and keep walking, never breaking stride. Melt into the crowd.

You're a Yale man. Of course you can do it. Right? "For God, for country, and for Yale," as the motto goes—a list that everyone understands to be in ascending order of importance. God forbids murder, but you're from a social class that has always understood the Commandments to be more in the nature of suggestions.

No, your reluctance to commit murder isn't from God, but from yourself.

Your country wants you to do this. You're fighting Hitler, for God's sake. You'd put a knife in Hitler if you were given the chance, wouldn't you? And Yale would *definitely* want you to do this. The anchor point of the campus is a bronze statue of Nathan Hale, the young spy in the Revolutionary War who, as the British looped the gallows rope around his neck, supposedly said, "I only regret that I have but one life to give for my country." The statue, his ankles bound and his hands tied behind his back, gazes out to posterity, his brow noble and his shoulders square with resolve. This is how your alma mater wishes to see her sons.

A few nights later, you're walking down a dark road in the Fatih district. Your assistant is with you, there to help you get out of a fight if necessary. Trying to block out the noise and tumult, you drop your gaze to the ground: the yellow light from the streetlamps gleams off the cobblestones, shattered by strutting or sauntering or staggering feet. Suddenly, your assistant nudges you. You look up and see your target. He has a distinctive appearance, which you know from photographs: pomade-slick hair, a gentle, exhausted face.

The street is crowded with people. The streets always are, here. Istanbul has a population of more than eight hundred thousand souls, not counting all the smugglers and refugees who steal into the city uncounted. When you walk in the covered Grand Bazaar, the sound of hundreds of voices bouncing off the curved ceiling makes you think of the rushing of a river. Here, the sound is dry, the ordinary overloud chatter of nightlife, but you still feel like you're in a river's current, being pulled along by forces beyond your control. Or maybe that's wishful thinking.

You have a dagger in your pocket, with the handle loosely clasped in your hand—*loosely* because you're afraid your sweaty palm will make the handle slick.

The man is coming closer. You examine his clothes. A heavy jacket, close-cut worsted from a bespoke tailor, would be bad, too thick to pierce. But no, he's wearing a linen jacket, the kind of one-season special people buy off the rack.

Just as you pass him, he glances at you for the briefest moment. You see a glimpse of fugitive humanity in his eyes.

And then—

4

TOO CLEVER TO BE TRAPPED BY A WOMAN

The library is a whispering post.
—SUSAN ORLEAN

STOCKHOLM IN THE WINTER OF 1942 WAS A PRETTY ENOUGH picture to hang in a gallery. Redbrick buildings, as tidy as a painting, warmed the cool waterline of the Baltic Sea; their steeples reached into the clouds, as thin and delicate as finishing brushstrokes. One might look at the scene and think of the lacquered quiet of a Vermeer.

A neutral country, Sweden had escaped, so far, most of the deprivations of Occupied Europe. The stores were well stocked, the people well clothed, the streets of cities like Stockholm bustling with men and women alike—in contrast to France's and Poland's cities of "widows," whose men had been shipped off to the front or to work in factories in Germany. One could live without fearing one's neighbors; no spies were allowed to operate in Stockholm, by government decree.[1]

One of those prosperous streets was Strandvägen, a quiet waterfront promenade lined with elegant Belle Époque buildings. It was the site of the American Legation (at 7A Strandvägen) and the British Legation (at 82 Strandvägen). The American Legation, in particular, was a luxurious sight: grand, tidy, gleaming white, like a palace that had been washed and ironed.

Like most diplomatic headquarters, the legations were places to push their nations' power, but softly—with money and glamour. Before the war, the Americans held glittering balls at 7A Strandvägen, which the Swedish royals attended.[2] Even after the Americans entered the war, their legation building remained a picture of calm. On their doorstep, diplomats in suits walked past well-heeled urbanites who carried purchases from the nearby Svenskt Tenn, an upscale boutique that sold everything from pewter ashtrays to kidskin cushions, or Rönnells Antikvariat, an antiquarian bookstore that sold first editions of centuries-old books and handwritten journals by famous thinkers. Everyone seemed to be carrying on exactly as they always had.

Only if you looked carefully would you notice that some of these ordinary-looking figures in the crowd—perhaps a man making a show of using a camera to take photographs of the waterfront; perhaps a young couple pushing a baby carriage—were lingering outside the legation for a suspiciously long time. And taking notes in notebooks.[3]

But if you were in a position to read the notebooks, or hear the whispers that rippled through the city—in communities of refugees from Poland, Norway, Denmark, and beyond; in underground cells whose members were training to join the fight against the Nazis; in the secret offices of intelligence agents, who wrote them up to send home to Washington or London—you would know that even though Sweden was a neutral country, the war had reached every one of its streets. Even in calm, perfect cities, like this one.

The reason that spies stood outside the American Legation, taking notes and photographs, was that everyone knew that the United States must be taking advantage of this foothold in Europe to conduct secret operations. And it was: the legation building was the secret headquarters of the OSS in Sweden. That's where Adele Kibre, who spied for both the OSS and the SOE, worked. It was at once the safest and the least safe place in the city to conduct spycraft. Because right across the stone courtyard, at 7C Strandvägen, was the Office of the German Military Attaché.[4]

A WILDERNESS OF MIRRORS

Outside of Sweden, in Occupied Europe, the war was being waged openly and brutally, and had been so for some time. In Poland, German planes flying over Warsaw circled back around to bomb, specifically, a little group of women and girls who were digging in a field for potatoes because they had no food. In Wiśniewo, German soldiers forced civilians to lie in the mud and rolled over them with tanks; during the massacre in Bydgoszcz, where more than ten thousand people died, German soldiers reportedly laid out the corpses of civilians, many times, in the shape of a swastika.[5] As the occupation continued, soldiers shot adults who stayed outside after the 6:00 p.m. curfew and grabbed children off the sidewalks to force them to give blood at hospitals for transfusions. Children were learning a new culture of childhood that was as grave and dutiful as adulthood; by 1944, a Polish refugee testified, "There are many forms of childish sabotage about which the children are very serious. If a German asks the way, a child will reply, 'I don't know,' or will misdirect him."[6]

In Norway, the Germans requisitioned fish from the fishing boats, winter clothes from the stores, even cutlery from civilians' homes. A Norwegian reporter said in an English newspaper that he'd "seen Norwegian workers paying daily visits to German soldiers' dustbins in order to still their hunger."[7]

In France, Catholic clerics helped their parishioners to hide Jewish children from the French police, since even in unoccupied France, the police took their mandate from the Gestapo. "Between five thousand and eight thousand Jewish children whose parents have been deported are homeless in unoccupied France," a British intelligence report of the time said. "It is about their fate that the immediate struggle between the Laval Government and the masses in unoccupied France is now going forward."[8]

In July 1940, Vichy France passed a law that directed the Ministry of Justice to examine the case of every foreigner who had received French citizenship for the past thirteen years and to revoke that citizenship if the adjudicators decided it was "not in the national interest." Thousands of French Jews lost their citizenship under this law.[9] By 1942, the Vichy government was taking away papers without even the pretense of judicial supervision; its policy for the Jewish children it sought in unoccupied France, noted one intelligence report, was "to deprive these children of any identity papers, so that their parents can never recover them."[10] Many of these Jews, both adults and children, were ultimately sent to concentration camps and murdered.

The purpose of revoking papers wasn't to force Jewish people to *leave*, as Jewish people trying to flee occupied countries realized. The Jewish physicist Lise Meitner fled Germany in 1938 in a terrifying train ride to Stockholm—terrifying both because Nazi stormtroopers regularly hunted through passenger trains to find Jews trying to leave, and because she didn't have a passport, since the German government didn't let Jews have them.[11] The purpose of revoking papers was to give the police and the Gestapo a justification for doing as they liked with their victims: arresting them, shooting them, sending them to prisons or concentration camps.[12]

And what happened in those camps? In the winter of 1942–43, not many outsiders could say. Outside of Europe, passages of Hitler's playbook for what he had the world's press calling "the Jewish problem" were becoming disturbingly clearer—but this section of the playbook was still secret. The Nazis kept the activities in the camps hidden even from those who worked nearby. In 1943, the historians Walter Laqueur and Richard Breitman later wrote, an official working for the Deutsche Reichsbahn railway system remarked that so many trains had carried passengers to Auschwitz, without any trains carrying passengers out, that the camp must, by now, be "one of the biggest cities in Europe." Ultimately, some 1.1 million people would die in Auschwitz.[13]

The bureaucratic efficiency that we associate with the Nazi regime relied on the recognition that paperwork can hide accountability for even the most abominable acts. This is, in part, because of what the paperwork *doesn't* say, because of the space off the record where workers can take initiative. Bureaucracy fosters a competitive environment where subordinates compete in the gaps between regulations to further the goals of their superiors, and their superiors in turn reward them for their loyalty. In the Third Reich, at every level from the top down, Nazi bureaucrats competed to further their superiors' goals of cruelty and genocide. Then, later, they claimed they were merely following orders.* Adolf Eichmann, one of the chief architects of the Holocaust, even said at his 1961 trial—in an effort to convince people that he hadn't *wanted* to commit genocide—that, had his superiors ordered it, he would have murdered his own father.[14]

Of course, paperwork itself was a tool in the genocide. At Eichmann's trial, prosecutors submitted some sixteen hundred documents, most of which Eichmann had signed, as evidence—each one of those documents a wheel in a relentless machine of death. And the Nazis weaponized the kinds of paper that criminalized being the wrong type of person just trying to exist—or to run: identification papers, work cards, ration books, travel permits, passports, visas. As a witness who testified at his trial recounted, the Jewish people who tried to escape Austria after Germany annexed it in 1938 found themselves caught in a labyrinth of paperwork that was designed to take away whatever money they still had, trap them behind a bottleneck of applications so they couldn't leave anyway, and then criminalize the fact that they hadn't left: "At one end you put in a Jew who still has some property, a factory, or a shop, or a bank account, and he goes through the building from counter to counter, from office to office, and comes out at the other end without any money, without any rights, with only a passport on which it says: 'You must leave the country within a fortnight. Otherwise you will go to a concentration camp.'"[15]

---

* This explains the rise of Adolf Eichmann, historians argue: "Eichmann—like innumerable other Nazi subordinates—was a competitive entrepreneurial bureaucrat in a very competitive bureaucracy. It was this combined with his loyalty that explains his efficiency. And it is the fact that there were thousands of Eichmanns, all entrepreneurial and competitive and all fiercely loyal to their superiors, that explains the terrible efficiency of the Nazi bureaucracy of murder." Albert Breton and Ronald Wintrobe, "The Bureaucracy of Murder Revisited," *Journal of Political Economy* 94, no 5 (1986): 909. See also Franklin Mixon, Jr., *A Terrible Efficiency: Entrepreneurial Bureaucrats and the Nazi Holocaust* (New York: Palgrave Macmillan, 2019), 8–9.

And yet the Nazis missed something essential. You might think they had figured out every way paper could be used as a weapon. They held book burnings to rile up their supporters, stole valuable Jewish books to build their own war chest, and used identity papers to keep people in line.*

But they remained oblivious to a crucial dimension of paper as a weapon. Perhaps the best way to illustrate what this was, and how they missed it, is a story—apparently true—that William Donovan loved to tell after the war: a French countess, American by birth and lucky by marriage, was traveling on a train during the war. When she entered the train's restroom, she used newspaper pages as a toilet cover to avoid touching the very public surface. Unbeknownst to her, the newsprint came off on her *derrière*. At the next stop, the passengers were ordered to disembark so the Gestapo could conduct a random inspection. The men and women went into separate rooms in the train station, where they stripped and presented themselves for inspection. When the Gestapo saw the countess's elegant bottom, they got very excited, believing they'd discovered a new method for Allied spies to carry secret messages. Only

---

* For this reason, Allied spies in the field fought back with an unlikely paper weapon of their own: "pocket litter," or oddments in their pockets that were designed to support their covers. Pocket litter included official papers, like ration books, travel permits, labor registration papers, and Nazi Party membership cards. But it also included straight-up trash—papers that were convincing because you wouldn't expect a forger to waste his time on them. Café receipts, ticket stubs, shopping lists, letters from the bank.

One of the forgers who made fake papers for the Allies later described his operation as an "artist's studio," which he set up in a garret on the Left Bank of Paris. ("Artist's studio" wasn't just a metaphor, it was a cover: on the shelves where he stored jars of chemicals for treating paper, he also placed paintbrushes, implying they were jars of painter's solvent. He and his associates would enter and leave the garret carrying painter's palettes. And they made real paintings, although they conceded that their true artistry lay in bureaucratic *trompe l'oeil*.) He made not just identity cards, but also library cards, movie tickets, store receipts, and other bits of pocket litter to serve as props to aid the performances of people the war had turned into actors. He was such a craftsman that he made his own paper to use in his forgeries: "closely woven, nice and compact, or fine, textured or untextured, depending on the nature of the documents to be made." Sarah Kaminsky, *Adolfo Kaminsky: A Forger's Life*, trans. Mike Mitchell (Los Angeles: DoppelHouse Press, 2009), 7–14, 68. On pocket litter, see also "SOE Group B Training Manual Regional Supplement," Special Operations Executive, manuscript number HS 7/66, National Archives (1940–1945), 145–46.

after they translated the French words into German did they accept the countess's explanation and order her, moodily, back onto the train.

Donovan always ended this story by saying that the Germans were so worked up about the supposed message on the countess's bottom that they forgot to inspect the lining of her purse. Which was stuffed with slips of paper intended for the OSS.[16]

But what the Nazis missed most significantly wasn't the intel in her purse. They at least *knew* to look for that—even if, in this case, they forgot. And it wasn't the newsprint, which they found and then dismissed as a red herring. It was the newspaper itself.

If Eichmann and his superiors had known what the OSS could do with a newspaper, they would have done far more to lock down the press than they did. For the transformative insight of the OSS was that most of what they needed, *really* needed, they could get from public sources.

In the right hands, paper could be more effective than bombs as a weapon in the war. Paper could tell the right reader what factory—detectable only by comparing minute fluctuations in railroad rates—to destroy in order to land a blow on the enemy that was more damaging than carpeting a whole city with bombs. Paper could tell the right reader the location of a hidden German garrison via some bubbly little reference in a local society column. The Axis didn't suspect that paper could reveal so much, because the right reader was a new species in intelligence: the analyst—those poor harmless drudges in the Chairborne Division of R&A, the recruits from the ivory tower who loved paper dearly and knew how to read its secrets.

"Analysts born rather than merely assigned to the job," the intelligence expert Thomas Powers wrote decades after the war, "have a glutton's appetite for paper—newspapers and magazines, steel production statistics, lists of names at official ceremonies, maps, charts of radio traffic flow, the text of toasts at official banquets, railroad timetables, photographs of switching yards, shipping figures, the names of new towns, the reports of agents, telephone directories, anything at all which can be written down, stacked on a desk, and read."[17] This is the traditional task of the historian: sitting for days and months in archives, riffling through the evidence until the evidence starts to whisper.

IN THE NAME OF FAIRNESS

To be sure, the Nazis did try—*try*—to lock down the press. Censors in occupied countries strove to ensure that information that might be damning or sensitive didn't make it into newspapers. Even in some neutral countries, like Switzerland, censors ordered newspapers not to publish rumors of horrors abroad that had no solid backing: "This, the censors said in their internal guidelines to the editors, was 'atrocity propaganda' of which there had been so much in the First World War."[18] If you were hunting in the newspapers for clues to secret events abroad, you had to be an uncommonly good reader.[19]

Sweden had no formal system of press censorship. Instead, newspaper editors censored their own papers in the name of maintaining neutrality, which some historians have argued better served the interests of the Third Reich than flagrant government censorship would have done. In 1938, Germany began pressing forcefully for the media in neutral countries to observe total neutrality on the acts and ideas of the Third Reich. Ernst Hermann Bockhoff, a Nazi "neutrality expert," argued in the Nazi Party's official newspaper that any criticism of fascist Europe would be "discriminating" against the fascists, and that the fascists had no choice but to treat such discrimination as an act of war. A neutral country that didn't force its media and populace to be neutral about fascism wasn't *really* neutral, he said—and Germany would respond with military force, as was proper when dealing with military opponents.[20]

"We shall in future assert our point of view with ice-cold consistency," Bockhoff wrote. "For the democratic small states, the problem of neutrality has become, in the twentieth century, a question of life and death."[21]

The Swedish government warned the press to speak carefully about the Nazis, and on occasion it pulled out of circulation particular books or periodicals that it thought crossed the line the Third Reich had drawn.[22] In 1940, the government forbade movie theaters to show the Charlie Chaplin comedy *The Great Dictator*, since the film ridicules Hitler—and ends with Chaplin breaking character to say, "I don't want to rule or conquer anyone. I should like to help everyone if possible. Jew, gentile, black man, white."[23] In 1942, when Swedish newspapers published refugees' firsthand accounts of Nazi brutalities in Norway, Sweden's Minister of Justice, "terming these affidavits 'horror stories,' and speaking of 'alleged' atrocities, ordered the papers to be confiscated and criminal proceedings to be instituted against their publishers."[24]

Even beyond these political pressures—which the Swedish government sought to apply quietly from behind the scenes—professional and financial pressures were strong enough to keep the country's media, for the most part, away from that line. The government could stop the national railroads and mail service from delivering a publication, which would drive almost any publisher to bankruptcy. And Swedish authors often made most of their book sales in Germany. All of this, not to mention the pride that Sweden took in being the country of the Middle Way, the neutral player in a world gone mad, the peaceful northern paradise, led to one inevitable result. "The persecution of Jews in Nazi-held countries was soft-pedaled, the horrors of the concentration camps were wholly dropped out, blitzkrieg, invasions, and all the endless atrocities committed by the Nazi hordes were reported and commented on only in the meekest undertones," an observer who had been living in Sweden wrote in 1943. "Perhaps the most curious phenomenon of Swedish press policy was that every, even the tamest, bit of criticism directed against the Nazis had to be invariably compensated by a corresponding poke at the Allies, so as to safeguard Sweden's 'neutrality.'"[25]

Is there a safe place on the sidelines of a conflict like this one? Can a newspaper stand aside and observe both the tolerant and the intolerant without condemning either group—and refrain, thereby, from *helping* either group?

Hitler's government argued that newspapers in neutral countries *certainly* could, and in fact *must*. The Nazis demanded that the press in Sweden normalize—treat as credible and give equal time to—Nazism. That strategy extended to newspapers, but also libraries, bookstores, and universities. These efforts worked to legitimize ideas that were once abhorrent.

The media's behavior had consequences. When Sweden's government signed a series of trade agreements with Germany, the public, figuring Germany couldn't be all that bad, assented. These agreements gave Germany definite advantages in the war. Sweden sent Germany almost all of its production of iron ore, together with massive shipments of cellulose, lumber, paper, and wood pulp, essential for keeping the Reich's printing presses rolling during the wartime paper shortage. Sweden also sent Germany arsenic, insiders claimed—one thousand tons of it in 1941 alone, produced as a by-product of Sweden's copper mines. The Nazis had a lot of uses for arsenic, none of them good.[26] Sweden even allowed Germany to use Swedish trains and railway tracks to carry troops and military equipment to Norway.

Again and again, Sweden tilted its neutrality in Germany's favor, to the point where onlookers suggested that Germany accepted Sweden's neutrality because it benefited Germany more than occupying Sweden would have done. Though the public assented to these measures, opinion on all of this was split. The labor unions opposed the Nazis, the police favored them, and the prime minister seemed willing to make any concession that would keep Germany from invading Sweden for a little while longer. ("He is made of the stuff that has produced the Scandinavian diehard isolationists of Wisconsin and Minnesota," one writer said of the prime minister. "As long as his little Sweden is safe and sound, Per Albin doesn't give a damn if the world goes to bits.") The king, meanwhile, opposed the Russians so strongly that he sometimes personally pressed the government to make choices that favored the Germans. The Swedes circulated a joke that played on the king's name, Gustaf Adolf V: "Once Sweden was ruled by Gustav Adolf, but now it is ruled by Gustav and Adolf."[27]

As Sweden continued to lean toward Germany, Allied sympathizers in the country found themselves in ever more danger. The Norwegians and others who were training in secret to fight for the Allies in Occupied Europe had to take great care to avoid the notice of the Swedish government and the Swedish police. So did the American and

British intelligence agents who were working in Sweden. If the Swedish police caught them, they faced arrest, imprisonment, deportation, even Gestapo-style beatings and interrogations.

For the Swedish police—and the Swedish *secret* police—had aligned themselves with the Gestapo. They had *trained* with the Gestapo. In the mid-1930s, they collaborated with the Gestapo in Berlin on an investigation into methods of "telephone tapping and recording conversations." During the war, Allied agents in Stockholm assumed that the police monitored their phone lines and filled their phone conversations with false leads. The Swedes also read messages sent by mail and telegraph, not just from suspected intelligence agents, but from anyone in the country; as the SOE pointed out drily in an internal report, Enigma, an encryption machine that the Germans relied on for much of the war, was perfected with the help of Swedish engineers, and the Swedes had personnel who were excellent at decoding messages. In time, British diplomats in Stockholm even discovered that the police had planted listening devices in their apartments. "From evidence now available," the same SOE report said, "it is fairly certain that conversations overheard by this means were made full use of by the Swedes and in many cases passed on to the Germans."[28] Stockholm was neutral, but it wasn't impartial—and it was far from a safe place to be a spy.

In order to survive, you had to keep ahead of those tracking you, watching you, filtering your information sources. You had to find new sources of information in places and pages that your opposition didn't expect.

THE SECRET BOOKS

When Adele Kibre landed in Stockholm in August 1942, she was very much alone, even for a spy.[29] As a foreigner, she knew from the jump that the authorities would view her with suspicion and watch her movements. She did keep that professional address in the American Legation, and that appears to be where she took the photographs she sent, shrunk down to microfilm, to the SOE in London. The SOE shared those photographs with the OSS; recall that Kibre's mission in

Stockholm was a joint operation between the American and British intelligence agencies. Her task was to find and photograph any document they asked her to capture, using a lightweight Contax microfilm camera.[30] She was an experiment: the very first agent to go into the field to acquire documents for the Interdepartmental Committee for the Acquisition of Foreign Publications, a tiny outfit in the OSS that had just seven people on staff.[31]

The police seemed to be everywhere in the parts of the city that diplomats frequented. Two officers stood in uniform at all hours outside the British Legation. The ordinary-looking pedestrians who lurked on the street in the diplomatic districts were members of the Swedish secret police, who liked to use, as proof of their ordinariness, props like baby carriages or dogs. One point that the British had in their favor was that the Swedish secret police were not especially good at staying secret. They wrote notes and took pictures; they set up a secret observation post in a barn across the road from the legation building, then moved the observation post to a construction crew's shelter down the road, so they could monitor the traffic that passed the building. They drove by in cars, thinking they'd disguised themselves because they kept changing the license plates—but the British knew who they were because they drove gasoline-powered cars that only the government could afford, while other drivers in Sweden by then had moved to cars powered by generators that ran on charcoal or wood.[32]

Upon her arrival, Kibre moved into the Grand Hôtel, a building with an immense neoclassical facade whose staff had a reputation for infinite politesse. The Grand Hôtel was the home base of the international press; so many foreign correspondents lived there that they nicknamed their set of hallways "Fleet Street."[33] The hotel, like the country it was in, was beautiful, practical, and clean; it had blinding white linens, grand dining rooms, a café, a barbershop (where, one journalist reported, diplomatic staffers from enemy countries sometimes sat beside each other in "deadly silence"), a telegraph room, a billiard room, smoking rooms, reading rooms stocked with newspapers, and a much-loved bar.[34]

The OSS cautioned its agents not to meet sources at the Grand Hôtel. It would be hard to find a dust bunny there, even with a white-glove search, but the place was infested with spies, despite the law. A lot of the hotel's staffers were Swedish counterespionage agents. Swedish police officers—and Gestapo officers—regularly searched the rooms. Foreign intelligence agents who lived at the hotel also got in on the game. An OSS officer named Wilho Tikander paid a hotel staffer to bring him the ink blotters they collected when cleaning the rooms, together with the names of the guests who had used them. The OSS also paid for the trash in the rooms' wastebaskets.[35]

The Americans in Stockholm who *weren't* spies sometimes used the hotel's reputation as a place with a million eyes and ears to play jokes. After the war, an American airman named Herman Allen—whose plane went down in Sweden, forcing him to spend the war there under the Swedish government's supervision—liked to recount a story about sharing a meal with his friends in one of the hotel's dining rooms. "They spotted two Germans at the next table and decided to play a familiar prank. The airmen began an animated discussion about some elaborate military plan. While they talked, Herman drew a map on a napkin and threw it on the table. As they walked away, Herman glanced back and watched one of the Germans grab the napkin and put it in his pocket."[36]

In all, the Grand Hôtel must have been an utterly strange place to live, at once genteel and bloody, crowded and isolating, filled with enemies who were trying to know all about one another, yet remain strangers to one another. But the world of booksellers, archives, paper, the world Kibre had been sent to infiltrate as a bibliographic detective—that would have been as familiar as home. Which must have been at least a small consolation.

MANY CUNNING PASSAGES

If someone asked Kibre, at the hotel or elsewhere, why she was in Stockholm, she said she was an attaché for the American Legation. She also mentioned that the Library of Congress had sent her on a book-collecting mission unrelated to the war—more or less the same cover story that Joseph Curtiss brought to Istanbul.[37] Sherman Kent's abiding problem, back in his R&A Division in D.C., was that the Library of

Congress had few foreign books, and the new method of intelligence he was building relied on reading books. Kibre turned this problem into a cover: the Library of Congress, with the majestic inefficiency of any government agency, had finally gotten approval to build up its collections—and was going to do so, war be damned.

Sometimes, depending on the situation, it seems Kibre told people that she was a press reader—perhaps to explain why she would have been buying lots of newspapers. The job of press readers was to write up abstracts of the stories they read in the European press and send them back to their home country by telegraph. Press attachés weren't supposed to send home anything that looked like intelligence—just abstracts of stories in the press—and the Swedish government monitored the telegrams that Stockholm's assorted legations sent home to make sure the press readers were sticking to their scripts.[38]

As a press reader, Kibre would have had an excuse for hunting out news in Stockholm. But Kibre wasn't sending home abstracts. She was sending home, by secret pouch, microfilm copies of entire newspapers, including newspapers from Occupied Europe that the Nazis had banned from circulation in Allied countries. She was sending home scientific journals that Allied scientists could no longer acquire, underground newspapers from Norway, secret photographs of sabotage in Occupied Europe, books that even Swedish libraries refused to lend out because, as the German Legation told a library about one title, "This publication from 1940 onward contains information of value to the enemy and therefore of interest to spies."[39]

In short, Kibre was tracking down and sending home anything and everything that the OSS asked her to find—and the OSS had some very big asks. When she arrived, the legation's press office, called the Special Reporting Section, subscribed to 89 newspapers (well, some of those subscriptions actually belonged to the British Legation, but they shared their copies) and a handful of technical journals. You might think those would be enough to reveal anything that a newspaper was going to reveal. But Allied intelligence wanted much more. Just as a start, they wanted 172 more scientific and technical journals than they were getting. They wanted German propaganda newsletters and provincial newspapers that were on a "restricted list" and went only to certain vetted subscribers. They wanted a copy of an illegal pamphlet on how to become a deserter that students published in Munich, titled *Ich Will Nicht Mehr* ("I will not go on any longer"). They wanted books that had been privately printed, books that had been printed by underground presses, and books that the German government had designated "secret books" and pulled from circulation. They wanted, in addition to the current newspapers, back copies starting from 1940. They wanted atlases, directories, maps, and telephone books, all of which would be used to help plan air raids and ground operations. They wanted publications on aeronautics, banking, bibliography, electronics, governance, finance, international relations, labor, law, legislation, metallurgy, mining, politics, regulations, shipbuilding, statistics, synthetic petroleum, and scientific publications of every description. Because the right piece of paper, in the right hands, might hold the secret to winning the whole war.

If the new kind of intelligence operation they were building in Washington was going to work, they needed a special kind of intelligence agent, part book expert, part detective, who could deliver whatever they might ask for—no matter how guarded, no matter how rare. How exactly they were going to *read* everything, make sense of everything, was a problem they would have to solve themselves. Kibre's job was to first give them the world.

In 1943, when Kibre's contact in Washington, Frederick Kilgour, wrote to her about the latest being asked of her in Stockholm, he admitted that the Americans' hunger for documents, especially among OSS R&A agents working in the Library of Congress, would make it very difficult for her to acquire all they asked for and still look like an innocent civilian: "As for the Library of Congress, they really want everything. I imagine that this is the most difficult type of request to fulfill. I would certainly hate to have someone in Sweden tell me that he wanted a copy of everything published in and around the United States. In the first place I, personally, would feel somewhat like a goop walking into Brentano's"—a bookstore chain in the United States—"picking up one copy of everything in sight, and saying, 'I want to buy these.' But this is what the Library of Congress wants you to do."[40]

Many of these items were so valuable that the Allies didn't want people *on their own side* to know they had them. Kilgour cautioned her to include in the frame, when she took pictures of certain newspapers and technical publications, a card that said something to the effect of "Copies of the newspapers noted below are restricted to Interdepartmental Circulation. In making quotations from the restricted titles one should never use the title of the publication, and the source must be disguised."[41] That way, if R&A reports based on those publications ever fell into enemy hands, the enemy at least wouldn't discover where the data was coming from and cut it off at the source.

Kilgour didn't care, at first, *how* Kibre got those items. She was the expert bookhound, the archive hunter whose civilian job was to find rare publications that even professors couldn't find. In late 1942, shortly after she arrived in Europe, Kilgour wrote to her, "I don't care how you go about acquiring this material. . . . If you can spend $1,000.00 by going around the newspaper stands and book shops, go ahead and please keep a fairly accurate account of these expenditures."[42]

THE GREAT BOOK HUNT

What would you do, knowing that you were being watched from all sides and that your base of operations was the least surreptitious place in the city? Kibre started by getting library cards. She went around to the library for Sweden's Royal Institute of Technology; the Karolinska Institutet Bibliotek, the oldest medical library in Stockholm, which held all manner of medical journals as well as a marvelous archive of rare books; the library for the Royal Veterinary College of Sweden, which had the medical books that the Karolinska Instituts didn't; a civil statistics office; and all kinds of local libraries, because you never know when a book will wash up on the hidden shore of some neighborhood library nobody bothered to check. She made friends with librarians, too, which is evident from the huge numbers of books that she started to send back, in microfilm, to the OSS with the notation "confidentially borrowed."[43]

The library of the Karolinska Instituts had, in its archives, rare and extraordinary medical texts. It had *Notes on Nursing* by Florence Nightingale; an eighteenth-century French study of venereal diseases, which was illustrated by huge full-color lithographs of the affected body parts, and which was a huge bestseller in its time; a seventeenth-century book by a German doctor, Engelbert Kaempfer, who visited Japan and reported on medical tools and practices there, which included tea, acupuncture, and a resin called "dragon's blood"; and more. The library's reading room, however, was quite humble. Low ceilings; yellow lights; long narrow rooms that were occupied by long narrow tables; and walls with packed bookshelves—books under the windows, books jutting from odd corners.[44]

The Karolinska Instituts was a case of too much science with too little funding and too little room. It wasn't just the library: the embalming lab was in the basement, right next to the furnace and the vents; the bacteriology lab, where researchers worked with dangerous bacteria, was also in use as a lecture hall; the chemistry classrooms were crowded with distillation rigs and jars of who knows what. The students took a certain cheer in pretending that they were mad scientists; wags put up posters outside the anatomy halls that advertised "skeletons . . . available for rent at good prices—with or without skulls."[45] In short, it was a place you might go to find Doctor Frankenstein, but not to find James Bond.

None of the places Kibre haunted were places you'd expect to find a spy. But that was the point: the places you'd expect to find a spy were precisely where agents of the Swedish Police Bureau looked for them. Nightclubs, officers' clubs, drinking holes, legations, train stations, ports, hotels. In the city's libraries, Kibre could work without attracting attention. The libraries held hundreds of stories about spies, but none of them, ironically, were about spies in libraries.

Kibre built relationships with seemingly every library and bookstore in Stockholm. Her correspondence from these years, some of which is preserved in the National Archives, includes letters to a medical school library, a civil statistics office, and the library of Sweden's General Export Association.[46]

She bought books from Henrik Lindstâhls Bokhandel, an obscure little shop in central Stockholm, and from Nordiska Bokhandeln, the city's largest bookstore. Since 1851, Nordiska Bokhandeln had occupied a prominent corner in the city's shopping district, a cheerful building with granite columns and narrow windows. The word for *cozy* in Swedish, *treflig*, carries with it a whole world of meanings: a warm little nook to sit in after you've been outside in weather so cold that the air hurts your face; a good book; a cup of mulled wine; warmth; solitude; respite.[47] Nordiska Bokhandeln was *treflig*.*

Kibre sent messengers—cut-outs, in spy parlance—to Nordiska Bokhandeln and other stores to pick up the orders she made for the OSS, to add an extra layer of misdirection to her operation.[48] Sometimes, she placed orders for more books than she actually bought. She would order from some fancy antiquarian bookstore, say, a large set of books to look over at the legation, then keep the ones she wanted to buy and send the rest back with a friendly note. ("Dear Sirs: Thank you very much for the highly interesting books contained in your packet on approval, dated May 29. The rejected items (6, previously procured from you) are herewith returned. Very truly yours, Attaché Dr. Adele Kibre.")[49] One suspects that she microfilmed the books that she didn't buy, then returned them to the bookstore and sent the microfilms to London.[50]

Sometimes, Kibre's work as an intelligence agent required her to pretend to be a very different version of herself. Consider Rönnells Antikvariat, a huge antiquarian bookstore in the center of Stockholm. In later years, the lore passed down through the staff of Rönnells was that the bookstore sided with Germany, not the Allies.[51] And yet Kibre did regular business with them: buying books, having books delivered so that she could look them over, exchanging friendly letters with the staff.[52]

As a literary detective who searched for rare orders in bookish spaces, perhaps Kibre, to gain the trust of bookshop owners who sided with the Germans, paid close attention to the propaganda about the United States that the Germans were pushing in Sweden. The Germans

---

* After the war, a writer noted that the bookstore kept on display by the door a pincushion stuck with tiny flags: "If a visitor pins a white flag in his lapel, it means 'I'm just browsing,' and clerks don't bother him; a red flag means 'I'm in a hurry, please wait on me.'" A very Scandinavian conception of coziness: *Please don't talk to me, I want to be alone with your books.* Herb Bailey, quoted in "New Wrinkles," *Reader's Digest* 63 (1953), 132.

very badly wanted Swedes to believe that Americans were ruffians who had no concept of culture—that if they won, they would tear down the libraries and concert halls of Europe. And so the Germans sent to Stockholm, as proof of their own elite *Kultur*, professors in round glasses to give lectures, conductors in white ties to wave their batons over performances of *The Magic Flute*, fashion designers to strut through banquet halls amid flocks of women in dirndl skirts. They made sure their scientific and technical journals flowed, without wartime interruption, into Stockholm's libraries and universities, so that Swedish students and intellectuals understood that scientific progress spoke the German language.[53]

The Germans also spread the word—over the radio waves; in daily German newspapers, which they sent for free to Swedish addresses; in German military newspapers; and in dedicated propaganda newspapers, many of which appeared in multiple languages—that Americans are braggarts, reprobates, thrill seekers, big spenders, and all-around impertinent puppies. American troops, the Germans said, were stealing treasures from European churches and precious books from European archives, a result of their simultaneous envy and incomprehension of European culture. Finally, the Germans did all they could to launder propaganda into seemingly neutral sources. They offered carefully slanted news summaries to Swedish newspapers, knowing that newspapers reprinted items of this kind from one to another without attribution. An organization called the German Library of Information, which claimed to be nonpolitical, promoted as the essential library of classic German literature a list of titles that covered sixty-six closely typed pages. "Of these," a report in the U.S. Congress said, "more than a quarter are outright propaganda."[54]

Perhaps that was the secret to Kibre's successful cover. She might have passed herself off as someone whose sympathies lie with *culture*. The Library of Congress hired her to acquire books in Europe, and she was looking for pro-German books.

It's easy to imagine Kibre strolling up to a bookseller to explain her new job at the Library of Congress. Perhaps, if she was asking after a particularly sensitive book, she would pretend to be nervous. Maybe she'd be asking for one of the presentation copies of *Mein Kampf* that Hitler gave to top-ranking members of the Nazi Party. (Of course, she would refer to that group as the NSDAP. A *shibboleth*, a little signal that marks the speaker as an insider. Someone who respected the Nazi Party wouldn't call it *the Nazi Party*. The word *Nazi* was a nickname that opponents used; it meant, roughly, "hick." Instead, they'd call party members *Nationalsozialisten* and the party itself *the NSDAP*.[55])

"It's a large book, with a white leather cover, and a golden Reichsadler stamped on the front," she'd say. "You wouldn't happen to know where I could find a copy?"

THE HOLLYWOOD VOICE

Adele Kibre—a hard-nosed literary detective, a brunette from a Hollywood where blondes have all the fun, a woman serious about being taken seriously—was strangely well positioned to pull off a charm offensive on these particular targets.

Americans, as a group, have a reputation for being extravagant, boastful, cynical, and jovial. Swedes are none of those things. Instead, they're known to be excruciatingly polite. Swedish authors have compared Swedes to the Japanese in the high regard they hold for modesty, simplicity, and restraint.[56] In diplomatic settings in other countries, people would give the Swedish representatives nicknames like "the Quiet Men." In the 1940s, they tended to dress formally, even in settings where Americans would dress down, like dinner with friends; they often greeted each other with a bow and the slang word *tjänare*, "servant," as in "I'm your humble servant." The problem was often getting them to talk in the first place.[57]

Before the war, Kibre could present herself to the booksellers and librarians of Europe as a fast-talking Hollywood dame. But Swedes tend to be easily embarrassed by the grand gestures that make movie characters so appealing for most of the world. When film studios dub Hollywood films into Swedish, they often tone down the dialogue so that dramatic lines become mild—what one commentator called "Swedifying" the language. Even the word *love*, in real life, is too much, a Swedish commentator says: "Instead of saying 'I love you,' which to Swedish ears sounds artificially Romantic—as in a cheap romantic novel—one says, 'I like you.'"[58]

But Kibre had another persona waiting in the wings. One that, perhaps, came closer to method acting, drawing on her own feelings and experiences. A woman whose career depends on getting men to respect her at work—in an academic world where it's a foregone conclusion that she can't become a professor despite having the requisite PhD—can't spend all her time playing the fast-talking Hollywood dame. Men *want* women to smile, which means that getting them to treat you like a man often means not smiling. Don't laugh. Don't say little reassuring things. Be curt in a way they'd read as normal in a man but as arrogant in a woman. Or as *angry* in a woman.

In her correspondence with Swedish bookstores, libraries, and scholars, Kibre speaks in a way that's consistent with the brusque standards of Swedish etiquette. In many letters, she practices the Swedish custom of repeated thanking—saying, for instance, "Many thanks" at the beginning and "With renewed thanks" at the end.[59] But she also gets to the point and loses the chitchat in a way that American readers would be apt to see as cold. She tells them, usually, that the Library of Congress wants such-and-such publications, or that she has received the publications they've sent and is returning the ones that, on reflection, aren't up to her standards. She always signs, with her name, the title "attaché."

An exchange she had in February 1944 with Axel Boëthius, a professor of archaeology at the University of Gothenburg in Sweden, shows just this. The professor, who had a professional connection with the Swedish newspaper *Allsvensk Samling*, wrote in a letter that the paper would be a fine addition to the Library of Congress and that he'd be glad to add whatever address she preferred to the newspaper's subscriber list, no charge. She wrote back, with thanks, that she would tell the Library of Congress the good news. And she added that she was trying to get subscriptions to various art history journals with the help of other Swedish professors, but that the war was interfering with the delivery of those issues even in Sweden, as well as keeping her from the archives she used to visit: "Contact with my own pre-war field of research (medieval writing and art centers) seems long ago. So far, even a brief visit to the Royal Library has been impossible. However, I did procure (for the Library of Congress) the presently published facsimile editions of two MSS of the Library's collection."[60]

Kibre used every skill she had from her prewar life to succeed in her mission. For the professors, she was a tweedy medievalist. For the rare book dealers, she was a no-nonsense library worker. But her adventures also took her into company she hadn't had before. The underground, for example. Or the company of Nazi sympathizers. She was curt enough, by nature, to please the Swedes. But one imagines that her background in Hollywood gave her the ability, when she needed it, to charm anyone who needed to be charmed. Kibre connected with members of the Norwegian underground, who gave her underground newspapers to share with the OSS. And she connected with the Germans—on friendly enough terms that they sent her, directly by mail, materials that they sent only to their allies. Well, that's one way to keep your enemies from getting suspicious when you sneak around: persuade them that, yes, you *are* sneaking around, but you're sneaking around *for them.* Kibre didn't tell her superiors how she got in with the Germans, so we're left to wonder how she used her background and training to do it.

We might imagine, for instance, Kibre wandering around a party in an expensive-looking apartment in the fashionable district of Östermalm. The host might be a Swedish civil servant who's known to have fellow-feeling for the Germans. Perhaps she has persuaded her contact at a pro-German bookstore that she collects rare editions of *Mein Kampf.*

Her goal is to get her name on a subscription list for propaganda publications from Germany. The Swedish government doesn't allow such publications to be sold at newsstands, and the Germans don't send them to anyone who might do anything with them except repeat the propaganda as news or rumors to friends and strangers. Parties like these are, at least superficially, a nonsectarian affair—the people walking around with glasses of *julmust*, dressed in black ties and Cleopatra gowns, are of all nationalities. Kibre runs a substantial risk just being there. If her targets mark her as a loyal American who is trying to get access to enemy publications, not only will she fail at her objective, but they'll certainly realize she wants to use those publications for intelligence. Her cover as a spy will be blown.

She stands close enough to her target for him to overhear her accent. It works: "You sound like Hollywood," a German-accented voice from behind her says.

Kibre turns around. The man smiling at her is tall and stocky, with blond hair that she'd know anywhere as bottle dyed.

Of course Kibre sounds like Hollywood; whenever she goes to parties in Europe, she puts on a zing of the artificial accent that actors used in movies, which people around Los Angeles call the General American accent. Hollywood is America's charm offensive, a circuit of invisible influence that runs like an electric current through a world full of moviegoers. When people hear the Hollywood voice, they want to talk about their screen idols. Often enough, she can turn that conversation into an offer to get her some rare book or show her the uncatalogued part of an archive. Because they aren't just talking to her when she uses the Hollywood voice. They're talking to Myrna Loy and Greta Garbo and Claudette Colbert.

From there, the conversation progresses amiably, conspiratorially. Kibre has a cover: she explains that she left Hollywood, where she was once an aspiring screenwriter, after certain parties, a certain element that has its hooks in the film industry, kept turning her down for writing jobs in favor of their own people, so she fell into a job as a press reader in Stockholm. She's learning a lot from all the newspapers she has to read for work, for instance how the British are in secret talks to give Ireland to the Americans as a thank-you gift when the war is over.

Here, the man, whose eyes brightened when she told him about her job writing up abstracts of local newspaper stories to send to the American press, interrupts her: No, no, that sounds like British propaganda. The British will never give up territory to the Americans, as they just want to use the Americans to conquer Europe for themselves. If she wants to do her job right, she needs to have the proper context to understand which stories she reads are true. He knows someone who manages subscriptions for the Reich's Foreign Press Service, which shares informative bulletins with certain journalists from abroad. These are restricted publications, of course, and she shouldn't mention them at work, lest the Swedish authorities find out. Will she give him permission to add her to the subscription list?

She will.

THE "ILLEGALS"

Kibre did much of the detective work of tracking down books herself, since that was her area of expertise, using every trick at her disposal. But she also built an office of staffers, called the "Kibre Unit," who helped her with photography, deliveries, keeping up with the news in foreign languages, and other essentials. When Kibre arrived, the legation already had a small, dedicated staff of people whose job was to read foreign newspapers. However, these staffers weren't spies, but rather press readers, tasked with keeping the American media up to date on events abroad. They usually sent home capsule summaries of important stories, which newspaper editors would read and adapt for their own audiences.[61]

By contrast, Kibre sent information directly to Allied intelligence, and the Kibre Unit worked under her direction, taking pictures and reading foreign publications for useful morsels. They were a crew of refugees and other misfits. Like Knud Ditlef-Nielsen, a Dane with a roaring laugh and the face of a prizefighter. Nielsen grew up in Copenhagen as the son of a religion and philosophy professor. By the time he joined Kibre's crew, he was in his midthirties. Before the war, he traveled the world as a radio specialist working for General Electric, then took an office job in Copenhagen with the electronics conglomerate Philips.[62]

What exactly Nielsen did that motivated his abrupt departure for Stockholm—where he lived among strangers, held down a job that certainly paid far less, and was eventually joined by his father, whom Kibre listed in her records using the mysterious term "illegal"—the historical record doesn't say. Perhaps he was a member of the Resistance. Whatever the case, after the Nazis invaded Denmark in April 1940, Nielsen went "to the other side" (*hinsidan*), in the jokingly ominous slang that

Danes use for going to Sweden. (The term refers to the other side of the Øresund Sound.)

His family might have known where he'd gone, but his friends and colleagues apparently didn't; he was "only heard from again," a profile of him in a Philips company magazine later said, "after May 5"—referring to the date of Denmark's liberation in 1945. He spoke English—all of Kibre's employees would have—and he described himself to the magazine as a lover of American literature.[63] As a member of the Kibre Unit at the American Legation, Stockholm, Ditlef-Nielsen tracked down publications from Denmark, specifically, and took microfilm photographs of newspapers and other printed matter.

Another "illegal" listed as part of the team in Kibre's records was Professor Sigmund Huppert, an engineer who directed the Polytechnic Institute in Frankenhausen, Germany, until the city council, under growing Nazi pressures, dismissed him because he was a Jew. Huppert made it to Sweden in 1940, where he kept up with German-language and technical literature for Kibre's little group.

The Kibre Unit also included Beatrice Anderson, a typist who was the American-born child of Swedish immigrants; Ellis Janson, an office assistant and messenger; and Veronica Korjus, a typist and translator, Estonian by nationality, who had taken classes in English, German, and art history at the University of Stockholm. Kibre poached a lot of her employees from the British Legation, where they worked as typists before coming to work with her on something more dangerous.

Here as elsewhere, the diversity of the OSS staff was a great strength, enabling Kibre's team to read in different languages and provide useful information about all the different species of papers that Kibre was being asked to deliver.

WOLVES WITH SHEEPSKINS

In Occupied Europe, other book collectors, ones with very different methods, goals, and ways of valuing books, were plying an ugly trade. The Nazis often used whatever they could to further their ends, regardless of whether they actually respected the things they were using. Under the cover of building libraries and academic institutions, the Nazis seized an untold number of valuable books from Jewish bookstores, homes, libraries, and places of worship, which they instead used to build their personal wealth—or destroyed.

Two Nazi organizations, in particular, led the destructive collection of Jewish books. One was the Reichsleiter Rosenberg Task Force (*Einsatzstab Reichsleiter Rosenberg*, hereafter the ERR), a commission for looting books and artwork to stock the Reich's academies and libraries and museums (not to mention the homes of its leaders). The other was the Reich Security Main Office (*Reichssicherheitshauptamt*, hereafter the RSHA), an intelligence body that managed the planning and implementation of the Final Solution, and which collected Jewish books to use while working up a justification for wiping out the Jewish people.[64]

The leader of the ERR, Alfred Rosenberg, was a Nazi Party functionary who had a boyish, sulking face, which he disguised by posing in photographs with exaggerated furrowed brows. Rosenberg spent his early adult years kicking around the periphery of the worlds of art and publishing: getting a graduate degree in architecture (his thesis design was a crematorium); studying painting at an art studio; teaching art at a preparatory school; and starting at the age of thirty, working as the editor of the *Völkischer Beobachter*, the official newspaper of the Nazi Party. Even though the newspaper's circulation was tiny when he started, he managed to find a publisher for his book, *The Myth of the Twentieth Century*. He worked on the book for more than a decade and released it in 1930. The publisher was Eher-Verlag, the official publishing house of the Nazi Party, and the book was a massive, lofty, incoherent treatise on the history of the entire world, the Jewish corruption of culture, and the failures of modern art.[65] The book sold lots of copies, sat in prominent view on the shelves of Nazi officials, and—given that it was some seven hundred pages long—was probably rarely read. Hitler later referred to it dismissively as "that thing that nobody can understand."[66]

A biographer later described Rosenberg as "a deeply half-educated man." He had access to knowledge—in time, one of the largest libraries in human history, all of it purloined—and he clearly wanted to be a high theorist, but he wasn't good at thinking through what he read or even reading very widely. That didn't stop him from rising to the rank of Deputy of Ideology and Education, and then to the rank of Reichsleiter—the highest rank in the Nazi Party, save for the Führer himself—with the unabridged title Reichsleiter for the Office for Supervision of the Total Intellectual Schooling of the Nazi Party.[67]

In April 1933, shortly before Rosenberg settled into this position, Hitler's government issued a decree that purged from the civil service in Germany all non-Aryans and "politically suspect" individuals. Because the civil service included universities, thousands of university instructors suddenly found themselves out of a job. The instructors who remained knew that their job security relied on the fealty they showed to the Nazis. Students in their lectures took notes on the political leanings of what they said, and informers within the faculty even reported on what colleagues said in department meetings.[68]

As Hitler's ambitions grew, so did Rosenberg's opportunities. He knew that Hitler had dreams of building an international academy of Nazi art and intellect that would make the whole world gape in wonder. It would be an immense stone building, more than six city blocks across the front and almost as long down the sides, with stark rectangular walls and little dark windows that evoked the classics of prison architecture, and at the center, a tower almost four hundred feet tall, jutting stiffly against the sky. He would call it the *Hohe Schule der NSDAP*, the High Institute of the Nazi Party. Rosenberg told Hitler that he would be glad to assemble the institute's library, and Hitler agreed, writing in January 1940, "I order that Reichsleiter Alfred Rosenberg continue this preparatory work, especially in the field of research and the establishment of a library. The offices of the Party and the State organizations are required to support his work in every way."[69]

This became the mission of ERR. The agents of the ERR rode in army trucks and dressed in "uniforms resembling those of the SS," an OSS agent later caustically remarked.[70] Many of them had training in history and library science, the better to pick out valuable books in the smoldering cities of Europe—but as the historian Mark Glickman comments, they "wanted to be soldiers," and they acted with requisite swagger and brutality. As Hitler's armies swept across Europe, the ERR followed, seizing whatever took their fancy.[71]

The RSHA, meanwhile, was an umbrella organization that included the Gestapo, the SS, the regular police, and other police and intelligence services. Whereas the ERR could seize books only in occupied countries, the RSHA could seize books both inside and outside Germany. A section of the RSHA called Department VII was in charge of researching the Reich's opponents. The RSHA seized Jewish books so that the so-called scholars of Department VII could use them—with a backbreaking amount of reading against the grain—to "prove" that the Jews were conspiring against Western civilization.[72]

Franz Alfred Six, who taught political science at the University of Berlin before taking a position overseeing the RSHA's main library in Berlin, supervised sympathetic art historians, ethnologists, linguists, sociologists, and other scholars who worked with the library's materials. (At its height, the library held up to three million books.) The RSHA gave the scholars money and covered them with honors; in exchange, they wrote whatever the RSHA wanted them to. The funding for the library, its staffers, and the visiting scholars came from the money that the Nazis seized from the Jews they deported or sent to camps.[73]

The hard work of assembling the libraries of the RSHA and its sister organizations came, in large part, from the compelled labor of Jewish scholars, who were forced to identify their own cultural treasures. At the RSHA library, a team of Jewish scholars, working under threat of death, spent fourteen to sixteen hours a day classifying books, writing up bibliographic records, shelving books, packing and carrying crates of books, loading and unloading trucks, constructing bunkers, cleaning up rubble after air raids, cleaning the apartments of library staffers, shoveling snow, and doing everything else the library staffers didn't want to do. Many of them were older men, former university professors who might, by now, be looking toward retirement; even so, the SS guards who oversaw them made them work at a speed that would daunt young men, beating them when they didn't work fast enough and saying things like "I'll finish you off," or "Don't look at what you've packed, or you will be shot." In 1943, the Nazis sent most of them to Auschwitz and brought in a fresh group of Jewish forced laborers.[74]

O LORD GOD TO WHOM VENGEANCE BELONGS

Perhaps it is no surprise, then, that the Nazis were so vulnerable to forms of attack that took advantage of those disregarded disciplines and those refugee scholars. The ERR and the RSHA were hunting down books as an excuse for hunting down people, and as a result, the books themselves were often barely an afterthought. The Gestapo, which carried out the book collecting for the RSHA, told the furniture dealers who confiscated the contents of Jewish homes to set the books aside for them, but the dealers "lost" many obviously valuable books, and often the Gestapo didn't even bother looking through the books they did receive, sending them all to be pulped at the paper mill in Guben. (Dr. Ernst Grumach, the leader of the team of forced Jewish laborers at the RSHA library, later wrote that the Gestapo handled Jewish books "in a perfectly arbitrary and . . . an absolutely irresponsible way.")[75]

There was no Nazi efficiency in this endeavor. The Nazis took their gains through dishonesty and betrayal, and often they squandered their resources in the service of cruelty, because the cruelty was the point. In September 1943, the Gestapo told the representatives of Rome's Jewish community that they would be safe—all twelve thousand of them—as long as they paid a fee of fifty kilograms of gold. At the time, the paperwork for their deportation was already being processed. The day after Rome's Jews paid the extortion fee, military officers started going through the synagogues and Jewish libraries of Rome, removing the books on the grounds that the Jews had been accused of conspiring against the state, and the Nazis needed the books in order to investigate. The books disappeared from history and have never been recovered. A few days after this, the historian Mark Glickman writes, "Nazi soldiers rampaged through Rome, gathered all the Jews they could find, and sent them to Auschwitz. Many Jews escaped, but more than a thousand did not, and they were murdered soon after they arrived at the camp."[76]

As for the ERR, it claimed at first that it was only seizing property that had been abandoned by its owners. But the war turned whole cities into piles of "abandoned" property, as Julien Bryan, an American journalist who was in Warsaw during the siege of Poland, explained: "Everywhere one looked, there were hundreds of people on foot, on bicycles, pushing wheelbarrows and even baby carriages loaded down with their bedding and a little food. . . . Poor and rich mixed together, but money no longer had any meaning. . . . Blankets, mattresses, and bread were the most precious possessions."[77]

Later, the ERR dropped those justifications, sending units of ERR soldiers and SS officers to rip apart bookshops, libraries, synagogues, and homes while the owners were still very much present. In a typical scene, ERR soldiers waited for Shabbat to burst into a Jewish place of worship where they intended to seize books, the better to terrify as many people as possible while grabbing their loot. (One of the worshippers called, in despair, the words of Psalm 94: "O Lord God to whom vengeance belongs; O God to whom vengeance belongs, shine forth.")[78]

Even ghettos and concentration camps were sites for the Reich's obscene book collecting. Theresienstadt, in Czechoslovakia, was the site of an infamous ghetto and transit camp. At a given time, some thirty-six thousand Jews lived there; by the end of 1945, one hundred forty thousand Jews passed through, most of them bound for death camps.[79] When prisoners arrived carrying books, as most of them did, the Nazis took away the books and sent the prisoners on to the ghetto or their deaths.[80]

BONE MILLS AND PAPER MILLS

In the midst of all this death, real scholars and real teachers, as opposed to the pseudo scholars of the ERR and the RSHA, were doing their best to preserve documents and protect their students. One such scene unfolded in the Kovno ghetto in Lithuania, where the Nazis forced some thirty-five hundred Jews from all over the country to manufacture goods for Germany. In 1942, the ERR arrived there and sent out an order for the ghetto's inhabitants to bring their books to a house the

ERR had selected as a book collecting point. The Jews of Kovno had little food and no running water; their children were offered no schooling outside of the trades, like carpentry, that their forced labor would one day require. Now the Nazis would take even their books, in the hope that amid the truckloads of schoolbooks and potboilers and family heirlooms and religious books would be something of monetary value. "Anyone caught with books after the deadline would be executed," Solly Ganor, then a child in the ghetto, later recalled of the ERR's orders.[81]

Ganor and his friend, Cooky, got up to a scheme that in any other time and place would be classified as childish hijinks, scouting out overlooked books and hiding them in an abandoned house in what they called "Operation Library." They started sharing the books in secret with fellow prisoners of the ghetto. One day, their carpentry teacher, Mr. Edelstein, who had once been a math teacher, asked whether they could find him any books on mathematics. When Ganor brought him one, he embraced the young book smuggler, saying, "Do you know what a treasure this is? Look! It's in Hebrew and was printed in Tel Aviv only a few years ago. Where on earth did you get it?"[82]

Though he was only thirteen, Ganor firmly believed that he and everyone he knew was going to die soon, no matter what they did. By contrast, Mr. Edelstein believed "that good would eventually triumph over evil," Ganor said. This despite the fact that Mr. Edelstein "came from a small town where Lithuanian partisans locked the Jewish population into the synagogue, then set the building on fire. His whole family had been burned alive."[83]

On his way home from school on the day that he gave Mr. Edelstein the book, Ganor saw a guard shouting at his teacher at a checkpoint. He'd found the book. An SS officer arrived and asked Mr. Edelstein where the book came from. Mr. Edelstein spotted his student and gave a small signal for him to run. Ganor obeyed. "I was turning into a side street when I heard a shot," he said. "I looked back to see Mr. Edelstein fall to his knees. The German put the pistol to his head and fired again, and Mr. Edelstein fell over and lay still."[84]

"Me and my stupid books. For the first time, I realized the danger I exposed everyone to with my foolishness," Ganor wrote after the war. "Now Mr. Edelstein was dead. To this day I remember his feeble gesture waving me away from there. All he had to do was point in my direction to save himself, but he would not."[85]

In time, the Nazis would transform the Kovno ghetto into the Kauen concentration camp.

For the men who shot Ganor's teacher, paper was a pretext to kill. And beyond that, just a raw material to be pulped and turned into more copies of *Mein Kampf.* The crime of withholding books from them was the crime of withholding raw materials from the Reich.

For Kibre and her accomplices, however, paper was a weapon. Those pages wound up, we now know, in theaters of war that the Nazis couldn't have imagined *as* theaters of war. A set of basement corridors beneath the Library of Congress, unsuspected by the ordinary library patrons walking around above, where professors who have suddenly become intelligence agents sweat over reports that will guide the paths of armies. A boy running through the streets of Manhattan, from the New York Public Library to a secret intelligence headquarters at Rockefeller Center, carrying, to the amusement of everyone he passes, an atlas so large that he might as well be carrying a table. A cheap, rickety library in a town that nobody's heard of, Los Alamos, where a librarian spends her days writing up lists of desperately needed texts that are nowhere to be found in the United States.

In the hands of those trained to use it, paper was a weapon, humble and unsuspected, that would help to tear down all the world-spanning dreams of the Reich.

5

BREAKING CODES AND READING TRASH

R&A controlled the most powerful weapon in the OSS arsenal: the three-by-five index card.
—Robin Winks[1]

IN WASHINGTON, D.C., ON A LITTLE ROAD NEAR THE PO-tomac River, behind the Heurich Brewery—an old brick pile that, as one observer said, "sprawled like an amiable bum" in a dismal corner of the genteel capital—stood a cluster of buildings that housed the nation's espionage headquarters. You wouldn't have guessed it if you drove by. You would have seen crumbling warehouses and weed-choked riverbanks, and looming above it all, the massive steel tanks of the city's gas works.[2] But if you tacked behind the brewery and approached one of those buildings, you might have noticed that there were bars over the windows and guards at the door. This was the main campus of the National Institutes of Health. During the war, it was also the main campus of the Office of Strategic Services.[3]

It was not a glamorous place to work. One OSS agent described it as a labyrinth of humble toil: "The ancient corridors creaked and the tiny boxlike offices, crammed with filing-cabinets and clacking typewriters and paper-littered desks, might have resembled a small-town law firm on a busy afternoon."[4] When those tiny offices got too crowded, the OSS made more space for its employees by building temporary structures next door—"Paper-thin," as an agent later described them, made of plywood and tar paper, held together with cheap nails, wood glue, and hope.[5]

This unassuming stage was the site of something new in the world of spycraft: the Research and Analysis (R&A) branch. As we've seen, what we tend to think constitutes spycraft even today comes from a totally different sector of the trade. The Research and Development (R&D) branch of the OSS was a long-established type of institution in other countries and employed researchers in the applied sciences—chemistry, engineering, ballistics—fields that prepared one to build weapons and spy gear. When you think of the clichés of spy fiction, you're likely thinking of toys from R&D: poison pens, buttonhole cameras, exploding cigarettes.

By contrast, R&A pulled researchers from humanities departments in universities, and it had no equivalent in other spy agencies. R&A was the destination of all those documents that Kibre and Curtiss and other field agents sent home: the novels, newspapers, train schedules, walking maps, postcards, freight inventories, shipping news reports, and other bits of trash and treasure.

More than two thousand R&A analysts worked on the little campus by the gasworks—called "the E Street Complex," since the address was 2430 E Street Northwest.[6] Others worked in the Library of Congress and its annex, some twenty minutes from the E Street Complex by car, and this, at least, was a workplace with style. Observers have compared the Library of Congress to the Paris Opera House: outside, a granite palace topped with an imperious green dome; inside, gilded interiors rich enough to house the sun.[7] Alas, the R&A analysts who worked there often worked in the basement.[8]

THE HABITUAL MADHOUSE OF WASHINGTON

While Kibre was hunting through archives in Stockholm, Sherman Kent worked at the E Street Complex as an R&A analyst. Of all the ink-stained drudges who worked in and around those plywood palaces, Kent was the one who did the most and climbed the highest. Like Curtiss, he was a professor at Yale. And like Curtiss, he spent a stint training at Area B. But unlike Curtiss, Kent could probably catch the attention of a waiter. This was, recall, the man who could "throw a knife better than a Sicilian" and swear meaner than a sailor.[9]

Almost everyone who recalled Kent in their memoirs described him as a man of cheerful belligerence, of superb and outrageous profanity. Kent "was as down-to-earth as chewing tobacco," said Russell Smith, an OSS agent who later worked for Kent in the CIA, and he liked to slash through the politesse of government meetings with pointed phrases that cut to the chase. For example, he described one foreign regime's attempts to control a mess as "gathering piss with a rake."[10]

The OSS recruited Kent before the United States even joined the war.[11] In the fall of 1941, Kent was working in his office in the history department at Yale when the phone rang with a surprising invitation from an acquaintance, Conyers Read, a Renaissance historian at the University of Pennsylvania. The U.S. government was building a new kind of intelligence agency with an eye to improving the country's readiness for war, Read said. The agency (then called the Office of the Coordinator of Information) was recruiting the best historians in the profession, and they wanted Kent to join them.[12]

Read baited his hook with prestige, with the promise that Kent's name would appear with the names of the great, which is the most conventional enticement in academia. But the agency he lured Kent to was anything but conventional. The idea that spies could make use of a library, or that professors had anything to offer the military, was entirely new. And so Kent joined an agency with no reputation, no obvious directive, no institutional memory—not even, when Kent started, a proper headquarters. In his earliest days with the agency, he worked in the Apex Building near the Library of Congress, still unfinished and with no desks or office equipment. One of the first inquiries that he made of his new bosses was "Where do I sit?" After that, "Do I have access to a telephone?"*

He soon figured that out. In the years to come, Kent would become the father of a new field called intelligence analysis—the intellectual foundation of the present-day CIA. The central conceit of intelligence analysis is that intelligence work should follow the university model of scholarship, with analysts working separately from policymakers and striving for the highest degree of objectivity.

In other words, intelligence analysis, as Kent conceived it, is espionage transformed into an academic discipline like literature or art history.[13] Building the OSS, then the CIA, in the image of the university he left behind, Kent revolutionized the world of spycraft. But he didn't achieve this on the strength of his ideas alone; his path to the top was a hurricane course of arguments, insults, threats, provocations, and sabotage—the happy place of a man who kept knives as comfort items.

HORSE-AND-BUGGY ESPIONAGE

The military, the State Department, and the Foreign Service all regarded the newly formed OSS with disdain. After all, these organizations had *experience*. They had protocols, procedures, settled ways of doing things. They had institutional wisdom, and that institutional wisdom said that the training these new professors brought with them was not the kind of training that real intelligence officers gave a shit about. OSS agents later recalled their skepticism: "Even the Foreign Service was dedicated to the proposition that the experience and intuition of ambassadors and Foreign Service officers was the best possible basis for policymaking and that systematic research was sometimes useful but not an essential ingredient for understanding foreign affairs."[14]

---

* One of his colleagues in the agency, the economist Calvin Hoover, commented that the confusion would eventually settle, that the government loved to start new initiatives without knowing how to run them: "This is the habitual madhouse of Washington." Sherman Kent, unpublished memoir, Yale University Archives, Series II, Tape 5, pages 1–4.

True, these organizations didn't have dedicated intelligence staffs in place. The U.S. government had never performed serious espionage in peacetime—and, recall, after World War I, Secretary of State Henry Stimson shut down any branch of them that would.[15] But they still had procedures for gathering intelligence that they thought were quite good. Before the war, the State Department funneled in news from American embassies overseas. The ones doing the reporting were embassy staffers and military attachés. The State Department had more than 160 years of experience with this method, called "foreign situation reporting." Ben Franklin did it in Paris in the 1770s; John Quincy Adams did it in St. Petersburg in the 1810s.[16]

But that was a problem. The State Department's method of intelligence gathering hadn't changed in any substantial way since the colonial era. In 1945, Dean Acheson, then under secretary of state, told Congress that, at the start of the war, the State Department's "technique of gathering information differed only by reason of the typewriter and telegraph from the techniques which John Quincy Adams was using in St. Petersburg and Benjamin Franklin was using in Paris."[17]

Another problem was that people tend to nurture wildly different ideas about what's newsworthy. The letters that Franklin and Adams sent home from their diplomatic posts tell us as much about the personal interests of the writers as about the political situations they observed: Franklin, for instance, wrote detailed accounts of how the women of Paris applied their rouge.[18] The embassy staffers of the 1930s likewise followed a gut preference for which items were important enough to report home. And these staffers had a long list of responsibilities to carry out, on which foreign situation reporting ranked low.[19]

OSS analysts argued that the information the United States needed went far beyond what the old methods could provide: "Somehow our horse-and-buggy ideas of international espionage must be brought up to date."[20] But the diplomatic and military corps didn't want to hear from a bunch of long-haired professors who climbed down from their ivory towers and started talking about how the men with experience, the men with well-honed instincts, were out of touch.

THE COLLEGE OF CARDINALS

So Kent and his fellow drudges worked in quiet mortification in rattling plywood offices and dim library basements. William Donovan, the head of the OSS, expected the Library of Congress to be a place of pride for the R&A branch. It would provide the agents with a landscape for gathering intelligence that no other country's agents had ever explored. As Kent later said, "It was their research skills and the Library's collections that were to fill up the gaps of information which had accumulated in intelligence work between World War I and World War II, when virtually no analytical work was done anywhere in the Federal Government."[21] Kent, like Donovan, believed in R&A's mission from the start. But the dismal offices given to his researchers suggested that not everyone shared his faith.

Kent later guessed that he was the thirtieth researcher R&A had hired.[22] The director of the R&A branch, James Baxter, was a historian who had been the president of Williams College. The deputy director, William Langer, had been a historian of Europe at Harvard. The branch was divided into regional sections, above which reigned a small Board of Analysts that reviewed any reports that R&A researchers produced that seemed important enough to forward to the White House, and that included the bibliographer Wilmarth Lewis, the economist Edward Mason, and the geographer Richard Hartshorne.[23] (The Board of Analysts was also called the College of Cardinals.)

R&A analysts worked for other groups across the branches of U.S. intelligence, military, and government, depending on who needed them and requested reports. The analysts worked in subdivisions based on region: Europe, Africa, the Far East, and so on. Their job, in the words of one intelligence expert, was "to turn information into intelligence—to take the mass of incoming material and get the truth out of it." (He added, explaining what he meant by *intelligence*, "It ranges from estimates, say, of the political intentions of a revolting party in some country to the most detailed of information, such as the depth of water at a particular point on a beach where conceivably military operations might someday occur.")[24]

The term for the reports they produced for these parties was "estimates."[25] An intelligence estimate could comprise an answer to a specific question, an evaluation of alternatives in a set of choices or a set of explanations for a scenario, or a summary of known information on a topic.[26] For instance, when R&A analysts wrote estimates for the OSS Morale Operations Branch, which dealt with propaganda, they might summarize and assess Japanese radio propaganda. They didn't make policy; they only advised the people who did.

Before long, R&A put Kent in a leadership position, appointing him chief of the division of R&A that focused on researching Africa. This was a hugely important appointment. North Africa offered to whoever could control it—the Axis or the Allies—an essential source of petroleum and other raw materials, as well as a potential launching point to invade Occupied Europe. As early as July 1942, the Allies knew they would attempt an invasion of North Africa before the end of the year.[27]

In Washington, Kent found himself fighting on two fronts: planning for an invasion of North Africa, a task that required breathtaking amounts of research, and arguing to the U.S. military that the research his section was producing was good and usable. Kent and his fellow station chiefs had to make the case for R&A to the military again and again. A colleague recalled that Kent's "amazingly colorful and imaginative profanity was an asset in any tense negotiating session on an intelligence estimate."[28]

Those same colleagues were chary about *recording* Kent's profanity—perhaps afraid that his language was unseemly even in a military context; perhaps careful of the dignity of a man who was, by the time they wrote their histories, the boss of just about everyone in intelligence; or perhaps just unsure of how to spell his more imaginative coinages.

If we want a glimpse of those early negotiations between Kent and his military counterparts over whether to escalate R&A's research to the higher brass, we will have to imagine it. Picture, for instance, Kent meeting a general while the OSS and the military were jointly scouting strategic locations for an invasion of North Africa:

"Look, Professor, I'm sure your work is impressive to undergraduates scratching their pimples, but I'm fighting an actual war. Stop sending me reports; I won't read them. My men are giving me everything I need."

"'Everything you need' will be thousands of coffins if you don't read this. Would you rather read reports or obituaries?"

"How about you call me 'officer'?"

"How about I call a doctor to remove the stick up your back? Here, take a look at this."

"What the hell is this?"

"It's a telephone directory for Casablanca."

"A telephone directory. You brought me a telephone directory."

"All the way from the New York Public Library. Just look inside, why don't you?"

"I don't speak French."

"That's too bad, because that means you can't order off-menu from the world's finest whores. But I'll translate. These are street addresses for every Casablanca business that you need to sabotage or occupy. 'Materiel de chemin de fer.' That's railway equipment. 'Société française des munitions de chasse, de tir, et de guerre.' That's French for munitions factory. Listening now?"

Kent flipped through the book's pages, gesturing like a general nudging flags around on a battle map. "Here are all the post, telegraph, and telephone offices that could give up the whole goose. The electric works. The Red Cross pharmacy. A full map of every borough, port, and railroad that runs from Morocco to France. I've labeled the 'fastest route,' 'cheapest route,' and 'romantic route for when you wanna get laid.' You've got lives on the line and you haven't even researched this enough to take a fucking family vacation."[29]

"Jesus Christ. That's—that's—hold on. Who says we're landing in Casablanca?"

"No one told me. I figured it out. That's what working in intelligence means. Your boats are practically named *Sink Me Offshore of Casablanca*. I can promise the armies waiting there have figured it out too."

"Well, Professor, I concede this might be useful. So why not stop wasting my fucking time and get me an English translation of this? My men don't speak Two-Faced, Cheese-Eating, Wine-Drinking, Negligee-Wearing, Mistress to the Prince of Fucking Versailles."

THE TRANSATLANTIC ESSAY CONTEST

The choice of North Africa for an invasion was not immediately obvious. "In mid-1942," writes the historian William Breuer, "Adolf Hitler stood on the threshold of a quick victory over the Grand Alliance—the United States, Great Britain, and Russia."[30] Nazi Germany held much of Europe as occupied territory, and Hitler's troops had beaten a thousand-mile path into Russia. All of Europe might soon be in hand, as Hitler's head of propaganda, Josef Goebbels, boasted in his diary: "The Führer is well on his way to his goal of world conquest."[31] Surely the only way to weaken him was to first break his hold on the Continent.

In April 1942, President Roosevelt's military advisers argued that the U.S. military, as its first major action in the war, should help Britain to mount a cross-Channel invasion of France. Roosevelt agreed, which threw the British into dismay. The Americans didn't seem to understand that the Allies didn't have the *capability* for a cross-Channel assault—not against the immense German forces that waited on the other side.[32] For such an invasion to work, so many things would have to be in place: the German forces would have to be thinned across a far larger area; the French, still mired in the bitterness of defeat, would have to be more emboldened to resist their occupiers through sabotage and outright fighting; the Germans would have to have less fuel, fewer planes, fewer tanks, fewer supplies all around.[33]

Churchill's own adviser, Sir Alan Brooke, suggested sending the Americans to the shores of French North Africa instead. If the Allies took that territory, they would have an excellent perch from which to send planes to bomb Occupied Europe and ships to obstruct Axis ports. To defend against those planes and ships, Hitler would have to spread his forces across thousands of miles of shoreline. The Allies would control North Africa's supplies of petroleum, and their spies would have access to new intelligence pipelines from Occupied Europe.[34] Then—*then*—the Allies would be ready to start thinking about a cross-Channel invasion of France.

But North Africa was almost as daunting a target as France. Germany's Afrika Korps, commanded by General Erwin Rommel, was in the process of devastating Britain's forces in the region. In just fourteen days in the summer of 1942, some seventy-five thousand British soldiers fell or were captured. On July 1, as Rommel's troops advanced on Cairo, British military staffers hastily burned their papers, just as Japanese diplomats burned their papers in advance of Pearl Harbor. "Such quantities of secret papers were hastily burned in anticipation of Rommel's arrival," Breuer writes, "that on a day to become known as Ash Wednesday, the sky over the Egyptian metropolis filled with black smoke."[35]

After the British persuaded the Americans that French North Africa should be their target, the two nations launched an intense discussion of logistics, sending wires back and forth that proposed all manner of plots and stratagems. One of Roosevelt's military planners, a general named Dwight Eisenhower—little known at the time, but soon to be quite famous—nicknamed the bickering "the transatlantic essay contest."[36]

At last, a plan fell into place for the ambitious operation, which the Allies gave the code name Torch. The Allies would send a surprise wave of invading forces to Algeria and Morocco, which the French military held on behalf of the French Vichy government. They would hit the ground simultaneously at Algiers, Oran, and Casablanca, and would follow up by pushing east to take the entire region. And the Americans would make the landings alone.[37]

The reasoning on this last point was solid: French hostility toward the British ran high, not just because of historical enmity, but also because in recent months, the British had targeted French forces in attacks that killed thousands of French soldiers. The Americans hadn't been in nearly as many such fights; and so the French, who liked the Americans anyway for sticking it to the English during the American Revolution, might be inclined to welcome a purely American invading force as friends and liberators.[38] But giving Torch to the Americans meant staking the operation on a military that had little experience with global warfare. "Never had a major invasion been mounted from 3,000 miles away," a historian later wrote:

> There were no textbooks, and no precedents. [Their] mission was to assemble an untested, partially trained force of some 38,000 men, move the force and its vehicles, weapons, ammunition, and supplies to another continent across an ocean infested with German U-boats, storm the defended shores of North Africa, defeat whatever hostile force might be encountered, secure a large beachhead, and prepare to drive hundreds of miles eastward.[39]

And they had only two months or so until D-day, which, though we now associate the term with the landing at Normandy, was a term that applied to any mission's start date.

In August 1942, just after the military appointed Eisenhower as commander in chief of the Allied Expeditionary Forces, putting him in charge of Operation Torch, a colleague in Washington told him, "There is a unanimity of opinion of Army officers here that the proposed operation appears hazardous to the extent of less than a 50 percent chance of success."[40]

THE STUDY GUIDE

Invading a foreign shore is a huge undertaking, and the U.S. military couldn't do it by simply pointing ships and planes at the Moroccan shoreline. They needed detailed information. Where were the airfields, electric stations, municipal offices, police offices, post offices, railroad stations, telegraph offices? (During an invasion, American troops would need to capture these *immediately*, possibly in the dark.) Where could the army find hotels and schoolhouses to set up temporary quarters? Where could the Medical Corps establish hospitals? What were the roads like, and what kinds of vehicles could the troops drive over those roads? What was the capability of the ports and docks, and how should the navy organize convoys to best be served at those ports and docks? What was the climate like, and what equipment should the troops be given to deal with that climate? What would the troops need to know in order to get along with the locals? The list of questions ran on and on.

Kent became friendly with the G-2 (army intelligence) officers who dealt with African intelligence. One day, one of G-2's section heads came to Kent and asked him to do some research just for them: "How would you boys like to do a railroad study of Algeria? We need it in the worst possible way, and you people are just the ones to undertake it."[41]

Now, a study of the railroads in Algeria might seem like the least romantic task imaginable. Find out where the railroads run: past what cities and ports and mines, through what natural hazards. Find out whether different sections of railroad use single tracks or double tracks, electrified tracks or nonelectrified tracks, standard gauges or narrow gauges, wood ties or metal ties. Find out the answers to the most meticulous questions about gradients, freight traffic, axle loads, passenger loads, schedules, security measures: so many questions that the resulting report will fill more than three hundred pages.[42] But for a library rat, this kind of task can be positively thrilling. You never know, in the archives, when you'll find the solution to a mystery. The driest materials can catch you up in a conflagration. You just have to know how to work the records.

Kent knew how to do just that. The Department of Commerce had a records office where they found "an endless number of reports by commercial attachés on such things as railroads, ports, and telecommunications systems." The Association of American Railroads had "a magnificent library of foreign periodicals dealing with, among other things, railroading all over the world." R&A was pioneering what later became known as OSINT, or "open source intelligence." They didn't need to send secret agents on a mission to Algeria to steal confidential documents and interrogate railroad employees in dark rooms. Instead, R&A's triumphs "came in large part," Kent later said, "from articles that had already been written, usually in French, and infrequently in English on these very railroads."[43]

When Kent's team handed G-2 the finished study of Algerian railroads, G-2 was so delighted with the results that they asked for more railroad studies set in other locales: Morocco, Nigeria, Tunisia, and beyond. And for studies of transportation broadly. And for studies of topographic conditions. Then for studies of Turkish railroads, of railroads in Europe. Truth be told, G-2 got a little drunk on the possibilities. James Baxter, the chief of R&A, made sounds of annoyance about how many requests G-2 was piling on his researchers, but he let almost every request go through. Soon enough, R&A was fielding intelligence requests from all corners—the military, the State Department, and an alphabet soup of other government agencies.[44] Kent and his team were in high demand.

Soon, a State Department officer who knew about Kent's work, one Harry Villard, made an important introduction. An acquaintance who had moved to the United States from Morocco told Villard that his father was coming to join him. This was noteworthy because his father "had been the construction engineer for the whole Moroccan railroad system and had been in charge of the Moroccan railroad system for many years."[45]

"Villard was kind enough to tip me off and ask me if I would like to see the man," Kent later wrote. "Of course, I would, and Villard accordingly invited me out for a drink at his house in Georgetown."[46]

A railroad engineer might be able to divulge significant details that could help the Allies hobble the occupying forces that held Morocco's rails. Which rail lines seemed most likely to carry major troop movements? (Reconnaissance agents might need to keep these under surveillance, in order to keep track of enemy plans, and sabotage agents might need to "cut" them in order to keep troops from reaching a particular place.) Which rail lines transported freight from ports and factories? Where were the bridges, the tunnels, the signal stations, the workshops and repair plants where damaged train equipment was fixed? Kent was especially keen to learn the answer to a rather niche question: did Morocco's railway system have any sidings—that is, places with double tracks, which allowed trains to pass each other? Sabotaging double tracks took extra work and extra planning.

The challenge was to get these answers without looking suspicious, since Kent didn't want his intentions to be known. By the time he wrote his memoir, he had forgotten the man from Morocco's name, so he called him Monsieur X. When Kent visited Villard's home to see Monsieur X, he brought with him a questionnaire booklet that R&A's researchers were using to standardize their research on the Moroccan railroad. The booklet included all the questions above, and more. When he arrived, Kent kept the questionnaire hidden in the belongings he left in the entryway: "I knew that I was asking him the most delicate kind of questions," he later said, "and that he should know at once that the sort of questions I was asking were of a high intelligence value." Villard told Monsieur X that Kent was a history professor who studied North Africa, and who was naturally delighted to have the chance to talk with a native.

Kent began his questioning with as much misdirection as he could. Perhaps he opened the conversation with a litany of grievances against his students; perhaps he hummed and crossed his legs and tapped a pipe against his knee. In any case—he was an aggressively ordinary history professor, and he had come to ask dry questions about Morocco's economics and politics. Villard served daiquiri cocktails, and Kent shotgunned a few of them while he worked up the courage to shift the conversation from these ordinary topics to something more delicate. He asked about a well-known problem in Morocco, namely the difficulty of getting enough fuel to run its industries. Monsieur X replied that Morocco relied largely on coal, and depended, lately, on local coal mines. Oh, Kent said, but coal is so difficult to transport—how could Morocco possibly set up its railroads to haul such heavy loads? Which set them safely on the dangerous topic of railroads, Kent later wrote:

> I asked him a few more pointed questions, and then said,
> "Monsieur X, it just so happens that I have in the hall a
> number of papers here with these questions written down,
> and I wonder if you would be so kind as to help me fill out
> some of the gaps."
> "Why, sure," he said in effect.

I returned from the hall with this bundle of forms, one for each division point of the Moroccan railroads, and started to ask about sidings. I had previously discovered that the word for *siding* in French, because our conversation was in French, was *embranchment*, and instead of falling dead at the mention of so sensitive a matter, he said, "Why, certainly, let's see your forms."

And, right there before my eyes, he went through the forms for each division point and wrote with his own hand where every single siding occurred and how long they were. As I remember it, they were all or mostly all about one full kilometer in length. What he had given me was among the most priceless kind of information that a man could have furnished, and with my bundle of papers, I had another daiquiri and hurried back to the office.

By then, the time was 8:00 p.m. No matter: Kent called a G-2 colonel right away and explained the data he'd gotten hold of. The colonel asked for a write-up *immediately*—before the city woke up the next morning, if possible—and when Kent delivered, the colonel sent off the write-up at once by telegram.[47] A professor had delivered urgent wartime intelligence.

FRONTLINE LIBRARIES

R&A's work turned the strangest places into intelligence hubs. Libraries, for instance. One day in early 1942, government agents—likely R&A analysts—marched into the New York Public Library and demanded to see its collections of maps. The same scene was playing out at libraries all over the country: a librarian at UCLA later recalled hearing stories from his elders "of coming to work and finding that the map library had suddenly become a top security area protected by 24-hour armed guards."[48]

R&A wasn't the only agency that took an interest in maps. It was constantly fighting for jurisdiction over cartography and geography, among other fields that could be put to intelligence purposes, with other entities such as Army Intelligence and the State Department. The leaders of R&A sought, from the start, to run R&A so that it avoided merely duplicating the work of other intelligence services and instead provided them, and their parent entities, with information they couldn't get themselves. When COI became the OSS in 1942, President Roosevelt moved the OSS under the command of the Joint Chiefs of Staff, a council of senior officials from the Armed Forces, in part to make it easier for military leaders to use R&A's insights early in their strategic planning.[49]

Maps provide an especially potent example of the knowledge deficit that R&A was designed to address, the reason that R&A agents were hunting through libraries and confiscating whatever scraps they could. In 1941, when the United States entered the war, the country's stockpile of maps was, in the words of one onlooker, "utterly deficient." The Army Corps of Engineers, which at the time made most of the maps the military used, had a budget that provided for two cartographers. The whole of the United States contained just two portfolios of maps showing all of Japan.[50]

For this reason, making maps was a huge component of the work of R&A geographers, who passed endless hours copying historical maps in places like the New York Public Library. (The geographers in R&A were generally called analysts, like many other R&A staffers.)* They drew situation maps every day for the War Department; they drew reference maps and thematic maps to accompany the reports that R&A wrote at the request of military and government officials; they drew maps to propose strategic elements of upcoming military operations.[51] (As it happened, the headquarters of R&A's Map Division was Sherman Kent's complex at 25th and E streets.)[52]

---

* Most of R&A's geographers were university instructors, but Arthur Robinson, the head of R&A's Map Division, grew increasingly desperate for people he could train as mapmakers. "He found that piano players, for example, had greater finger flexibility than other people, and that he could often make decent cartographers out of them." Keir Sterling, "American Geographers and the OSS During World War II," in *The U.S. Army and World War II: Selected Papers from the Army's Commemorative Conferences*, ed. Judith Bellafaire (Washington, DC: Center of Military History, 1998), 224–25.

The map deficit was just one part of a wider knowledge deficit that tormented the military and government officials leading the war, a deficit that explains why R&A and, to a lesser extent, other intelligence services put so much effort into recruiting the kind of knowledge workers who knew how to cobble together information from scraps. Intelligence agencies, following the direction of their researchers, took all kinds of items from the libraries they annexed: old books, magazines, newspapers, postcards, telephone directories, travel guides.[53] They also took librarians. Every day, for instance, Walter Ristow, a librarian who headed the New York Public Library's Map Division, worked until lunchtime in a Military Intelligence office at Rockefeller Center, then walked to the NYPL, spent an hour or so performing his regular duties, and then returned to Rockefeller Center for the rest of the day. The library had given him partial leave so that he could help U.S. Military Intelligence read historical maps as a civilian staffer. Other librarians at the NYPL scoured the shelves for books that might be useful to the war effort. One of the first maps the Map Service, a cartography unit in the army that collaborated with the OSS, asked for at the NYPL was a map of North Africa.[54]

But the humanities researchers who were recruited more than pulled their weight. Much of their work followed a premise that professors know all too well: the answers might be *right in front of you*, but you won't see them unless you do the reading. And another premise: nothing in the archives is unimportant.[55] Whimsical doodles of sea monsters or satirical maps that portray countries as wine-bloated buffoons farting on each other—you might think this sort of thing would be irrelevant to military intelligence. But historians and professional researchers take the word *irrelevant* as a challenge.

Consider the maps of the South Seas that the Wilkes Expedition published in the nineteenth century. Old copperplate engravings that sketch coastal depths with fluttery, curlicued lines, the Wilkes maps were designed to aid whaling ships. The surveyors got their measurements by firing guns from their ships and "noting the elapsed time between the flash and the report."[56] Not ideal lumber for the age of radar and fighter planes, but the historians made it work. American soldiers did indeed skirmish, reportedly, on South Sea islands that military intelligence had needed to study using the Wilkes maps.[57]

The value of maps was obvious: before you can put boots on the ground, you have to put ground under the boots. But Research and Analysis based the claim for its importance on the idea that you can get vital combat intelligence from all kinds of unpromising sources, not just laughably outdated maps. R&A researchers just kept working out new ways to pull usable intelligence on every aspect of the war from the snips and scraps that crossed their desks.

Kent and his team in R&A's North Africa section were no exception, devouring photo albums, old books, movies, magazines, and most of all, newspapers, which—though censored—turned out to be gold mines, if only you knew how to read them right. (One staffer summed up this philosophy with the phrase "Ninety percent of all so-called secret information comes from the newsstands.")[58] Kent's team had just eight members. But in mid-1942, when the military started planning, in earnest, an invasion of North Africa, the military was so desperate for any kind of usable intelligence that it was willing to rest substantial responsibility on their shoulders. Kent and his little team—which had been created scarcely a month before—worked around the clock, writing reports that higher-ups used to make and revise plans for the invasion, which seemed to change from minute to minute.

The OSS had never helped to direct a major operation. American soldiers had never parachuted into combat. Operation Torch wasn't just the first big test of the Research and Analysis division; it was the first big test of the OSS as a whole.[59]

SECRETS AREN'T SECURE

The challenge that Kent and his team faced during the planning of Torch was the perpetual challenge of intelligence more broadly: their success depended on their staying one step ahead of the enemy's knowledge of how intelligence works.

The concept of a secret is an easy way to show this precept in action, because a secret isn't just information; it's an idea *about* information. The idea is that you can keep information out of enemy hands by protecting it behind a key that you keep secret, like a cipher key or a code word or a password. Or, on a more general level, by treating the information like water that must on no account leak out from your protective container.

Certainly, the U.S. military used these principles to hide their own plans. In Washington, the Torch planners had their offices in a temporary war building near the Potomac River. Staffers put out gossip that they were in charge of planning troop movements to the UK, and they reinforced this gossip by referring—even within the supposed safety of the building—to Algeria with the code word "Britain" and to Morocco with the code word "Ireland."[60]

In Maryland's National Harbor, leading up to the launch of Torch, soldiers loaded port warehouses with innumerable crates labeled with seemingly random numbers and letters—the result of Kent and his team's research. Many of these crates held maps: marine maps, road maps, topical maps, topographic maps, maps of every description for hundreds of locations in North Africa. The soldiers who crated these maps and carried them from publishing house to warehouse "were given no leaves and were, in fact, more or less under arrest."*

But the fact is—to borrow a phrase from today's information security experts—that *secrets aren't secure.* A secret is actually a dangerous way to keep something secret. Or, to put it another way, if you have assets or information that you want to hide from others, you should try as much as possible to keep whatever system you use to hide those assets from depending on secrets like passwords. Because people are *terrible* at keeping secrets.

Consider the most urgent secret that the United States kept during the war: the location of the Manhattan Project at Los Alamos, the secret site in New Mexico where scientists worked on designing the first atomic bomb, and the work that went on there. By 1943, university

---

* R&A innovated new technologies for publishing maps. Sterling, "American Geographers and the OSS During World War II," 224; William Breuer, *Operation Torch: The Allied Gamble to Invade North Africa* (New York: St. Martin's, 1985), 34–35.

researchers around the country noticed that scholars and grad students in the sciences were disappearing from their labs—going *somewhere* to do war work, but nobody knew where.[61] But at least one researcher figured out where his colleagues went when he checked out a guidebook to New Mexico from his university library: "At the back of the book, on the slip of paper on which borrowers signed their names, I read the names of Joan Hinton, David Frisch, Joseph McKibben, and all the other people who had been mysteriously disappearing to hush-hush war jobs without saying where. I had uncovered their destination in a simple and unexpected fashion. It is next to impossible to maintain absolute secrecy and security in war time."[62]

At Los Alamos itself, the researchers required, in order to do their work, all kinds of scientific books and journals. The Manhattan Project's librarian, Charlotte Serber, ordered most of those books, as she had to, as loans from the University of California library system, since many of the titles they needed were out of print. "By July 1945," one historian writes, "the Library included approximately 3000 books, 160 journals per month, and 1500 microfilm reproductions of specific articles and portions of books." Had enemy spies walked into those libraries and looked around the stacks for missing books and journals, they would have found that hundreds of books and journals on chemistry, metallurgy, and physics were missing—and therefore that some sort of scientific project on those topics was under way.[63]

Further to the work at Los Alamos, the scientists were required to keep confidential papers in combination safes in their offices. ("The Project must have had more safes than all the banks in New York," a Los Alamos scientist later commented wryly.) But the scientists often chose combinations that were easy to remember. Richard Feynman, a celebrated physicist who was then a young scientist at Los Alamos, helped scientists who forgot the combinations to their own safes to open those safes, simply by guessing nerdy numbers: pi (31-41-59), Euler's number (27-18-28), the *c* from the equation $E = mc^2$ (29-97-92), or Planck's constant (66-26-07). The protection of the papers was reliant on a *secret*—the safe combination—that, often, was all too easy to guess.[64]

All of which is to say that Kent and his team understood something about intelligence that the enemy didn't, something that even most people on their own side didn't know. That something was the extent to which secret keepers leak their secrets in the form of disclosures, available to those who are willing to do the most serious, laborious, tedious digging. For as long as R&A could follow paper trails that the enemy never considered, the Allies had a good chance of winning the war of intelligence.

RUSE DE GUERRE

The Allied militaries tried mightily to keep their own secrets. Their success was spotty. People sedulously stamped documents with the words *SECRET, TOP SECRET, PERSONAL & MOST SECRET.* They warned each other constantly not to talk about things they knew or even suspected. When you opened an American newspaper, you might well see, between the articles, a warning in bold letters: "**Don't spread rumors.**"[65]

Nonetheless, accidents and near-misses proliferated. In London, a general was almost sent home when he left his office window open and a top-secret memo about the plans for Torch, which was sitting on top of his desk, blew onto a lawn outside the building. And an officer drunkenly groused in a pub about spending all his time on an upcoming sea-to-land invasion. (Eisenhower told his staff, "Send the son of a bitch home—on a slow boat!")[66]

The biggest disaster of all would happen on September 25, 1942, a little more than a month before the planned North African invasion, when German fighters shot down a British seaplane en route from London to Gibraltar. On board was a courier, J. H. Turner, who was carrying a letter to Gibraltar's governor general that disclosed all manner of confidential details about the planned invasion of North Africa: "D-day, targeted areas, troop and sea strength—the works."[67] The case that held the letter was equipped with a bomb that was supposed to explode if the plane went down, so the enemy wouldn't get hold of the letter. But when the plane went down, the bomb didn't go off. Soon afterward, fishermen found Turner's body bobbing in the water off Cádiz, Spain. Spanish police arrived and picked up the body and its cargo.[68]

When representatives of the Spanish government gave the corpse and its cargo to British intelligence at Gibraltar, the Brits panicked. Did anyone open the case? Did some Spanish functionary take a photograph of the secret letter and give or sell it to the Germans? Did the plans for Operation Torch make their way to the Spanish government, to the German consulate, to Adolf Hitler himself? Ultimately, the Allies decided to continue with Torch as though this terrible exposure never happened—though the possibilities gave them plenty of sleepless nights.[69]

So how do you keep secrets if you can't keep secrets? A time-honored method is to flood the enemy with bad intelligence. Drown information with disinformation. In the case of Torch, this was the job of a British counterintelligence outfit called the XX Committee. This committee did similar work to that of Curtiss's X-2 unit in Istanbul; the name XX, like the name X-2, was a pun on "double-cross."[70]

The XX Committee sent instructions to agents and double agents working on four continents to murmur confidentially—over beers or in diplomats' cars or under the high gilded ceilings of the Vatican—that the Americans couldn't handle the war and the British were worn to a nub with fighting.[71] They wouldn't be invading *anywhere* soon—perhaps ever. Or perhaps, the agents murmured, the Americans and the British were making preparations to invade Norway. That would explain why lots of new vessels seemed to be congregating in British waters. Just to add some oomph to the story, one of General Eisenhower's aides set out a winter coat and snow boots in plain view in his office when he met journalists. Sure enough, news pieces started theorizing that the Allies were headed for Norway.[72]

Like all good lies, this one was tinctured with truth. There *was* a reason for all the new vessels in British waters. And the Americans *were* in over their heads—more than the Americans would admit to themselves. Ironically, when American spies crept into North Africa to make ready for Torch, they were so clumsy and unsubtle that the German spies already in North Africa assumed the Americans were playacting in "an elaborate *ruse de guerre* to deceive the Germans into believing that an invasion of French Northwest Africa was being prepared."[73]

Another method of keeping secrets when you can't keep secrets is to snow, sucker, and stonewall your own people. People can't spill what they don't know. When American and British troops boarded ships to launch the operation, they had no idea where they were going. A hierarchy of security classifications allowed personnel in Class I to know exactly what was going on, personnel in Class II to know a broad time and place, and personnel in Class III to know "only that a general offensive action is contemplated." Personnel in Classes I and II were advised to lie to personnel in Class III, and the lies they told differed depending on whom they were talking to: troops and sailors from Britain were told they were sailing around the Cape of Africa; troops from America were told they were going to Syria; flyers were told they were going to the Middle East; troops headed to Gibraltar were told they were going to Malta.[74]

Even among the higher-ups who were in the know, some crucial details remained a mystery. Weeks after D-day had been decided, the Allies were still writing up official plans for Torch that said, "The date of assault (D Day) will be communicated at an appropriate time to all concerned."[75]

THE ALL-NIGHTER

Kent likely didn't know the date of the Torch assault, but he knew it was coming and that he had to work fast. In later years, he recalled with great clarity the crunch session in which they worked up all their research on North Africa into a master document, "which was to be . . . the R&A Branch's major contribution to North African planning." They started on the morning of August 13, 1942—a hot day, even in the early hours, and promising to be absolutely sweltering by noon in the stuffy building where they worked. Some fifty analysts worked shoulder to shoulder, shuffling papers, taking notes, talking over each other. "Everybody was working like beavers all that day and into the night," Kent said.

As the clock went past midnight, I well remember, a short break that a number of people took for coffee and perhaps a donut. I especially remember my dear friend, Herman Liebert, called Fritz, who was the editor of the Economic Division and a gifted editor, too. Liebert was something of a dandy in his dress, and always wore, even in the summertime in Washington, a high stiff collar. That day he had on a white Palm Beach suit and a stiff collar, and by midnight his white figure had been splotched with this, that, and the other of the commodities we had been throwing around, including a generous amount of coffee.

About six or seven in the morning, Fritz retired to the men's room without a razor, and his face still unshaven, he nevertheless changed his dirty white collar for a spandy clean one, which gave the most amazing contrast to his general comportment that you could imagine. Nature had endowed him with the kind of beard that turned blue ten minutes after a close shave, and here he was, eighteen hours or so from his last shave, his face a quarter of an inch covered with black hair, filthy white suit, filthy shirt, and this startling, sparkling white collar, which did no more than emphasize the general disarray all the rest of his person.[76]

You've heard of all-nighters, but this was a marathon study session with stakes far higher than passing a midterm. A full thirty-six hours after they began, Kent dismissed most of his subordinates and started to put the final touches on the report. By then, the date was August 15. Working with R&A's brilliant secretaries, who knew how to make mess look like method, Kent assembled the pages and submitted them to the high command. The work, at least for now, was done.[77]

As the convoys prepared to depart, a general named Ernie Harmon visited an admiral on a cruiser lingering in port, carrying a "highly secret book of instructions," he later said, "as thick as a Sears Roebuck Catalogue." The admiral looked at the report in Harmon's hand and held up his own copy. "Harmon, have you read this book and do you understand it?"

"No, sir. I haven't read it and I doubt if I'll have time to before we reach Safi," Harmon said, referring to a city in Morocco. "I don't even know who wrote it."

In the end, nobody needed to know who wrote it. Nobody needed to know the names of any of the poor library rats who built high, teetering towers of pages, or the war planners who laid them out as crisp, practical orders. But Harmon and the admiral sat down together and worked through their reading. "When I left Davidson's ship," Harmon said, "basic agreements were condensed on a single typewritten sheet and I had a complete understanding of what we were going to do."[78] Months of steady grinding among the library stacks would now be tested in battle.

THE FINAL EXAM

The invasion was hell, as war always is. When American troops began wading ashore on November 8, 1942, machine-gun bullets were sprayed at them from forts defending the beaches. The numbers were against them: 107,000 Allied troops against 200,000 Frenchmen.[79] Some of the French chose to fight back; some didn't.

All told, the fighting lasted six months before the last Axis soldiers on the Continent surrendered. But the Americans started seizing remarkable victories on the very first day, and the operation quickly turned into a resolute offensive. The story became a story of triumph: the Americans had stepped onto the world stage, and they were ready to throw down with any and all challengers. The newest fighter for the Allies was a ringer.

"A tremendous gamble, and it won! Hostilities ceased in Algiers at the end of the first day; in Oran on the third and in Morocco on the fourth. Within eight days, French troops were battling the Germans in Tunisia, and before the month was out, the whole of French West Africa's military strength and facilities were at the disposal of American commanders," boasted a 1946 article in *Collier's* magazine. "None of these results were accidental. True, we had some lucky breaks, but preceding the invasion, and responsible for its success in no small degree, were weeks of secret negotiations and daring intelligence work." Before D-day, the U.S. military estimated that the first push of the invasion would entail sixty thousand Allied casualties; in the actual event, Allied casualties numbered fewer than fifteen hundred.[80]

"Professor! I was about to go liberate you from that plywood coffin you work in. We pulled it off, and no small thanks to you, you beautiful, bow-tied, smart-mouthed son of a bitch! We walked right into North Africa like a pig walking into a pastry shop. It'll be easy flying from here, mark my words. German morale is finally hitting the shitter. I wouldn't be surprised if they break apart in their own shitstorm in three months, just like they did in 1918."

"Slow down. I'm glad about North Africa, but let's not count our shitstorms before they've hatched. My staff—"

"Nuts to your staff. Just admit that we've won and pour a drink with me to celebrate. Your staff aren't the only ones who've ever seen a history book, and everyone knows how this chapter of history goes."

"If everyone knew, then you wouldn't be paying me—for this."

"What horseshit clever-ass report did your staff come up with now? Did they find a secret source of information in used German toilet paper? Did they figure out how to read Hitler's plans from the flutter of ribbons in little girls' pigtails?"

"No, they thought they'd break U.N. custom and actually apply intelligence to their intelligence. Everybody big enough for a nonplywood office thinks this will be another 1918. But my staff were professors before they came here, and before *that* they were poor miserable grad students who spent their whole lives studying political science instead of getting laid. At least out of pity, listen to them. They say public morale matters in a democracy, but not in Hitler's Germany. Morale means fuck-all when a totalitarian tells you to march."[81]

"So, you're saying what? Hitler says he's invincible, we just proved he isn't. That's not enough to get some cracks going through his foundation?"

"You've got a good launching pad for hitting the Continent, but that foundation won't crack unless we get inside. We've got to sabotage pieces of the machine and stoke resistance from within. Blow up Gestapo offices and give tactical training to dissenters. Labor already hates Hitler, so we should get them to work slower and take more days off to fuck their wives. Or, in France, to fuck each other's wives. If they're *real* patriots, to fuck *soldiers'* wives. Sabotage will weaken the control of the totalitarian state. *Then* public morale will make a difference."

6

THE DIRTIEST WORK THAT CAN POSSIBLY BE IMAGINED

A *stands for atom; it is so small*
No one has ever seen it at all.

B *stands for bomb; the bombs are much bigger,*
So, brother, do not be too fast on the trigger.

S *stands for secret; you can keep it forever*
Provided there's no one abroad who is clever.

—An alphabet the physicist Edward Teller
created for his child at Los Alamos[1]

ON AUGUST 2, 1939, JANET COATESWORTH, A FREELANCE
stenographer who often typed up papers for professors at Columbia
University, received a call from a gentleman at the King's Crown Hotel
in New York City. The gentleman asked her to come to his hotel room

and type a letter for him. This was not an odd request in 1939; typing was a woman's job, and most men didn't know how to do it. When she arrived at the hotel room, she met a young man with disheveled brown hair who was pacing back and forth in an agitated state.[2] He insisted on closing the door. The historical record doesn't say what he was wearing, but he was a physicist, so I like to imagine that his clothes were good as individual pieces but didn't make sense in combination. As soon as Coatesworth set up her typewriter, he began to compose aloud a letter to "F.D. Roosevelt, President of the United States, White House."[3]

Still pacing, the young man described, in a Hungarian accent, the possibility of constructing "extremely powerful bombs," and he felt it was "his duty" to warn the president: "A single bomb of this type, carried by boat and exploded in a port, might very well destroy the whole port together with some of the surrounding territory."

"That convinced me!" the stenographer later said. "I was sure I was working for a nut."[4]

The stranger advised the president to find someone he trusted with such a mighty secret, "a person who has your confidence and who could perhaps serve in an unofficial capacity," to supervise laboratories that could make the extremely powerful bombs and to obtain for the United States a special chemical element that the bombs required. Germany, he warned, had already stopped the export of this element from some of its mines. Then he got to the signature line.

"Yours very truly," he said, "Albert Einstein."

Coatesworth—who knew, as everyone did, that Albert Einstein was actually a little old German man with white hair—left the meeting believing the man she'd been trapped in a hotel room with was "deranged," a self-deluding phony. Decades later, historians tracked her down. It turned out the letter she typed was the real thing: it did go to President Roosevelt, and the signatory was indeed Albert Einstein.[5] Einstein wasn't an expert in nuclear physics, but Leo Szilard, a refugee scientist and the man who dictated the letter, was. He drafted the letter for Einstein to sign.

Janet Coatesworth didn't know it, but her letter changed the course of the war.[6] Though World War II ended with the atomic destruction of cities, during most of its course, the general public didn't know about the discovery of nuclear fission and thus the power to create an atomic bomb. No doubt many people, had they been told the secret, would have thought, as Coatesworth did, that the notion was insane. Even within the scientific community, the ingredients that went into making an atomic bomb were a desperately guarded secret.

But President Roosevelt knew—because men who were in a position to know delivered the letter to him—that the note really did come from Einstein, and that any scientific discovery that alarmed him was worth taking seriously. Roosevelt formed an advisory committee to investigate the weapons potential of uranium, which the letter named as the element that could be harnessed to create that catastrophic explosion. Their work led to the creation of the Manhattan Project.

The intense secrecy that the Allies and the Axis alike tried to maintain over the race to build an atomic bomb meant that the agents who were dispatched to play roles in that race—say, by surreptitiously photographing scientific journals, as Kibre did, or by sabotaging the other side—often didn't know why they were asked to do what they did. For spies during the war, the idea that their actions mattered for reasons they couldn't know was often the one conviction that kept them going. They had to trust, small though they were individually, that their stories connected in larger actions that made a difference in the war.

This chapter tells one of those stories—and, in the process, tells a story about something that Hitler and his confederates never truly understood: the power of power from below. The OSS and the SOE learned early on that lone saboteurs can take down their targets more effectively than fleets of bomber planes; that small groups of people on foot can go where squadrons of tanks can't; that ordinary people with local knowledge can foil the plans of occupying generals—that, in short, the monumental power Hitler's regime worshipped could be outmaneuvered by precisely the weakness he despised in others. It's a story about the SOE and the OSS needing to get rid of a problem so big that only small people could be entrusted with the task. To do so, they enlisted agents on the ground, as they did often, to carry out a mission whose purpose was kept secret from the agents themselves.

Our story begins in early 1943, when the SOE, at one of Britain's spy-training schools, gathered a small group of men from the Norwegian underground and told them that they must travel in secret to the hydroelectric plant at Vemork, Norway, and destroy it with their own hands. They didn't explain why, although a refugee scientist named Leif Tronstad, who helped them prepare for their mission, gave them an ominous hint.

"It's the heavy water," the scientist said. "It's manufactured at Vemork, and can be used for some of the dirtiest work that can possibly be imagined. If the Germans can solve the problem, they'll win the war."[7] The spies on the ground didn't grasp the significance of this information, but their superiors in London and Washington did with chilling clarity. Heavy water, their scientist sources told them, is an essential ingredient for making an atomic bomb.

A SECRET ARMY

Industrial sabotage, as a weapon of warfare, is an invention of the Second World War. War has always entailed destroying the enemy's resources, but only during WWII, when the Nazis ordered manufacturers in occupied countries to fuel the Nazi war machine and conscripted workers from those countries to work in factories in Germany, was the opportunity for sabotage significant enough to shape the whole war.[8] (The training materials at Beaulieu note: "The seven million foreign students in Germany are the 'secret army' right in the heart of the enemy's country, who only need to be trained and coordinated." This statement refers, in large part, to industrial sabotage.)[9]

At Brickendonbury Manor, a grand house just north of London, the SOE ran a secret facility, called STS 17, for developing methods of sabotage. The man in charge of sabotage training there was Major George Rheam, whom historians now call "the founder of modern industrial sabotage."[10] As stiff and inflexible in his manner as the machinery he devised ways to dismantle, he taught his students that sabotage must be as precise as good engineering is.[11]

"Anyone trained by him," one historian says of Rheam, "could look at a factory with quite new eyes, spot the few essential machines in it, and understand how to stop them with a few well-placed ounces of explosive; to stop them, moreover, in such a way that some of them could not be restarted promptly by removing undamaged parts from comparable machines nearby."[12]

Brickendonbury Manor received a steady flow of students who had escaped from occupied countries, since they were especially well suited for the work, being able to return home, blend in with the local population, and carry out secret sabotage missions.[13] Rheam remarked of his foreign students that "the Norwegians impressed him the most, for bravery, for readiness to run risks, and for steadiness in facing the dangers of sabotage."[14]

A BOOK CIPHER

The news that the Nazis were up to something nefarious at a hydroelectric plant in Norway came to the SOE through Stockholm. After the Nazis occupied Norway in 1940, Stockholm became, for practical purposes, the communications gateway between the resistance in Norway and SOE headquarters in London. Maintaining secret radio contact between Norway and London turned out to be distressingly difficult, whereas the British Legation in Stockholm, because Sweden was a neutral country, could communicate with London openly, via telegram. From there, couriers could carry messages by hand to Norway and back, using fishing boats to cross the Skagerrak strait under the cover of darkness.

Captain Malcolm Munthe was a British intelligence agent who grew up in Sweden and joined the British military—as his ancestry allowed him to—after Sweden declared neutrality in the war. He worked at the British Legation in Stockholm as an assistant military attaché, where he looked after the exchange of messages with Norway.[15] Munthe communicated with his counterpart in London, Sir Charles Hambro, using a cryptographic system called a book cipher. Each man had, in his personal library, a copy of the same book: *Ruskin's Works*. In their telegrams, they simply listed the location in the book of every word in the message: for instance, "98, 2, 5" might be the fifth word on the second line on page 98, or "kill." (One reason a book cipher is so effective is that one can use different locations in the book to repeat the same word, which means codebreakers can't look for patterns in repetitions.)[16]

Stockholm was also a place where sabotage missions in Norway were planned and where members of the Norwegian resistance gathered to prepare their next steps. Norwegian loyalists traveled by foot from their homes to the Norwegian Legation in Stockholm, a journey that could take months, in the hope of being trained and given a mission. There, Munthe and the British intelligence scooped them up, trained them, and sent them back on sabotage missions planned by the SOE.[17]

Knut Haukelid, a Norwegian sabotage agent, recalled in his memoir his disappointment at winding up in a camp in Öreryd for Norwegian refugees after he fled to Sweden. He also recalled his joy at receiving a summons, thanks to a friend's machinations, to visit the British Legation in Stockholm: "To be summoned to Stockholm was the greatest thing that could happen for a refugee at Öreryd. Stockholm meant the possibility of getting over to England and getting into the war again."[18]

UNKNOWN APPLICATIONS

Lief Tronstad, the scientist who told the small band of saboteurs that they must destroy the hydroelectric plant at Vemork, was a Norwegian who, like the saboteurs themselves, escaped to Allied territory through Stockholm.[19] Tronstad knew that the plant's heavy water program held dangerous potential because he developed the program himself. Tronstad was twenty-eight years old when, in 1931, American chemist Harold Urey set the scientific community abuzz with his discovery that hydrogen, which famously consists of just one electron and one proton, has an isotope—a variant of the element with a different number of neutrons—that also contains a neutron. (Urey won the Nobel Prize for his discovery in 1934.) We can find that isotope most easily in heavy water: "heavy" because the extra neutron increases the hydrogen atom's atomic weight.[20] Heavy water exists in nature, but only in miniscule amounts; if you want enough heavy water to use in a weapon, you need to manufacture it.

Tronstad wanted to study the new substance, even though its uses weren't obvious: "Technology first," he liked to say, "then industry and applications!" So, in 1933, he approached Norsk Hydro, the company that owned the plant at Vemork, and asked whether he could set up a lab there to produce heavy water. He needed water and electricity, which the hydroelectric plant had plenty of. Norsk Hydro said yes.[21]

After the Nazis occupied Norway, Tronstad fled to Stockholm—staying there for a month, then allowing the British to spirit him away to the UK.[22] In a report that he later compiled for the SOE, Tronstad wrote, "Even before my departure from Norway in the autumn of 1941, it was quite clear that the heavy water plants at Vemork would be of great importance in the war effort. . . . It was, however, at that time not considered a matter of urgency."[23]

At the time, only scientists understood the scale of the destruction the atom could unleash. They recognized that a nuclear reactor—a device that created a controlled chain reaction of atomic splitting—was almost certainly an essential part of the path to build an atomic bomb, and that heavy water could be useful to building a reactor. (We'll see how heavy water facilitates that chain reaction shortly.) But that path seemed long, and the end product—the bomb itself—seemed far off. In the end, however, the creation of the atom bomb turned out to be much like how Ernest Hemingway described going bankrupt: gradual, then sudden.

PUBLISH AND PERISH

In 1934, the sequence of discoveries that led to uncovering the secret of atomic fission kicked off in Rome, where the physicist Enrico Fermi reported that by firing neutrons at the element uranium, he could create new radioactive elements; he'd discovered a new kind of artificial radioactivity.[24] This caught the attention of two lab partners in Berlin, the physicist Lise Meitner and the chemist Otto Hahn, who had worked on radiation for years.*

Meitner and Hahn learned from their work that radioactive particles could indeed produce new kinds of atoms, but they didn't realize they were working on something with weapons potential.[25] When Germany annexed Austria in 1938, and Meitner, a Jewish Austrian citizen, fled to Stockholm, the German authorities tried to stop her, not because of her knowledge, but because she was Jewish.[26]

In Stockholm, Meitner corresponded with Hahn, continuing the work she'd left behind.[27] Meanwhile, in 1937, Fermi had achieved an interesting result by once again firing neutrons at uranium atoms, this time creating new elements with properties different from the original uranium, but he didn't quite understand what he'd produced. In 1938, at Meitner's urging, Hahn replicated Fermi's experiment and sent Meitner a letter that described the results. She understood the results in a way the experimenters did not. Meitner proposed that the uranium atoms were splitting into pieces, releasing some neutrons in the process. Not only was it possible to split the atom, but scientists had inadvertently been splitting the atom for the past few years, starting with Fermi's experiment with uranium in 1934.[28]

As soon as Meitner shared this idea with Hahn, her old lab partner, he rushed to get it into print. He took the opportunity that her lack of status provided to give himself all the credit for the discovery. In 1939, he published a series of papers announcing "the splitting of uranium." These papers do not mention Meitner. In 1944, he won the Nobel Prize, alone, for discovering the atom can split.[29]

The revelation that the atom can split—a process that Meitner's nephew, also a physicist, named *fission*—had terrifying implications that Meitner grasped immediately. She and her nephew coauthored a

---

* Meitner and Hahn tried to run a safe lab in keeping with knowledge of the time. When they started hands-on work on radiation, they made a policy that anyone in the lab who touched radioactive material had to use toilet paper as a shield while touching anything else, pulling squares from toilet paper rolls that were scattered around the lab. Laura Fermi, *Atoms in the Family: My Life with Enrico Fermi* (Chicago: University of Chicago Press, 1961), 155–56; Stiffler Barron, *Lise Meitner: Discoverer of Nuclear Fission* (Greensboro, NC: Morgan Reynolds, 2000), 9–11, 37–38.

paper that explained not only the mechanics of fission, but also how much energy the process must unleash: "the fission products must fly apart with kinetic energies of the order of a hundred million electron-volts each."[30] In other words, a pound of fissioning uranium will explode with the force of some twenty million pounds of dynamite.[31]

Scientists tried, at first, to keep outsiders from learning what they knew, at least until they managed to feel out the size of the new discovery. Niels Bohr, a Nobel Prize–winning physicist who fled to Sweden and then the United States from Occupied Denmark, was the first scientist in the United States to know about uranium fission. He was friends with Meitner and her nephew, and learned the findings from them before anything was published—he started talking about fission to the colleagues picking him up even as he went through customs at New York Harbor.[32] But when he gave a talk soon afterward at George Washington University, switching topics at the last minute in order to explain the discovery to his colleagues, the audience of physicists, realizing the terrible, tremendous implications of what he was saying, immediately kicked out the journalists who were there to cover the talk.[33]

What the general public didn't know, the military refused to believe. Even after President Roosevelt read the letter from Einstein that Miss Coatesworth typed up for Leo Szilard, even after Roosevelt ordered up a military committee to look into the atom's potential, the U.S. military dismissed it as crackpot. When, in October 1939, refugee scientists tried to explain fission to a group of bigwigs from the army, the navy, and a weapons research facility called Aberdeen, they got exactly nowhere. "There was a high-ranking officer from Aberdeen," one of the scientists later recalled, "and he did not believe a word of what we were talking about."[34] Nonetheless, the scientists persisted, trying to persuade their own government that they could build a world-breaking weapon while keeping governments abroad from learning what they knew.[35]

The first problem was figuring out how to weaponize the splitting of the atom; the second problem was keeping that secret. Leo Szilard solved the first problem when he realized that, because a uranium atom throws off two or three neutrons for every neutron that penetrates its core, you can use uranium to start a chain reaction: one atom, when punctured, punctures two more, and so on through the whole mass of atoms. This chain reaction means uranium can detonate on a large scale.

Quietly, Szilard and a group of trusted colleagues at Columbia carried out experiments that proved him right.[36] They sent reports of their findings to *The Physical Review*, asking the editor to keep their reports on record but not publish anything in the journal itself. They also wrote to colleagues proposing that *everyone* cooperate to keep information about fission out of the public pages of journals.[37] One colleague they wrote to, the Parisian physicist Frédéric Joliot-Curie, ran a similar experiment—and then published a letter right away in *Nature*.[38] A colleague frantically telegrammed him, begging for secrecy. Joliot-Curie telegrammed back: "QUESTION ETUDIEE SUIS D'AVIS MAINTENANT PUBLIER AMITIES JOLIOT." This meant, loosely translated,

> I have considered the question and I think I will publish now.
> 🦪 Joliot

There was no hope, then, of keeping this dangerous discovery secret from the Nazis. Left without a reason to withhold their paper, in April 1939 Szilard and colleagues published the findings they'd secretly filed with *The Physical Review*.[39] Soon scientists throughout Germany, Britain, Russia, and the United States were pushing their governments to fund research on nuclear weapons.

In March 1940, the heavy water lab that Tronstad founded at the Vemork hydroelectric plant got its first big order, ever—"The first time I got the impression," a scientist who worked there later said, "that the product seemed to have achieved any kind of special interest." The order was from Paris, and it demanded the lab's entire inventory of heavy water, some 180 kilograms of it, to be delivered "as soon as possible," the scientist said. "The case had to be dealt with in secrecy. Thus I had to take the whole lot to Oslo in a motorcar myself. From Oslo the product at once was sent directly to Paris."[40]

Joliot-Curie had evidently figured out the use for heavy water.[41] Others would soon follow—Germany included.

WHITEOUT

What Joliot-Curie realized in early 1940 was that heavy water can be a moderator to make mass fission possible—and mass fission is how you cause an atomic explosion. So far, scientists had only produced fission on a small scale, splitting small numbers of atoms at a time—not nearly enough to cause the chain reaction at the heart of an atom bomb. Because of the way uranium atoms work, if you want them to fission on a mass scale, and then to get caught in a chain reaction, you need a moderator to slow the fast neutrons produced by the splitting uranium atoms so that the neutrons become slow enough to split *more* uranium atoms. In principle, heavy water is ideal for this purpose. Once Joliot-Curie figured this out, he started ordering heavy water from the only facility in the world that produced heavy water at a large scale: the Vemork plant in Norway.

It took until early 1942 for the militaries of Britain and the United States to accept that atomic weapons were a real threat and that they must, at all costs, keep the enemy from assembling the ingredients for such a weapon. Britain was finally listening to Professor Tronstad's urgings that the heavy water facility he'd built at Vemork, Norway, must be destroyed.[42] But by March 1942, agents in Stockholm reported to London that the Vemork plant had already delivered 300 kilograms of heavy water to Germany in 1941, then another 300 kilograms in *just the first two months* of 1942.[43] The Germans were pushing the scientists at the Vemork plant to escalate the production of heavy water as much as they could, and to sell to nobody but the German government.[44]

The Germans didn't tell the scientists at Vemork what they wanted the water for. (Tronstad, remember, built the heavy water lab before the product had commercial applications, out of a spirit of scientific curiosity.) One Vemork scientist, in a report that he secretly sent to the SOE in 1944, said that, although he "understood the Germans must need the Z for an important purpose"—he used the letter *Z*, clearly intuiting that the substance was, for some reason, the stuff of secrets—they told him that they were using it for harmless scientific experiments.* And that they needed more of it: four to five tons a year, preferably.[45]

If you want a factory destroyed, send a bomber plane. If you *need* a factory destroyed, send a saboteur. The Allies needed that factory destroyed—and so they arranged, at last, for a sabotage party to leave for Vemork, which included none other than Knut Haukelid, the refugee who had escaped from Norway and trained in an SOE camp in Scotland for this exact type of purpose.

On the night of February 16, 1943, the six men climbed inside a bomber plane in Scotland and took off for Norway.[46] "The hum of the powerful engines rose and fell, and inside the aircraft conversation was almost impossible," Haukelid later recalled. "For that matter, no one wanted to talk. We sat on our parachutes and packs of equipment or silently jostled for the one tiny peephole that gave us a view over the North Sea."[47] The plane took a circuitous route in order to avoid witnesses and radar stations, keeping at a high altitude over the coast of the Skagerrak strait and then dropping low, once they crossed into Norway itself, to follow the protective troughs of the valleys. Perhaps because facing death can sharpen our awareness of the beauty of existence, or perhaps simply because this might be his last homecoming, he felt the pain of love for a familiar landscape as he looked out the window.

"There was the snow, the forests and the mountains, which we had so sorely missed during our time in England," Haukelid said. "Never had the country been so beautiful as now."[48]

After they landed, the men set out on skis for a long journey in the wilderness. They wore white snowsuits—to camouflage with the snow that contoured every part of the landscape—and did their best to keep out of sight.[49] The equipment they hauled in their packs included explosives, guns, sleeping bags, and bundles of food and clothes. They

---

* The same scientist said that Joliot was working with heavy water for the Nazis in Occupied Europe—where he was "treated almost as a prisoner, working under supervision of the Gestapo." HS 8/955, 90.

brought a toboggan to help them carry heavier items over the snow.[50] They would have to camp outdoors; a sabotage party couldn't exactly check in to a hotel. But the very fact that the men had to make their way in the wilderness—the fact that they *could* make their way in the wilderness, because they knew the woods and snow of their country in a way the invaders could not—gave them a remarkable advantage.

"It is marvelous what skis can mean in Norway. They give a king's soldier his choice of maneuverability," Haukelid said. "Now we were back, and with good equipment, we would show the Germans that possession of the roads was not enough in a country such as ours."[51]

A PLACE NOT UNLIKE HOME

Like all the Norwegian resistance fighters who worked in collaboration with Britain, Haukelid trained in the Scottish Highlands, where the weather, altitudes, and terrain resemble those of Norway more closely than anywhere else in Britain.[52] This training area, called STS 26, was in Inverness-shire. The terrain included Rothiemurchus Forest—ancient, eerie, a place so defiantly wild that the locals swore fairies still lurked—and the Cairngorm Mountains, a range that holds snow, in some places, all year round.[53] Few people lived in the area, so the students could train for battle without worrying about the neighbors, and they lived in three huge hunting lodges that were repurposed as training facilities.[54]

Between the German invasion of Norway in 1940 and the surrender of Germany in 1945, some 530 Norwegian men and women served in the Norwegian branch of the SOE, many of them training at the school in Scotland.[55] Their training included courses in demolition, disguise, parachuting, planning operations, propaganda, wireless telegraphy, and the use of weapons from different countries. (Often, a spy couldn't carry a weapon, since that would be damning—so, in a pinch, he had to know how to steal and use an enemy's weapon.) And, of course, sabotage.[56] In the field, these agents supervised underground cells, held down wireless stations, recruited civilians to the cause, ran messages, sank boats, carried out raids. Sometimes a raid had no purpose except to keep up the morale of Norwegian civilians: *Ah, det er godt, we're sticking it to the occupiers.*[57]

After Haukelid left Norway to train as a sabotage agent in Britain, the Gestapo, which tried to keep track of the Norwegians who were disappearing to join the Resistance, visited his parents and asked them, as a not-so-veiled threat against the household, whether they knew where their son was. His mother said he was camping in the mountains.

"No, he is in England," a Gestapo officer said. "Our contact in Sweden tells us he has been taken across the North Sea in a fighter plane. And what do you think he is doing there?"

"You will find out when he is coming back!" his mother replied.[58]

"IF ANY MAN IS TO BE TAKEN PRISONER, HE UNDERTAKES TO END HIS OWN LIFE"

Haukelid was soon on his way. Poor flying weather delayed the mission again and again, but it also gave the men extra time to practice and go over logistics. By the time they landed in Norway, Haukelid's sabotage party, code-named Gunnerside, had a meticulously detailed plan of attack. A small advance party, code-named Swallow, had been watching the Vemork plant since a year prior and transmitting to the SOE every detail they could see or hear. So Haukelid's party knew exactly where the guards and sentries would be and what routes inside the plant would lead them to the machines they meant to destroy. (They'd even practiced destroying mock-up machines that the SOE built at the Scotland training school—with the help of Professor Tronstad.)[59] A lesson that the SOE had learned from prior operations in Norway was that "No point is too small to be overlooked." So the sabotage party set out with a plan, a backup plan, *other* backup plans, and a nothing-left-to-give-but-my-breath plan, to wit: "If any man is about to be taken prisoner, he undertakes to end his own life."[60]

The distance from the landing point to Vemork, just thirty miles, might take a good skier a day to travel in good conditions. But for the sabotage party, crossing that distance took a week of struggling against storms, wind, and blinding snow. A plane crash the previous fall had let the Germans know the Allies wanted to carry out an attack in the area and had prompted them to step up the security around Vemork. More soldiers came to patrol the area; the *Reichskommissar* himself, the Nazi governor of Norway, visited the plant; fresh orders went out to watch for saboteurs.[61]

On February 23, while preparing to leave a cabin they'd broken into to take shelter from a storm, they were caught off guard by a stranger. He had skied right up to the cabin. The party immobilized him easily—it was six against one—but the obvious next step, eliminating him as a witness, was far more unpalatable. "The situation was really pretty desperate for us," Haukelid said. "We could not take him with us, and we could not let him go; nor could we kill him, unless he should prove to be a member of the N.S."—referring to Nasjonal Samling, the pro-Nazi party.[62]

"Are you a member of the N.S.?" asked one of the saboteurs.

After a long pause, the stranger said, "Well, I'm not exactly a member, but that's the party I support."

"The boys were now generally in favor of shooting him. He had indeed plainly declared himself an N.S. man," Haukelid later wrote. A search of the stranger's belongings revealed identity papers that showed he lived in a nearby village; easy enough for him to warn the authorities about the strange men in camouflage uniforms who were using his cabin. Yet the stranger's hesitation—his waffling—gave Haukelid pause. Did he think he was speaking to Germans? So Haukelid asked whether the man's neighbors would vouch for him as a Nazi.

After another pause, the stranger said, "I've so many enemies down here that they're sure to say I'm not a Nazi. Just to make things difficult for me."

Ah, so he did *think* he was speaking to Germans. "It was anything but easy to convince him that we really were Norwegians," Haukelid wrote, but at last he spoke to them in dialect and they replied as *landsmenn*.[63] Celebration on both sides: they wouldn't have to kill him after all! Instead, they cheerfully kidnapped him: *You're coming with us, friend, until we figure out what to do with you.*[64] They tied him to his toboggan, presumably to make him look like an enemy prisoner, instead of a friendly prisoner, if they came across real Nazis.

A few hours later, the sabotage party and their captive neared their destination. The weather had cleared, the world shone with the dazzling whiteness of sun on snow, and on the mountain plateau they were traveling across, you could almost see forever, Haukelid later said.[65] As they approached a valley, they saw two skiers climbing the valley slope toward them, about six hundred feet away. They were in civilian clothes, but in suspiciously good shape.[66]

Haukelid pulled on a civilian toque, tucked a pistol under his jacket, and skied down to talk to the men, planning to pass himself off as a reindeer herder. Everyone else hid.[67] While the party waited—hands on their pistols or, in the case of their captive, hands uselessly bound—they no doubt considered, in some form, the full meaning of the motto that the exiled king of Norway had given to the underground: "Alt for Norge"—*All for Norway*.[68] "Then, suddenly, above the noise of the wind," said a later SOE report on the mission, "sounded what Joachim, the Gunnerside leader, describes as 'three wild yells of pleasure.' Gunnerside was in touch with Swallow."[69]

The men of Swallow—the advance party that had been hiding in Vemork for months, sending the Allies information on the plant's security—looked *terrible*. It turned out they'd almost run out of food while waiting, as storm after storm delayed air missions, for a sabotage party to join them. They'd started eating reindeer lichen.[70] When they took the men of Gunnerside back to their little base, their guests shared rations that seemed, to them, like an impossible bounty: "They sat chewing chocolate and raisins, and could not believe the truth of this fairy story—that somewhere else on the earth there was food enough. Their eyes shone like little children's on Christmas Eve," Haukelid said.[71] (The Gunnerside party carried a page of extra messages for the Swallow party, typed on rice paper so the messenger could eat it in an emergency. After the messages were read, a Gunnerside agent moved to throw the paper in a fire, but a Swallow agent ate it, explaining that his party never wasted food.[72])

Having reunited, eaten, and found a safe place to rest at the Swallow base, the Norwegians were feeling pretty good. As the evening set in, they decided to let their captive go; he'd borne his kidnapping well and seemed, they decided, trustworthy. They gave him some money, a package of rations, and a stern order to stay away from his village for three days and to keep silent about his adventure after he returned.[73] Apparently, he did just that.

WHERE TO KEEP YOUR CYANIDE PILL

After a few days of rest, reconnaissance, and hiding the equipment they would need near the plant so they could travel light, the sabotage party was ready to go. Maps that remain in the SOE's archives—which bear a small label, "Stockholm," to show where the SOE got the information—show the layout of the site that the agents were set to move through.[74] Barbed-wire fences encircled the entire plant, and land mines protected a zone that happened to be right next to the heavy water lab. Once the agents got onto the property, they were to enter the northeast building and seek out the door to the basement. The door would be locked, of course, but they had to get into that basement however they could. There, they would find the lab they needed to destroy.[75]

At 8:00 p.m. on February 27, 1943, nine men left a cabin in the Fjøsbudalen valley—less than a mile west of Vemork—that they were using as an advance base. The night was windy but clear, with just a few clouds illuminated around the half-moon. Forbidden to use flashlights while carrying off the operation, the men would have to work entirely in the dark. They carried bullets, but their guns were unloaded, for fear that a stray discharge would attract attention.[76] They also carried cyanide pills. These were in rubber capsules; the SOE recommended that agents hold these pills inside the mouth, tucked between the gums and the lower teeth. If the enemy captured them, they should bite through the rubber.[77]

The men wore British uniforms for their mission. If the enemy captured them, the uniforms *should* entitle them to the rights of prisoners of war, which included protection from execution, but they knew that was optimistic. The men in the plane crash the previous fall had also worn British uniforms, but the Germans shot the survivors anyway. Hitler had announced that saboteurs didn't count as soldiers, even if they *were* soldiers, and that they should be dealt with as though they were members of the Resistance, who could expect no rights at all.[78]

This fact didn't worry the men of Gunnerside and Swallow. "Hitler's order to shoot every commando or sabotage soldier had little effect on us. We had agreed that if anyone was wounded, the best thing he could do was to take the pill and finish himself off," Haukelid said.[79] They wore British uniforms not for protection, but as disinformation. Better to let the Nazis think the British blew up the lab than to reveal that Norwegians were weaponizing local knowledge.

The route to the hydroelectric plant was long and steep. The Germans treated the hostile landscape that surrounded the site as part of the plant's defenses. The only way to approach the plant from the front was to cross a seventy-five-foot-long suspension bridge, which stretched over a gorge that fell more than six hundred feet below. Two guards with firearms waited at the far end of the bridge to pick off any unauthorized visitors. Behind the plant, a steep mountain bank blocked off all intruders who didn't want to tumble down a slope of ice almost as vertical as the gorge. One could descend the slope by taking a set of stairs near the water pipelines that ran down from a mountaintop lake, turning the turbines that generated the electricity of the hydroelectric plant. But land mines studded the ground around the pipelines, and the guards could use searchlights to light up the stairs, and machine guns to drop whoever they saw descending.[80]

The saboteurs knew of a single weakness in this Piranesian network of fortifications: a small railroad that connected Vemork with the next town over. The Germans used the railroad rarely, to move heavy equipment; reconnaissance suggested they didn't bother to guard it. The railroad ran in a furrow cut into the mountain. This is the path the saboteurs took—skiing *past* the plant by several miles, turning right and crossing a river to get to the railroad, and then turning right again to follow the tracks back to Vemork.[81] Eventually, they had to abandon their skis: the snow was so soft and deep that they sank to their waists and had to walk. The railroad passed close to the plant's end of the suspension bridge, and when they came near enough to the bridge to see the traffic on it, they hid, eating food from their pockets and waiting for their moment. A pair of buses rolled in—carrying, they knew, the night shift guards they would soon have to sneak past or shoot.[82]

THE BLOWING-UP PARTY

At half past midnight, the party split into two groups: a "blowing-up party," which would focus on demolishing the lab, and a "covering party," which would focus on giving the other group cover. Haukelid led the covering party.[83]

The covering party took the lead; the blowing-up party followed, waiting for the covering party to check each obstacle in turn before moving forward. First the covering party crept up to the factory gates, where one of the men used a pair of armorer's shears to cut the iron chain that held the gates shut. Then the blowing-up party advanced to another gate about ten yards past the first, cutting its chain while the covering party protected their backs.[84]

"I stopped and listened. Everything was still quiet," the leader of the blowing-up party, Joachim Rønneberg, later said of this moment. "The blackout of the factory was poor and there was a good light from the moon."[85]

With the second gate open, the covering party moved across the plant's yard to a guard hut next to the hydrogen factory—the building that hid the heavy water lab in its basement. Perhaps a dozen guards were hanging out there, they estimated; another twenty or so guards would be walking around the factory site.[86]

While the covering party watched the guard hut, the blowing-up party sought out the door to the basement of the hydrogen factory. It was right where their intelligence said it would be: just outside the building. The door was locked, as they expected. Professor Tronstad had said that if they couldn't break through the door, they should try to break into the ground floor of the building and look for another route inside. Failing all else, they would find, at their feet somewhere, the entrance to a cable tunnel, which they could crawl through to get to the basement.[87] The basement door and the front door wouldn't budge, so the blowing-up party split up to search for the entrance to the cable tunnel. They saw, in a window of the building, the silhouette of a guard.[88]

At last, Rønneberg spotted the entrance to the cable tunnel. He crawled in, with another party member following him "over a maze of tangled pipes and leads," he later said. "Every minute was now valuable. As there was no sign of the other two demolition party members, we two decided to carry out the demolition alone."[89]

They emerged from the cable tunnel in a basement room next to the lab. The door to the lab was open; they rushed in, surprising a guard who was keeping watch down there. Rønneberg's partner held him at gunpoint by the wall, out of the way, while Rønneberg closed and locked the door to the lab and then started planting explosive charges on the machinery.[90]

"I had placed half the charges in position," Rønneberg said, "when there was a crash of broken glass behind me. I looked up. Someone had smashed the window opening onto the backyard. A man's head stood framed in the broken glass."[91]

In the meantime, the covering party waited uneasily for something to happen. The buzz of the generators was so loud that Haukelid, hiding behind some barrels near the guard hut, found he could talk quietly to his partner without the guards hearing them. They were ready, if shouts rang out, to run into the guard hut, firing Tommy guns and throwing hand grenades and working up a distraction. ("You must remember to call out 'Heil Hitler' when you open the door and throw the bombs," said Haukelid's partner, who must have seen a lot of action movies.) But they saw nothing, heard nothing. Just the buzzing of the generator, nervous, intent, like the murmur of innumerable bees.[92]

THE LITTLE BANG

Luckily, the head in the basement window belonged to one of the two remaining members of the blowing-up party—who, unable to find the tunnel entrance or their missing teammates, decided to break into the lab through a window they *did* find. As they crawled in and started helping Rønneberg place charges, Rønneberg's partner started showing off his uniform to the guard. Perhaps he wanted to leave a witness with the certainty that the saboteurs were British soldiers, which was the whole point of wearing British uniforms.[93]

"Have a good look at this," he told his captive, flashing the badges on his sleeve. "If you look carefully, you can tell the Germans what an English uniform looks like. I don't expect there are many of the master race in Rjukan who have had the chance of getting so close to an Allied soldier."[94]

Finally, the charges were ready to go. Rønneberg set the alarm-clock fuses to go off in thirty seconds, then activated them. The blowing-up party threw open the lab door, ordered the guard to run for his life to an upstairs floor, then shut and locked the door from the outside as fast as they could.[95]

Now the only question was how the hell to get out. Up the stairs and out the basement door, to start. And then—across the yard, with some men splitting off to grab the members of the covering party while the others headed for the gates. Haukelid, waiting by the guard hut, later recalled hearing an insultingly small *bang*, the only sign of the explosion underground. ("Was this what we had come over a thousand miles to do?" he asked.) The guards in the hut also seemed unimpressed, perhaps thinking that a land mine went off; a lone guard emerged from the hut and walked lazily in the direction of the sound, passing Haukelid and his partner without seeing them.[96]

After some squabbling over the passwords (two of the men joined their comrade without giving him the security word; he groused, "What's the good of our having passwords if we don't use them?"), both parties slipped out the gates they'd entered through, hiked over to the railroad, and started back, silently, on the tracks in the snow they'd made earlier.[97]

"For a moment I looked back down the line, and listened," Rønneberg said. "Except for the faint hum of machinery that we heard when we arrived, everything in the factory was quiet."[98]

They couldn't go back entirely the way they came. They had crossed a bridge on the way here, roughly an hour away. When the Germans finally became wise to the attack, they would surely send soldiers to patrol it.[99] So the men crossed the river by walking directly on the frozen surface, sloshing through a stinging layer of cold water above the ice. They were moving through a wooded valley when air-raid sirens started to wail. The Germans had finally discovered the sabotage. Soon, the saboteurs saw the shine of flashlights along the railroad route on the mountainside; soldiers were following their tracks in the snow.[100]

"That did not much matter to us," Haukelid said. "To capture nine well-armed men in a dark wood at night would be difficult enough for people with local knowledge; for Wehrmacht men it should be quite impossible."[101]

"THE BEST COUP I HAVE EVER SEEN"

The operation was a remarkable success. The saboteurs not only destroyed machine parts whose loss would keep the Germans from manufacturing heavy water for perhaps six months, but also managed to spill to the ground more than half a ton of the stuff.[102] Production was disabled, the stockpile was gone, and the saboteurs escaped without a single shot fired. It was teamwork that relied on the kinds of scrappy outsiders that the Allies embraced so skillfully: experts to teach the right methods of sabotage, analysts to draw up maps using whatever intel could be smuggled over, refugees with insider knowledge, *résistants* willing to slip through the eye of the needle. General Nikolaus von Falkenhorst, the general who led the Nazi forces in Norway, toured the plant to survey the damage and called the raid, grudgingly, "the best coup I have ever seen."[103]

For Britain's government and military, which still regarded the SOE with suspicion—after all, the SOE was Britain's newest intelligence organization, and its whole premise, the study of "ungentlemanly warfare," struck British lordlings as *infra dig*—the success of Gunnerside helped to persuade skeptics that the organization's unlikely alliance of British eccentrics, American professors, and foreign refugees could accomplish feats worthy of admiration.[104] A 1944 report to the

British Cabinet describes the success of the mission with slightly giddy pride. A mark of the secrecy surrounding anything involving heavy water, even in the offices of power, is that someone used a pencil to censor a draft of the report before the final copy went to the Cabinet, crossing out every reference to it and writing in aggressively vague substitutions:

> Gunnerside's . . . men passed unseen into the basement of the five-storied concrete building where the ~~heavy water high concentration~~ **most delicate** plant was installed, silently overpowered the Norwegian guards, and laid their charges on the ~~special containment cells~~ **machinery**. Swallow acted as a covering force for the withdrawal. The German guards saw no one and heard nothing, until a cataclysmic explosion announced the destruction of ~~3,000 lbs. of heavy water~~ **the target**.[105]

The Nazis were furious, as the Cabinet report records with some glee. Higher-ups punished the guards on duty that night; the Gestapo knocked on doors throughout the region, looking for the saboteurs; soldiers patrolled the mountains, occasionally mistaking each other for the enemy. The captive guard doesn't seem to have bought the claim that the saboteurs were British soldiers, but the Germans' search for men who fit the right profile seems to have lifted the morale of local Norwegians: "To the entertainment of the inhabitants, posters appeared offering rewards for information about 'tall young men with fair hair and blue eyes speaking Norwegian.'"[106]

NO MORAL DECISIONS

The sabotage mission of February 1943 was not the last time the Allies sent a strike against Vemork's heavy water facilities, but it was the decisive blow. Had the Allies tried to destroy the lab by dropping bombs from the air, they could never have reached the basement, as Professor Tronstad explained to some American generals when he was first trying to convince the Allies to attack the lab. Sabotage allowed the Allies to hit not just the lab, but the most critical machines in the lab, preventing the Germans from simply moving those machines to a lab elsewhere.[107]

Unfortunately, after the raid, the Germans intensified the plant's security so much that follow-up sabotage missions would be impossible. All that remained to the Allies was sending in planes to bomb the factory, which they started doing as soon as they heard the lab was running again.[108] But this time, air bombing could, and did, have an effect: the Norwegian scientists and engineers who worked at the plant—whose job was just to produce electricity and heavy water, not to ask questions—complained that they knew, because of the previous sabotage raids, that the bombings had to do with the heavy water lab and demanded that the lab be shut down. After all, the lab fulfilled no military purpose, right?—or so the Germans reassured them. Or did heavy water have some special use that made the Germans fixate on producing it at all costs?

Of course, some of those scientists were collaborating with the SOE and the Resistance, sending secret reports on the plant's activities to Stockholm. One of those secret reports records an argument that the Norwegian director of the Vemork plant made during a meeting with the Germans—namely, that the plant's real business was making nitrogen for farmers to use in fertilizers, and that they couldn't afford to put that business at risk: "In view of the German statement that production of SH-200 [the German code for heavy water] was not directly important to the war effort but was for scientific investigation purposes in the future, it must . . . be absurd to expose to destruction such an important producing plant as Norsk Hydro's, which was of such value to Norwegian agriculture and Norwegian export."[109]

Eventually, the Germans relented. In 1944, they shut down heavy water production at Vemork, dismantling the lab and shipping the equipment to Germany—where, apparently, not much happened with it.[110] Resistance works.

Soon after, Haukelid, who was still in the region causing mischief, learned of the plans to send the remaining heavy water to Germany.[111] On the evening of February 19, 1944, he and two fellow saboteurs walked aboard a ferry that was scheduled to carry the barrels over a lake, planted bombs with alarm-clock timers in the bilge, and then walked back onshore, telling the ferry's watchman they'd stowed illegal contraband aboard and would return to take the morning ferry.[112] (That last part was to explain why they wouldn't be taking the evening ferry, as that was the one that was set to be blown up.)

The ferry watchman who let them "stow the contraband" proved, by that action, that he supported the Resistance, and Haukelid agonized over whether to warn him to flee. After the bombs went off, the Germans would surely interrogate the watchman—and probably worse. (After the raid at the Vemork plant, the Germans transported the few Norwegian guards who were on duty that night to a concentration camp.) And there were further moral dilemmas: one of Haukelid's two fellow saboteurs knew that a friend planned to take the ferry that evening. The other saboteur knew that his mother planned to take the ferry that evening. Should they warn the people they cared for not to take the ferry? Even if they said nothing specific, even if they said not to ask questions, the people they warned might warn *their* loved ones in turn, and in just a few rounds of warnings, the Germans might learn of a plot under way.[113]

There were, in this instance, no moral decisions: only immoral decisions and more immoral decisions. They'd known from the start that civilians were going to die.

In the end, the saboteur whose friend was going to take the ferry didn't warn his friend. The saboteur whose mother was going to take the ferry paid her a visit and drugged her food so she couldn't make the planned trip. And Haukelid just shook the watchman's hand and expressed his gratitude, probably with more emphasis than the moment seemed to warrant—"Which puzzled him," Haukelid said.[114] On the morning of February 20, as the ferry was passing over the middle of the lake, an explosion blew open the ferry's hull, and the ferry, along with its cargo of heavy water, sank. Eighteen people died, fourteen of them civilians.[115]

The Germans never did succeed in using heavy water to make an atomic bomb. Whether any of the people who died would have gone willingly, knowing that was the end of the story their deaths were part of, is impossible to say.

ALT FOR NORGE

Is a good spy a good man? This whole episode illustrates the difficult moral problems that the spies and saboteurs who fought for the Allies confronted at every step. Would you kill the skier your team stumbled across in the wilderness? Blow up a ferry full of civilians? Let your mother sail on the doomed ferry? Or warn her of its doom and risk your plans getting out? Is it more moral to decide, when you become a spy, that you've given up being able to make moral choices—that you'll never know what your superiors know, and therefore trying to outthink their orders risks causing problems beyond your comprehension? Or is it more moral to try, whenever you can, to reduce the collateral damage of your missions through clever scheming, accepting that doing so might put your missions themselves at risk? What if the stakes of the war you're fighting are as high as you can imagine—life or death, survival or annihilation, the fate of the world?

Jean-Paul Sartre, a philosopher who fought in Paris with the French Resistance, later wrote about a young man he knew who was faced with the choice of staying at home to help his mother or leaving to fight for the Resistance. No principle can help in such cases, Sartre said. Nor was the young man's choice really a question of morality. Instead, it was a question of humanity. The person decides what kind of person they are—a dedicated spy, or someone who puts family above patriotic duties—by the decision they make. Morality doesn't decide; the person does.[116]

What the *résistants* in this chapter decided was to join the Resistance, even though in some cases it got their families in trouble with the Nazis, and to carry out missions that put themselves, and sometimes others, in danger, without the consolation of knowing what those missions were for. But their concern for human life was such that they chose to save lives whenever it was within their power to do so while still fulfilling their missions. Perhaps these choices are inextricable from the Norway they grew up in, the side they chose to fight for, the lives they'd led when they *weren't* at war.

Leif Tronstad could have left Norway, as others did, early in the occupation, but he chose to remain and gather information for the Allies for as long as he could.[117] The choice, one might say, of a consummate scientist: someone who believed that science was powerful enough to make a difference in the war and was willing to risk his life to put that science in the service of the Allies.

In late 1944, Tronstad returned from England to Norway, where he helped to train Resistance fighters and maintained communications with contacts at Norsk Hydro as well as other Norse corporations. His aim was to help the Resistance use the same principles he'd used to advise this sabotage mission to prevent the Germans from sabotaging Norwegian assets—factories, airports, railroads—as they retreated. Tronstad's turn to counterscorching must have given him some satisfaction; it meant the Nazis were getting ready to run, and that he could finally use his talents to defend, not destroy, his country's resources.[118]

But on March 11, 1945, while Tronstad's unit was questioning a Nazi collaborator, the man's brother burst in and either shot Tronstad or beat him to death with a rifle—the record is unclear. The man and his brother escaped; before fleeing, Tronstad's unit sank Tronstad's body under the ice of a frozen lake, hoping to shield him from the rough handling of the Germans, who were still in charge. The Germans found him anyway. They examined his body, took pictures, splashed him with gasoline, burned him, and threw what was left in a river.[119]

In August 1943, Tronstad had written, from England, a letter to his ten-year-old daughter, Sidsel:

We have to do everything for our land to make it free again.
When we say "Our Fatherland," we don't just mean the
land, which is beautiful and we also love, but also everything
we love at home: mother, little boy and you, and all the
other fathers and mothers and children. I also mean all the

wonderful memories from the time we ourselves were small, and from later when we had children of our own. Our home villages with the hills, mountains and forests, the lakes and ponds, rivers and streams, waterfall and fjords. The smell of new hay in summer, of birches in spring, of the sea, and the big forest, and even the biting winter cold. Everything.[120]

In the end, Tronstad got everything back, but he paid everything for it.

7

SURRENDER ON DEMAND

Tangle within tangle, plot and counter-plot,
ruse and treachery, cross and double-cross,
true agent, false agent, double agent, gold
and steel, the bomb, the dagger, and the firing
party, were interwoven in many a texture so
intricate as to be incredible and yet true.
—Winston Churchill

LONG AFTER HIS FLIGHT TO THE UNITED STATES, THE WRITER
Hans Sahl recalled the circumstances of his escape from occupied
France. A friend had sent him to the Hôtel Splendide, telling him an
American was waiting there for him—an American who somehow,
miraculously, had Sahl's name on a list of people to be helped out of the
country. "Imagine the situation," Sahl wrote:

> The borders closed; you are caught in a trap, might be arrested
> again at any moment; life is as good as over—and suddenly
> a young American in short sleeves is stuffing your pockets
> full of money, putting his arm around your shoulders, and
> whispering with the conspiratorial expression of a ham actor:
> "Oh there are ways to get you out of here," while, damn all,
> the tears were streaming down my face, actual tears, big,

round, and wet; and that pleasant fellow . . . takes a silk
handkerchief from his jacket and says: "Here, have this. Sorry
it isn't cleaner."

"You know," Sahl added, "since that day I have loved America."[1]

The young American was Varian Fry, who had stumbled into the
world of covert operations just the year before. In 1940, Fry was studying
as a graduate student at Columbia University when his friends invited
him to join a new group called the Emergency Rescue Committee. This
was not the same committee as Oswald Veblen's Emergency Committee for the Rescue of Foreign Scholars; rather, the group Fry belonged to
devised a plan to deliver U.S. visas directly to refugees trapped in France
who were writers, musicians, and other cultural luminaries.[2] They had
managed, through strenuous networking, to persuade Eleanor Roosevelt to help them get the necessary visas.[3] Now all they needed was for
someone to deliver them.

Fry volunteered.

Fry could visit Marseille openly, his own visa in hand, because the
United States wasn't yet in the war. Nonetheless, he had a complicated
task: his committee had obtained visas that allowed refugees to enter
the United States, but the Vichy government would not give refugees
exit visas that allowed them to leave France. Fry could tell the Vichy
government and the U.S. consulate that he was in France to give hu-
manitarian aid to refugees, to buy refugees clothing and help them pay
for food, but he could not tell the Vichy government that he was there
to help refugees *escape*—and the U.S. consulate would not go so far
as to help him with this rebellion against the authorities. Fry would
have to work covertly.[4]

Game but utterly green, Fry figured that delivering visas to the
people on the committee's list would be the work of just a month. "Since
I had a month's vacation coming up in August," he later wrote, "I told
the Committee, 'I'm not right for the job. All I know about being a
secret agent, or trying to outsmart the Gestapo, is what I've seen in the
movies. But if you can't find anyone else, I'll go.'"[5]

Varian Fry is one of the most American characters imaginable. A bright-eyed rookie who watched a bunch of movies and then, armed only with the examples of James Cagney and Humphrey Bogart, went off to fight the Nazis. While he was working this audacious scheme, he even talked out of the side of his mouth like Bogart, according to people who knew him in France. But what also seems to be particularly American about his adventures is the way he managed, with reckless optimism and confidence and generosity, to turn a small band of outsiders into a Resistance operation that won spectacular victories against the Third Reich.

Movies can only teach you so much. They can teach you a style. The style—the wry and worldly persona—that Fry learned from the movies deeply impressed Hans Sahl, who spoke often in later years of the young man who, when Sahl arrived at his hotel room door, "welcomed me in, put his arm around my shoulders, tucked money into my pocket, and whispered out of one corner of his mouth, like a rather poor actor playing the part of a plotter: 'If you need more, come back again. Meanwhile I'll cable your name to Washington. We'll get you out of here. There are ways. You'll see—oh, there are ways . . .'"[6]

But movies don't teach you the particulars of running a human trafficking operation. When he landed in Europe, Fry later said, "My pockets were full of names of men and women I was to rescue, and my head was full of suggestions from everyone on how to go about it. But would any of these suggestions work once I was in France, under the very nose of the Gestapo?"[7] Ultimately, the responsibility of making the committee's big ideas work in the real world was his alone.

What would you do?

Fry began by letting it be known that he would—under the auspices of the International Young Men's Christian Association (YMCA), which had given him a letter to confirm this story—be giving aid to refugees by dispensing charity money and helping them fill out the paperwork for exit visas. (To keep refugees from panicking, the Vichy government often promised them exit visas once their paperwork was processed. The paperwork was rarely processed.) This much was legal, so Fry could meet refugees openly.[8]

The day after he made this announcement, refugees began visiting his hotel room. "Many of them had been through hell," he said. "Their nerves were shattered and their courage gone. Some of them had been in concentration camps, escaping only at the last moment as the German troops marched through France. They had joined the great crowds of people streaming south. Sometimes they had walked hundreds of miles to get away from the Nazis."[9]

The heavy traffic in and out of Fry's hotel room soon prompted a visit from a local police officer. After questioning him in detail about his charity work on behalf of the YMCA, the officer told him that everything seemed to be in order. Then he dropped his voice. "If I had found anything suspicious, it would be necessary for me to arrest you here and now." He waited a beat and then asked, "You understand?" Fry understood. His cover story was acceptable, but he would have to proceed with care to ensure that sympathetic onlookers like the officer before him could pretend not to notice his actual work.[10]

Fry named his charity operation the American Relief Center and hired a small staff to help him run it. They turned out to be a team of remarkable talent and dedication. His first hire, Albert O. Hirschman, a German-born refugee who held a doctorate in economics, understood the region's black markets intimately. He helped the Relief Center to launder money—a necessary step to disguise its financial dependence on rescue groups in New York. Next came a posh Austrian, Franz von Hildebrand, who had already helped a refugee aid organization in Paris and therefore knew, in Fry's words, "how a relief committee should be run."[11] Lena Fishman, a cool-headed Jewish woman who spoke English, French, German, Polish, Russian, and Spanish, served as the team's secretary, reading and answering letters and sometimes helping Fry to interview visitors. Miriam Davenport, a Smith alumna who was in France to learn painting, gave an expert's backing to the committee's mission to help leading cultural figures: "If a refugee came to us claiming to be an artist, and Miriam had not heard of him, she would send him out to make a drawing. When he brought the drawing back, she would look at it and decide right away whether or not he was telling the truth." Finally, Charlie Fawcett, a young artist from the American

South who seemed, Fry commented drily, to have come to France to study its feminine beauties, served as doorman and receptionist. He wore an ambulance driver's uniform, which had the intended effect of soothing the ragged nerves of the visitors who waited for an audience with Fry.[12]

Fry ended up staying much longer than his planned-on month. Over the course of the next year, Fry's little operation succeeded in smuggling hundreds of refugees out of France. This achievement is all the more remarkable given that visa rules were perpetually shifting, rendering worthless the loopholes and false travel documents that the team had relied on just a moment before. France, Portugal, Spain, and the United States required different documents and changed their requirements constantly; the Spanish border closed entirely; secret paths across the mountains were discovered and had to be abandoned for new ones; allies vanished or were thrown into internment camps. The Vichy government ruled that the police could "intern, without trial, anyone who was thought to be 'dangerous to public safety.'"[13]

The American Relief Center thus needed a constantly changing array of false identity cards, letters of transit, passports, residence permits, and visas.[14] Hirschman, already the Relief Center's man for getting money laundered with the help of his contacts in the local mafia, put the center in touch with people who could produce these documents: for example, a refugee artist who could paint exact simulations of identity card stamps. Hirschman knew from false identity papers, for he carried a stack of them himself; a German Jew, he had joined the French Army to fight against the Nazis, which left him liable to a traitor's death when the French surrendered. His senior officer saved his life by calling him to a private meeting and declaring, "I am going to make you a French citizen." After Hirschman chose a new name and birthplace—the clever man gave himself a birthplace in Philadelphia, making himself, on paper, also an *American* citizen— the lieutenant filled out and stamped new military papers attesting to his French identity. While working for the American Relief Center, Hirschman carried almost a dozen documents that bore his new name, Albert Hermant: military discharge papers, an identity card, a substitute birth certificate, and membership cards for all kinds of local clubs and organizations.*

Hirschman sometimes expressed wonder at the turns his life had taken: "First I was a soldier. Then I was an underground smuggler. Now I am a gangster. What next?" (Lady Fortune has a sense of humor. After the war, he became an infinitely eminent professor of economics and politics at the Institute for Advanced Study in Princeton.)[15]

Fry's team members never planned to belong to a criminal syndicate. But their squeaky-clean backgrounds, which must have seemed so distant from the lives they now led, gave them an unexpected advantage. They were easy to overlook, since they were, after all, merely scholars and artists. It was that same training, however, that gave them the forms of expertise that made them dangerous to the Vichy regime: forgery, languages, textual cultures, the economics of the black market. Hirschman could run the numbers in a classroom or a criminal hideout; he just needed to switch up his identity cards. It turns out the difference between a scholar and a gangster can be as trivial as a piece of paper.

The need for false identity papers grew as more and more people applied for aid from the Relief Center. The Vichy government made an increasing number of categories of affiliation illegal, driving Jews, leftists, dissenting politicians, and others out of their jobs and homes.[16] Eight months in, the staff calculated that more than fifteen thousand people had visited or sent letters.[17] Any one of them could have been an undercover spy for the Germans; while managing this crowd, Fry looked out for agents of the Gestapo by evaluating applicants' stories and asking them for references, but ultimately, he said, he tried "to give each refugee the full benefit of the doubt. Otherwise we might refuse help to someone who was really in danger and learn later that he had been dragged away to Dachau or Buchenwald because we had turned him down."[18]

---

* Fry later commented—using his nickname for Hirschman, Beamish, which referred to the man's wide smile—"Beamish would smile and say in his German-accented English, 'I've overdone it, I guess. I have so many papers, the police would suspect me right away. I'm like a criminal with too many alibis. I should get rid of some of them.' But he never did. He loved them too much, just because they were so grandly false." Varian Fry, *Assignment: Rescue* (New York: Scholastic, 1945), 27–29, 39–43.

In the end, the person who brought down Fry's organization was not one of his applicants, but one of his contacts in the criminal underground. In a memoir, Fry recalled his unease with one mafia underling who often ran errands between the mafia and the Relief Center: "Dimitru was a short, oily little man, with over-polite manners, who could turn his smile on and off like an electric light. When you shook his right hand, it felt like an empty glove."[19] Eventually Dimitru double-crossed Fry by revealing his secret operation to the police; Fry figured out Dimitru's betrayal when Dimitru approached one of Fry's employees on the street and shook his hand—a signal—in the full view of police officers. Soon afterward, the French police put him on a train out of France and let him know that he was not welcome to return.[20]

The date was September 1941. He had been in France for only thirteen months. In that time, he'd helped some fifteen hundred refugees to escape Europe.[21]

Fry's adventures demonstrated a truth that would prove to be disastrous for the Reich's globe-spanning ambitions. Small groups of people really can change the world. Call it the power of small numbers: the unreasonable, improbable, wonderful ability of small groups of outsiders to challenge huge powers precisely because they have strengths that those powers see as weaknesses.

Hitler's impression of America's weaknesses started with the fact that it was a nation filled with what he saw as lesser races.[22] Hitler also despised intellectuals, regarding any career that entailed digging through libraries as particularly pointless.[23] But that type of thinking was why the very people Hitler's Reich sought to exclude or destroy were singularly equipped to defeat him.

Authoritarian regimes, in the words of Robert Hutchings, a scholar of public affairs and the former chair of the U.S. National Intelligence Council, are prey to "intellectual pathologies" that drastically narrow what they're capable of thinking: intense conformity, resistance to contrary information, the overestimation of insiders, and the stereotyping of outsiders.[24] Authoritarianism is a catastrophic intellectual handicap.

By contrast, the refugees who fled Occupied Europe and joined the Allied cause *valued* contrary information and questioned established ways of doing things. And America's young intelligence service listened to what they had to say, even when their ways of doing things seemed as far as you could get from how spycraft was supposed to work. As the OSS would discover, success didn't come from emulating the archetype of the spy, good or bad—it came from individuals using their own strengths and expertise in surprising ways. Like Fry's team members, whose unlikely backgrounds turned out to be superb training for running a Resistance cell, the professors and scribblers who worked for the OSS turned out to be superbly trained in what intelligence work *really* requires. And thanks to the man who turned their labors into a new form of intelligence, the spy game would be changed forever.

INK KNIGHTS

Now we turn back to Washington—to the secret ink-spilling labors of the type of poor bookish wretches whom Hitler scornfully called "*tintenritter*," or "ink knights."[25]

If you were able to take a bird's-eye view of all the people who were fighting the war in secret, rather than out on the battlefield, you would see an immense and intricate picture. Varian Fry, in Marseille, got substantial help from Alfred Barr, the director of the Museum of Modern Art in New York City, who would later advise James Sachs Plaut and Lane Faison, two art historians with an important part to play in this story. In New York, Hannah Arendt, one of the writers Fry rescued (and later a famous political theorist), helped to gather lists of stolen Jewish treasures for the Allies to hunt down—an important military undertaking, since the Nazis were selling valuable books and artworks on the black market to help pay for the war. Adele Kibre, working in Stockholm, sent photographs of scientific journals to her superiors in London, who sent them to their colleagues in Washington, who sent them to Los Alamos—where they might be picked up, for example, by the refugee physicist Niels Bohr, who was working on the atomic bomb in secret. Bohr's brother, Harald, who stayed behind in Europe, hunted all over the continent for scholars in need of rescue, sending news by wire to a civilian committee in New York that sought, like Fry's, to help refugees escape.[26]

Very few people *got* that bird's-eye view, or anything close to it. Secrecy demanded that undercover operations—for the OSS and otherwise—be splintered among different factions that didn't know about each other. Or at least *tried* not to know about each other. The military tried to avoid knowing that the OSS was breaking into neutral embassies. The American Legation in Sweden pretended not to know that Adele Kibre was running an intelligence operation under its roof. The U.S. government pretended not to know about Fry's rescue operation, but in fact, the First Lady herself was abetting it.[27] A paradox of spycraft is that gathering good intelligence necessitates working alone, but *making good* on that intelligence necessitates working together. And the knowledge that's necessary to coordinate that teamwork is dangerous to grant to any one person.

One of the few people who got anything approaching the full picture was Sherman Kent, the irascible Yale historian. After the extraordinary success of the Allied invasion of North Africa, Donovan promoted Kent from the head of R&A's North Africa division to the head of R&A's whole Europe-Africa division.[28] Donovan knew that if the Allies were to win the war, Kent would have to replicate, across the whole field of combat in Europe, the miracle he'd pulled off in North Africa.

And remarkably, he did just that. Kent managed the analysts who sifted through the mountains of paper that Kibre and others like her sent home. He commissioned their reports. He persuaded the military to heed their often counterintuitive insights and defended those insights even when they contradicted the findings of other spy agencies. In the process, Kent and R&A revolutionized the world of secrets, creating a new field of intelligence that became the foundation of modern spycraft. Today, historians call Kent "the father of intelligence analysis."

LITERARY REMAINS

What was the background that prepared Kent for this job? To begin with, long experience working with massive amounts of data. If a dissertation is an autobiography, Kent's dissertation is a story about a life in the archives. Completed in 1933, the dissertation focuses on the July Monarchy, a turbulent period when France was roiled with conflicts between monarchists and republicans. Perhaps the subject appealed to Kent's taste for political warfare. But his writing makes abundantly clear that, even more so, he relished the opportunity that French history provides to work with a superabundance of archival records. The French love to write things down.

Again and again, Kent returns, in his study, to the point that a historian is a bibliographic detective who must assume that evidence can be anywhere. He read seemingly everything that bore on his subject, and he talks in great detail about how to turn up evidence in different kinds of paper. Books that exclusively focus on an era's politics, he says, are insufficient to understand that era's politics. Personal correspondence is a useful political resource. It's best to read historical accounts that have conflicting biases, which will make their respective limitations clear. A public figure's enemies often keep detailed records of their doings. The underground press may record granular numbers that the official press doesn't bother with. Memoirs are interesting but untrustworthy, since most memoirs—which Kent calls, with a touch of ghoulish humor, "literary remains"—focus on huge political events, which means they ignore the tiny essentials, and also because they're written to shape the author's legacy: "Men cannot and will not tell the truth under these circumstances." Newspapers say more about the prevailing narratives of the time than what really happened. Compare the data in a minimum of three newspapers for accuracy. Read every part of the newspaper. Political coverage, market coverage, advertisements—it's all useful.[29]

All of this would help, no doubt, when he was managing intelligence analysts who *also* read everything.[*]

---

[*]   In fact, the hundreds of cartons of documents Kent went through in the Archives Nationales and elsewhere included many of the kinds of documents his analysts later prized as vital sources of intelligence: reports by the secret police, propaganda, seditious literature, documentation of underground organizations, and less obvious intelligence sources, like atlases.

But because Kent was a man whose personality played a role in the wartime politics of the OSS, it may be worth spending a moment to consider what this scholarly debut reveals about his temperament. For one, Kent writes far more candidly, far more *caustically*, than most graduate students would. His work is full of searing appraisals: "Emile Bourgeois's short work partakes of the evils of the Cambridge Modern History for which it was written"; "Two characteristics stand out as typical of these newspapers. The first is their overwhelming devotion to political news, the second their equally overwhelming devotion to typographical error." No institution is too sacred for his acid pen: "The catalogue of the Bibliothèque Nationale is an imposing monument to human incompetence."[30]

If Kent's dissertation has a hero, it's the irascible French journalist Armand Carrel. Dark-haired, slightly built, with immaculate manners and a mouth that got him challenged to several duels—the last of which killed him at the age of thirty-six—Carrel resigned from the French Army after a coup fizzled out and joined the opposing side in Spain. In 1829, Carrel and two friends founded *Le National*, a leftist newspaper that many called "a personification of Armand Carrel." His contemporaries said that he seemed to write with the point of a sword.

"Always seeking a fight, always attacking the administration, always misinterpreting its every move, Carrel left a great tradition in French journalism," Kent wrote. "His paper, devoted to political news of the most controversial kind, is filled with his brilliance and unreasonableness, his complaints and misconstructions. It is a mine of information and misinformation, and still the most valuable single document on the period."[31]

It's not hard to understand the appeal of such a man to Sherman Kent. Here was a man for whom the only words were fighting words, for whom politics was war by other means. He had no patience for the dogma "My country, right or wrong." He was idealistic and irritable. He regularly put himself in peril for important causes, but he died in a fight that contemporaries described as "a wretched quarrel not worth a hair of his head."[32] Perfect.

In short, by the time he joined the OSS, Kent was already thoroughly trained in what a new era of intelligence would require. Bibliographical detective, resolute contrarian, Kent was ready to lead an army of ink knights who, like him, had been training without knowing it for a global conflict. One that required them to work through huge amounts of information in a short time, to find new arguments in what everyone thought they'd already seen, and to use unlikely forms of expertise to solve problems that other people couldn't.

IMPLAUSIBLE OPERATORS

In some superficial aspects, Kent's operation was a Washington bureaucracy like any other. It was a hierarchical institution set in a stuffy world of office etiquette and cheap government furniture. As the head of the Europe and Africa section of R&A, Kent still reported to Bill Langer, the Harvard historian who served as the head of R&A, and Bill Langer reported to Bill Donovan. Standards could be even stricter than ordinary Beltway standards: according to one of Kent's R&A analysts, the economist Richard Ruggles, the analysts who had been working on the North Africa invasion were locked inside their buildings for the week prior to D-day, lest they reveal some crucial bit of intelligence on their way home to sleep.[33]

But something made this seemingly ordinary government agency different from others like it. We can find a good testimonial of what that something was in an article that Donovan wrote in 1946 to make a public case for the permanent establishment of a centralized intelligence agency. As the leader of the OSS, Donovan was in a better position than anyone to see what was truly new about his new intelligence service. Before the United States entered the war, he said, the State Department already had a small intelligence service, as did the War Department and the navy. But these services focused strictly on military intelligence—which, at the time, meant facts about other countries' military affairs. The tonnage of French naval vessels, or what new ships the Germans were building, or casualty numbers in the Spanish

Civil War. After all, what besides military facts could possibly be useful for military intelligence?[34]

When the war started, the limitations of those services immediately became obvious, Donovan said. Nobody in Europe was willing, any longer, to let outsiders snoop on their military affairs, and the United States had no legations in occupied countries. The government had to rely on the information that neutral countries were willing to share, but they lacked the means to know if it was trustworthy.[35] How did Sweden, for example, get hold of an especially hot tip? Did German agents plant it? Did the Swedes make it up for their own purposes? It was impossible to know.

So in 1941, when President Roosevelt asked Donovan to build a new intelligence service, Donovan had a prime opportunity to study firsthand why the prior system had failed. And he knew he couldn't succeed by just trying to match what America's allies and enemies were doing. The British had a reputation as wise old spymasters, heirs to an unbroken tradition of cryptic codes, concealed daggers, and posh secret agents that went back to the time of Christopher Marlowe and Good Queen Bess. (Never mind that the reputation was exaggerated, and that the British had let their intelligence infrastructure fall into neglect after World War I.) The French had been in the business for so long that they gave the English language the words *cipher, covert, espionage, surveillance,* and *spy.* Meanwhile, the Germans had spies everywhere—especially within their own borders, since, being a police state, they spied on each other.[36] There was simply no way for Donovan's new agency to catch up to these countries on their terms.

So it didn't. The only way out was to find entirely new sources of information. And to find experts who could decipher, evaluate, and piece together that information in order to turn it into *intelligence.* This is what Donovan's agency, and specifically the part run by Sherman Kent, did. They expanded—dramatically—the very concept of what *counted* as intelligence and what kind of person would make a good spy.[37]

Spycraft itself goes back for centuries, for millennia—for as long as we have stories. But the idea of having civilians, not militaries, run intelligence was fairly new.[38] And the idea that those civilians could find new sources of intelligence in telephone books, industry directories, in columns of numbers that economists drew up and then made dance—well, it was an idea that could save the world. The dramatic shift in intelligence during the war was the shift from collecting haphazard anecdotes on the ground to collecting and studying published facts.[39]

Which also meant bringing two new groups of civilians into the spy business: civilians to go out into the field to collect these new sources of intelligence, and civilians to stay in Washington to analyze it. The metaphor that Donovan used for the analysts who worked under Kent in Washington was that of an operator at a telephone switchboard. A telephone switchboard is a single control panel that connects people who want to communicate with each other, but can't call each other directly and may not even know each other's numbers. The spies who worked all over the globe on behalf of the Americans, the British Commonwealth, and the governments-in-exile of Occupied Europe operated in small, isolated cells of as few as three members apiece, who didn't know of each other's existence and could exchange messages only with Washington or London.*

In a telephone exchange, the caller contacts the operator, not the person they're calling. So it was for the men and women of R&A, who were, Donovan said, the switchboard's "highly implausible 'operators'—scholars and research men, economists, engineers, experts on European labor movements, historians, linguists, anthropologists, and sociologists learned in the lore of strategic regions." They alone saw all the nodes on the switchboard, and they alone knew how to transfer an urgent message from some remote fishing village in Norway to the White House.

---

* Even within these cells, the spies played cellular, specialized roles designed to protect the group from unexpected blows. Three-member cells, for example, had the minimum number of roles needed to run a sabotage or information ring: an organizer, a courier, and a wireless operator, or "pianist." If the Gestapo picked up any one member of the team, the OSS or the SOE could send in a replacement. No spy did everything, and therefore, in theory, no spy was irreplaceable. Noreen Riols, *The Secret Ministry of Ag. & Fish: My Life in Churchill's School for Spies* (London: Macmillan, 2013), 38.

What distinguished the "implausible operators" of R&A from telephone operators was that they transformed the messages they passed along. They studied the newspapers, the underground newsletters, the propaganda mailings, the "secret books," the restricted scientific journals, the telephone directories, the policy documents, the covertly taken photographs, and the rest of the documents that agents in the field sent home, and they figured out how to turn it all into actionable intelligence. As researchers, they did what they did best: they studied vast amounts of information and presented arguments about it.

THE MAP AND THE TERRITORY

Sherman Kent's desk at the war's great switchboard in 1943 and 1944 looked nothing like his desk at Yale. In a rather literal sense, the world that surrounded Kent was gray, rickety, and crowded with ad hoc office lumber. In addition to raising temporary plywood structures in odd corners of Washington, the OSS requisitioned space in all sorts of buildings, like theaters and orchestra houses, that one wouldn't normally expect to house government work. The office address of Frederick Kilgour, Adele Kibre's superior, was Stage Auditorium 532, which was presumably a repurposed performing-arts space. Kent's office address was #702 Annex #1, designating him as an inhabitant of one of the plywood "tempos."[40]

But to the imaginative faculty, which for a scholar like Kent often seems quite as real as the room he sits in, that world might have looked like a great, vibrant web, with each strand radiating to some crucial arena of combat. The spymasters of the OSS and the SOE spun connections between the stately government buildings of London, the leaky plywood tempos of Washington, the lively bazaars of Istanbul, the neat little bookstores of Stockholm, the seedy cafés of Marseille, and the crowded, cheaply furnished scientific library at the Manhattan Project site in Los Alamos, where refugees from every corner of Europe, standing at steel bookshelves under naked fluorescent lights, read the latest publications from Berlin and elsewhere. These strands connected people with innumerable histories and different backgrounds, who had been—to borrow a phrase from Charles Dickens—very curiously brought together.

Along these strands, in both directions, information flowed. Objects too. In Stockholm, OSS agents bought more ink than they needed and sent the surplus home. Why? They were buying *German-made* ink, which was available in neutral Stockholm, and which the OSS used to make convincing forgeries of German documents. And the franc notes that Allied spies spent in France were actually forgeries that got their realistic "used" appearance—which made them look like notes that had long been in circulation—from lying on the floor in government office buildings in London. Every day, clerical staffers in those offices walked around on top of millions of francs, crumpling them underfoot.

Anthropologists working for the R&A in Washington, collaborating with a historian at Yale, worked up a database of survival techniques from cultures and climates around the world. The navy drew on their knowledge to produce a handbook in 1943, titled *How to Survive on Land and Sea*, that sailors who washed up on foreign shores would be able to use to stay alive.[*] By early 1945, the military had given almost a million copies to servicemen in the Pacific.[41]

In Los Angeles, William Donovan asked the German-born movie star Marlene Dietrich to record a set of songs in German—about soldiers missing their girlfriends—that the OSS hoped radio stations in Germany and Italy would play, demoralizing Axis listeners. (This was known as "black propaganda": media disguised as the enemy's own

---

[*]   Some of the book's advice: if you must swim in a fast-flowing shallow river, swim on your back with your feet first, having inflated your trousers with air to help support your legs. If you want to climb a palm tree in search of coconuts, "do it native-style," tying a loop of rope around your ankles to help you shimmy up the tree. Look inside rotten logs for grubs to eat. If you're stranded on a raft at sea, you can attract fish at night using a light and then scoop them up in a net. If your plane has gone down in the far north, lichen are edible, but they may give you a stomachache unless you boil them first. Because some people are more susceptible than others to the effects of plants that harm you by touch, you should experiment at home with poison ivy to find out whether you're one of those people. If you meet natives of any region, "Treat them as equals, be eager to learn, and show enthusiasm and admiration for their skill and proficiency in guiding and supplying you with the necessities of life." It goes without saying that this advice may be inaccurate or outdated, and that you should use up-to-date guidance in survival situations. Robin Winks, *Cloak & Gown: Scholars in the Secret War, 1939–1961* (New York: William Morrow, 1987), 46–77; United States Navy, *How to Survive on Land and Sea: Individual Survival* (Annapolis, MD: United States Naval Institute, 1943), 2, 20–23, 90, 136, 181, 215, 220–21.

media that aimed to lower morale.) Dietrich agreed. The operation was a success; the U.S. government later found that "black radio" damaged German morale as much as air raids did.[42]

The nickname of R&A was the Chairborne Division, but in spite of this, Kent and his colleagues did sometimes leave their desks. In fact, the researchers went out on all kinds of odd adventures. Some of them went to the front lines to gather information. Sidney Alexander, an economist, led a team across the deserts of Tunisia to examine broken and captured German tanks. They collected serial numbers and other identity markings, which they sent back to London and Washington for analysis.[43] Another team sent home tires from enemy vehicles, which researchers used to figure out how reliant Germany was on synthetic rubber. Others snooped around railroads in D.C. to learn how trains performed in the bitter cold—say, in the Russian winter— and visited factories to find vulnerable points that similar factories in Germany might have.[44]

They pieced together what they learned from these adventures— and what they could learn from the seemingly endless scraps of paper that swirled through their reading rooms—to answer questions that were enormously important and dauntingly specific. By the end of the war, R&A researchers gathered over a hundred thousand documents and wrote more than three thousand reports.[45]

These reports went to the Pentagon, to the White House, to Donovan's office on E Street NW. They went to London, where Winston Churchill presumably read them as he *liked* to read intelligence reports: while sitting in bed, wearing a nightshirt and a silk robe, puffing a cigar. (Once, the prime minister was so immersed in his reading that he didn't notice that his cigar was dropping hot ash on his robe, which started to smoke. "Excuse me, sir," said a polite underling who was in the room to take dictation. "You are on fire. May I put you out?")[46]

A DIAMOND IN THE ROUGH

What made Kent an ill-fitting professor made him a great intelligence officer. "Sherm has been called a rough diamond aristocrat," one of his colleagues later said. In a world of bow ties and tweed jackets, he stood out with his shirtsleeves and red suspenders, his eternal quid of spit tobacco, and his extravagantly vulgar language.[47] At Yale, his demeanor, which better suited a drill sergeant than a history professor, both enthralled and exasperated students; they reveled in his profanity-laden lectures, but they dreaded his merciless grading.[48]

In the OSS, Kent's unorthodox personality finally found a perfect match. The intelligence analysts he ferociously pressed to do better *wanted* to do better. There was a war on, after all. And his training as a historian taught him ways of dealing with evidence that turned out to be invaluable now that oceans of evidence, literal tons of paper, were pouring in from all over the world. In the 1930s, long before he imagined that he would be asked to use his training as a historian to alter the course of history, Kent wrote a book on the historian's craft. There, he described principles of historical analysis that would go on to shape how he ran *intelligence* analysis, his OSS colleagues said: "When the evidence seems to force a single and immediate conclusion, then that is the time to worry about one's bigotry and to do a little conscientious introspection into why this particular conclusion stands out. Was it in the material or was it in you?"[49] The evident is rarely so evident as it seems—a wise principle for a historian, and an imperative one for a spy.

Another secret weapon that scholars like Kent brought to bear on their work for the OSS was their almost superhuman resistance to boredom. Scholars don't recognize as boring things that most people would justifiably *think* are boring. Who wants to read through a pile of industry directories? Or trade magazines, railway schedules, lists of serial numbers from tanks, and local newspapers from small towns abroad? What about paperwork from American insurance firms who did reinsurance for properties overseas? Or books with titles like *The Universal Directory of Railway Officials* or *The Railway Year Book 1936*?

Boredom is often overlooked as a security strategy—a way of keeping secrets. But it's effective. A secret can be published in the newspaper, and it will stay a secret if nobody bothers to read it. But there is a certain type of person—if you're reading this book, you may be that type—whose heart beats faster at the thought of so much paper, evidence, information. Nobody knows what causes this syndrome. Usually, libraries and universities help to contain it—to provide a green pasture for the gently mad. The OSS figured out how to weaponize it.

But the same quality that makes scholars so valuable as intelligence analysts—their ability to thrive amid boredom—can also lead them to write analyses that nobody wants to read, including the decision-makers they're trying to reach. (When he was national security adviser, Henry Kissinger, a Harvard professor who was no stranger to academic jargon, groused that intelligence analyses forced him to "fight his way through 'Talmudic' documents to find their real meaning.")[50] Kent was a rare scholar who could make the theoretical practical. And with his distinctive rough manner, he could make a case for his analysts' results that military decision-makers would listen to.[51]

In his postwar writings, Kent often discussed the importance of tailoring analyses to decision-makers' interests. But in practice, he often battled decision-makers on behalf of his analysts. If a decision-maker chose not to listen to an analyst, he said, his job as the analyst's champion was to make that decision-maker suffer for it: "Let him be uncomfortable—thoroughly uncomfortable—about his decision to heed this other."[52]

Kent's success, and his analysts' success, proved that "scholars and research men" were the right people for right job at the right time. And Kent came to regard intelligence analysis itself as a discipline that belongs in the humanities or social sciences. For him, what gave those fields of study value for intelligence was that they specialize in examining evidence and making informed judgments in cases where data is poor and evidence is ambiguous. A war isn't a controlled experiment. Strategic intelligence estimates are unprovable. We have to act in wartime anyway.[53]

Kent later argued that no matter what cool toys and gadgets we invent for espionage, nothing will ever replace the importance of the human analyst: "Whatever the complexities of the puzzles we strive to solve, and whatever the sophisticated techniques we may use to collect the pieces and store them, there can never be a time when the thoughtful man can be supplanted as the intelligence device supreme."[54]

NINETY-NINE PERCENT PERSPIRATION

The thing about world-changing discoveries is they don't always come in world-shaking forms. Kent's researchers worked on problems that, at first glance, might seem laughably trivial. What's the best number of pellets to put in an antiaircraft shell? What parts of a plane are worth reinforcing with extra armor? What percentage of rubber in German tank tires is synthetic? The scholars of R&A showed that working on supposedly small problems could yield big results.

Consider the case of the tank serial numbers. Initially, Allied intelligence tried to use sources like prisoner-of-war interrogations to obtain numbers concerning other countries' production of military vehicles—numbers that the Allies desperately needed in order to guess, for example, how Germany might counter a push into new territory, or whether Germany was vulnerable to an attack based on overwhelming force. However, these sources often provided exaggerated figures—say, ten times as great as the reality.[55]

Likewise, estimating production based on factory size produced estimates that were far too high, since the same factories that produced tanks also produced trains.[56]

It was in April 1942 that the scholars of R&A found a solution to this problem. The factories that produced German tanks affixed the chassis of each tank with a serial number, which indicated the model of the tank, the factory that produced it, and the order in which it rolled off the assembly line. So the OSS instructed troops to photograph these serial numbers whenever they captured German tanks in battle, allowing R&A to work out, on an ongoing basis, the total production numbers for each model.[57]

Prior to R&A's analysis, intelligence agencies guessed that the Germans were producing, in 1943, a million tires a month. R&A scholars estimated that the true number was 186,100. (It turned out to be 175,500.) They also figured out that more than 70 percent of German tires came from just five manufacturers, and all of Germany's tanks came from just two manufacturers, that far fewer factories were *assembling* those tanks than anyone had expected, and that only two factories produced gearboxes. Naturally, this was valuable information for bombing operations.[58]

R&A scholars often arrived at conclusions that went against the prevailing wisdom of other intelligence groups. Early on, for instance, military intelligence predicted a terrible food shortage in Germany, but an R&A study found that German soldiers were in fact receiving *larger* food rations, and German civilians were still eating enough calories to get by. (This was because they were stealing food from the populations of occupied countries, as the economic historian Adam Tooze notes.)[59]

Likewise, while military intelligence anticipated that Germany would suffer a deficit of munitions and raw materials, R&A scholars said this was unlikely to happen.[60] Instead, they said, the deficit that would cause the Germans real trouble would be a deficit of men suitable to enlist in the military, since the birth rate had been low during the previous world war. As it turned out, this prediction was accurate; in 1944, more than 25 percent of German soldiers were over the age of thirty-four.[61] The military took R&A's new calculations into account, to its benefit.

Structurally, R&A might have been a stuffy Washington operation, but when the time came for those at the top to make decisions, they valued the insights of the outsiders and oddballs they'd brought into the fold rather than valuing only their own ideas. And that made all the difference.

HAVING NEW EYES

The power of an outside perspective in R&A wasn't limited to the professional novelty of scholars in the world of spycraft. The staff of R&A was filled with immigrants and the children of immigrants. One of Kent's subordinates, Eugene Anderson of the Central European Section of R&A, commented, "In the Central European Section the *lingua franca* is broken English."[62]

Consider the case of Abraham Wald. A mild-mannered young mathematician with a mind that was forever wandering above the clouds in the high, cold air of abstraction, Wald grew up in Romania in a large, financially struggling Jewish family. His father supported the family with a job as a baker, but young Wald showed such a gift for mathematics that his family worked up the money to send him to university. But when he took his PhD from the University of Vienna in 1931, he had no chance, as a foreigner, to secure a university position in Austria. He found a low-paying job as a researcher working in Vienna for Oskar Morgenstern, a German-born economist who would become one of the inventors of game theory.[63]

Morgenstern's politics as an anti-Nazi made him unpopular in Vienna, so in 1938 he left Austria to take a teaching position at Princeton. He helped Wald to follow him to the United States, where Wald taught statistics at Columbia University. This is how he wound up working for the OSS in the Statistical Research Group (SRG) of R&A, which was a secret little band of economists and mathematicians who worked down the block from Columbia, in a gray apartment building on West 118th Street, applying their expertise to wartime problems. "This was a group where Milton Friedman, the future Nobelist in economics, was often the fourth-smartest person in the room," the mathematician Jordan Ellenberg later wrote. "The *smartest* person in the room was usually Abraham Wald."[64]

In 1943, the military brought a question to Wald. They had been taking down meticulous records of American bomber planes that returned from combat missions, recording where bullets hit every plane. What they were trying to work out, based on that information, was where they should install more armor plates. (They couldn't just add more armor everywhere or the planes would get too heavy.)[65]

The military analysts assumed they should put the extra armor on the parts of the planes that took the most damage. The records clearly showed that the fuselage tended to come back with the most bullet holes, then the wings, then the tail. Really, they were just asking Wald about the optimal amount of armor to add to those places. But Wald told them that under no circumstances should they do as they were planning. Think about it, he said: these were the planes that *made it back*. What the records proved wasn't that the fuselage was the most vulnerable part of the plane. They proved that the fuselage could take *a ton of bullets* and still bring the plane home in flying condition. The engines, by contrast, must be terribly vulnerable, since few planes made it home with bullet holes in the engines.[66]

Wald drew a diagram for the military analysts that showed a bomber plane, adding spots to represent where bullet holes often appeared. He pointed at the parts of the plane *without* spots, the engines among them. *This* is where they should add the extra armor, he said.[67]

Wald's insight was more than a brilliant display of counterintuitive reasoning. He based it on heavy-duty statistical analysis, producing page after page of dense polynomial equations. His statistical methods of estimating plane vulnerability proved so useful that the U.S. military was still putting them to use during the Vietnam War. He was able to see under the surface of the problem because he lived in a mathematical world of abstractions, which meant he recognized the power of adding tiny advantages to that fundamental insight through additional calculations. The power of small numbers. And the power of small numbers is how nations win wars, as Ellenberg writes: "The winners are usually the guys who get 5 percent fewer of their planes shot down, or use 5 percent less fuel, or get 5 percent more nutrition into their infantry at 95 percent of the cost. That's not the stuff war movies are made of, but it's the stuff wars are made of."[68]

The Germans didn't want someone like Wald. After all, he was Jewish. They had no place for a large portion of the members of the Statistical Research Group, including Wald, Jacob Wolfowitz (a Jewish immigrant from Poland), Meyer Abraham Girshick (a Jewish immigrant from Russia), and Milton Friedman (the son of Jewish immigrants from Hungary). They had no place for the large number of women who worked for the group as computers, solving differential equations and churning out statistical tables. After all, the German phrase for a woman's place was *"Kinder, Küche, Kirche"—children, kitchen, church.* Nor did they have a place for the group's Black members or its members with serious disabilities.[69]

That being said, the U.S. government had a complicated relationship with the refugees who worked for the war effort. Because Wald, who wasn't yet a citizen, was therefore legally an "enemy alien," he was officially forbidden from reading the papers he wrote, which were classified. ("The joke around SRG was that the secretaries were required to pull each sheet of notepaper out of his hands as soon as he was finished writing on it.")[70] The military head of the Manhattan Project, General Leslie Groves, was so suspicious of the refugees who worked for him that he had the FBI follow some of them around. After a long day tailing Leo Szilard, the refugee physicist who helped write the Einstein letter to Roosevelt, around Washington, the FBI wrote up the following report: "The Subject is of Jewish extraction, has a fondness for delicacies and frequently makes purchases in delicatessen stores and eats his breakfast in drug stores . . . speaks in a foreign tongue and associates mostly with people of Jewish extraction. He is inclined to be rather absent minded and eccentric, and will start out a door, turn around and come back, go out on the street as if he were watching for someone or did not know for sure where he wanted to go."[71] In other words, the FBI expended considerable shoe leather investigating Szilard just to figure out that he was an older Jewish man.

Nonetheless, the United States won, in no small part, because it was willing to accept the help of Wald, Szilard, and all the others who had no place in the world Hitler was trying to make. The refugees, like Hans Sahl, who, when rescuers smuggled them out of Occupied Europe, insisted on bringing along documents that might help the Allied cause. The refugee physicists who spent nights poring over journals that had just been delivered to the library in Los Alamos.[*] The young women who, freshly graduated from the math department at Vassar, spent their days crunching numbers in that gray apartment building in Manhattan. ("When we made recommendations, frequently things happened," Allen Wallis, a member of SRG, later said of his group's work in that building. The air force loaded the guns of fighter planes,

---

[*]   One refugee physicist at Los Alamos, Gregory Breit, had the presumably quite stressful job of calculating, over and over, the odds that igniting an atomic bomb would set the Earth's atmosphere on fire and destroy the world. His task was to make *absolutely sure*, you see, that the odds were zero. Stanislaw Ulam, *Adventures of a Mathematician* (New York: Scribner's, 1976), 150.

and the navy prepared propellants for rockets, in keeping with their suggestions.)[72]

Even refugees who weren't working in military and intelligence services eagerly offered their expertise, however unorthodox, to the war effort. Consider a story later told by Donald Downes, the man whom Joseph Curtiss met in the Yale Club those years ago. When Downes began working for the OSS in early 1942, he received his first assignment at a meeting in Washington with one of Donovan's closest aides.

"We want, and the request is from the highest possible military level, the codes and the ciphers of four neutral embassies here in Washington," Donovan's man said, according to Downes's memoir. "We have reason to believe they are handling information for the enemy. We want to be able to read their cables. You will be given a completely free hand, technical advice and aid from the British, and whatever sums of money are needed subject to our approval, that is Allen Dulles and mine. You can count on us for all help and aid possible, *unless you are caught*. Then, we agree, we have never heard of you."[73]

The hardest embassy to steal codes from was the Spanish embassy, Donovan said—a job that wouldn't have been possible without the help of some savvy refugees. First, they needed to have someone working on the inside. They asked the president of a prominent women's college whether he could spare one of his Spanish instructors for the war effort. He could. And so the instructor, whom Downes calls only "Mrs. G," moved into a D.C. boardinghouse where many of the secretaries from the Spanish embassy happened to live.*

Next, the OSS got a company to put a help-wanted ad in the *New York Times*, looking for a secretary who had exactly the same background as one of the secretaries from the embassy. Mrs. G showed her the ad, and she took the job, since it paid a whopping $400 a month.

---

* Donald Downes, *The Scarlet Thread* (London: Deriek Verschoyle, 1953), 88–93. Who was Mrs. G? Alas, Downes doesn't give us enough clues to know for sure. Perhaps she was Germaine Guillén, the wife of the Wellesley Spanish professor Jorge Guillén, who herself sometimes taught at the college. She happened to be Jewish, which is why Jorge moved from Spain to the United States.

(Over $7,000 a month in today's money.) Mrs. G took the position she vacated. And now the OSS had someone on the inside.[74]

Then Downes went to New York City to meet a safecracker named G. B. "Sadie" Cohen. Cohen ran a shop near the Lower East Side that sold locks, keys, and safes, but that was just a front for his real business: masterminding robberies for hire. Downes had a colleague in army counterintelligence, a major who used to work for the New York Police Bomb Squad, who praised Cohen's talents to the heavens. ("Sadie's spent a lot of time in Sing-Sing, but we always spring him early and hold back an indictment or two over his head so he works for us," the major told Downes. "There's nothing Sadie can't open!")[75]

Cohen didn't *look* like a criminal mastermind, Downes wrote. He was slight, potbellied, "with curly gray hair on which his battered derby sat like a chicken on its nest," a Jewish immigrant who ran a small business on what seemed to be a shoestring budget. (Downes said the place looked like a "junk heap.") But looks can be deceiving, as every spy knows. When Downes and the major walked into his shop, Cohen greeted them cheerfully: "Val, lootenant, how's bombs? Vat can I do for you?"*

Downes described the situation. "Sadie listened, like a doctor in consultation," and then explained exactly what they should do: they should give their secretary a little gilder's hammer. She should sneak it into the embassy hidden in "her woman's national bank, her bosom." Then, when unobserved, she should use the hammer to strike the dial of the embassy safe. (The hammer, having a rubber head, would be silent.) When the Spanish realized the safe was broken, they'd call the manufacturer, which would send a repairman to fix it. The OSS should tell the company to send Cohen himself as the repairman. Then, while fixing the safe, Cohen would examine the lock and make a duplicate key.

The whole thing was simple, clean, and elegant. Cohen had solved, as easily as one might solve a basic times table, a problem that had stumped America's intelligence agencies. But when Downes asked how much Cohen wanted to be paid, the criminal responded with indignation.

---

* This dialogue is reproduced from Downes's memoir.

"Paid!" Cohen shouted. "Paid. You've come into my place to insult me. Don't I have two nephews in the army? Ain't I an American as much as you? Aren't you ashamed? Pay me? You can't even tank me. Even a ticket to Vashington you can't buy me, or a Coca-Cola."[76]

Sadie Cohen was a criminal, but he wasn't a Nazi. For the honor of helping the Allies, he gave his services for free. The OSS knew they could trust him because they knew that there is, in fact, honor among thieves, and because they understood that if you want to get something done right, there's no good substitute for an expert.

In order to steal the codes from the Spanish embassy, they depended on Cohen's help as a consulting criminal. But they also relied on the help of two charming socialites from Philadelphia, Sidney and Eleanor Clark. At the OSS's behest, the Clarks, who were refugees from France, befriended the embassy's diplomats and took to entertaining them in high style in their suite at the elegant Wardman Park hotel. On the night that the OSS used Cohen's copied key to get into the embassy safe, they knew that the diplomats were away from the embassy, because they were at a party with the Clarks.

The success of this mission hinged on a few powerful lessons. First, no one can be an expert in everything. The key to success is to value and leverage the distinctive talents of those around you. Cohen knew how to use a gilder's hammer to quietly break a safe; the Clarks knew how to use caviar forks to spear down the embassy's staff at the crucial moment. And second, in the fight against the Nazis, refugees like Cohen and the Clarks ultimately helped turn the tide of the war. Nazi Europe based its whole identity on forming an in-group that violently excluded these people. America, when it honored its best values, welcomed them. It's the American way: welcoming strangers, seizing the practical gains of diversity, finding common cause between aristocrats and thieves.

CONDEMNED TO REPEAT IT

The historians of R&A knew that to understand the future, we must look to the past. So they looked to see how the Germans assessed their own successes and failures during the previous war. Unless humans had become far more sensible in the past two decades—and unless they'd learned, specifically, to appreciate the uses of historical research outside of universities—many of the problems that had arisen in the past were likely to arise in the future.

The search paid off. The historians found, in a German booklet on railroads published in 1939, an essay by an official in the German High Command that described a curious and important association between Germany's railroads, its expansionist ambitions during World War I, and its ultimate defeat in that war. The author pointed out that Germany's early victories in the war actually caused an escalating series of problems with railroads—which were essential, in both wars, for moving armies and transmitting military messages—that helped to strain Germany's resources to the breaking point. As German armies in World War I pushed farther outside of German territory, they needed ever greater numbers of locomotives and train cars to carry troops and messages. The rolling stock they already had from peacetime didn't stretch nearly far enough, and they couldn't easily swap German trains and rails with trains and rails from other countries. Germany's problems with transportation compounded again and again, to the point where "building locomotives," the essay said, "became just as important as manufacturing guns."[77]

The OSS report on this essay noted that German officials seemed not to have actually read the essay or put its lessons into practice—which meant that once analysts started looking, they could find the same problems building as Germany conquered territory now: "Strange to say, these conclusions did not lead in time to action; therefore history repeated itself."[78]

There was more. Studying two of those aforementioned books with infinitely boring titles, *The Universal Directory of Railway Officials* and *The Railway Year Book 1936*, allowed the historians to compare the network of railroads in Russia with the territory that the Germans captured in Russia in 1941. Which in turn allowed them to estimate how the Germans would try to move troops and supplies out to the furthest front lines, and how quickly their rail stock would deplete. R&A scholars realized that the Germans were falling into a trap of their own making.

Soon, two pieces of damning news returned from the field. First, the Germans were forcing Russian prisoners of war to lift and move Russian railroad tracks in order to convert them from the wide Russian gauge to the European standard gauge. Second, the Germans were already running out of locomotives to send to Russia on the converted tracks. Ahead lay supply, military, and even political problems between Axis countries, as the Germans had promised to transport a massive amount of coal to Italy by freight every winter.[79] All of this from studying some railway reference books.

The railway problem illustrated an important point about Germany's war planning: Germany was counting on the resources of captured territory and the compelled labor of captured people to keep its war machine running. But even when Germany got what it wanted, those very victories became a source of weakness. Capturing railways meant German troops needed more cars to run on those railways, just to hold the territory they passed through, than peacetime needs had provided, and they couldn't build new cars as fast as they needed them. Capturing huge swaths of land meant Occupied Europe had a tremendously long exposed coastline: if the Allies were to try to push their forces onto land somewhere on that coastline, the Germans had no way of knowing where it would be, and they didn't have enough equipment or manpower to guard the whole coast. That vulnerability would go on to give the Allies a huge advantage—and Allied spies a crucial role to play—in the Normandy invasion.

History had indeed been destined to repeat itself. A willingness to look to the past—and to do the "boring" legwork—gave crucial insights to the Allies that enabled them to weaponize the historical shortsightedness of the enemy.

STRATEGIC SABOTAGE

Throughout 1943 and 1944, in the United States embassy in London, a genteel brick building in Grosvenor Square, a team of OSS researchers was working to identify targets for strategic bombing. Called the Enemy Objectives Unit (EOU), the team collaborated with representatives of the U.S. military, although it often disagreed with the military's initial assessments. Thirteen of the EOU's fifteen members were research analysts from R&A.[80]

The British and the Americans disagreed about how to use the new technology of air bombing. The British championed a strategy they called "area bombing." The concept was simple: drop bombs en masse over whole cities, with the aim of sapping enemy morale. (It turns out this doesn't work. Bombing civilians just makes them more determined to resist.)[81]

The Americans favored a more targeted approach, called "pinpoint bombing," which involved striking specific factories, railroads, and other "bottlenecks" on which the German war effort depended. The factories targeted didn't produce what you'd expect, such as tanks or submarines or fighter planes. Instead, they produced the parts that you'd need to *make* tanks and submarines and fighter planes. Parts like ball bearings. If you destroy a ball-bearing factory, the theory went, you'll *also* render useless all the factories that rely on those ball bearings.[82] And bombing just those factories, just those bottleneck locations, would do maximum damage to the enemy's war effort while reducing civilian lives lost as much as possible, the Americans argued.[83]

Of course, this approach would require knowing which factories produced ball bearings. And that's where Adele Kibre's library hunting came in.

Consider, for example, an R&A report from April 1944 that lists every known ball-bearing factory in Occupied Europe.[84] It names its sources of information on these factories, and those sources include many books that Kibre acquired in Stockholm. For example, the *Deutsches Reichsadressbuch für Industrie*, which listed the names and addresses of businesses all over Germany. This title was listed as the source for information about ball-bearing factories in Aachen, Beckum, Berlin, and beyond, provided addresses, company names, and details about the specific ball-bearing components that the factories produced. From these facts, the Allies could presumably deduce what machines were in the factories, and therefore how best to destroy those machines.

In practice, pinpoint bombing didn't work. Not the way its proponents said it did. The air force boasted that its secret bombsight technology enabled airmen to drop "a bomb into a pickle barrel from thirty thousand feet." But they knew this wasn't actually true. Reconnaissance showed that some *80 percent* of the bombs the Americans dropped failed to get within *a thousand feet* of the target.[85] Moreover, it turns out that you can't really disable a factory by dropping a bomb on it from an airplane. A report that the U.S. government released in 1945 confirmed that bombing factories from above—even using that secret bombsight technology—didn't really do much to slow their production. It might damage the buildings, sure—but often, it didn't damage the machines *inside* those buildings.[86]

As the historian W. Hays Parks notes, the air force came to use phrases like "precision," "pickle barrel," and "pinpoint bombing" as a way to sell itself as being more ethical and efficient than it really was. (The air force even used the term "marshalling yards" to describe a common target, which outsiders presumably read to mean railroad yards. In fact, "marshalling yards" was just a sugarcoated term for *cities*.)[87]

But if pinpoint bombing wasn't the hoped-for solution to taking down the German war machine, that didn't mean the people who came up with the idea of precision attacks were wrong. It just meant that precision attacks couldn't be achieved through pinpoint bombing. The OSS came to realize that the same effect could be achieved far more reliably, with even fewer civilian lives lost, through sabotage.[88]

A saboteur could target a piece of equipment with a level of precision that the men who boasted about hitting a pickle barrel from thirty thousand feet only *wished* they had. Properly trained saboteurs could target bottleneck machines they knew to be crucial to production; destroy identical components of machines that had multiple units, rendering them irreparable; and tailor their sabotage techniques to cause the most damage possible. For instance, setting up the sabotage to trigger when the machine was moving, so the machine used its own power to destroy itself. Puncturing the fuel line of an idle machine and sealing the puncture with wax, so that when the machine heated up later on, the wax melted and the hot fuel started a fire. Or putting sand in a machine's lubrication system, which would destroy, with no further effort, every one of its moving parts.[89]

And they only needed a few people to accomplish this, with the cheapest of tools: a knife, a lump of wax, a handful of sand.* Germany's antiaircraft defenses might stop bombers from flying overhead, but they couldn't stop saboteurs—who had on their side inconspicuousness, agility, and the ability to strike their targets with unmatched precision. A smaller, weaker group using its disadvantages as advantages to overcome a larger, more powerful group. The power of small numbers.

Sabotage operations often took their personnel from resistance movements in Occupied Europe and their directions from the OSS or the SOE. Secret agents who trained at Beaulieu, at Area B in Virginia, or at other such training camps would drop into enemy territory and set up a little *réseau*, or cell, often with just three members: a courier, an organizer, and a radio operator. The spy cells would then train *résistants* to break apart factory equipment or blow up sections of railroad or change road signs to misdirect foreign occupiers. Another advantage of using sabotage operations rather than bombing raids was that sabotage operations rarely hurt or killed civilians, which made it far easier to maintain the goodwill of the local population.[90]

R&A economists and historians helped to write the sabotage handbooks that instructors at training camps used to teach spies, and which spies in the field then used to teach *résistants*. They were an improbable but remarkably effective pairing for teaching the secret arts of destruction: historians, who know that what we remember often omits the most interesting and dangerous details of the past. And economists, who know that what *seems* to keep the world around us moving is often different from what actually does. Sabotage is, after all, a tactic with

---

* "Where destruction is concerned," an OSS sabotage handbook declared, "the weapons of the citizen-saboteur are salt, nails, candles, pebbles, thread, or any other materials he might normally be expected to possess as a householder or as a worker in his particular occupation. His arsenal is the kitchen shelf, the trash pile, his own usual kit of tools and supplies. The targets of his sabotage are usually objects to which he has normal and inconspicuous access in everyday life." Office of Strategic Services, *Simple Sabotage Field Manual* No. 3 (1944), 1.

a history we can learn from. It's also a tactic that succeeds in proportion to the damage it does to the production of specific goods as well as to the economy at large, which economists are in a special position to know about.

The handbooks divided sabotage into two main forms: *coup de main* attacks, which were dedicated operations performed by a team in the dead of night; and the slower, less obvious, but still very effective "simple sabotage" of workers loitering on the job or damaging their own machines. (As an OSS handbook described the latter, which the British termed *ca'canny*, a Scots phrase meaning *go slow*: "Slashing tires, draining fuel tanks, starting fires, starting arguments, acting stupidly, short-circuiting electric systems, abrading machine parts will waste materials, manpower, and time. Occurring on a wide scale, simple sabotage will be a constant and tangible drag on the war effort of the enemy."[91])

These, too, were ways for victims of Hitler's regime to fight back. Perhaps, out of fear for their families, they couldn't rebel openly, but they could refrain from sharpening their tools, act dull and careless on the job, forget to lubricate machines that needed lubrication. Just as spies, in real life, didn't carry James Bond gadgets because those gadgets were liable to discovery during a search—as the saying went, you could have a weapon or a cover, but not both—civilian saboteurs had to use tools that would seem innocent to the police: "A knife or a nail file can be carried normally on your person: either is a multi-purpose instrument for creating damage. Matches, pebbles, salt, nails, and dozens of other destructive agents can be carried or kept in your living quarters without exciting any suspicion whatsoever."[92]

What made a great spy wasn't gadgets; what made a great saboteur wasn't bombs. It was cleverness, cunning, an ability to believe in the power of small acts of rebellion.

Sabotage was a big reason why Germany's reliance on forced labor—on prisoners in concentration camps, prisoners of war, workers in occupied countries whose labor Germany conscripted to the war effort, and foreign workers whom Germany imported against their will—proved to be such a mistake. Forced workers, who were already slow and weak due to illness, bad treatment, and poor nutrition, had to be watched constantly lest they commit sabotage—and they found all kinds of ways to commit sabotage still.

But the Nazis had no way out; their whole economic system required them to pile ever more forced labor onto their economy.*

"IMPORTANT ENDS JUSTIFY MINOR SINS"

The Allies would have faced a very different war if not for the efforts of their spies, saboteurs, and the university-in-exile that was R&A. But there are further lessons to be learned from the intertwined fates of all these unexpected secret agents. As the example of Donald Downes and his colleague, the selfless safecracker, shows, times of crisis can be crucibles in which villains become heroes and heroes become villains. In general, the people who decide to make it all about themselves are at risk of becoming the latter. Lacking experience as an undercover operative, Varian Fry sought role models in the movies. It's probably for the best that James Bond wasn't one of them.

But consider the case of Carleton Coon, the Harvard anthropologist who went off to work for the OSS in North Africa. Ever since a shadowy government man in a suit visited his office to recruit him on the day of the Harvard-Yale game in 1941, Coon had been making the most of what must have seemed like a wartime career right out of a spy novel. ("Since childhood I have wanted to do the kind of work I have been doing for the past year," he wrote around this time—already drafting his memoirs. This was also when he wrote that "it is probably

---

* At the height of Germany's use of forced labor, one economic historian says, "Some 26 percent of the German labor force comprised either civilian workers from Western Europe, who worked in Germany under contract, or various categories of forced labor from the east. The argument is plausible that the German war economy would have collapsed as early as 1942 had it not been for the system of forced labor. Virtually no sector of the German economy was not at least partially dependent on it." But this system never *worked*, except superficially. It just meant Germany was dying a slow death from self-administered poison rather than an immediate collapse. The Nazis weren't exactly master strategists. Hans Mommsen, "The Impact of Compulsory Labor on German Society at War," in *A World at Total War: Global Conflict and the Politics of Destruction, 1937–1945*, ed. Roger Chickering, Stig Förster, and Bernd Greiner (New York: Cambridge University Press, 2005), 181.

the secret ambition of every boy to travel in strange mountains, stir up tribes, and destroy the enemy by secret and unorthodox means.")[93]

After Operation Torch, the OSS was strained to the seams trying to hold—and expand—Allied territory in North Africa. A deal with the British left the Americans in charge of much of North Africa's military governance, which meant the OSS ran a large share of intelligence there. But the SOE was still plenty active in the region. In Tunisia, a country on the continent's north coast, bordering the Mediterranean Sea, the SOE ran five camps dedicated to teaching locals how to fight as *résistants* in the continuing skirmishes against Vichy forces. The OSS helped. Which is how Coon, who spent the months before Torch smuggling guns into Tangier, found himself teaching sabotage and covert operations in one of those camps. He dressed in a British combat uniform, belted and sage green, with officer pips on his shoulders that he'd fashioned from billiard-table felt—presumably to make himself look more impressive, since he wasn't an officer. He went by a *nom de guerre*, although this, too, was likely an unnecessary flourish: Captain Retinitis.[94]

"Here's Carl Coon," a colleague said when he arrived in camp; "now the company of rogues and cutthroats is complete."[95]

In his Harvard classroom, Coon had espoused a low view, as a professor of anthropology, of everyone who wasn't of Northern European descent. In a book that he later compiled from his lectures, he wrote that, although people of other races can't help the fact (which isn't a fact at all, of course) that they're less intelligent, they must bear up anyway and change their ways to become more like Northern Europeans, for the good of humanity: "Overpopulation can be reduced and epidemics controlled only when the peoples of all nations have reached a satisfactory level of modern culture."[96] Maybe his experience in the classroom was what made his superiors give him a teaching job now. Regardless, what he was accustomed to teaching at Harvard informed what he taught in a training camp for spies and saboteurs. *World affairs are a great game that white men must guide. The only useful kind of power is power from above. The hero in a crisis is the man who makes his decisions most known and felt.*

Coon "took a tough view of war: if policy required that someone be assassinated, he favored it," the historian Robin Winks later said.[97] That "tough" view also played out in his approach to intelligence gathering.

Coon decided to have his students in Tunisia kidnap boys from outlying villages and bring them back as hostages, leaving word that the boy's father must come alone to negotiate his son's release. "The old man inevitably came with gifts, demanding his son," Coon later wrote. "He was sent back to get good information about enemy positions, and when he came the second time his son would be released if the information was satisfactory."[98]

Now, getting information about enemy positions was important. The military called it combat intelligence: simple, concrete tactical details about how many men were ahead, and where, and with what kinds of weapons. In Europe, some 60 percent of the credible combat intelligence that the U.S. Army obtained came from a remarkable group now called the Ritchie Boys, named for their training school, Camp Ritchie in Maryland. Typically, a team of Ritchie Boys traveled with an army unit and, as the soldiers pushed into new territory, interrogated local civilians.[99]

But the Ritchie Boys used their language skills and local knowledge to get intelligence from civilians—they didn't kidnap those civilians' children. That seems to have been Coon's innovation, and he was proud of it: "This use of hostages was our chief source of intelligence aside from the work of our own patrols."*

Coon had a few other innovations as a training camp teacher. He came up with the idea of hiding little bombs in mule turds. You would plant them on the road, and then, supposedly, they would blow up

---

* The back cover of Coon's memoir, which he published in 1980, displays a photo of Coon standing with a handful of his students in the camp, which was in the green hills of Cape Serrat. Coon is wearing his British uniform and a sapper cap that, he writes in a caption, he took from the head of a fallen Greek officer. Coon is standing proudly with his hands behind his back. Most of the young men around him are smiling, although two of them look nervous. In the caption, Coon writes offhandedly, "I am with eight men, of whom at least six were members of the *Corps Franc d'Afrique*, and two more were Arabs, possibly hostages." Carleton Coon, *A North Africa Story: The Anthropologist as OSS Agent, 1941–1943* (Ipswich, MA: Gambit, 1980), back cover.

German tanks. However, none of the turd bombs ever actually stopped a German tank. They only ever made two kills, Coon later wrote: "one Arab and one cow."[100] In his memoir, Coon writes about this time with a sense of grandeur; he seems to have felt closer than ever to his old dream of being an adventurer among savages, a Lawrence of Arabia.

But Coon's dreams of glory came to an end in December 1942, when he had to leave the country abruptly under suspicious circumstances.

After Operation Torch, a French admiral named Jean-François Darlan was left standing as the de facto leader of French North Africa.* Darlan was a power-hungry weasel, despised by prominent Allied leaders and the OSS alike, as they feared his continuing presence would poison the Allies' relationship with French *résistants*.[101]

On December 24, 1942, just over a month after Torch, Darlan was assassinated. The assassin, a *résistant* named Fernand Bonnier de la Chapelle, received his training at a sabotage school whose senior American instructor was Carleton Coon.[102]

The OSS immediately recognized that the optics of all this were very bad. Bonnier had a clear connection to Coon. And a subsequent investigation revealed that the gun Bonnier used to shoot Darlan wasn't a standard-issue weapon. It was a Colt Woodsman pistol. The same kind of gun as Coon's.[103]

---

* The United States was the reason Darlan was left standing—not the first or last time the U.S. would create its own nightmare in a foreign government. After Torch, an American diplomat named Robert Murphy traveled around North Africa, secretly trying to persuade French leaders to rebel against the Germans when the Allies invaded—which would make the invasion far easier for the Allies. Murphy didn't particularly care which French leaders he got cozy with, as long as they promised to help him out. That included figures from the far right: men who hated the British, collaborated gladly with the Nazis, and only made a deal with the Allies to save their own skins. Murphy liked to say, "Important ends justify minor sins."

Darlan wanted to be more powerful than De Gaulle if he was going to switch to the Allied side, and he was willing to put the Allies at risk in order to get it. For days after the start of Torch, Darlan refused to tell his men to lay down their arms unless the Allies agreed to make him the leader of French North Africa. At stake was a significant swath of territory that Darlan's troops guarded. The Allies could win without Darlan, but not without a significant cost. Finally, the Americans agreed to his terms. Winks, *Cloak & Gown*, 180–85; Peter Tompkins, *The Murder of Admiral Darlan: A Study in Conspiracy* (New York: Simon & Schuster, 1965).

Coon's superiors ordered him to get out of Dodge. An OSS man couldn't be suspected of involvement with the assassination of a Free French official. And so, while Coon's training camp fell into chaos—as he described it later, "Captain Sabbatier, the head of the camp, hid for several days and then went to jail; my instructors either hid or were jailed, and the camp and my instruction program blew up"—he fled to northeast Algeria, where he kept his head down for a while.[104] On December 26, the French executed Bonnier by firing squad. In his memoir, Coon mentions Darlan's killing, but not that anyone thought he had something to do with it—which is odd, given how eager he is to present himself as a glamorous spy at the center of dramatic escapades. Being falsely implicated in an assassination is the *height* of dramatic escapades. Instead, Coon passes over the period hastily, saying of it, "Little of importance either to the war effort or to me happened as far as my personal activities were concerned."[105]

As it turned out, this wouldn't be the last time Coon seemed to put his own adventures before the interests of his comrades-in-arms. Nor was he finished playacting the glamorous spy. A few months later, he was back in Tunisia—in the ancient little town of Sbeitla where, on the evening of February 16, 1943, French and American soldiers were clogging the streets, fleeing from advancing German troops.[106]

As the Americans ran, one division was tasked with defending Sbeitla long enough to allow the others to retreat. Orders came down to "hold the line until 1100 the next morning."[107] Hamilton Howze, the operations officer for that division, begged Coon to help fight. To get into a foxhole and throw Molotov cocktails at the approaching German tanks.

Coon declined. He and the other OSS men threw a few turd bombs onto the road and then returned to the safety of their bunker. They spent the night playing cards, pushing around rifle cartridges as poker chips, while Howze's division held the line.[108]

"We didn't want to," Coon later said, explaining why he didn't fight. "It was not OSS work."[109]

FREE AGENTS

In an article that he wrote for *Life* magazine after the war, William Donovan praised the scholars of R&A as "amateurs" who made good: "These amateurs in intelligence showed what intellect, diligence, courage, and willingness to get around can accomplish in a supposedly esoteric realm."[110]

Looking back from a longer view of the world they made, we adjust his argument a little. These scholars weren't amateurs in intelligence. They were *experts* in intelligence. It's just that the intelligence world didn't know it yet. They were perfectly suited for the kinds of intelligence gathering and decision-making that, when they started out, hadn't been invented yet. The kinds that they, in fact, invented.

Everyone else thought they knew what a spy must be like: a glamorous, mysterious figure who skulks around corners, speaks in hushed tones, and carries a cloak and dagger. People put this archetype to different uses: Varian Fry used it to give himself courage while he was behind enemy lines, while Carleton Coon used it to justify refusing to join his comrades in frontline combat. But the scholars of R&A defied the archetype entirely. Which is the real point of Donovan's words: That Americans know how to start fresh. That Americans know how to make a stunning advantage of what people like Hitler consider to be a disadvantage.

This is why, in the same breath, Donovan also praised the "hyphenated Americans" who did so much for the war effort: "An unusual circumstance that helped us was the melting-pot nature of the American population. No other nation has in its population so many diverse national strains as are found in ours. During the war, some thought the unassimilated admixture would prove a weakness that our enemies would penetrate and exploit. Instead, the vast pool of linguistic skills and special racial and regional knowledge became one of our prime assets. No matter what region was involved, we were always able to muster for intelligence work either American citizens or friendly aliens versed in its language, politics, history, and customs."[111]

The refugee mathematician Peter Lax later wrote, naming just some of the refugees who worked on the science side of the war, "Everybody was painfully conscious that we were in a race against the Germans, and people noted with grim satisfaction that the great contributions of recent refugees from Hitler's tyranny, such as Bethe, Fermi, v. Neumann, Peiris, Szilard, Teller, Ulam, Wigner, to name a few, tipped the scale in favor of the free world. If ever there was divine retribution, this was it."[112]

8

THE LONGEST DAY

The war will be won or lost on the beaches.
We'll have only one chance to stop the enemy,
and that's while he's in the water.... Believe
me, Lang, the first 24 hours of the invasion
will be decisive.... For the Allies, as well
as Germany, it will be the longest day.
—Germany's general Erwin Rommel to
Captain Hellmuth Lang, on the expected
Allied invasion of Continental Europe

MAJOR WILLIAM MARTIN OF THE ROYAL MARINES WAS QUIET, shy, and tremendously competent. Thirty-six years old, he had won the devotion of far more senior superiors. Whenever Admiral Lord Mountbatten, the commander in chief of the Mediterranean Fleet, sent him off on a mission with some other unit, he begged the men Martin would be working for, only half joking, not to keep the industrious officer for themselves, but to "let me have him back, please."

Not bad for a boy from Cardiff. In Britain, God knew, you couldn't rise to become the man who kept the world spinning, the man everyone depended on. *That* was handed out at birth. The upper ranks of His Majesty's military were filled with lords who'd got officer status at the moment of joining up, simply because of the titles they were born with. Even in uniform, they wore, on their souls, a signet ring, an old school tie. No bones about it: to get on, a man had to be clubbable. And Martin was perhaps a little too shy, a little too down-at-heel, to be clubbable.

No, you couldn't rise to become the man everyone depended on—but you *could* become the man *that man* depended on. That's what Major Martin wanted. Why, on the mission he was setting out on now—he was flying to North Africa to train troops for a devilishly secret, war-changing operation—his superiors entrusted him, not only with letters that bore on the secret operation, but also with letters they dare not let their colleagues see because they were gossiping so frankly. Giving him state secrets was trust, but giving him personal secrets was *trust*. Perhaps one day the chief of the Naval Staff, or the president of the Grosvenor Club, or the King, would look at him and say, "I couldn't get it done without Martin."

On a dismal afternoon in late April 1943, Major Martin, wearing his battle dress uniform and a peaked cap, fastened the end of a long metal chain around his chest, like a harness. At the end of the chain was a briefcase. This contained the letters that Martin was to deliver in North Africa; the chain ensured that nobody could take the briefcase from him without—well—killing him.

Soon he was boarding a distressingly rattly little aircraft. Inside, he pulled on a Mae West—a life vest that, if the wearer pulled the right cords, would inflate into two bosom-shaped floats—and gave a reverent thought to his fiancée, Pam. He touched a cross necklace he wore under his uniform for luck. Time to leave the little country with the low skies and join the vast skies of Africa.

At 0400 hours, the plane, which was now somewhere near the coast of Spain, suddenly gave a sickening jolt. The pilot shouted for everyone to strap in. Martin, who had removed the metal chain from his chest to feel more comfortable, clipping the end to the belt of his trench coat, barely had time to process that they'd come under fire when the whole back of the aircraft—with a deafening bang—ceased to exist. The plane had no tail end. He was looking at black sky. This wasn't survivable.

As the plane screamed down toward the Atlantic, Martin experienced something that he never expected from his final moments, as often as he'd imagined them during his training. He knew, vaguely, that he ought to be thinking about his duty as a soldier, or about Wales, or even his fiancée—Pam, lovely, madcap Pam—but instead he was surprised to find that an avalanche of rage tore through him. He'd never imagined that what he'd read about as a schoolboy, in Homer's *Iliad*, might be a *fact of war*: the rage of young warriors who, dying in battle, go down to the underworld with a scream of fury. He'd thought it was a literary device. He knew that he had good reason to fight in this war, that this was a war good men had to fight in. But all of his youth, all of his life, was being taken away now, and the *wrongness* of that enveloped him with a terrible roar.[1]

A little while later, a body drifted vaguely in the direction of the shore, pulled by the tidal streams that flowed toward the Spanish coast. The tides pulled along, too, attached to the body by a chain, a briefcase full of secrets.

THE GHOST WAR

Major William Martin of the Royal Marines never existed. The Germans thought he did, though. And why wouldn't they? After all, they had a body, and they had all the records that he carried on his person, which their friends in the Spanish government shared with them. Player's cigarettes and a box of matches. An invitation to join the Cabaret Theatre Club, an avant-garde little nightclub in London. Two love letters from Martin's fiancée, whom he'd met that very year—well, wartime romances were notoriously reckless. A cheesecake picture of her in a swimsuit. (Well done, Marty: coy, shrewd dark eyes, cheekbones that you could slice paper with.) A notice from Lloyds Bank warning him that his account was in overdraft. An identity card that had recently been reissued to replace one he'd lost, bearing a smiling picture of the man himself.[2]

Major Martin was a *ruse de guerre*: a ploy that British intelligence agents put together in order to convince the Germans that the Allies— who, after they invaded North Africa in 1942, began mustering their forces in Tunisia to push across the strait and capture Sicily—actually planned to attack Greece and Sardinia. The ruse entailed inventing a fictional man, planting details on a corpse that corroborated this fictional identity, and sending the corpse adrift off the coast of Spain, where

Spanish authorities were sure to find him and to share their discovery with the Germans. The briefcase of "secret documents" that washed ashore with the body of Major Martin convinced the Germans to move their resources to Greece and Sardinia, which made invading Sicily, which the Allies did in July and August of 1943, far easier. It worked so well that the operation, code-named Mincemeat, is famous today.

But although Operation Mincemeat is, today, the most famous ruse of the Second World War, it was far from the biggest one. Throughout the spring and summer of 1944, the Allies orchestrated and deployed a series of deceptions that, aligned with the invasion of Normandy, led them to victory in the war's most important battle.

The Germans knew that sooner or later, the Allies would try to invade Occupied Europe. But Occupied Europe had a long, exposed coast; the Allies might strike anywhere along it. So the question was when—and where.

The Allies chose the Normandy coast, but they needed to divert the Germans from gathering their forces there before the invasion. And *during* it. And after. If the Germans brought their full forces to the invasion point, Allied soldiers would have no chance.

And so, as the Battle of Normandy raged for almost three long months, Allied spies around the world, judging this battle to be important enough to risk everything on, pulled out all the stops. From London to Marseille to Istanbul to Stockholm, spies burned their covers, worked up dazzling distractions, told more extravagant lies than they'd ever dared, sent false information through double agents whose credibility they had been building up for years and now had to risk destroying utterly. The Allies combined real military operations with deception operations and the guerrilla work of saboteurs.[3] It was a "ghost war"—an invisible war, fought alongside the *actual* war.

"WE SHALL FIGHT ON THE BEACHES"

Here's the war that everyone saw—the war you've heard about.

The invasion of Normandy was, and remains to this day, the biggest amphibious landing in history. It began at 6:30 a.m. on June 6, 1944.

By the end of that day, more than 150,000 troops had crossed the English Channel and landed on the beaches of France, including 73,000 Americans, 61,715 Brits, and 21,400 Canadians. More than 5,000 sea vessels carried them across, with more than 11,000 airplanes backing them up from above.[4]

German soldiers met them as they did.

The Allies had the advantage of numbers: the troops landing on the beaches outnumbered the Germans defending those beaches many times over. But the Germans had the advantage of geography: the high cliffs and bluffs over the beaches gave them secure posts from which to fire on the Allied troops, who had to climb rocky inclines while being strafed with machine-gun bullets. The Germans also had better protection: they fought from bunkers, from concrete forts called pillboxes, and from artillery batteries in trenches and dugouts, fortified with land mines, nests of barbed wire, and "Belgian gates," or spiky metal contraptions designed to tear up the hulls of landing craft.[5]

Because of this, the beaches of Normandy were killing fields. Even with the advantage of numbers, the Allied losses were enormous. On Omaha Beach, 2,374 Allied troops were wounded or killed on D-Day; on Juno Beach, 805; on Sword Beach, 630; on Gold Beach, 413; on Utah Beach, 197.[6]

Those who made it through faced still more obstacles. One soldier who landed at Omaha Beach recalled the difficulty of running, in full gear and under fire, across a beach that was not sand, but smooth, slippery pebbles: "It was like running on a bed of marbles that would displace as you ran on it, and the footing was very bad. You couldn't dig a slip trench because the stones would just slide right back into the hole. You couldn't find any shelter for yourself on that beach." When he finally climbed, through barbed wire, to the crest of a hill that gave him a little shelter, wheezing from smoke inhalation, he saw a landing craft in the water below go up in flames: "Before the men started to disembark, a shell hit that ship, and I have never seen anything go so quickly. I don't think there was a living soul that was able to get away from that vessel alive. It went up just like a charcoal fire. Poof! It was a mass of flames. I don't know how many men in the [landing craft] perished, but by the size of that ship, there must have been about two hundred men on that vessel. We lost two hundred men in one instant."[7]

But the Allies had one last advantage that day: the element of surprise. The officers in charge of the landings—General Dwight Eisenhower, the leader of the invasion force as a whole, and General Bernard Montgomery, the leader of the ground troops in the invasion—kept the date and place of the landings a secret; and this secret, which the invasion's planners protected using strict security measures, like code names, kept the Germans from massing even stronger forces on the target beaches. (The code name for the naval landings was Operation Neptune, and the code name for the invasion itself was Operation Overlord.[8])

When the sun set on D-Day, the Allies had secured a tentative foothold on all six of their target beaches. The Battle of Normandy would continue for another eleven weeks, but thanks to superior numbers, firepower, and payment in blood and bullets, it ultimately ended in victory. The battle was a turning point in the war, shifting the balance of power in Europe in the Allies' favor.

That's the war that everybody saw. And this war was, in almost a historical first, *the war that everybody saw*: thoroughly documented, publicized, analyzed, with the new technologies of photography, film, radio, telephony, telegraphy, radar, and more. During the D-Day landings, a huge share of Americans listened to the radio broadcasts of George Hicks and Wright Bryan, who reported live from the Normandy coast.[9] As early as D+1, June 7, readers of American newspapers could follow the movements of Allied troops the day before in nearly ten-minute increments. The dispatches described, in addition to what beachheads had been seized, how many German divisions were generally thought to be in France, where the next landings would likely be, the curtains of dark smoke that hung over the coast, the hiss and splash of enemy shells hitting the water, the continuous din of guns, and the ominous crimson explosions that lit the beaches at night. Images accompanied the stories.[10]

So much was seen by so many that one might wonder what an intelligence service could possibly know that the rest of the world didn't.

But what everybody saw wasn't the whole picture. In the midst of the most visible war in history, in the midst of the most visible *battle* in history, that ghost war was also raging—invisible to all but the spies whose world this book has been exploring. Because if observers were everywhere, then you had to fool them into making a mistake by believing what they saw.

FAKING IT

What is a ghost war? A ghost war is a war of deception, a war of phantoms. It's a war in which the enemy fights against phantoms that *you* deploy. Phantoms made of greasepaint, made of chicken wire, made of tinsel and burlap and chattering unattended radios. Phantoms made—and this is the edge that makes the knife sharp—of the enemy's own beliefs and desires. (A number of groups were involved in dreaming up and coordinating ghost war tactics, including the OSS and the SOE.)

According to Barton Whaley, a postwar scholar who specialized in military deception, what most people think of when they think of military deception is what he calls *security*. Security means all the different forms of keeping things secret. Hiding your real plans. Like the date and place of the landings for the Normandy invasion. If someone asked you how to plan a military operation in such a way that you surprise the enemy, you'd probably start describing tactics that fall under the rubric of security, Whaley says. But the truth is that security can't hide a truly large operation: "With rare exceptions, even the tightest security measures guard against disclosure only to the most naïve, preoccupied, witless, incompetent, or unlucky enemy."[11]

If secrets won't protect a large operation, what will? Whaley's answer is deception: the active spreading of falsehoods. The French call this act *intoxication*, a word that suggests how falsehoods can impair or disable. The word also suggests how falsehoods can have a kind of allure, like drinks at a party.[12]

"The ultimate goal of stratagem," Whaley says, referring to military deception, "is to make the enemy quite certain, very decisive, and *wrong*."[13]

However, he cautions that everyday exposure to deception—even everyday *practice* in it—won't necessarily make someone good at military deception. The insincerities that get you by in the office, on the cocktail circuit, or on the campaign trail are of little help when you want to send an opposing army in the wrong direction.[14]

To see how awkwardly someone can fumble a deception operation if they don't have the right training, consider an event that happened in 1943 in New Mexico. J. Robert Oppenheimer, the head of the Manhattan Project, had a problem: he worried that the residents of the nearby city of Santa Fe might be getting curious about the top-secret work being done at Los Alamos. So he ordered one of his physicists, Robert Serber, to spread a false story in Santa Fe.

Oppenheimer's plan was simple: visit a bar and talk loudly about how the scientists at Los Alamos were building an electric rocket. But when Serber and some of his colleagues went to the bar and struck up their conversation, they found that nobody seemed to care what they were saying. They talked louder. Nothing. Finally, Serber walked up to one of the bar's patrons and shouted in his face, "Do you know what we're doing at Los Alamos? We're building an electric rocket!"

Even after this memorable display, word did not go around Santa Fe that the scientists at Los Alamos were building an electric rocket. (The FBI and Army Intelligence were keeping an ear out.)[15] Good deception requires more than a loud voice and a lie. Good deception is an art.

WAR PAINT

During World War II, the Allies didn't have extensive training in military deception. But they had a brilliant idea to bridge that gap in their knowledge, which was to turn to artists for help.[16]

That's because effective deception requires two things, and the first is the skill with which false signals are deployed. This is where artists excel. A photographer knows the tricks of photography, a painter knows the tricks of creating illusions, a set designer knows the tricks of building realistic props, an actor knows the tricks of maintaining a fake persona, and a writer knows the tricks of creating compelling characters.

In fact, one of the great innovations in modern military deception—camouflage—came from an artist, a painter named Abbott Handerson Thayer. Thayer, a graduate of Brooklyn Art School, spent his school years sketching animals in the Central Park Zoo and started his professional career by selling paintings of them.[17] In 1896, he began publishing articles in biology journals about what he called "protective coloration," and in 1909, he published a book with his son that described, with an artist's sensitivity, how animals use coloration to camouflage themselves in different environments.[18] The book made a splash; it even caught the attention of Theodore Roosevelt, the former president, who wrote a response arguing that Thayer overestimated the importance of coloration due to his "artistic temperament." (Roosevelt, a big-game hunter who took pride in his manly reputation, seems to have taken offense at the idea that animals might use something as froufrou as coloring to survive.)[19]

Soon after World War I broke out in 1914, combatants realized they had a new kind of problem: how to hide troops on the ground from airplanes.[20] Some artists who were fighting in the French infantry remembered Thayer's principles and started smearing paint on their uniforms. The gambit worked, and soon everyone was talking about the new military strategy that the French called "camouflage," after a slang word for *disguise*.[21]

But despite the successes of camouflage during World War I, many military leaders were skeptical of anything that came from such a bohemian source. (In 1918, a U.S. Army officer, seeing French camouflage specialists at work with their paintbrushes, groused, "Oh God, as if we didn't have enough trouble! They send us artists!")[22] They thought of disguise as cowardly, frilly, even womanly.[23] Nonetheless, artists took pride in their contribution to the war effort. In her 1933 autobiography, the poet Gertrude Stein recalls strolling through Paris in 1915 with Pablo Picasso. They spotted some military equipment painted with camouflage patterns, which neither had ever seen. Picasso was delighted. "*C'est nous qui avons fait ça,*" he told her. "It is we that have created that."[24]

And so, during World War II, it fell to artists once again to invite the muses to war. The ghost war relied not just on painters, but on set designers, directors, and professional actors: habitués of the stage and screen who made the theater of war a literal *theater of war*.

But set design only works if it fits the play. First, the Allies needed to tell a story that would captivate its audience.

HITLER'S INTUITION

The second key to effective military deception is finding the lie that your enemy already believes. This relies not just on the art of storytelling, but on the science of psychology. Research has found that people often assess new information with a considerable bias, and sometimes they simply refuse to believe information that doesn't match their existing opinions. (Confirmation bias, psychologists call it: one of the most famous, most stubborn human flaws.) This means that even a crude lie, an obvious lie, can succeed in fooling the enemy, if it fits your enemy's beliefs. You just need to understand which of the enemy's beliefs will work on your behalf. "The fact is," wrote Cynthia Grabo, an intelligence analyst who stayed with the CIA after the war, "the most successful of all deception plans and operations are those which capitalize on and actively encourage the enemy to believe his own preconceptions."[25]

Here's what the Germans believed about the planned invasion. They knew, once Allied forces started gathering in England, that the assault would hit the coast of France, right across the English Channel. After all, the Allies would need to use fighter planes, and these had a relatively short flying range. And besides, all those troops and ships hanging around the English coastline were clearly preparing for something. But they weren't assembling in England in order to start a trip all the way around Spain, Portugal, and the boot of Italy and then attack the Continent on the coast of Trieste.*

---

* An MI5 officer later lamented, "By the early spring of 1944, it was utterly impossible to disguise the fact that the major attack would come somewhere between the Cherbourg peninsula and Dunkirk; the true preparations, which could not be wholly disguised, indicated this beyond all doubt, and the distance from the base at which fighter cover could be supplied helped define the limits." Ben Macintyre, *Double Cross* (New York: Bloomsbury, 2012), 2; Seymour Reit, *Masquerade: The Amazing Camouflage Deceptions of World War II* (New York: Hawthorn Books, 1978), 33–37.

However, the Germans also believed that the Allies would need to claim a large port early on, which made them assume that the Allies wouldn't target the Normandy coast, which is exactly where the Allies were planning to land. The coast was too shallow and dangerous, the Germans thought, to moor the huge ships they'd need for an invasion. They didn't know that the Allies had devised floating artificial ports— called Mulberries, made of steel and concrete and pulled by a fleet of tugboats as big as the Spanish Armada—that would give the ships the deep-water ports they needed.*

High-ranking Nazis praised what they called "Hitler's intuition": his supposed ability to anticipate his enemies' every move on the battlefield. Hitler himself took great pride in his military instincts, which he regarded as almost supernatural.[26] His intuition told him, now, that the Allies would direct the invasion at the Pas-de-Calais, a little coast opposite Dover. The towns there had harbors deep enough to accommodate huge military ships, and the roads provided excellent access for an army to roll toward Paris. No other target could be as strategically advantageous, Hitler said: "It is here that the enemy must and will attack, and it is here—unless all the indications are misleading—that the decisive battle against the landing forces will be fought."[27]

Hitler also believed that Norway would play a crucial role in the coming fight. Well, this was more than a belief; it was a preoccupation that he held for reasons that went beyond the actual evidence. Sometime in the 1930s, Hitler read a book by a German admiral, titled *The Naval Strategy of the World War*, that argued that Germany lost the First World War because much of its fleet was trapped in a corner of the North Sea. The only way to win a world war was to hold Norway and its ports, the book said.[28]

---

* In fact, Allied engineers devised all kinds of clever contrivances to make the invasion work on that unforgiving coast: Mulberries; Gooseberries, or lines of ships that the Allies planned to sink around the Mulberries to create breakwaters as protection from rough surf; unrollable steel netting to make airfields of soft beachfront land; fuel pipelines that Allied submarines made ready to lay under the English Channel—in a project code-named Pluto, for "Pipe Line Under the Ocean." Macintyre, *Double Cross*, 3–4; Hans Speidel, *Invasion 1944: Rommel and the Normandy Campaign* (Chicago: Henry Regnery Company, 1950): 20–33.

And so, with the monomania of a man who has Read an Important Book, Hitler guarded Norway with some of his strongest, fiercest forces—including, for a while, the majority of his submarines and every one of his flagships. In November 1943, he had in Norway some 380,000 troops, a tank division, and a substantial air fleet.[29] During the winter and spring that followed, as he waited for the Allies to launch their invasion, he expanded his force in Norway to 400,000 troops.[30] Perhaps the Allies were planning to strike Norway while the Germans were distracted with the upcoming fracas in the Pas-de-Calais: a one-two punch.

He also amassed tremendous forces in the Pas-de-Calais. More than that, he made the Pas-de-Calais the launch site for the "secret weapon" that his engineers had been building, which turned out to be the V1 pilotless flying bomb. The V1 was, indeed, impressive: it could travel a distance of 160 miles, and it detonated with the strength of a four-thousand-pound bomb. In May 1944, Hitler finalized a plan to launch these weapons from the Pas-de-Calais. London, his target, would be utterly obliterated, and the invasion would end before it began. He chose a launch date that, according to his intuition and his intelligence services' very best findings, would be the eve of the invasion: June 16, 1944. He was off by ten days.[31]

But we're getting ahead of ourselves. Hitler believed a lot of untrue things about the Allies' plans. But we can change what we believe when we see new evidence. Hitler didn't. The genius of the Allies was their ability to keep him believing those untrue things even after new evidence contradicted them. They used the science of psychology against him and his generals and his intelligence agents. Because, as they had learned from Operation Mincemeat, we love to see our assumptions confirmed.

THE THEATER OF WAR

That was the story. Now, back to the set design.

Let's start in the world capital of deception: Los Angeles, California. Or, to be accurate, a few miles outside of Los Angeles, where, in 1942, the air force set up a camouflage training school. The school resembled a studio lot, abounding, as one historian observes, with "art directors, scenic designers, painters, animators, landscape artists, lighting experts, carpenters, and prop men" who had worked, before the war, for film studios such as Disney Studios, MGM, Twentieth Century Fox, Universal Pictures, and Warner Bros.[32]

"None of those people had the slightest bit of know-how," a military staffer later said, referring to their fighting experience, "but they sure made up for it with their energy."[33]

The reason these Hollywood types were suddenly in demand was that advances in film media had changed the game of military camouflage. During World War I, the U.S. military only needed to hide things from enemies at ground level, so they painted zebra stripes on their tanks and ships, which made it hard for enemies observing from the side to tell the direction a given vehicle was moving. By World War II, the problem was how to hide things from pilots who took photographs from above.[34] So camouflage experts needed to design new tricks to fool cameras. (The word for someone who creates camouflage, wonderfully, is *camoufleur*.)

The black-and-white cameras of the 1930s and '40s rendered color in shades of gray that didn't match up with how the human eye perceives colors. This is why, if you see color photographs of actors wearing makeup for old films and television shows, the colors they're wearing might look unsettling: bluish lipstick, yellow foundation. (Rudolph Valentino, an Italian actor who became Old Hollywood's definition of *tall, dark, and handsome*, had a dark complexion that kept him from getting cast as a hero until the visionary makeup artist Max Factor came in to devise a makeup solution. Valentino had tried to lighten his skin using pink foundation, which, on film, looked white as a drowned corpse; Factor switched it out for deep yellow. When the director saw him applying the foundation to Valentino for a screen test, he shouted, "Not that! Not THAT! . . . He's too dark as it is." But Factor knew his business, and the screen tests showed Valentino with a skin tone that matched his costars. The yellow foundation stayed.[35])

So a camoufleur who wanted to paint a tarp to match a grass lawn would choose gray, not green, since the green paint that would fool a human eye would show up lighter than the grass on film.[36] The instructors at the Los Angeles camouflage school knew this principle as well as they knew dailies, marks, lighting, and blocking; at other camouflage schools around the country, the instructors likewise tended to be professionals in fields that required them to know not just color, but value and hue: painters, Broadway set designers, fashion designers, interior designers.[37]

Camouflage has two main forms: *concealment* and *confusion*. Concealment entails hiding the offending object altogether—for instance, using canvas, chicken wire, and foliage to hide an ammunitions dump in a forest. Here, again, World War II camoufleurs often worked with an eye to aerial photographs, ensuring that a camouflage never cast a shadow that looked like, say, the profile of a tank.[38]

Confusion entails dressing up the offending object so it looks like something innocent. A 1941 article in *Life* magazine, written by an army camouflage expert, shows, as an example, a photograph of what looks like a farm shack in the countryside, with a farmer and his wife, who wears a short-sleeved dress, resting in the sun beside it. Another photograph shows the shack's walls and roof unfolding like the sides of a stage set: "The roar of an airplane is heard in the sky so down come the walls and out pops an anti-aircraft machine gun." Finally, we see a figure in a cotton dress aiming a huge anti-aircraft gun at the sky, ready to shred: "the farmer's 'wife' turns out to be the crack gunner of the outfit."[39]

Operation Mincemeat was arguably confusion camouflage, too, though its misdirection went the other way: dress up something innocent so it looks like something dangerous. One of the lessons of Mincemeat for this kind of deception was that even fake clues can put real people in mortal peril. Forge a few papers to plant on a corpse, what's the harm in that? But then—how do you forge the corpse? "Does anyone know whether we can get a body?" was the first question that agents raised during the planning for what became Mincemeat, and getting a body that would pass for a soldier who had died in a plane crash at sea turned out to be remarkably difficult. For a time, the agents running the operation thought they would need to kill someone in order to get the forensic details right: "to do a Burke and Hare," in one agent's words.[40] Luckily, they found a body that would do the job before they decided to get some poor soul drunk and suffocate him with a pillow, as the murderers William Burke and William Hare famously did in the 1820s when—seeking forensically "clean" cadavers they could sell to medical schools, which used the cadavers for anatomy lessons—they killed and sold sixteen victims.

The Allies started talking about Normandy as their target in November 1943, when Franklin Roosevelt, Winston Churchill, and Joseph Stalin met in Tehran to plan the great Overlord invasion. During the six months that passed between the Tehran conference and D-Day, the Allies used all kinds of confusion camouflage to persuade the Axis, as they had with Mincemeat, that they planned to attack somewhere other than where they really did. While Mincemeat gave a false identity to a dead body, the Normandy deception operations used living bodies, sending around whole corps of soldiers, called "deception units," that sought to mislead the enemy about the Allies' plans and positions. In this ploy, a lieutenant might stick extra stars on his field jacket and do his best impression of a general—riding around in a jeep, visiting cafés, barking orders at comrades who had to salute him even though he didn't really outrank them.[41]

Traveling with the deception units were "camouflage battalions": units of engineers charged with deceiving enemy eyes, either by hiding real military assets or building fake ones. These battalions drew on the lessons of the theatrical set builders who taught at the camouflage schools. In theaters, as in theaters of war, set builders valorize speed, efficiency, and the clever use of materials. Camouflage troops building decoys often had to make do with what was at hand: burlap, canvas, cardboard boxes, chicken wire, tin cans, and wooden crates. With these unlikely materials, they could work miracles: creating, for instance, what a pilot looking down from thirty thousand feet saw as a fully operational airfield, complete with fuel tanks, planes, and runways, but was in fact a pile of garbage arranged in a *trompe l'oeil* sculpture.[42]

All over Europe, deception units made maneuvers that suggested the Allies planned assaults on Norway, Italy, the Pas-de-Calais—

anywhere but the Normandy coast. After the Allies took over Corsica in late 1943, for example, they made a big show of moving a handful of fighter planes and assault ships to the harbor town of Bastia, which offered an obvious launching point for an assault on the coast of northern Italy. A small group of wireless operators worked up enough radio traffic to simulate the communications of a whole army. Allied intelligence soon noted, with gratification, that the Luftwaffe had greatly increased its surveillance of Corsica, a sign that the Germans thought the island was an important Allied air base.[43] It wasn't.

In March 1944, General Patton's Seventh Army—which was part of the force that captured Sicily, thanks to Mincemeat—secretly decamped from Sicily to Naples in preparation for the Normandy invasion. Not wanting the Germans to find out they were assembling closer to France, they left behind a deception unit that aimed to give the impression that the Seventh Army never left.[44] Patton got in on the fun, visiting Cairo for a week and wandering around gawking at the pyramids like a wide-eyed sightseer, with the aim of making the Germans think his Seventh Army in Sicily was coordinating with the Polish Corps in Cairo. Just in case the informants who saw him in Egypt failed to make anything of the show, a photograph of Patton in Egypt found its way—*whoops*—to a picture magazine in Istanbul, the city of spies. The photograph showed Patton sharing a laugh with the general of the Polish Corps. On the Polish general's shoulder—barely visible, but people like to feel rewarded for having sharp eyes—you can see the insignia of the Seventh Army, surely another sign that the two forces were coordinating.[45]

In Algiers, intelligence agents printed fake pamphlets—like the ones they passed out among troops in new regions, explaining things like how to get along with the locals—titled "THINGS WORTH SAVING AND WHAT TO DO ABOUT THEM." The pamphlets described monuments in Livorno and Pisa that the troops must take care not to damage when they entered those cities. They sent the pamphlets to Patton's deception unit in Sicily; the actor-soldiers were dutifully careless about leaving them where civilians could find them.

Historians later judged that the pamphlet trick probably did a lot of good in advancing the Allied deception.[46]

THE UNDERSTUDY

Just as the stage dressing of camouflage was often the work of Hollywood and Broadway professionals, many of the players who animated the scripts of the Allies' deceptive maneuvers were professional entertainers. To hold the attention of the Germans, the Allies deployed actors to march around, playing soldiers and generals in places where the real soldiers and generals weren't.

One such entertainer was M. E. Clifton James, an Australian actor who was working as a pay clerk in the British Army when he received a call, in May 1944, from the Hollywood star David Niven. Niven, then a colonel in the British Army's film section, told James to report to London straightaway, as he would be needed to help make some army films.[*]

But this was no ordinary acting job. Allied intelligence had been searching for someone who could pass for the British general Bernard Montgomery, whose movements the Germans watched closely. James had an uncanny resemblance to Montgomery. An officer in British intelligence who had been a drama critic in civilian life remembered seeing a photo of James in a newspaper and dug through Fleet Street's morgues until he matched the face with a name.

"You have been chosen to act as the double of General Montgomery before D-Day," James was told at the meeting in London. "It is our business to trick the enemy and perhaps save the lives of thousands of men."[47]

After studying Montgomery's voice, his manner, his personal habits—the general had a habit of folding his hands behind his back, which was fortunate for James, who had a fake finger to replace a

---

[*] The call was so out of left field that James wondered whether it was an enemy hoax: "I had an imaginary preview of a thrilling screen drama in which a glamorous enemy spy spread alarm and confusion by vamping a pay clerk and persuading him to falsify the accounts." M. E. Clifton James, *I Was Monty's Double* (London: Rider and Company, 1954): 5–6.

missing one—James posed as Montgomery on a tour of Gibraltar and Algiers, pretending to be on a secret mission to plan an invasion of southern France from North Africa.[48] The ruse worked, and Hitler's spies reported back to Berlin on Montgomery's plans in Africa—which proved to be a great help on D-Day, because it distracted them from realizing what would be happening in Normandy, making them focus on this potential invasion instead.

Throughout his memoir about the operation, James describes using his knowledge of the theater to whomp up relevant experience in a field, spycraft, that he had never worked in. For example, he says of his landing at Gibraltar: "It was like the setting for one of those large-scale dramas which, in the old days, were staged at Drury Lane. In the background, like a vividly painted backcloth, rose the Rock. On the stage were the actors awaiting the entrance of the Leading Man. Behind were the troops, and on my left the high-ranking officers of the three Services drawn up to attention. On my right was another group and a line of cars with their drivers standing to attention beside them. There were even the 'Villains of the Piece,' Hitler's agents disguised as honest Spanish workmen."[49]

The ruse worked so well because it played on what the Germans already believed about Montgomery. The Germans knew that "Monty" was given to surprising moves. They knew that rumors were going around that he was engaged in some sort of secret undertaking: "These rumors had been spread all along the African coast through indiscreet telegrams, whispered reports in native bazaars, and even unguarded talk in brothels."[50] They also knew that he had a distinctive twin-tap salute, walked about with a leisurely gait, wore a gold watch chain, and was a dry, confident speaker.[51] The Allies simply gave the Germans one and one and one, and let the Germans add them up to three.

The Germans' delight at their own cleverness no doubt helped to sell them on the story. What reader doesn't love to guess the ending?

THE PEARL OF THE BOSPORUS

The ghost war waged in every theater, and Istanbul was no exception. And no one could craft a plot twist like Joseph Curtiss. When Curtiss set up the double-cross unit in Istanbul, he was preparing for exactly this kind of moment. He knew the enemy's beliefs intimately, because his unit was expert in the art of turning enemy agents into double agents. The German agents whom his unit (and others like it across Europe) turned into double agents gave the Allies valuable information about how the enemy's intelligence worked; shared the questions that the Germans asked them to find answers to, which gave the Allies insights into the enemy's plans; and of course, sent home answers that *shaped* what the Germans were planning.[52] So, when the time came for the war's most high-stakes deception, the pieces on the enemy's side of the board were broadly where the OSS wanted them to be, and the people responsible for moving those pieces had ideas about how to play the game.

But Curtiss's unit didn't just turn enemy agents into double agents. It also convinced many to become outright defectors. The defections were the real masterstroke of Istanbul's X-2 agents. Within a single year, six German Abwehr agents in Istanbul defected. These open rebellions must mean, Hitler realized, that even more Abwehr agents were working with the Allies in secret.[53]

These defections infuriated the Führer. Perhaps the last straw for him was the defection of Erich Vermehren, a young German lawyer who was hired in 1943 by the head of the Abwehr in Turkey, Paul Leverkühn, to join the office in Istanbul. Leverkühn, his position in the Abwehr notwithstanding, was an anti-Nazi, and he knew perfectly well that Vermehren was an anti-Nazi, too. (When he was a teenager, he lost out on a Rhodes Scholarship for refusing to join the Hitler Youth.)

Perhaps Leverkühn intended for Vermehren to quietly undermine the Abwehr, as he himself was doing. Instead, Vermehren got out of Dodge altogether, flying to London in January 1944. (Vermehren called in sick to the office, then left town with his wife and an Allied escort. He was "out sick" for a week before the Abwehr realized anything was amiss.)[54]

Vermehren's defection was a very public embarrassment for Germany, since the Allied press quickly started circulating stories about the highly placed young German couple who defected "because they were disgusted with Nazi brutality."[55] For some time, Hitler had been unhappy with the Abwehr's performance, especially in Turkey. Now, he decided to cut off the problem at the head. In February 1944, he fired the head of the Abwehr—Wilhelm Canaris, who until now had been Hitler's chief of intelligence—and dissolved the Abwehr altogether, moving its agents into the Reich Security Main Office (*Reichssicherheitshauptamt*, or RSHA), a police intelligence organization under Heinrich Himmler. (For good measure, he also fired Leverkühn and yanked him out of Istanbul.)[56]

It was a drastic move at the worst possible time for the Germans. Right when the Allies were preparing for what everyone agreed might well be the decisive battle of the war, Hitler started making major changes to the Nazi intelligence system, destabilizing the Nazis' flow of intelligence. The work of integrating the two services was, as one might imagine, a huge bureaucratic hassle, only settling down in May. That is a dangerously long time to have one's intelligence services in disarray. The Abwehr's move to the RSHA disrupted the work of least twenty-two thousand agents, German informants said after the war.[57]

More than this, Himmler's favored branch of the RSHA, the SS Security Service (*Sicherheitsdienst*, or SD), purged thousands of Abwehr officers to make room for its own. Yet, as a police organization, the SD was predictably better at policing than military intelligence. Its agents tended to be the kind of men who want to go into police work in a police state, which is to say they enjoyed conducting brutal interrogations and exerting control over civilians, but didn't care so much for the kind of subtle, ink-stained analysis that modern spycraft relies on.[58]

After the war, history would sing the praises of the double-cross system for its successes in maneuvering the Germans to play the game as the Allies wanted. But the double-cross unit in Istanbul managed to achieve something truly remarkable: it convinced Hitler to remove some of his own pieces from the board.

"THIS IS LONDON! THE FRENCH SPEAKING TO THE FRENCH . . ."

In France, the Allies used different tactics. Maurice Buckmaster, the head of the French section of the SOE, later described the long con that British and American intelligence pulled on the Germans in advance of D-Day by carefully contaminating the messages that they sent out over the radio and through the currents of rumor that passed from mouth to mouth in France.[59] Every night at 7:00 p.m., the BBC aired a special program for France, spoken *en français* so that French people could understand it. The French authorities forbade anyone to listen, under threat of punishments that went up to twelve months of hard labor; but plenty of civilians took the risk of listening anyway, with the lights off and their windows shut tight to keep the sound of tinny voices from making its way to the street.[60] (The broadcast always began with the opening bars of Beethoven's Fifth Symphony: da-da-da-*dum*, or dot-dot-dot-dash, which is Morse code for the letter *V. V for victory.*)

Along with encouraging messages that Charles de Gaulle, the leader of the Free French Forces, and others worked up for the French populace, the BBC broadcast always included what Allied intelligence called *messages personnels:* personal messages for a selected number of the 306 Resistance cells that were listening in from all over France. These messages took the form of code phrases, so that the Germans, who were also listening in, couldn't tell what they meant. *The cassoulet has gone cold. The winters of my childhood were long seasons.* That sort of thing.[61]

The Resistance cells didn't know about each other, or at least about each other's members; that way, nobody could give his compatriots away even if he was under arrest—even if he was being tortured—and the Germans couldn't infiltrate the whole network even if they infiltrated a single cell. The cells also didn't know when the long-expected invasion of Europe would arrive, although they knew what *message personnel* would tell them it was imminent, and they knew what tasks they must carry out as soon as that message came. "In almost every *département* of France," Buckmaster said, referring to the nation's administrative districts, "our men waited—waited for the signal that the great day was at hand."[62]

While they waited, saboteurs destroyed bridges and railroads, following the directions of those *messages personnels*, that the Germans might try to use later to send reinforcements to Normandy. Allied war planners were careful when choosing targets for the saboteurs to attack. They needed the sabotage to support the coming invasion at Normandy, but they needed the *pattern of sabotage* to *look* like they were preparing for an invasion in the Pas-de-Calais. So, for example, they took out bridges over the Seine River—a whopping thirty-six of them between late April and early June—but not bridges over the Loire River, which offered access to Normandy but not the Pas-de-Calais.[63]

Though the planners of Mincemeat did not, in the end, need to commit murder to obtain their body, the planners of this campaign of sabotage did commit to sending innocent civilians, as well as their own people, to their deaths. In fact, when they commissioned a professor named Solly Zuckerman to write up "a plan for a ninety-day attack against eighty rail targets in western Europe," he estimated that the casualties in France and Belgium would be twenty thousand deaths and sixty thousand injuries. The British War Cabinet objected to the plan, saying that enacting it meant "we should build up a volume of dull hatred in France which would affect our relations with that country for many years to come," but Dwight Eisenhower, the man in charge of all things Normandy, deemed these casualties a necessary sacrifice. Destroying those railroads could keep the Germans from bringing their full strength to Normandy for a full month and a half, according to Zuckerman's estimates.[64]

All of which is to say that ghost wars have real casualties; that, in the theater of warfare, scriptwriters and stage designers and actors might be called to dress a set with fictions and props, but when the curtain falls, real bodies lie on the stage. A French railroad official whom the Allies snuck over to London from France to help plan the sabotage campaign quit in May after he heard a Nazi-controlled French radio station report the troubles he was causing: "The French railway system is in complete chaos. The Allies have successfully pulverized into rubble whole marshalling yards. . . . The temper of the population, especially that of Paris, is rising because no food is available, nobody can travel, and there are severe restrictions in the use of electricity."[65]

In fact, before D-Day, Allied fighters and saboteurs got killed more often in the fictional target areas than the actual target area. In a military strategy that may at first seem counterintuitive, the Allies conducted sabotage and aerial bombing missions in the Pas-de-Calais with frequency equal to, and often greater than, those in Normandy, in order to keep the Germans believing the Pas-de-Calais was the target.[66] Precisely because the deception was working, the Germans had stronger defenses in the Pas-de-Calais than in Normandy, which meant that the Allied pilots who flew on missions over the Pas-de-Calais to drop bombs, perform reconnaissance, or drop supplies for underground Resistance cells got hurt and killed at higher rates than the ones who flew on preinvasion missions over Normandy. The pilots on these missions didn't know their missions were in the service of fiction; and their deaths, of course, were very real.[67]

LE FAUX SEMBLANT

Throughout the ghost war, and especially in the lead-up to the invasion of Normandy, deception principles from Mincemeat served the Allies well. An important one: Secrets aren't secure. The planned invasion of Sicily, which Mincemeat sought to obscure, could only happen after the successful invasion of North Africa. But by the same token, the invasion of North Africa made it inevitable that the Allies would use North Africa as a launching point for further operations. "In spite of all that could be done in the way of security, it was apparent to everyone that the Allies would not just sit back indefinitely: there must be an invasion somewhere," said Ewen Montagu, the operation's leader. "Therefore we could not hope to prevent the Germans knowing that there *was* an operation afoot."[68]

But even if the Germans learned that Sicily was the target of the invasion, the Allies had a plan for that too. Major Martin's letter said that, though the Allies planned to invade Greece and Sardinia, they would send the Germans false intelligence that their *real* target was Sicily. "It seemed to me that the beauty of this was that if there were any actual leakage of our real plans, the Germans would think that what was in fact a leakage was only part of the cover that they had read about in the letter," Montagu said. "If they swallowed our deception—that one letter—they would disbelieve any genuine information that might leak through."[69]

They even referred, in the letter, to the fake operation against Greece by the code name Husky—the actual name of the Sicily plans. If the word *Husky* had reached German ears, they would be all the more likely to believe the fake letter.[70]

So it was with the nightly sabotage coups and radio broadcasts that went out throughout France in the days and months ahead of D-Day. The *messages personnels* included real messages, but they always included a lot of fake messages too. In this way, the Allies distracted the Germans, aiming to keep them busy with useless information and prevent them from finding patterns that would help them interpret the legitimate messages. (Buckmaster, the head of the SOE's French Section, called these fake messages "blinds."[71]) Flooding the information stream with garbage was one way to hide items that were available to everyone; you couldn't keep them secret, but you could make decoys look more significant.

Montagu's job was to give his audience such an appealing interpretive through line that they'd treat such pesky details as outlying data. The satisfaction of assembling the pieces of Major Martin's life into a good story might well prompt the Germans to ignore any incongruities that lingered in his death. So Montagu planted details all over the body that aimed, he said—quoting the dramatist W. S. Gilbert—to give "artistic verisimilitude to an otherwise bald and unconvincing narrative." Martin wasn't just carrying a letter from one superior to another; the letter was, in Montagu's words, "the old boy type": a chummy bit of back-channel slander where the sender and recipient talked over the heads of those who hadn't gone to public school. Martin didn't just have a fiancée, he had a fiancée he got serious with too quickly, as happened so often under the pressure of the war, and her father didn't approve of the match. His "pocket litter," to use the term that spies applied to the documents that agents kept in their pockets to corroborate their cover stories, showed that he had trouble with money, that he was so keen to buy an engagement ring that he did so even though his bank account was already overdrawn, and that he smoked a brand of cigarettes whose advertisements celebrated the glories of the British navy.[72]

Humans are remarkably willing to lie to themselves in order to preserve a story that entertains them or aligns with their understanding of the world. Journalists, for instance, often use the phrase "too good to check" to refer to stories that nobody wants to fact-check because they're so fun to believe that people actively fight for them over the truth. Montagu gave Martin a piece of pocket litter with an address written on it ("The Manor House, Ogbourne St. George, Marlborough, Wiltshire") that was so English, he thought, that the Germans would love it and *want* to believe it.[73]

The Allies did the same thing in the weeks leading up to the invasion of Normandy. The British knew from American intelligence, as well as from their own decryptions (called Project Ultra) of secret German radio traffic, that much of the German military brass believed, with Hitler, that the Allies were planning to land at Pas-de-Calais. So they asked their most trustworthy agents to confide to their least trustworthy confidants that, in the nightly BBC broadcast, "any reference to soup was to the Pas-de-Calais." The news was sure to reach the secret police; after all, double-dealers are popular because they talk to everyone. And then—to sweeten the bait—they started referring to soup *constantly* in the blinds. *"Monsieur Gérard aime le potage"*—Mr. Gerard likes soup. *"Caroline démande du bouillon"*—Caroline asks for broth. Now the blinds were doing double work: giving the Germans useless work *and* dropping a breadcrumb trail away from the truth. The Germans dutifully rerouted more troops to Calais.[74]

Another truth about deception that worked in Mincemeat: people aren't inclined to believe what the historian Anthony Cave Brown calls "a lie too easily obtained."[75] If you drop an official letter containing a false narrative outside an embassy, the diplomats will probably figure out the letter is a plant. But though we may suspect that our enemies lie, we tend to believe that our *friends* tell the truth. Or at least that they have good judgment. One of the hooks that made the Mincemeat story plausible to the Germans—even though the idea of a body washing onshore chained to a suitcase of secret letters was, as Mincemeat's planners acknowledged, implausible—was that the Spanish got hold of the body, not the Germans. The Spanish provided an extra layer of supposed due diligence between the lie and its intended audience.

HOLLYWOOD NORTH

Here's an example of those deception principles at work—an example that also shows the Allies using Hollywood less covertly than usual as a weapon, this time as a glamour offensive. In the spring of 1944, Stanton Griffis, a fifty-five-year-old Paramount executive with a round face and the perennial smirk of a man who has mastered the Hollywood party circuit, went to Stockholm to broker a deal. He had already visited the city soon after the United States joined the war, ostensibly as a talent scout for his film studio. But his public duties of drinking *brännvin* with pouty blondes concealed a secret OSS mission: behind the scenes, he was gathering information on Sweden—in particular, its trade with Germany in iron, steel, and those all-important ball bearings.[76]

Now, he was in Stockholm to charm the Swedes into stopping the flow of ball bearings. "How do you know that any of our ball bearings have ever helped to kill an American boy?" a Swede asked Griffis at one point in the negotiations. Griffis's colleague whipped some ball bearings from his pocket and placed them on the table, asking, "Where were these made?" After a moment of scrutiny, the Swede said, "Yes, these were all made in our factories, where did you get them?" Griffis's colleague replied, "Every one of these was taken from a German airplane shot down over London."[77]

The Swedish government believed the Germans would win the war, and thus didn't want to lose a friendly trade agreement with the

Third Reich, but Griffis and his colleagues got them to agree to stop shipping ball bearings while the trade negotiations with the Allies took place. A small grace—but timing is everything, and in early 1944, that small grace was worth a lot. Right when Hitler was trying to ramp up war production to make ready for the biggest fight of the war, he lost his best supply of a little part that his fighting machines couldn't do without. Eventually, Griffis wore down his opponents with his very best Hollywood boardroom tactics—what a historian later called "a judicious mixture of black-list threats, promises of compensating Allied commercial orders, and businessman-to-businessman persuasion." The Swedes sold the Americans some $6 million worth of ball bearings—around $100 million today—and promised to satisfy its German quotas with ball bearings that didn't suit the needs of war manufacturing.[78]

That wasn't the end of OSS maneuvers in Stockholm. At the same time that Griffis was wheeling and dealing, OSS agents all across the city were whispering about Norway. Recall that Hitler thought holding Norway was key to winning the war, and that he therefore kept a huge number of troops stationed there. The OSS aimed to tell a story that played on that belief and made sure those troops *stayed* in Norway.

American engineers went around Stockholm asking, not too discreetly, how much weight Swedish trains could bear, and made noises that hinted they were thinking about the particulars of moving freight from Norway to Sweden. Swedish photographers took pictures of British surveyors measuring the height of railway tunnels between Stockholm and the Norwegian border. The British flyers who were residing, for the duration of the war, in Swedish internment camps—most of them had made emergency landings on Swedish soil and were allowed to make weekend trips away from the camps, although their British superiors warned them not to sleep with any Axis spies while they were out—allowed themselves to be seen examining local airfields.[79]

Once again: one and one and one made three. Members of the Swedish government who were in a position to see all these pieces no doubt took satisfaction in putting together the story of the Allies' designs on Norway. And the Germans who moved in Stockholm's political circles no doubt believed the story all the more because it came from their Swedish friends.*

One last breadcrumb, based on a truth that Americans know well: money talks. *Loud*. The OSS had Wall Street traders buy Scandinavian stocks, to give the impression that Scandinavia was about to be invaded by the Allies, and the SOE had High Street traders do the same. When Swedish journalists caught wind of this disruption in the markets, they made a great noise about it, thinking it must prove an Allied invasion was on the way. Surely if anyone knew how to buy or cheat his way into dependable insider information, it was a Wall Street trader.[80]

DER TAG

By spreading themselves thinner and thinner—by rerouting troops to Calais, to Norway—the Germans were exposing their forces to hits from Resistance saboteurs in those places. Hit by hit, piece by piece, tanks, armored cars, and other military equipment that was merely inconveniently located disappeared off the map entirely. The SOE had to tell the Resistance to *lighten up* on the attacks, lest the cells run out of explosives and ammunition before the invasion.[81]

Then the day finally came. On the evening of June 5, 1944, people listening on secret radios to the BBC's nightly 7:00 p.m. broadcast in France heard the code message *"Les carottes sont cuites"*: "The carrots are cooked." To those in the know, the message was a signal that the Allied invasion of France was at hand.[82]

After this highly anticipated declaration, the BBC broadcast a whopping 306 *messages personnels*. This time, not a single one of them was a blind. Instead, they gave a specific coded instruction to every

---

* More breadcrumbs for the Germans to follow: Bruce Hopper, a Harvard professor of government who was Stockholm's OSS station chief, managed to befriend Himmler's private physician, who resided in Stockholm and visited the Reichsführer-SS in Berlin every month. Soon, the doctor had several OSS agents in his circle of friends, though he had no clue that these Americans were OSS. While talking about business, they dropped clues that seemed to confirm that the Allies planned to invade Scandinavia. Anthony Cave Brown, *Bodyguard of Lies* (Guilford, CT: The Lyons Press, 1975), 470–71.

Resistance cell in their network—setting off a pattern of coordinated destruction all over France that the cells, despite not knowing each other or where and how the invasion was happening, could carry off in perfect harmony, as Maurice Buckmaster later wrote:

> To men huddled in mountain huts, to men in bistros in
> crowded towns who hid behind drawn blinds and locked
> shutters from the patrols which scoured the streets, to men
> in the Landes, in the Haute-Savoie, in the Jura, in Lille, in
> the Massif Central, in the heart of Paris, in tiny hamlets on
> the Gironde, the Dordogne and in the Correze and in the
> black factory country of the Nord and the Somme, in the
> forests of the Ardennes and the barren hills above Grenoble,
> in Marseille, Bordeaux, Toulon, Dijon, Besançon, in
> Clermont-Ferrand, Chartres, Le Mans, Orléans, and Rennes,
> every message carried deadly meaning. "*Vilma vous dit oui*"
> meant "Destroy all German rolling stock on the railway line
> Angouleme-Bordeaux." "*Madame dit non*" meant "Bring down
> all telegraph wires between Caen and Alençon and Caen and
> Évreux." All over France, similar tasks were started. Arms
> were brought down from lofts and dug up from beneath cellar
> flagstones. Uniforms were brought out and buttons polished.
> France was ready to help in her own liberation.[83]

All over France, saboteurs in the underground Resistance swung into action: this was a moment they'd waited for and prepared to act upon in each of their separate cells. Between the time that message went out over the airwaves and the time, some hours later, that the first boots hit the beaches of Normandy, Resistance saboteurs and their companions from the OSS and SOE sabotaged *more than nine hundred sections of railroad*.[84]

And not just railroads, either. Saboteurs dug cables out of the ground, yanked telegraph wires out of the air, drove spikes into underground telecommunication cables, and threw grenades at signal relay hubs. Switchboard operators abandoned their posts. As a result, Nazi military bases all over France started losing their communications.[85]

Many of the men and women who did this last-minute sabotage had trained at Beaulieu.[86] One of them was Violette Szabo, a French-woman who, during her first mission in the field, established her cover as an above-it-all local by trying on evening gowns in an haute-couture shop that Nazi officials frequented and walking out with a stunner. Szabo dropped into Limoges, a city with rail and telephone networks that the Allies wanted to disrupt, by parachute less than forty-eight hours before the Normandy landings. On June 10, D+4, she was carry-ing sabotage instructions among local Resistance cells—together with a Resistance leader named Jacques Dufour, code name Anastasie—when a German patrol party ambushed them. Szabo used a submachine gun to hold them back while Anastasie got away. After she ran out of bul-lets, the Germans arrested Szabo; she was executed in the Ravensbrück concentration camp.[87]

Robert Maloubier, whom a Beaulieu instructor later called the "greatest saboteur" of the French agents who worked for the SOE, per-sonally destroyed eight different bridges using explosives in the days following the Normandy landing.[88]

In mobilizing those cells of *résistants*, the Allies were taking a leap of faith. They had no way of knowing if the weather would allow the ships to cross the Channel that morning. In their secret planning, the architects of Overlord had set D-Day for June 5. But June came in like a lion, with gale winds and storm clouds and high, roaring waves on the Normandy coast. They could gather all the intelligence in the world, but they still couldn't predict the weather. Reluctantly, fearfully, the operation's leaders delayed the launch for a day and prepared to delay it for more. Because the invasion required the cooperation of army, navy, and air force troops, it was dependent on ideal weather conditions.[89] This was complicated still further by the fact that the tide, too, had to be at a certain phase.[90] This meant that if the storms remained strong enough to prevent the invasion from taking place as planned, the Al-lies would have to wait two weeks to try again. By then, as Eisenhower noted, "Secrecy would be lost": having sprung the mousetrap, they couldn't very well spring it again.[91]

Suddenly, on the evening of June 5, the meteorologists detected a break in the intensity of the storm. The lull would be short, but it was just enough for the Allies to launch their fleets for France.

And so they went—flying against storm-force winds, struggling past waves that surged so violently that the distance from the cap of one wave to the next was 150 feet, with a deep drop in the middle. The ships took on dangerous amounts of water; some capsized.[92] Near the beach, the waves reached four feet in height, flooding some of the landing ships; "others were kept afloat only by vigorous bailing on the part of soldiers who used their steel helmets as buckets."[93]

But as it turned out, the storms worked in the Allies' favor. The German leadership looked at the weather and agreed that an assault on Fortress Europe was unfeasible for the time being. "The entire German high command," a historian later said, "was unanimous in its judgment on the eve of D-day: whatever the Allies intended, the weather was too bad to permit an invasion during the first week of June." In fact, on June 5, General Erwin Rommel got in his car and started driving to Germany for a vacation.[94]

The determining factor in this decision was their preconceived ideas about the timing of *any* invasion. The Germans had studied past landing operations by the Allies and found that the Allies attempted invasions only in good weather. "To the methodical German mind there was no deviation from this rule," one historian says. "All along the chain of German command, the continuing bad weather acted like a tranquilizer."[95]

As a result, the invasion of Normandy caught the Germans by complete surprise. On June 5, their reconnaissance efforts were limited to a single, cursory flyover near Holland, and the ships that should have patrolled the Normandy coast stayed in port. During the pivotal first few hours of the invasion, the Allies crossed the Channel unchallenged. An Allied general later commented, "In this capricious turn of the weather, we had found a Trojan horse."[96]

D-DAY, H-HOUR

At last, the time came for the ghost war and the real war to come together.

In the early hours of June 6, the full moon shone bright, lighting the way for the ships that pushed through the Atlantic Ocean on the way to the coast of France: first the minesweepers, vessels that dragged electric cables to set off magnetic underwater mines, sailing in wedge formations that cleared twelve-hundred-foot-wide lanes for the rest of the fleet to sail through; then trawlers that marked the lanes for others to see using buoys; then landing craft crowded with troops.[97]

And then—after the minesweepers cleared their first lanes—the fighter planes swooped in. "Almost on the stroke of midnight," a crewman on a Canadian minesweeper later wrote, "the whole coast in front of us awoke to a frenzy of brilliant white flashes and thunderous detonations."[98] The sneaking was over; the secret was out; the fight had begun.

D-Day and *H-Hour*: June 6, 1944, at 6:30 a.m. So important did the Battle of Normandy prove to be in the turning of the war that those two terms left their former general usage—where military planners used *D-Day* and *H-Hour* to refer to the start of *any* operation—and became historical terms referring to this single event. But that day and hour only mark when the first Allied soldiers staggered ashore. The offensive really started at midnight, if not before, and it continued for eighty-four harrowing days.

For the soldiers on the ground, those eighty-four days were filled with terrors. Men staggering through hip-deep water as mortar shells explode around them. Men incapacitated with panic, drowning in water just four feet deep.[99] A man crouching, a hundred yards from shore, in a crater that an exploding shell left in the ground atop the cliffs; one of his fellows crawls into the crater with him, steals a peek over the rim to see what's ahead, and drops backward, a bullet in his forehead.[100]

But the Allies made it through, not just the eye of the storm, but the eye of the needle, arriving—partly thanks to the weather, partly thanks to disinformation—in a place and at an hour that the Germans didn't expect. By the end of D-Day, the Allied divisions that were landing on the targeted beaches—the shores near Sainte-Mère-Église, Carentan, Isigny, Saint-Laurent-Sur-Mer, Port-en-Bessin, Courseulles, and Ouistreham—had established, between them, a beachhead that spanned fifty miles.[101]

Fifty miles, and the area of Occupied Europe was more than six hundred thousand miles. It was a start.

THE FINAL INNINGS

Now that the invasion had begun, the goal of the game the war planners were playing had changed: they must keep Hitler from sending reinforcements to Normandy. They would have to trick him into keeping his forces elsewhere in Europe, to the north and northwest. They would have to send false story after false story after false story, and have Hitler believe all of them, even as each in turn proved to be false. They would have to play on every one of his frailties. If they could succeed in doing this, they could win the battle, which would turn the course of the war. A historian later called this stage "the final innings of the great game against Hitler."[102]

To do all this, the Allies continued to rely on ghost war tactics. The distractions started small, close to the action. On D-Day, Allied planes flying over the Cherbourg Peninsula dropped eight real paratroopers and two hundred "dolls"—dummies that were half the size of real men. As the dolls fell, the planes also dropped flares and noisemakers that made sounds like rifles and machine guns. The real paratroopers, when they landed, turned on speakers that played prerecorded sounds of the shouting and swearing of soldiers. They kept this up for half an hour, then disappeared into the French countryside.[103]

The same thing was happening all over the French coast, wherever the Germans had substantial mobile units. Whole brigades of Allied paratroopers seemed to be dropping behind the front line of German defenses, then turning out to be props when antiparatroop units searched the fields and orchards where they'd landed. In Paris, German military leaders tried to make sense of the barrage of frantic radio reports on these phantom brigades. Meanwhile, some distance away, real paratroop brigades hit the ground unmolested. These deception units superbly demonstrated the power of illusion to magnify not just a fighting force's perceived size, but its actual impact on the battlefield. With just a few men—and a little fakery—they achieved the results of a much larger fighting force.[104]

Meanwhile, in Edinburgh, an army made of bluster and chicken wire was having a fine time. The British Fourth Army had 350,000 men, subsidiary corps in Dundee and Stirling, and a headquarters in Edinburgh Castle. Except that it didn't. Since March, a few wireless operators in Edinburgh had been chattering away, pretending to run training exercises for the attack on Norway that Hitler firmly but mistakenly believed was coming any day now. Around sixty men had the job of working up a story, published one day at a time over the wireless, on the radio, and in local newspapers, about the adventures of this formidable fighting force. Bagpipers were visiting Edinburgh Castle to give a special performance for the British Fourth. A major in the British Fourth was engaged to be married. The British Fourth had set up a footie league and was giving a splendid showing on the pitch. The British Fourth was getting ready to join with American and Russian forces and launch an invasion of Norway—the main event for which the little hubbub in Normandy was just a preliminary distraction.[105]

When German reconnaissance planes flew over Edinburgh, they saw what appeared to be bustling airfields, complete with bomber planes, fuel drums, and antiaircraft guns. The truth was that they were looking at a set. The planes were wooden facsimiles, the antiaircraft guns were poles slathered in green paint, and the fuel drums held nothing but audacity. A few real antiaircraft guns were in place to take shots at the German planes, but they deliberately missed; their only purpose was to discourage the Germans from flying too low.[106]

The dummy tanks that the Allies used in Edinburgh and beyond came in lots of materials, from springy rubber to sturdy wood. No matter the material, the artists who crafted them put meticulous effort into ensuring their shadows, as well, had the right shape for tanks in aerial shots. (If you're fighting a shadow war, your shadows must be immaculate.) Sometimes the camoufleurs whose job was to arrange the fake tanks as set dressing hung camouflage netting over them, as if they were trying to disguise their existence, but they did so poorly, on purpose. To give the illusion of tank tracks, they simply dragged around bicycle trailers that had rubber tank tracks on their wheels.[107]

Along the Scottish coast, camoufleurs floated dummy fleets of ships. These were true masterpieces—all the more incredible considering they were made of cloth, lumber, and chicken wire, as the historian Seymour Reit notes. Here, the set designers gave it their all, leaving no telling detail missing from the stage. They rigged up chimneys that produced genuine smoke. They strung clotheslines over the decks that bore the laundry of the fictitious crews, with each garment no doubt telling its own story. They planted radios on board that played the BBC news or the catchy tunes of the *Hit Parade*, like "Don't Sit Under the Apple Tree."[108]

After D-Day, these fake fleets ramped up their feigned activity. After all, the Allies wanted Hitler to believe that the Normandy invasion was just a diversion and the real assault would soon follow in the Pas-de-Calais. During the day, camouflage troops put on a show of loading crates onto the ships. And at night, they used moving lights to give the appearance that they were still busy on the docks, loading the ships around the clock.[109]

Erwin Rommel and Gerd von Rundstedt, who were in charge of German defenses in France, asked Hitler to let them bring the infantry and tank divisions at the Pas-de-Calais down to the battlefront at Normandy. Hitler replied that not only could those divisions *not* leave their post, but the Germans must send *more* troops to the Pas-de-Calais. The field marshals later described that as the moment they realized they would lose the Normandy coast to the Allies. Hitler had swallowed the Allied deception hook, line, and sinker. For another month, he believed vehemently that the Allies would be landing any day now at the Pas-de-Calais.[110]

The only disadvantage of using artists to build decoys to draw the enemy's eye is that artists can get emotionally attached to their creations. During the Battle of Britain, the months in 1940 when the Luftwaffe waged a furious campaign in British skies, an airman and his superior had a frantic conversation on a field telephone, punctuated by the sound of explosions, that a Royal Air Force officer later recalled with amusement:

> FLIGHT SGT. (AGITATED): Sir! We're being attacked!
> PILOT OFFICER: Splendid, Sergeant. Good show.
> FLIGHT SGT.: They're smashing the place to bits!
> PILOT OFFICER: Yes, excellent. Carry on.
> FLIGHT SGT.: But, sir—we need fighter cover! *They're wrecking my best decoys!*[111]

The notion that a ghost army can defeat a real army might seem fanciful, but the numbers speak for themselves. On D+4, sixteen Allied divisions were fighting to hold the beachhead at Normandy. If the Germans had brought all the troops they could over the shattered railroads of France, twenty-one and a half German divisions might have been in Normandy fighting against those sixteen. Instead, the number of German divisions in Normandy was ten and a half. In total, a staggering ninety divisions of German troops that could have joined the fight in Normandy remained elsewhere, locked in a ghost war that never fully materialized. The substantial force in Norway was still there when the Germans surrendered in May 1945.[112]

As for that secret weapon, the V1, that Hitler stashed in the Pas-de-Calais in preparation for the assault: after the Normandy invasion started, Hitler could have directed his V1 rockets at port cities like Southampton, which was a major launching area for Allied ships. But in the weeks before the invasion, the Allies had a streak of air raids so successful that Hitler, furious, began talking about the V1 bombs strictly in terms of *hurting* the English by bombing London, rather than *fighting* the English by bombing the coast. "Soon we can begin the attacks on London with the V1 and the V2," he told his aides in early June. "The British will suffer. They'll find out what retaliation is!"[113]

Once again, the Führer's intuition was a boon to the Allied cause. Soon enough, the Allies figured out how to use radar and other technologies to protect London from most of this assault; and in the meantime, the Allies' assault on the Continent continued largely un-threatened by the weapon that was supposed to stop the invasion at the starting point.[114]

NORMANDY BATTLE HINGES ON IT

On the morning of D-Day, very few people in France's capital city knew the invasion was even happening, just 170 miles away.

That morning, one and a half hours after H-Hour, a local politician who had a hand in Resistance activities received a telephone call. The caller had just a few words to say: "My mother-in-law has arrived."[115] Meaning: the invasion was under way.

The few Parisians who, like him, knew what was happening ob-served that the faces on the city streets looked as they did on any other day—though every so often, two faces would exchange a cautious ex-pression of "sweet joy," one later said. The Germans, meanwhile, looked more and more flustered as the morning progressed. At 1:00 p.m., Winston Churchill announced the invasion on the BBC—and then, at last, the news was out.[116]

But even then—such is the power of a compelling story—lots of German military leaders and intelligence agents had trouble believing the reports coming in from Normandy. A German intelligence officer in Paris observed that the city's generals couldn't reconcile the news with what they believed about the bad weather, the inhospitable coast, the chatter about targets further north: "Why that place? Why this time?"[117]

Civilians, meanwhile, ran to the city's bookstores and bought up every book and map they could find that mentioned Normandy, emp-tying the shelves.[118] It was a hopelessly belated way to get the news of the day, but in a certain sense, they were better informed than the Ger-mans, simply because they were willing to adapt to unexpected news while the Germans still weren't.

Perhaps the reason the Allies were able to use spies and saboteurs to such brilliant effect during the Battle of Normandy was that they understood the value of information asymmetry—and that playing a game of information asymmetry often means accepting the unknown.

Spies in fiction can see all the pieces on the board, but spies in real life only ever know what's happening on their own square. This is the uncomfortable part of total secrecy: it really is *total*, and as a consequence, even within one's own organization, it's often the case that the left hand doesn't know what the right hand is doing. You can only do your job and trust that the game on the board will work out as it should. If it does, all those individual actions will form a collective that will help turn the outcome for your side.

As Allied soldiers fought their way, step by step, toward Paris, *résistants* in the city fought guerrilla battles in the streets to wear down the German military before the Allies arrived.* They broke into the wine stores of known collaborators to steal wine bottles for making Molotov cocktails.[119] (Frédéric Joliot-Curie, the scientist who revealed the secret of fission to Nazi Europe just so he could get a publication—and then found himself under Nazi watch in a laboratory in Paris, where he was "treated almost as a prisoner, working under supervision of the Gestapo," according to an SOE report—gave his expertise, now, to the Resistance, supplying chemicals to make the explosive cocktails.[120])

And the philosopher Jean-Paul Sartre urged his fellow Resistance members in an underground newspaper: "We all know the order: attack a German and take his revolver. With that revolver seize a rifle. With that rifle seize a car. With that car, seize a tank."[121]

In this phase of the fighting, every individual action had consequence, and even saboteurs found themselves playing important roles in *ruses de guerre*. The role of a mailman, for example. Fifteen days after the first soldiers staggered ashore on the beaches of Normandy, General Eisenhower sent a message—labeled "Most Urgent"—to the SOE's French Section. A corps of German tanks was on the way to Normandy, big enough, when it arrived, to crush the Allied forces that

---

* You may be wondering, by the way, where the money the French Resistance used for its activities came from. Much of it came from Hollywood—from film studios like Paramount. The OSS couldn't easily get hold of banknotes from (or foreign assets in) occupied countries, and although it solved the problem, in part, by forging bills and by trading currencies in neutral cities like Istanbul, it also got Paramount to share the notes and assets the studio was using in its own international dealings. Stanton Griffis, *Lying in State* (New York: Doubleday, 1952), 102.

were still struggling to hold the coast. The only way to stop the tanks was to sabotage a bridge at Évreux that they would be compelled to cross, since the Resistance and the RAF had blown up every other bridge they might use.[122]

The SOE's French Section telegraphed a desperate message to the French underground: "BRIDGE AT EVREUX MUST REPEAT MUST BE DESTROYED NORMANDY BATTLE HINGES ON IT HAVE YOU EXPLOSIVES FOR JOB REPLY MOST URGENT MESSAGE ENDS."[123]

That same evening, a mere three hours before the Germans arrived at the river, a member of the underground, Robert Hanote, *nom de guerre* Hervé, sent back a reply. Hervé was thirty years old and lived in Lille, although he happened to be near Évreux that evening. Until now, his job in the underground had been to pick up refugees in Lille who were fleeing to Belgium. As it happened, only one refugee ever came upon Hervé's route and tried to make contact with him, but at the crucial moment, Hervé didn't reply to the refugee's password—out of fear, he told his handlers later. The refugee managed to get to Belgium anyway; but perhaps Hervé's moment of fear, his failure to answer when the call came, weighed on him. Perhaps he felt that he'd missed his chance to do something for his country.[124]

This time, he replied as follows: "MESSAGE RECEIVED AND UNDERSTOOD WILL DO IMMEDIATELY EXPLOSIVES AVAILABLE VIVE LA FRANCE VIVE L'ANGLETERRE." He ran to the house of a local mailman and borrowed his uniform, mailbag, and bicycle, explaining why only with the words "*Pour la France.*" He put on the uniform, packed the bag to bursting with blasting agents, and rode onto the span of the bridge at Évreux, passing a German sentry who was keeping watch over the bridge. Then he stopped, pushed a button, and brought down the whole bridge, killing himself in the process.[125]

THE DAY ENDS

On August 30, 1944, the Battle of Normandy formally came to an end. In Paris—where the French Resistance forces had been fighting with terrible desperation, watching their fighters drop by the hundreds as they waited for the Allies to arrive, until finally American soldiers entered the city with overwhelming force—the Germans withdrew from their positions and retreated eastward, leaving the city to the Allies.[126]

As the American soldiers who liberated the city later recalled, entering Paris was a bittersweet experience, as the streets were filled with joy but also starvation, grief, bombed-out buildings, and other horrors of war: a time of celebration, but also of terrible reckoning. The fight to get this far into the Continent, far enough to reclaim the City of Artists, had been hard won on every front. But it *was* won in part because artists helped to fight: painters, actors, writers, set designers, and other followers of the muses fought the leaders of the German armies using the weapons of their arts. The dramatic deceptions that transformed the theater of war deserved a standing ovation as the curtain came down on this act.

And so, the most pivotal battle of the war was won. France was liberated. The streets of Paris veritably flowed with wine—as celebrants uncorked the bottles that Resistance fighters hadn't emptied to use for Molotov cocktails—and the air rang from dawn to dusk to dawn again with uproarious toasts: *Vive les Américains! Vive la France! Vive de Gaulle! Vive la victoire!*[127] But liberation came too late for many. And millions more would die before the war ended.

9

LIES AND DAMNED LIES

One may smile, and smile, and be a villain.
—WILLIAM SHAKESPEARE

AFTER THE LIBERATION OF FRANCE, AS ALLIED VICTORY IN Europe became ever more certain, R&A's workload grew rather than shrank. Analysts swam against a swelling tide of documents—literally tons of paper—captured from the front. When the American army captured a new city, the Nazis, fleeing, would do their best to destroy or carry out their own paperwork as they left, but even when they partially succeeded, the archives left behind were so vast that they *slowed* the work of intelligence services: too much information, too much garbage to sift through.[1] On top of that, Kibre and her colleagues in the Interdepartmental Committee for the Acquisition of Foreign Publications (ICAFP) kept up the flow of documents streaming into London and Washington from all over the world. Every branch of the services seemed, by now, to depend on a harried tribe of readers.

In the summer of 1944, one poor bastard who worked as a research analyst at the Library of Congress, reading through publications the ICAFP sent home, wrote to his superiors begging for more staffers to help him with the reading. He calculated that he needed six more readers to help him with his job, which was to get through about eighty-five thousand issues of newspapers and other periodicals.

"From the enclosed reading estimate," he said, "it will be seen that I have been reading at about the rate of 12,000 issues a year."[2]

As it happens, this particular reader was tasked with finding in all those pages every stray piece of information he could to help the Allies track down paintings, books, and other treasures that the Nazis had looted from the countries they occupied. Don't be fooled by his focus on art; his mission was strategic and tactical, not merely sentimental. Masterpieces are money. Treasures are, well, treasure. The Nazis were trading silver for submarines and melting bronze statues into bullets, and the Allies feared that, as they gained ever more ground on the Continent, the Nazis would sell off Europe's greatest artworks—or would burn them, to prevent the Allies from turning them to the same advantage.[3] So the OSS set out to reverse the flow of treasure.

By the fall of 1944, the OSS had created a special intelligence outfit of art historians, the Art Looting Investigation Unit: the "Art Unit," as they called themselves. The Art Unit had just three field officers, all of them navy men who jumped at the chance to work in a role that featured art. The first, Lane Faison, Jr., was the quintessential rumpled professor. Thirty-seven years old, Faison had brown hair and an owlish, boyish face. He stood six feet tall and had a lanky frame. When he filled out his draft card in 1940, under a prompt that read, "Other obvious physical characteristics that will aid in identification," he wrote, "glasses."[4]

The second, Ted Rousseau, Jr., had Hollywood-handsome looks. Before the war, he worked as an assistant curator at Washington's National Gallery of Art; anyone could see that he was on an express train to the top of the profession, and he had the easy, glad-handing manner to match.[5] "I am not primarily interested in academics; enjoyment comes first," he later told the New York Times, explaining his curatorial philosophy.[6]

The third of the trio, and the director of the Art Unit, was a Harvard-trained art historian named James Sachs Plaut. Unlike Faison, who had to run through his first intelligence training in 1944, when he joined the OSS—he "had to go through the training that everybody did to get to be OSS, learning lock picking and code work and all that stuff," Faison later said—Plaut and Rousseau were already intelligence veterans. They did their training early on and had worked, ever since, for the Office of Naval Intelligence.[7] Where Faison was a little rumpled, and Rousseau was slick, Plaut was proper. (A newspaper profile of Plaut written after the war said that he and his wife, Mary Friedlander Plaut, ran their household "by rules that make Emily Post look uncivilized."[8]) At thirty-three, he already had the look of an elder dignitary, with appraising blue-gray eyes and a long patrician face.

The professor, the star, and the dignitary: these three were tasked with getting to the bottom of the most immense art theft in history. Scholars estimate that the Nazis stole more than one hundred thousand artworks from every corner of Occupied Europe.[9] And the U.S. government had decided that experienced art historians, who knew how to recognize masterpieces and interrogate their Axis counterparts as fellow experts, should carry out the work of finding the stolen art, tracking down the perpetrators, and unraveling the tangled skein of auctions, museum galas, thefts, threats, extortion, and murders to expose the crimes that could be prosecuted.

The adventures of this small but remarkable group would illustrate, once again, the pivotal role that scholars of the liberal arts played in fighting the war. Their adventures would also illustrate a paradox that seems especially pertinent to the problem of restoring peace after war: they were perfect for their mission, but not perfect soldiers. As we'll see, at the end of *this* war, in *this* field of contest, imperfect soldiers—men who were willing to defy orders—were exactly what the Allies needed. We need soldiers to win wars, but we need nonsoldiers to win peace.

BLOOD AND TREASURE

The Art Unit, which worked for the OSS, was separate from the Monuments Officers, the group of men and women who worked under the Allied military command to protect important documents, monuments, and art in territory the Allies captured. Both groups did work that had essential military value. The Monuments Officers, whom the army called "the Venus fixers," followed on the heels of frontline battalions to secure artworks—and to secure archives. Archives of the Nazi bureau-cracy could reveal the enemy's plans; archives of civilian desiderata, like property records, could help the Allies to rebuild the shattered cities of Europe; and archives of valuable manuscripts—well. The old phrase for a nation's spending on war is *blood and treasure*.[10]

The Monuments Officers found, in Sicily, shopkeepers using an-tique texts from the National Library in Palermo as wrapping paper.[11] (All of Europe was suffering from a paper shortage, and archivists in Italy and England alike fought mightily to keep their desperate coun-trymen from cabbaging their archives.[12]) In Benevento, they found the city's surviving legal records stashed in a stable.[13] In Montegufoni, they found priceless paintings, among them Botticelli's *Primavera*, propped up casually around the halls of a country villa. Professor Cesare Fasola, a librarian at the Uffizi Gallery in Florence, had walked thirteen miles to the villa from Florence to protect the paintings from German or British soldiers, whoever happened to be nearby. He remained there even when the exchange of gunfire made the grounds a "no-man's-land," begging the advancing British troops to shoot wherever they wanted, but not at the villa.[14]

Throughout all this work, the Monuments Officers relied on in-telligence that the Chairborne Division pulled together during their endless reading sessions in the Library of Congress. Anything could yield useful dope to send to the front: newspaper stories, sales listings, directories of public auctions, art dealer advertisements, field reports, government proclamations, books about famous archives, and more.[15]

The Art Unit had a narrower task. They acted as sleuths, tracking the oleaginous smell of paint and blood from murdered households to gutted archives to elegant auction houses to stately museums to stables and cellars and mines, working out where the Nazis hid the art they stole, who was involved in the thefts, the methods they used, and any-thing else the Allies might wish to know in order to recover Europe's treasures, identify war criminals, and pump the criminals they captured for actionable intelligence. They were a precision strike unit: the Monu-ments Officers had hundreds of members, but the Art Unit had just the three field agents.[16]

The Art Unit set up a headquarters in Washington and a field office in London, but the three agents traveled all over Europe.[17]

In January 1945, Rousseau started working his way through Spain. He tracked down a banker named Alois Miedl, who sold ill-acquired art to Hermann Göring and other Nazi leaders, and tried to casually shake down Miedl for information while pretending to be a Frenchman. He wasn't very good at pretending to be a Frenchman, it turned out, and he wound up conceding his real identity to Miedl. "Why didn't you say so?" asked Miedl, who promptly started regaling Rousseau with stories of his and his friends' dirty acquisitions. The downside to the unexpectedly easy interrogation was that Miedl was the kind of drinker who needed to drink just to stay upright, and he expected Rousseau to keep up with him, one brandy after another. "I just about had the DTs before I got all the necessary information," Rousseau later said.[18]

In another adventure, Rousseau found thousands of guilders' worth of Dutch paintings packed in sawdust in a port storage warehouse in Biscay, then unraveled the tangle of clandestine trades that put them there, exposing a criminal network that stretched across Holland.[19]

Plaut went to Italy to investigate art crimes in the Mediterranean. In March, he arrived in a prison-like interrogation center in Rome to begin an interrogation of a German spy named Wilhelm Mohnen that lasted almost two months. Mohnen, an art dealer who (according to a report on this interrogation) "managed by intrigue and scheming to worm himself into the confidence of a number of highly placed persons," handed out all kinds of incriminating tales about his associates. Soon, Plaut knew who spied for the Abwehr in France, who traded illegal weapons, and who tried to set up a secret pen-pal arrangement, using invisible inks, between the German ambassador and the pope.[20]

Even the man who held down the Art Unit's London office, an expert in colonial silver named John Phillips, got in on the action. While visiting a collection of looted art in the Bavarian Alps, Phillips stumbled upon an unexpected use for his expertise, according to the historian Robin Winks. While examining an early work by the seventeenth-century Dutch painter Jan Vermeer, one of the greatest artists in history, Phillips realized that something was off about the tableware. A pewter flagon in the painting had a handle that dated from the nineteenth century, not the seventeenth. The painting had to be a modern forgery.[21] By the end of the summer, the forger, who'd made a handsome pile selling fake Old Master paintings to prosperous Nazis—including Alois Miedl—confessed to his deception, an admission that rendered eight "Vermeers" as well as other priceless artworks suddenly worthless.[22]

By V-E Day—May 8, 1945—the Art Unit's London office had assembled a dossier of suspects, based on information from the field agents, that held more than two thousand names.[23]

OUR KIND OF PEOPLE

One reason the OSS found professional art historians so useful for the task of investigating criminals is the criminals they investigated often let down their guard around colleagues. Hermann Göring, the leader of the Luftwaffe and perhaps the most dedicated art looter in a network of graft, robbery, and murder that stretched across Nazi Europe, had had no problem finding a thousand art professionals to staff his extensive operations.[24] And those staffers seemed to think of themselves as respectable members of an elite profession—and seemed to assume that other members of the profession would surely protect them.[25]

Time and time again, the officers of the Art Unit and MFA&A (Monuments, Fine Arts & Archives Division) encountered scholars who had collaborated with the Nazis and took for granted that life would go on as before. Walter Farmer, a Monuments Officer who ran a "collecting point" in Wiesbaden, where the Allies gathered stolen art to be repaired and repatriated, later described with delight how the "arch-Nazi" Hermann Voss, a museum director who built the collection for Hitler's planned art museum in Linz, walked right into his office, expecting a collegial handshake. ("Dr. Voss . . . called my office and politely asked for an appointment," Farmer said. "I guess he was hoping to get back into his old job as director of the Wiesbaden paintings collection, but when he arrived I welcomed him with a detachment of military police who took him away to prison where he awaited trial for his war crimes."[26])

A similar lucky break presented itself one day to two Monuments Officers in Germany, Lincoln Kirstein and Robert Posey, who happened to mention their job to a dentist who was fixing Posey's teeth. The dentist was delighted to learn the Americans were *just like* his son-in-law, Kirstein later wrote: "We protected objects of art, and here the coincidence was extraordinary, because his own soldier son-in-law was in the same business."[27] Perhaps he could introduce them. (Yes, please, they said.)

The dentist hopped in their command car and showed them to a cottage hidden in the woods outside of town. "It was a pleasant house," Kirstein later said, "with photographs of Notre Dame de Paris, the Île St.-Louis, Versailles, books, flowers, and the agreeable atmosphere of a scholar's cultivated life—domestic, concentrated, a long way from war."[28]

When the dentist's son-in-law learned that his visitors wanted to talk about French art, he rushed to offer his expertise. He *loved* French art; he was a scholar of the subject; until recently, he'd lived in France with his wife and child ("which, they proudly explained, had been born *in Paris*"). As it turned out, the dentist's son-in-law was none other than Hermann Bunjes, Göring's personal art consultant. Bunjes wrote the pseudo-legal justifications that gave the Nazis leave to ship countless trainloads of French-owned art out of France.[29]

To an outsider, this interrogation would have looked like a pleasant conversation between fellow scholars. Apparently that's what Bunjes thought it was. "It was hard to believe," Kirstein said, "that this man had, for six years, been the confidant of Göring, the intimate of Hitler's closest guards; that he had been in the SS since before he graduated from college." He seemed to believe the Americans already knew everything and just wanted to go over details; Kirstein and Posey struggled mightily to play it cool. He revealed the locations of so many stashes of stolen art that the list they sent afterward to headquarters, which was numbered using letters, ran right from A to Z and then used double letters.[30] The greatest stash, he said, was in a salt mine in Alt Aussee, Austria. That was where Hitler and Göring kept their own collections.

Collegiality worked as an interrogation tactic because Nazi art experts believed that the American art experts who appeared at their doors would simply accept them as colleagues. But seeing Bunjes as Bunjes seemed to see himself was unsettling, Kirstein said: "Here, in the cold Moselle spring, far from the murder of the cities, worked a German scholar in love with France, passionately in love, with that hopeless, frustrated fatalism so marvelously described by Rilke. When did we think he could go back? He wished to finish his book on the twelfth-century sculpture of the Île de France which he had started at Cluny with Kingsley Porter and Marcel Aubert."

Bunjes told them that he sometimes found the Nazis repulsive, as when, during a meal at an elite club in Berlin, he learned that he was dining on silver plates that had belonged to a Jewish family.[31] Clearly, the experience stuck with him; perhaps it did disgust him. But he didn't quit Göring's service afterward. Eventually he was shuffled out against his will in one of the Nazi leadership's occasional bureaucratic upheavals. How did he justify to himself his claim to love the country he'd helped to loot and burn? How did he reconcile his crimes with a scholar's cozy existence?

THE PROTECTION OF ART

The history of art is a history of crime. In these years, even more so than usual. The Nazis used powerful art institutions—auction houses, galleries, museums, universities—as machines of expertise to sort and appraise their loot, and they worked with dealers, museum officials, and professors who performed confiscations, thefts, and forced sales on their behalf. They described these actions with the word *Kunstschutz*, which literally translates to "the protection of art."[32]

Military governments across Occupied Europe had departments called the Kunstschutz, often staffed by German art historians, which represented themselves as protectors of the art that belonged to occupied states. In 1941, at the request of the Kunstschutz in Paris, the Military Governor of Paris sent every substantial private collection of confiscated art, much of it belonging to Jewish families, to the Rosenberg Task Force, the looting organization that reported directly to the Nazi Party. He also helped the Kunstschutz staffers and consultants who were scouring the city for treasures: giving them papers, for example, that told authorities to show them all possible favor. He was then enraged to discover that the Kunstschutz took to Germany an art collection that was supposed to belong to the French state—something they'd promised him they'd never do.[33] But that was how they worked; they obliged *others* to take promises seriously, but they placed no such obligation on themselves.

In 1943, the Kunstschutz in Rome made an agreement with the Italian government to help ship almost 190 crates of Italian-owned art to the Vatican. A Luftwaffe unit that reported to Hermann Göring courteously took on the job; when the shipment arrived, it was fifteen crates short. When Vatican staffers examined the crates, they realized that Göring's men had opened them and taken things out.[34]

In 1944, the Kunstschutz in Bruges sent staffers to a church that held a marble sculpture, a Madonna and Child by Michelangelo. The Allies would soon reach Bruges, and the staffers "asked special permission to have one last look at the famous Michelangelo statue" hidden inside. A priest let them in. The next day, a group of German troops burst into the church and hauled the statue away. The wide-eyed visitors were apparently an advance party sent to scope out the joint.[35]

When the bishop of Belgium complained about the theft, the Nazis wrote him a high-handed letter explaining that Hitler had ordered it, "in order that the treasures might be saved from the dangers of destruction and removal from Europe by the Anglo-American enemy."[36]

The Rosenberg Task Force, meanwhile, marched through France at the heels of the invading German armies. They seized art, books, and furniture belonging to Jews and other enemies of the Reich, then shipped them off to furnish party offices or line the walls of German museums. The cream of the lot went to Paris, to be put on display for party leaders to inspect and pick out favorites for their own collections. The party leaders traded the art that nobody wanted for paintings that weren't among the seized goods; for example, trading tens of modern Impressionist paintings for one Old Master that was up for public auction. (The art dealers who accepted these trades were thrilled, because party leaders often had terrible taste, preferring third-rate paintings from Teutonic countries to first-rate ones from France.)[37]

And if the Reich's agents wanted to get a painting from an owner who seemed unwilling to give it up at any price, they could just apply leverage. *You have a son in a prison camp, don't you, monsieur? Surely you want to get him out. Madame, if you don't sell this painting for the reasonable price I'm offering—a modest but reasonable price, madame—then we'll just confiscate the painting and you'll get nothing.*[38]

The Nazis worked up all kinds of legalistic justifications for their thefts. Perhaps the original owners had fled, forcing the German state to extract a "refugee tax" from the belongings they left behind. Or perhaps German scholars could identify signs of "Germanic origin" in art that other countries possessed, which meant, the Nazis argued, that the art belonged to Germany by ancestral right.[39] From Belgium, the Nazis took the Ghent Altarpiece. From Russia, they took amber mosaics that Frederick I of Prussia had given centuries ago to Peter the Great.[40] From Italy, they took the Biblioteca Hertziana, a world-class library of books on art and architecture. From France, they emptied museums of "all objects of Germanic origin," which they defined very liberally. (A German professor whom Himmler assigned to study the Bayeux Tapestry, a famous embroidery that depicts the events surrounding the French invasion of England in 1066, said it actually depicts a "royal German saga expressing the Germanic traits of love of war and chivalrous respect for the enemy."[41]) Everywhere, the high rhetoric of self-defense and selfless cultural trusteeship: *We must rescue these treasures from the depredations of war. This is only retaliation for your crimes against the state. See what you're forcing us to do.*

A 1945 report on the Nazis' looting, written by a member of the Art Unit—the writer was anonymous, but he wrote with a superbly acid pen—described the agents who smoothed out acquisitions for the Rosenberg Task Force as a mediocre crowd of art world hangers-on who jumped at the opportunity, by working for the Nazis, to get to the other side of a velvet rope they could never otherwise cross: "the shadiest collaborationist art dealers and other such agents as shady lawyers, quasi-dealers, expert valuers and the like—all the riff-raff of the inter-national art market."[42]

Scholars who study collaborators in Nazi Europe often describe them as would-be kings of their own little hills. For example, some were fascist politicians who wanted to be leaders in a fascist France, a fascist Denmark, a fascist Greece, but hadn't had much success in winning elections on their own and believed the occupying Germans would put power in their hands. "They were, above all, though not exclusively, lo-cal fascists, none of them of any significant or lasting political weight in the late 1930s, but galvanized by German military victories into be-lieving their chance had come," writes the historian Philip Morgan. In other words, they persuaded themselves that the Germans would lift them onto thrones and then leave them alone to rule their own lands. The Germans, of course, expected otherwise: to create a German empire, a Third Reich where all other states obeyed the rule of Nazi Germany.[43]

In the art world, too, all kinds of would-be despots treated the Nazi takeover as a gold rush. Museums, galleries, and universities were little hills, too, and the collaborators who worked there saw opportunities for power. And they, like other collaborators across Occupied Europe, used Nazi leaders as models to imitate—sometimes quite literally. Wal-ter Andreas Hofer, who was the head of Göring's art collection and his foremost purchaser, demanded that everyone he met call him by his full title, "Director of the Art Collection for the Reichsmarschall." ("There is little doubt," one historian says wryly of Hofer, "that he not only was, but wanted more than anything else to be, Göring's alter ego as far as the collection was concerned.")[44] Josef Angerer, a dealer who funneled lots of dubiously acquired pieces to Göring, wore a Göring-like cos-tume for a time in the 1920s, complete with medals, and pretended to be Göring in order to scam people out of money. This peculiar fraud did not stop Göring from making Angerer one of his most trusted dealers during the Second World War.[45] Then there was Kurt von Behr, the chief of staff for the Rosenberg Task Force, who wore a German Red Cross uniform, a paper-thin bit of posturing for which the Art Unit ridiculed him in their reports.[46]

It's true that working with Göring gave agents access to dealers, galleries, and museums that would otherwise have been closed. It gave them leverage to use the kind of blackmail and threats that Göring was capable of delivering on. This meant that they got amazing paintings, not only for him, but also for themselves. It allowed them to travel, otherwise bureaucratically infeasible due to wartime restrictions on travel. And it allowed them to easily get money in the form of francs, gilders, kroner.[47] Many of his agents used these privileges to enrich themselves and live the high life.

Göring had a ready excuse when, in 1945, he explained to his interrogators at the Seventh Army Interrogation Center in Augsburg why he shook down cities across Occupied Europe for art to hoard for his personal wealth. He was simply planning to turn his hunting estate near Berlin into a state museum, to educate and inspire the people of Europe—after he was dead, of course. "After all," he said, "I'm a Renaissance type."[48]

Hitler also planned to create a state museum, using the art that his own private agents, as well as the Rosenberg Task Force and the Kunstschutz, stole on his behalf. He would build it in Linz, the city where he grew up, and it would be the wonder of the world: greater than the British Museum, greater than the Louvre, greater than all the cultural sites of Europe, because it would gather treasures from those sites in one place. When he was a teenager, the Academy of Fine Arts Vienna rejected him twice as an art student, giving the simple ruling, "Sample drawing unsatisfactory." Now the gatekeepers of the art world would have to spend all their time at a museum that bore his title: the *Führermuseum*, which would set the standards for whether a work of art should be hailed as a masterpiece or burned as degenerate. He would be the world's greatest patron of art—and the world's most important arbiter of taste.[49]

The fact that art has value and power that exists in a realm beyond economic value and political power—people risk their lives to preserve works of art they don't own and dedicate their lives to studying them, and we admire those people instead of calling them crazy—means that one can use the rhetoric of art's unworldly greatness to obscure all kinds of worldly motives. For Hitler, rage and jealousy. For Göring, a drive to obtain the security of wealth that became, by the end of the war, almost psychotic. (In the final months of Germany's defeat, Göring took his art collections with him everywhere he went, piled up in personal trains. Some observers said that, by the end, he focused on nothing but the acquisition of art, ignoring all his other obligations.)[50] Plenty of low functionaries who helped the Nazi Party might have seen in the upending of the art world a chance to have important people ordain *them* as important. Those who already *were* important might have seen a chance to gain better access to the cultures and treasures they told themselves they loved. After all, the British Museum is filled with plunder from the British Empire, and the Louvre is filled with plunder that Napoleon took from his French Empire. Now it was the German Empire's turn.

And yet the Nazi program for the future of art also called for the destruction of anything they deemed to be the wrong kind of art. In 1943, the Germans set fire, using gasoline and hand grenades, to the Royal Society Library at the University of Naples, reducing some two hundred thousand books to litter and ashes. In 1944, while retreating from the advancing Allied forces in France, they pulled a fleet of trucks up to a grand château in Rastignac, stuffed as many valuables into the trucks as they could, and then set fire to the château, destroying a collection of modern French paintings in the process.[51]

If Hitler couldn't put Europe's greatest art in the Führermuseum, he didn't want the art to survive at all. In November 1944, an archaeological adviser to the British War Office wrote an urgent letter to a member of the Cabinet, Lord Harold Macmillan, reporting that an agent in Munich had learned that Hitler "issued a secret order to all responsible authorities to the effect that in the last resort all historic buildings and works of art in Germany, whether of German or of foreign origin, whether legally or illegally acquired, should be destroyed rather than allowed to fall into the hands of Germany's enemies." The agent learned this information from Max Göring, a German art historian who worked for the Bavarian Commission for the Preservation of Art and Monuments.[52]

Did Max Göring (who wasn't related to the Reichsmarshall) really believe that Hitler's order was in line with the task of his commission for the preservation of art and monuments? At what point did he realize that his job was just to lend a sense of legitimacy to the tantrums and predations of his bosses? Or did he always know that's what he was there to do, given Nazism's explicit position that the state's duty was to follow the orders of the Führer, while the Führer had no duty but to follow his own whims? The art historian didn't survive to tell the Art Unit either way, as he died soon afterward in an Allied bombing.[53] The art-world elites who helped the Nazis to steal art under the lofty rhetoric of preservation were learning, in these final months of the war in Europe, that their collaboration had put the masterpieces they loved on a path to destruction.

PROPERTY OF THE FÜHRER

Even with the friendly dentist's unwitting help, the Americans almost lost the treasures that had been set aside for Hitler's and Göring's collections. By April 1945, a month before the Monuments Officers met the dentist in Trier, the Nazis understood that the mines near Bad Aussee would soon fall into the hands of the Allies. They decided to undercut that victory in the last way remaining to them.

On April 10 and twice thereafter, a Nazi functionary visited the mine at Alt Aussee with a small convoy that hauled eight wooden boxes stamped with the words "Mamor—Nicht stürzen." *Marble— Don't drop.* The functionary, who arranged to have the boxes stashed at different points around the mine, told everyone who would listen that the boxes held the property of the Führer. In fact, the boxes held airplane bombs that weighed hundreds of pounds apiece. August Eigruber, the provincial governor of Upper Austria, had issued an order to stash the bombs throughout the salt mine. When the bombs went off, the mine chambers would collapse and the equipment that kept groundwater from drenching the mine would break. The Allies might eventually dig their way in, but by then, not much would be left of the art. Hitler almost certainly gave his blessing to this plan. If Vermeer's most famous painting couldn't hang in his office, then it wouldn't hang anywhere.[54]

When the Resistance learned about the bombs, they took a chance on some of the mine staffers whose job was to help move and preserve the paintings underground. Would they help to blow up the tunnels before the Nazis could? The mine staffers would, and did; working under cover of bureaucratic obfuscation, so that everyone further up the administrative ladder was a few steps behind what they were up to, they removed the airplane bombs and blew up dynamite in the entrance shafts, blocking the tunnels while leaving the chambers full of art untouched.

Eigruber, incensed, demanded that soldiers find a way to break into the blocked chambers and torch the art with flamethrowers. But almost that same day, the Americans took Alt Aussee. Which meant, as Monuments Man Lieutenant Thomas Howe remarked drily, that Eigruber's orders didn't matter anymore.[55]

Meanwhile, as Patton's Third Army neared the Laufen salt mine near Alt Aussee, which held treasures second only to those in the Alt Aussee mine, SS officers crammed two trucks full of paintings and prepared to hit the road. "At the last moment a Viennese curator begged to go along to care for the art objects," a 1946 article in the *New York Times* said. "Permission was granted if he would let himself be bound and placed in the back of a truck." After "a chase as melodramatic as a Western movie," past the front line of Patton's troops, the Monuments Officers found the trucks sitting on the road shoulder, deserted; the paintings and curator were all in one piece.[56]

On May 8, the day after arriving in Alt Aussee, the Americans started to dig out the mine. The mine lay up a steep road above the village, on a ridge that jutted out hundreds of feet above a pine forest. The entrance looked more like a church than a mine, with a tiered roof and a horseshoe-shaped door.[57]

Behind this little entryway stretched a vast labyrinth of tunnels and chambers. The mine was so big—it had 137 tunnels in total—

that miners partitioned it into different named sections. The mine was always cold; the temperature hovered just above freezing. The guards in the tunnels wore heavy jackets even during the summer.[58]

The section called the Springerwerk held many of the mine's most important treasures, and the MFA&A officers started their work in that section, "picking out the cream of the pictures and getting them up topside," as one of them said. The Springerwerk alone held some two thousand paintings, stacked several layers deep; it also held books, drawings, furniture, prints, sculptures, tapestries, and antique arms and armor, like decorated breastplates and articulated barding for horses— all squeezed together in rough little rooms. Together, the chambers that held the art encompassed a space the size of eighteen football fields, but inside any one of them, the effect was claustrophobic.[59]

"It was a mole-like existence," Lieutenant Howe recalled of his work identifying paintings in the mine.[60] Some chambers were almost a mile from the entrance of the mine, and the most civilized among them had walls and floors made of raw planks. "Beyond those in which floors had been laid, there were vast unlighted caves of echoing blackness."[61] The mine held some ten thousand artworks, none of which had paperwork with them to indicate their owners, because, of course, they belonged to the Reich now. (Even today, twenty-seven hundred artworks remain in Alt Aussee because nobody knows who owned them.[62]) Slowly, working day and night in a place where the difference between day and night was negligible, Howe and his fellow moles sorted through the paintings and carried up those they considered the most important to load onto trains out of town. (They padded the paintings for the journey with bundles of cheap lace they found in one of the chambers, which they called "pads made from Hitler's window curtains.")[63]

Imagine it: you're underground, bundled up against the cold, walking in the dark through a narrow tunnel. Every two hundred feet or so, a hanging lamp throws a small circle of light on the cart track under your feet. The air smells faintly of briny wood; the walls are damp, and the ceiling glitters with drops of moisture.

As you walk, the walls transition from planks and red limestone to stubbly red salt rock. You reach a small, dark room that's filled with jumbled-up crates and canvases and furniture, the very picture of an abandoned storeroom. You turn on your flashlight to get a better look.

Then, suddenly, you see one of the most famous paintings in the world: the Ghent Altarpiece. The figures—Adam and Eve, the Virgin Mary, John the Baptist, a choir of singing angels, and others—are as lofty in their gestures as the pope leading a Mass, but the painter, Jan van Eyck, who found holiness in the mortal world God made, includes humble little details of humanity: if you look closely, you can see that Adam and Eve have pubic hair. The painting isn't just a sacred scene; it's an argument about sacredness.

Then a Brueghel, a rowdy feast at a wedding. A Botticelli, a portrait of a woman with rippling curls and disdainful eyes. A marble sculpture of Mary and her child that you know is supposed to be in Bruges.

And then, leaned up in a corner, forgotten, what Howe called "the rarest treasure of that collection." A painting that Hitler picked out for his personal collection in 1940, reportedly forcing the sale from a man in Vienna whose wife was born Jewish, paying for it with the proceeds from *Mein Kampf. The Art of Painting*: the only self-portrait by the greatest of artists, the seventeenth-century painter Jan Vermeer of Delft. The artist sits with his back turned to the viewer, silent, considering how to look at his subject.[64] This is a man who sees a painting not as a store of wealth, but as a gaze, a way of seeing.

Paintings are mortal. They're just layers of linen, wood pulp, gum, pigment, varnish, oil. Some of history's most celebrated painters, like Leonardo da Vinci, used experimental materials and methods that reflected their genius, but left their paintings more apt than most to flake apart without constant care. The mine at Alt Aussee was chosen as a storage space for Hitler's most treasured paintings not just because the underground tunnels kept them safe from air raids, but also because the moist, cold air helped to keep the art from decaying.[65] Even so, the paintings couldn't be expected to last, piled up as they were in that grave. Neglect destroys as surely as sun and rain.

Paintings are mortal. But they're also memory, an image of a particular time and place from a particular point of view, which is why we value them so highly, and why Hitler wanted to destroy many of them.

Without the museum of the past, without men and women of other times and places lending us their minds, our comprehension of the world is nothing more, as H. L. Mencken said, than a small flashlight beam in a large and murky room.

Now the Americans were bringing the art back into the light.

HOUSE 71

Bad Aussee is a little storybook town nestled in the mountains of Austria, some fifty miles southeast of Salzburg and three miles south of Alt Aussee. There, in June 1945, the Art Unit established a base of operations in a grand chalet called House 71. The chalet had high white walls, a turreted roof, gingerbread trim, and narrow windows that provided a perfect view of the mountain that held the salt mine, which locals called *der Schatzberg*, or "the treasure mountain." The building had been cocooned in barbed wire and turned into a prison for Nazi officials and collaborators. This is where Plaut, Faison, and Rousseau conducted most of their interrogations.[66]

The point of the interrogations was twofold: to learn where to find the art that the Nazis had stolen from the countries they occupied and the people they killed, and to work up criminal charges against the thieves, many of whom had committed war crimes that went far beyond the illegal confiscation of art. The Allies wanted to rack up Nazi leaders on as many charges as they could. The interrogations at House 71 were part of that plan.

Here's the thing about the art dealers and other high-culture functionaries who, after being captured by the Allies, were sent to be interrogated at House 71. They were arrogant. They were egotistical. Many of them believed, as one historian says of Bruno Lohse, a Nazi art dealer who called himself the "King of Paris," that they could speak as peers to white men who had attended elite schools like Harvard, since such men—and such men alone—were "worthy of their time."[67]

Plaut had attended Harvard. He also taught there before he was drafted into the navy. He knew the codes of Ivy WASP culture, and he could play on them beautifully. He used the assumptions of the men he interrogated against them. For example, the Allies brought in Hans Frank, the so-called "Butcher of Poland," for interrogation—Frank had committed unspeakable atrocities, and the OSS wanted to document his art thefts to add to his upcoming trial for war crimes. Frank had a plan for getting out of the situation: he would simply pretend he didn't speak English. (He spoke it just fine.)

No problem. Plaut spoke fluent German.[68]

GENTLEMEN THROUGH AND THROUGH

How do you interrogate a Nazi? A 1943 handbook published by the British SOE advises the interrogator to learn in advance what the target likes and use that knowledge to make the target feel comfortable: "Know your subject. Create a happy atmosphere: cigarettes, common ground, put at ease." The idea was to create the illusion of a friendly conversation between peers. "Do not overdo note taking," the handbook warns; that would lift the semitransparent film of amiable distraction that covers the reality that this is an interrogation. For the same reason, avoid "following logical sequence."[69] (Besides, following logical sequence would let the target more easily keep track of his lies.)

Instead, pretend to let the conversation wander. Have fun, laugh, banter. Maybe bring the target refreshments. (Cigarettes were so important that SOE interrogators sought funding for them from Britain's Ministry of Economic Warfare.[70]) But don't fall for your own bluster, and don't let your target lay your bluster on you: "Do not fall for the 'frank and honest' type, even if it is bona fide."[71]

For anyone with the most basic moral equipment, trading friendly commonalities with a Nazi will be a deeply unpleasant experience. In the introduction to a book about Bruno Lohse, the historian Jonathan Petropoulos, a peerless analyst of art theft in Nazi Europe, describes the unease he felt when he met Lohse more than half a century after the war ended, to learn more about the fate of the stolen art that never resurfaced.[72]

"Yes, I was friendly to him; that was necessary," he says. "Yes, I sometimes needed to have coffee or a meal with him, but that was a means to an end. . . . My meetings with Bruno Lohse were not *Tuesdays with Morrie* feel-good visits but a kind of game—I tried to pry information from him and he attempted to outfox me." After talking with Lohse, Petropoulos contacted the Art Loss Register, Christie's auction house, the Department of Justice, and the FBI about what he'd learned. But the whole affair never stopped feeling faintly dirty to him.[73]

Ironically, Lohse deigned to meet Petropoulos in the first place because Petropoulos was a Harvard graduate, and Lohse still remembered with pride his association with the "Harvard-educated art historians" who interrogated him in House 71.[74] They were essentially colleagues, Lohse believed. The interrogators of the Art Unit gassed him up so well that he was still falling for the trick decades later.

Maybe this is why the Art Unit chose as its base a beautiful chalet in Austria, the kind of mountain getaway that the *beau monde* frequented during the glory days of Habsburg rule.[75] The Art Unit also interrogated people at Neuschwanstein Castle in Germany—the so-called "Sleeping Beauty castle," which rises, like a mirage, from a basin of mist in the surrounding mountains. As with House 71, it was close to a stash of stolen art, but it was also a swell place that perhaps plumed the egos of the people who were held there. *We're all gentlemen here—I'll tell you where the art is, and then I'll be on my way.*

During the summer of 1945, Plaut interviewed dozens of people in Neuschwanstein Castle and House 71, sometimes stretching meetings with one person across a full month.[76] In his reports, Plaut was unsparing and acerbic. Of Karl Kress, a photographer who took pictures of treasures in the Jeu de Paume so that higher-ups like Göring could review the photographs and decide whether they wanted the treasures for themselves, he wrote, "Kress is a 'little man' with a weak personality."[77] Of Gustav Rochlitz, an art dealer who acquired art for Göring directly, he wrote, "Politically, Rochlitz had no genuine convictions. He appears to have acted at all times in his own interest as an unscrupulous opportunist."[78]

Faison and Rousseau, who also interviewed prisoners, didn't include these kinds of merciless character details in their own interrogation reports. Plaut, though, wrote with a pen dipped in acid—while during interrogations, he smiled and smiled and played the friend.

The men whom the Art Unit interrogated, in turn, played the friend too. Robert Scholz, an art historian who worked for the Rosenberg Task Force, told Plaut, who interrogated him at House 71, that his only job in the task force was "the orderly cataloguing and 'safekeeping'" of art. In fact, he led policy and directed confiscations.[79] Rochlitz told Plaut that he acted out of pure benevolence, as Plaut drily recorded: "Rochlitz stated that he had always felt that the day would come when he could make some agreement with the rightful owners of the confiscated pictures, and return them. (Note: These allegations by Rochlitz are refuted convincingly by other informants.)"[80]

Then there was Herman Voss, the director for the planned Führermuseum in Linz—and a man of such gall, and such confidence that the Monuments Men were art looters like him, that he was captured when he walked into the Allied collecting point in Weisbaden to ask for a job. Voss told Faison that he was an academic, "a 'scientific' man divorced from the obligations of practical life," and really too abstracted from whatever the Nazis were doing to understand or get involved in it.[81]

The Art Unit determined, however, that Voss knew what the Nazis were from the jump. He wrote an anti-Nazi poem in 1940—after his arrest, he showed a copy to everyone he could—and gossips in Paris said that after Voss first met Hitler in person, he said, "He is even worse than I expected." But that didn't stop Voss from working for Hitler when a plum directorship was on offer. "He was never a martyr to principle," Faison wrote of Voss. "It appears that Linz was the moral price that Hermann Voss was prepared to pay . . . in the satisfaction of his own vanity."[82]

Everyone suddenly seemed to be describing themselves as heroes of the Resistance. When investigators discovered that a Dutchman named Han van Meegeren had forged those Vermeers that he sold at sky-high prices to Göring and other Nazis, newspapers around the world trumpeted the exploits of the shrewd little dissenter who pulled one over on Göring. Van Meegeren basked in his new heroic reputation, but he *wasn't* a dissenter. He was a Nazi. He even had a little Hitler mustache. His motivation for faking the Vermeers, as he wrote in secret, was to get revenge on the art world, which called him "a third-rate painter," by tricking them into believing that his hand was the hand of the greatest painter in history.[83] But he was hardly special. In the summer of 1945, Europe was full of beaten men who had used the war years to try to climb to the top of their little hills, kicking down their perceived enemies along the way. They understood, now, that the game was over—and the time had come to try to pass themselves off, not as kings, but as heroes, if they could.

IMPERFECT SOLDIERS

The U.S. government started making plans to ship Germany's national art collections to the United States that summer, for "safekeeping." A military officer who helped with the planning explained to President Truman during a meeting in July 1945 that "an announcement [would] be made to the public, to include the German people, that these works of art will be held in trusteeship for return to the German nation when it has re-earned the right to be considered as a nation."[84]

These collections were vast and impressive. The Allied collecting point in Wiesbaden alone held "well over a thousand paintings from the Kaiser Friedrich Museum and nearly four hundred from the Berlin *Nationalgalerie*, not to mention cases and cases of other works of art belonging to the German peoples," the collecting point's director, Walter Farmer, later said. The artists included Botticelli, Frans Hals, Manet, Raphael, Rembrandt, Rubens, Titian, old and new masters from all over Europe.[85]

The United States had its eye on other German holdings, as well. An American official consulted a Monuments Officer about the possibility of moving to the United States a stadium that the Nazis had built in Nuremberg for holding rallies. When the Monuments Officer wanted to know why anyone would do that, the official gave him an odd look and said, "Because it's a damned good stadium." The real reason the government wanted the treasures of Germany's national museums was probably just as simple, an American curator wrote in a letter of disgust: "They're damned good pictures."[86]

The news traveled like a shock wave through the network of American art experts serving in Europe. *This* was what they were asked to do? Recover stolen art, indulge in fine lofty chatter about the immorality of stealing it, then turn around and steal some for themselves? "Plunder is the only word," Walter Farmer later said. "A mockery was being made of our entire operation. Not only was there no need to 'safeguard' these paintings in the United States, but in transporting them on the open seas in the dead of winter, these panel paintings and canvases would be exposed to the most pernicious climactic conditions that one could imagine." At the time, he wrote to his wife, "We are trying Germans as war criminals for what we are now ordered to do. One thing I know, we match every other country in being rotten, disgusting, petty and dishonest."[87]

That fall, Plaut wrote a position paper for the Commission, the government body that gave the U.S. military guidance on how to protect cultural treasures in war-torn areas, that said in no uncertain terms that the United States should not take Germany's art collections. The Roberts Commission's members included Francis Henry Taylor, the director of the Metropolitan Museum of Art; David Finley, the director of the National Gallery of Art; and Paul Sachs, a Harvard professor and Plaut's relative. George Stout, a member of the Monuments Men who wrote his own position paper for the committee, said that some of the committee's members tried mightily to keep such objections off the record.[88]

Perhaps it should have been easy for the U.S. government to take what it wanted, and to get, or manufacture, the assent that it needed to do so. After all, shipping treasures out of conquered territory had a long history. The Russians had already taken trains full of art out of the territories they occupied and back to the Soviet Union. They, too, used the language of safekeeping, but they also spoke openly about getting their pound of flesh from the Germans—about seizing "trophies" of sufficient value to reimburse the Russians for the tremendous costs of the war. The trophies they took home included paintings by Degas, El Greco, Manet, and Renoir, papers of the author Johann Wolfgang von Goethe, and a stash of gold artifacts that archaeologists then believed to come from Homer's Troy. Some of these trophies remain in Russia to this day.[89]

This sort of thing always sparked protests from the people who were losing the art—but consensus seemed to be that it was just how things were done. The winner in a war got to keep the spoils of war, which could be sold to offset the cost of fighting or simply displayed to show the world who was the newest title-holder in history's long line of conquerors. The U.S. government wasn't doing anything new when it ordered its art experts to gather works from German sites and ship them to American museums, to be kept in "protective custody."[90]

The government did try, at least, to find a justification that would fly. In September, the White House put out a press release that said the United States would keep the artworks "only as long as necessary to ensure their physical safety . . . At present these perishable objects are being stored under conditions which would bring about their deterioration."[91] Then an administrator for the National Gallery, working on behalf of the government, wrote a report on the facility in Wiesbaden that housed most of the German collections, saying (falsely) that the facility was in bad shape and the wise thing to do would be, in the words of one commentator, "to remove German paintings to America for safekeeping and return them if and when the German nation had earned the right to their return."[92]

Power is legitimating; if American art historians had let the U.S. government annex those German treasures, lawmakers would have made sure the justifications were polished and the paperwork was in order. And the art historians would surely have been rewarded for their loyalty. Lane Faison might have been able to score Rembrandts for his own museum at Williams College. James Plaut might have gotten a job offer from the Met or the National Gallery. Edith Standen, an art historian who assisted Walter Farmer at the Weisbaden Collecting Point, had something close to a standing offer to work at the National Gallery after her business as a Monuments Officer was finished, and she knew perfectly well that the National Gallery was keen on taking the German pictures.

The military did everything it could to put the squeeze on the recalcitrant scholars, down to reminding the scholars, mafia-style, that they had families to protect. A Monuments Officer named Charles Parkhurst later recalled a tense meeting with a colonel: "He summoned me to his room in Frankfurt and told me I couldn't afford to take this position. I said, 'Why not?' He said, 'You have a wife and two children.' I turned on my heel and walked out. I don't sit still for treatment like that."[93]

Nonetheless, the art historians who worked for the military and the OSS protested their orders, at great risk to themselves. They had learned to take orders like soldiers, but now, at the end of the war, they asserted their freedom again as scholars. They would not loot Europe. In November 1945, Farmer invited all the Monuments Officers serving in Germany to come to Wiesbaden and write a letter of protest. Almost everyone who received his invitation came—thirty-two men and women—and the resulting letter was forthright: "We wish to state that, from our own knowledge, no historical grievance will rankle so long or be the cause of so much justified bitterness as the removal for any reason of a part of the heritage of any nation even if that heritage may be interpreted as a prize of war."[94] (One of the Monuments Officers at the meeting said, "I feel like Thomas Jefferson when he wrote the Declaration of Independence."[95])

The art historians also published letters of protest in newspapers, contacted the press to publicize their dismay, and protested directly to bosses in the art world and the military. Some gave up serious career opportunities in the process. In August 1946, Standen wrote a letter to the National Gallery rejecting their tacit job offer because she objected to the Gallery's push to keep the German paintings. "I had always looked forward to working at the National Gallery when the war would have been won," she wrote. "But I now feel that I cannot possibly work under the roof that houses the paintings that were brought from Germany—with solemn pledges, indeed, of their eventual return, but with an absolute disregard for the people concerned, both American and German, and an ignorance of the actual conditions and probable consequences, which I consider unethical. . . . I am sure, too, that you personally will understand me when I say that I, as a good American, cannot accept a fiat from on high as justification of an action I consider morally wrong, or clear my conscience with the reflection that I was only doing what I was told."[96]

In November 1945, the U.S. government shipped about two hundred paintings from Germany to the National Gallery. Art historians understood this to be a trial balloon for large-scale confiscations; the government said, at first, that the paintings were being sent out of Germany for safekeeping and therefore wouldn't be exhibited, but once they were in the United States, they were exhibited with great fanfare and sent on a national tour.[97] But the art historians kept up their protests with such vigor that the tour's media coverage became a public relations disaster. At last, the government relented, quietly returning the paintings to Germany and abandoning plans to bring over more art.[98] Europe's treasures remain in Europe today.

Faison called this policy of returning stolen art to its place of origin "a brand-new policy, as far as I know, in the history of the world, instead of 'finders-keepers' in the Napoleon sense."[99]

AN UNDERCOAT OF CRIMSON

The history of art is a history of crime because art is wealth—and, as the author Honoré de Balzac said, behind every great fortune lies a great crime. The forgery of artwork is such a reliable profit turner that forgers can count on a better income than most legitimate artists. (Michelangelo, one of the greatest artists in history, got his start as an art forger in the fifteenth century.) Would-be looters have often funded archaeological digs. Patrons who donate wings to museums and sit on their boards sometimes use that same wealth to buy stolen art.[100] The Louvre is filled with paintings that Napoleon stole from Italy. The most famous treasure in the British Museum, the Elgin Marbles, is there because an English lord stole it from the Parthenon in Athens.

In the late 1930s, when the Nazis prepared a handbook to use as a resource for the invasion of Britain, they took special care to elaborate on the treasures in Britain's museums and the dubious origins of many of those treasures; without a doubt, the reason was to prepare a rationale for taking those stolen goods to Germany. "England has some of the largest museums in the world. Art treasures and cultural valuables have been collected or stolen for decades," the handbook says. "The biggest collections are to be found in the British Museum in London, which is organized with an international perspective and exhibits collections and treasures from all over the world, generally the very best that could have been obtained or stolen."[101]

The handbook offers other details that are clearly rationales for a planned program of looting. The National Gallery in London contains portraits of Jews, and therefore is an enemy of the Reich; the New Burlington Gallery hosted an "anti-German exhibition of 'degenerate art'"; the British Music Society, the Royal Society of the Arts, and other cultural organizations "have supported the fight against Germany"; Britain's libraries "contain the most important documents of European, and especially German, historical and cultural development." But, above all, the rationale the Nazis were preparing for when they stripped Britain bare of its paintings and statues and manuscripts seems to have been: *You did it first. This is how the art world works.*[102]

The scholars of the Art Unit and the MFA&A knew how often museums build their collections from theft, and they learned enough while hunting down stolen art to make anyone cynical. But despite every temptation, these art historians did something pure and unexpected that resonates to this day. Perhaps their experience as professors allowed them to make this audacious call: in the classroom, they talked about art, not as merely an asset, but as something that calls to the noblest part of us. Or perhaps the experience of interrogating Nazis and recovering art stolen from murdered Jews left them with the conviction that they couldn't repeat a crime that they had seen in its barest, ugliest form.

Regardless, the benefits of having an intelligence agency made up of scholars and experts, and of valuing scholarly insights more broadly, had this one last example, at the war's close: the scholars knew when to follow principles, not orders. In the process, they enacted the hope that the future of art—and of the world—would be different from the past.

NOT YET FINISHED

In September 1945, President Truman dissolved the OSS, saying it had completed its wartime mission. The Art Looting Investigation Unit dissolved along with it, although Plaut, Faison, and Rousseau continued their interrogations at House 71 until October of that year.[103]

In 1949, Lane Faison transferred to Munich and became the head of the city's Central Collecting Point, the last person to hold that position.[104] His job was to finish the work of sorting through the art that had been shipped over from Alt Aussee and other hiding places and returning it to whoever seemed to have the best claim to it.

The Munich Central Collecting Point was a stern-looking building, three stories tall, with impassive marble walls. It looked like a fantasy of classic Greek architecture by someone who had *read* about classic Greek architecture, but only ever *seen* concrete bunkers. The architect Paul Troost designed it in the 1930s as a kind of proof of concept for his boss, Adolf Hitler: this is what the Third Reich's architecture would look like. During the war, Hitler used the building for his party headquarters in Munich. After the war, the Art Unit filled it with the Reich's stolen pickings.

Before long, Faison realized that he had a problem. The Collecting Point held a lot of Nazi art, much of it from the confiscated estates of prominent Nazis who had been executed for war crimes. Watercolors by Julius Streicher, the publisher of the Nazi newspaper *Der Stürmer*. Sketches and paintings by Alfred Rosenberg, the Nazi functionary who gave his name to the ERR, and Baldur von Schirach, the leader of the Hitler Youth. Other items featured Nazi imagery—swastikas, soldiers, Hitler's scowling, puffy face—that somebody had bought to hang in their office or bathroom.[105]

What do you do with Nazi art? The responsible choice for a historian, surely, is to save it. Art historians like Faison know all too well how important small pieces of evidence become when scholars try to recreate the past. In the end, *nothing* is unimportant: that's the final lesson of the archives.

And for the historian, the ethical commitment to preserving the past does not depend on *liking* what we preserve. The art historians of the Art Unit judged the Nazi art in the Munich collection to have "no artistic merit."[106] Which was . . . reasonable. Streicher, a prolific amateur painter, painted watercolors at about the level of someone at a wine-and-paint party.[107] But historians the world over denounced the Nazis for burning "degenerate" paintings and books.[108] We lie to ourselves when we try to erase the past; and besides, it's a sin, surely, to deprive future generations of the chance to judge the merit of a work for themselves.

Here's what Faison did with the art. He examined it carefully; he weighed his options; he wrote around to make sure its fate was legally up to him, which, his superiors said, was indeed the case.[109] And then he threw it in the fire. Under his supervision, staffers chucked about five hundred pieces of Nazi art into the furnaces that kept the Munich Collecting Point warm.[110]

10

SEARCHING FOR A NEW PLOT

Me, poor man, my library
Was dukedom large enough.
—WILLIAM SHAKESPEARE

MEPHISTO: [Aside] Enough of
all this academic chatter,
Back again to devilry!
—JOHANN VON GOETHE[1]

IN EARLY 1945, WHEN AXIS AND ALLIED FORCES WERE fighting the Battle of the Bulge and the Soviet army was liberating Warsaw, Vannevar Bush—the head of the Office of Scientific Research and Development (OSRD), an agency in charge of coordinating war research at universities across the United States—summoned a Princeton professor named Henry DeWolf Smyth to a meeting in Washington. Bush asked Smyth, whose specialty was physics and who served as an adviser for the Metallurgical Laboratory in Chicago, a satellite campus of the Manhattan Project that focused on plutonium research, to write an account of the atom bomb—how it worked, how it was built—that could be given to the general public.[2]

The time was swiftly approaching, both men knew, when the United States would, in one way or another, make the atom bomb known to the world. The public would clamor for the story behind the weapon, and someone, a reporter or scientist who hadn't signed secrecy documents, would provide it unless the government told the story first. The benefit for the government in controlling the narrative was that the story could become an intelligence operation: it could shape people's ideas of the atom bomb in such a way that other countries would have more trouble building one. Smyth agreed to take on the task.

The resulting report, called *A General Account of the Development of Methods of Using Atomic Energy for Military Purposes Under the Auspices of the United States Government, 1940–1945*, was ready to go when atom bombs destroyed Hiroshima and Nagasaki in August 1945, killing hundreds of thousands of civilians and, shortly after, ending the war. Smyth wrote the report in his office at Princeton, which had iron grates on the windows, a safe to hold the documents he referenced, and soldiers on guard around the clock. (The guards sat outside Smyth's office when he was working and inside his office when he was at home sleeping. He later told *The New Yorker* that their job was to watch him, to make sure he didn't sneak out with nuclear secrets stuffed down his trousers, as much as to watch his visitors: "They did keep people from interrupting me, though. Sometimes I wish I had them back."[3])

It was an instant bestseller.[4] When Princeton University Press released it in hardcover in September 1945, it topped the sales lists alongside *The Manatee*, a steamy novel that, as *The New Yorker* pointed out, had a naked woman on the cover and therefore had more obvious, not to say heaving, selling points than a dry government report.[5]

Here is what Smyth did when writing the report that made its publication an intelligence operation—a misinformation coup so successful that it still utterly dominates the way we think of the atomic bomb today: he wrote it as a story about physicists, and almost *solely* about physicists, in order to hinder other people from figuring out how to build a bomb. The government knew that the physics of building an atomic bomb was the easiest part to figure out from basic principles—and also, from a certain perspective, the least important part. Far more important, at least for solving the problem of how to make the damned thing work, were the heroic labors of chemists, engineers, and technicians in Chicago and Los Alamos (who then had their contributions swept from history).[6]

Smyth's book tells the story that, today, we all *think* we know about World War II: a story of shaggy-haired physicists figuring out, step by step, how to split the atom, work up the result into a chain reaction, and then pack the ingredients into a steel alloy container that a bomber could drop onto whatever place the U.S. wanted to utterly destroy. For a long time, this was the sole narrative that storytellers had to work with; any alternatives were hidden behind classification. It became the basis for Hollywood pictures, magazine stories, and bestselling books: a genre in itself, crowded with images of men in white coats writing equations with shaking hands; rooms full of blinking machines; blackboards chalked up with diagrams of atoms splitting; the men in white coats again, crouching in the desert and shielding their eyes as a test blast turns evening to noon and crying, needlessly, "It works!"

Today, the popular term for World War II is "the physicists' war." After the war, physics departments found themselves the beneficiaries of soaring enrollments, a flood tide of government funding, and the kind of attention normally afforded to Hollywood stars: after all, everyone knew that the war was, at bottom, a triumph of physicists.[7] But what's important to understand is that in matters worthy of great intelligence security, *what everyone knows* merits a little healthy skepticism.

Because this was also the historian's war, the book collector's war, the artist's war. It was the professor's war. The bomb may have ended the war, but the research and analysis performed by the people described in this book won it. So spectacular were their contributions that they changed the future of intelligence.

There were other lasting repercussions. Behind closed doors, out of view, the aspects of the war that the government found useful to continue keeping somewhat secret unfolded in new postwar configurations. Universities found that the former spies who crowded their faculties allowed them to build relationships with American intelligence services. Those former spies recruited their students into the spy agency that succeeded the OSS, the CIA. They also accepted funding from the CIA in exchange for pursuing research programs that furthered CIA imperatives. And beyond that, they brought their wartime experiences back to their classrooms and faculty offices, reshaping their disciplines in the process.

A DIFFERENT KIND OF MURDER YOU CALL ART

In September 1945, less than a month after the war ended, President Harry Truman disbanded the OSS.[8] Donovan's agency was only ever intended for wartime intelligence. But the government didn't fail to recognize the agency's spectacular achievements—not least the achievements of its Research and Analysis branch, the civilian scholars who proved you can thwart the world's great intelligence services with a keen mind and a library card. Two years later, President Truman created the CIA, establishing a permanent civilian intelligence agency. That agency would go on to give a central role to intelligence analysis, a fancy phrase for what the scholars of R&A did. This was something entirely new: America's addition to the world of intelligence.

After the war, Kibre returned to the life she loved: traveling again from library to library as a freelance archival photographer, at home once more in a free Europe. She never married.

Like many women who fought in "the secret war," Kibre kept her secrets even after she returned to civilian life. She knew how to keep herself out of paper trails just as well as she knew how to follow those trails herself. And yet these women returned to a postwar world in which womanhood itself was different in great and subtle ways, in part due to their wartime adventures. When Selwyn Jepson, the SOE recruiter, returned to writing mystery novels after the war, he often wrote lines that seemed to reflect his acute knowledge of the women who went off to spy for the Allies.[*] In his first postwar novel, *Outrun the Constable* (1948), a man voices confusion that the protagonist, who looks like a

---

[*] Britain's Official Secrets Act would have prevented him from writing about the SOE's spies directly, but his postwar characters often think in ways a spy would think. Eve Gill, the protagonist of his major mystery series, tells another character that during the war, she worked for a government organization that trained agents to run resistance cells in France. Selwyn Jepson, *Outrun the Constable* (New York: Doubleday & Company, 1948), 117–18.

"nice girl," is on the wrong side of the law. She thinks, evidently reflecting on the war years, "I held my tongue with an effort; one day perhaps I would be able to explain to him in simple words that there are no longer nice girls and not-nice girls, whatever he had been brought up to believe, but merely girls—and furthermore that even they are women."[9]

Curtiss, too, never married. He took up his old place in Yale's English Department, where nobody knew—save for that senior professor who had called Curtiss into a secret meeting all those years ago—that he'd done anything during the war but collect books for the library. He'd pulled off a truly remarkable feat: working as a spy chief in wartime Istanbul, a city where everyone was presumed to be a spy, without once having his cover blown. He wasn't inclined to break his sterling record.

But when Curtiss went up for tenure at Yale shortly after returning, he ran into problems. Tenure is up-or-out: either the university judges that you've published enough deathless prose, enough field-defining works that will give your department a generations-long halo of renown, to have earned a permanent place on the faculty, or the university genteelly ends your employment and pretends you never existed. The trouble was that Curtiss hadn't published anything while he was away and Yale's administration didn't know about his work as a spy. After a great deal of fretting and consternation, Curtiss finally—quietly—broke his cover: the OSS brass contacted Yale's president and explained the situation. The university granted Curtiss tenure, and the ex-spy taught there for two happy decades before retiring in 1966.[10]

Sherman Kent also returned to Yale after the war and tried to make a go of it in his old department; but unlike Joseph Curtiss, who seemed quite content to teach and read for the rest of his career among the elms and gargoyles, he couldn't say, as Prospero does at the start of Shakespeare's play *The Tempest*, that his library was world enough for him. He'd always been impatient with students, according to his colleagues, and perhaps he found it tedious to be talking—now that he was in the classroom, not the conference room—to subordinates who hadn't done the reading but didn't have enough real-world responsibility to make that ignorance interesting. His battles with students, as he'd once described academic advising, had no real stakes; he was back to throwing chalk instead of knives.

After the war, publishers were hungry for books in a genre that some called "Now it can be told." In September 1945, the film company Twentieth Century Fox announced that it was offering, in a partnership with the publisher Reynal & Hitchcock, a writing grant to army journal-ists who could produce a five-page pitch for a fiction or nonfiction book that looked optionable.[11] One can easily imagine the kind of book that Kent might have written if he wanted to see himself played on the big screen by Humphrey Bogart; after all, he was right in the sand and dust of the arena of the OSS at war, and his irritable, world-weary demeanor would have delighted the right interpreter of tough-guy erudition.

Instead, Kent wrote a book on the art of intelligence analysis, titled *Strategic Intelligence for American World Policy*.[12] "Various editors had told Sherm to forget about such a project," a friend later said, "be-cause it didn't include any blood, guts, or beautiful spies, and because it wouldn't sell the 5,000 copies needed for a publisher to break even."[13] Kent didn't care. He wrote the book as though he were addressing only his former colleagues in the intelligence world. Princeton University Press published the book in 1949; reviewers praised its erudition while also pointing out that it was meant to instruct rather than delight. Wil-liam Jackson, who had served as an X-2 officer during the war, wrote in a review for the *New York Times*, "This book should be read by all high officials charged with responsibility for the security of the country and by all those who work in the field of intelligence."[14] He got the audience right: high-ranking bureaucrats in Washington did read the book, but few others joined them.

In the book, Kent makes the case for maintaining, in America's new intelligence service, the role of intelligence analyst and the prac-tice of recruiting intelligence analysts from the ranks of professional scholars—innovations that the OSS developed accidentally, but which had profound consequences for the intelligence world during the war. "The main difference between professional scholars or intelligence of-ficers on the one hand, and all other people on the other hand," he writes, "is that the former are supposed to have had more training in the techniques of guarding against their own intellectual frailties."[15] A human expert's knowledge is valuable partly because the expert knows the *limits* of that knowledge. Decades later, Kent wrote to a friend that no new technologies would put that thesis out of date—not computers or microdot messages or clandestine listening devices: "The heart of the book is as solid as ever; the game still swings on the educated, thoughtful man, not on gadgetry."[16]

The book was Kent's audition to return to the government, to the world of intelligence. And so he did, joining the CIA in November 1950, just eighteen months after the publication of his book. The CIA had failed to predict North Korea's attack on its southern neighbor that summer, and when China jumped into the fight, which the CIA also failed to predict, the agency's leadership decided to overhaul its methods. They set up a new division that would closely imitate the work that R&A had done during the war, and that would follow many of the specific policy recommendations that Kent set out in his book. The director of the CIA said he aimed for the division to "become the heart of the Central Intelligence Agency and of the national intelligence machinery." William Langer, the Harvard historian who had led R&A during the war and now worked for the CIA, became the head of the new division, the Office of National Estimates (ONE), and invited Kent to join the team as his deputy.[17]

Kent worked happily in the CIA until his retirement, rising to replace Langer as the head of ONE in 1952. In 1953, he began campaigning for the CIA to start its own academic journal—as though it really was a university, and as though intelligence were an academic discipline unto itself, like economics or art history. With his usual pugnaciousness, he explained to anyone who would listen that the CIA needed an in-house publication to preserve its institutional memory; without a dedicated literature, intelligence would languish as "a non-cumulative discipline." He also shared his "sense of outrage at the infantile imprecision of the language of intelligence." ("What kind of a way is this to run a railroad?" he asked.[18])

He got his wish in 1955, when the CIA established a quarterly journal, called *Studies in Intelligence*, with Kent as the editor. The role allowed him to cheerfully gore the subpar work submitted by scholars for publication, which he did for more than a decade.[19]

HOW NOT TO PROVE YOU'RE RIGHT

In 1951, Kent hit upon what he thought was a crackerjack way to prove his theory that well-trained scholars could find out 90 percent of what a country's intelligence service might wish to know about other countries. He enlisted a small group of historians at Yale—William Dunham, Morrell Heald, Basil Henning, Thomas Mendenhall, and David Potter—to spend the summer in Yale's Sterling Memorial Library reading through publicly available documents and working out, using those documents alone, a closely guarded military secret: the United States' "order of battle," or total military configuration, from the leaders to the troop units to the equipment. He also asked them to write up an "encyclopedia" that detailed the types, placement, and strength of all of the U.S. military's combat ships and planes. They did so, working together on the middle floors of the library, a sanctuary as secure, in its way, as the upper reaches of a defensive castle, reachable only after passing vigilant desk librarians, heavy oak doors, and coiling staircases with fire doors at every level.[*]

In due time, the historians presented Kent with a report, six hundred pages long, that did indeed describe the United States' order of battle with more than 90 percent accuracy. Kent decided to dazzle up the results with a little showmanship and asked a Sovietologist to reformat the report as if the Russians themselves had produced it. So a group of Yale historians who had no security clearances had produced a report that compiled highly classified information, and thanks to some magic with formatting and letterheads, the report now *looked like* it was written for the Russians.

---

[*]   I imagine the historians made jokes along the way by playacting as surly and darksyllabled Russians, since the instructions said to do the work as if they were "an informed and studious Russian team." Winks, *Cloak & Gown*, 457–61.

Kent gave the report to his superiors at the CIA—including the director of Central Intelligence, who didn't know he was undertaking the project in the first place—who, in turn, gave it to the president. "It was then," Kent later wrote, "that the shit hit the fan."[20]

In early October, President Harry Truman held a press conference to defend an executive order he'd signed that forbade the media from publishing classified information. At the press conference, he gave what he thought was the best possible example of how the media too often published stories that proved useful to "enemies of the United States": that Yale University had conducted a survey that "found—and they had no connection with the Government—that 95 percent of all our information was public property." When the reporters reasonably asked what Yale was doing conducting a survey of U.S. secrets if it had no connection with the government, Truman answered in a confusing way, probably because he didn't know the answer himself: "They got it out of the newspapers and magazines and sent it down here, and Central Intelligence came to the conclusion that they knew that 95 percent of it" was secret military information that the media had made public.[21]

The next day, the *Yale Daily News* published a scoop: "Unofficial sources have indicated that five members of the history department worked on what was described as an 'ultra-secret' project on the fifth and sixth floors of the library for a three-to-six-week period this summer."[22] What followed was a fair-size shitstorm in which right-wing commentators decried the long-haired radicals in Yale's professoriate for "subversively" hunting through America's military secrets.[23]

Kent and his CIA colleagues had to rush to do damage control before the story got worse, as the historian Robin Winks notes in an entertaining account of this whole episode. The five historians had made five copies of the report, which "were right now very hot potatoes," Winks says, because—and no one had quite thought this part through—they were full of military secrets. An official from the CIA presented himself at the Yale library and demanded the library's entire contents. (The librarians managed to persuade him to take only the historians' own papers and carbon duplicates.) A group of reporters assembled in the hallway outside the classroom of William Dunham, who had led the summer project, while he was teaching; Kent, unable to get him on the phone, called Basil Henning instead and said curtly, without stating his own name, "that the project had 'gone bad,' that Dunham should be warned, and hung up." Henning ran to the room where Dunham was teaching, walked past the reporters like he was going to teach the next class, and then told Dunham what was happening "under the cover of exchanging pleasantries as they erased the blackboard together." So when Dunham left the room, he knew to say essentially nothing.[24]

In the end, the furor died down, and Kent managed to keep his job. And ultimately, he'd proved that he was right—though he decided not to do anything like that again.[25] He'd accidentally turned his ideas into a good story, and as we've seen, a good story can be a dangerous thing.

AN ACADEMY OF ASSASSINS

Before all that, after the war but before the founding of the CIA, Carleton Coon returned to Harvard. Around the same time, he wrote a letter to William Donovan proposing that the OSS establish a secret assassination squad, under the leadership of someone like him, to eliminate foreign threats before they became dangerous.[26]

Coon had reason to feel restless and apprehensive at the prospect of returning to his old discipline. He had built his career as a scholar on the premise that humanity is divided into races that are irreconcilably different, some of which are naturally better than others, and that anthropologists have the important task of championing the "right" races in order to secure a future for humanity. After the war, this view had become rightly poisonous. Coon took issue with the dwindling prospects of his academic reputation. (Did he entertain the possibility that his old ideas were wrong? Did he hell. He viewed civil rights, as his memoirs make clear, as an *academic rival* that was trying to unseat him.)[27]

While writing his letter to Donovan, Coon saw an opportunity, perhaps, to appoint himself to something even higher and more secure than tenure. A way to preserve his authority as a scholar, even escalate it to the power of life and death. Because the folly of man is endless, he wrote, the public and public officials often decline to listen to "the clear and objective scholars who study the existing social systems and draw up the blueprints for a society to suit our technology." So, if the public didn't listen to scholars, clearly the most effective solution was to give a group of those scholars the secret and unanswerable authority to enact their scholarly ideas by force:

> Therefore some other power, some third class of individuals aside from the leaders and the scholars must exist, and this third class must have the task of thwarting mistakes, diagnosing areas of potential world disequilibrium, and nipping the causes of potential disturbances in the bud. There must be a body of men whose task it is to throw out the rotten apples as soon as the first spots of decay appear. If such a body had existed in 1933 its members could have recognized the potential danger of Hitler and his immediate disciples and have killed this group. This would have prevented the rise of a Nazi state in the peculiarly lethal form which it has taken.
>
> A body of this nature must exist undercover. It must either be a power unto itself, or be given the broadest discretionary powers by the highest human authorities.
>
> The only organizations in existence today which have even the rudiments of what is needed in the formation of such a body of men are the OSS and SOE. Agents of these two organizations are trained to act under cover, to act ruthlessly and without fear. We include objective scientists in our midst, and men of the widest experience in the political, economic and diplomatic fields.
>
> It seems to me therefore not too wild, too visionary, or too improbable a thought to suppose that from these two groups a smaller can be selected; a group of men, sober-minded and without personal ambition, men competent to judge the needs of our world society and to take whatever steps are necessary to prevent this society from a permanent collapse.[28]

Donovan pointedly refused to respond to the proposal. Coon's dream of a secret college of scholar-assassins was not to be.

After his proposal to Donovan failed, Coon settled unhappily into campus life. He stood in lecture halls, talking at faces that looked at him with skepticism, not admiration. ("Anthropology 1, which I was supposed to teach," he later complained, "was attended by a small clutch of conscientious objectors and minority students whose allegiance was more to other lands than to the United States."[29]) He sat in department meetings, drawing caricatures of his colleagues. In 1948, he left Harvard for the University of Pennsylvania, which promised him a museum job that had few of the faculty obligations that had become, in this new postwar world, vexations for him. "Mine was not a simple departure, but a second divorce," he wrote.[30]

Among his humiliations in this new world was the fact that his discipline started creating a body of professional ethics in response to the behavior of anthropologists like him during the war. While Coon's enthusiasm for kidnapping and murder was unusual among anthropologists working in Allied intelligence, they had all, to some extent, weaponized their knowledge for the war effort. And after the war, they learned with horror how thoroughly their counterparts in Germany and Japan had abetted war crimes.[31] (Josef Mengele himself, a physician who performed horrific experiments on prisoners in Auschwitz, had training in anthropology.[32])

The work of building up comprehensive ethical principles in America's anthropological organizations was slow and spanned many decades, but their members undertook it with great seriousness, and it was an implicit rebuke to the ways of old departments like Coon's at Harvard, with its jar of heads.[33] Before the war, American anthropologists plumed themselves as gallant adventurers who unearthed the secrets of exotic savages for the benefit of civilized men—savages who, being lesser breeds, they could treat as they pleased. Which is why these gallants, as a matter of course, robbed graves, stole artifacts, lied to their interview subjects, displayed corpses without permission in museums of natural history, and told doctors to keep dying patients—members of the local population in places they were studying—alive on morphine long enough to be interviewed.[34]

Coon simply refused to let go of that image of an anthropologist— even after the rest of his discipline had come to realize how harmful it was. So he played the role of gallant to the end—increasingly petulant, increasingly ridiculous. He railed against the political correctness of campuses in the late 1940s, wrote books that claimed (incorrectly) that white people evolved two hundred thousand years before Black people and therefore were superior, and wrote memoirs in which he gave others dialogue comparing him to Lawrence of Arabia.[35] Even a writer sympathetic to Coon could lament his inability to gracefully let go of outdated ideas: "Instead of retiring with honor, as a grand old man of anthropology, Coon went off, head high and back stiff, but disgraced in most of his colleagues' eyes."[36]

The moment that sealed his exile status in his discipline came in 1962, after Coon became the president of the American Association of Physical Anthropologists, largely because of his seniority in the field.[37] At the association's annual meeting in Philadelphia, he learned that some of the attendees wanted to propose a resolution condemning a new book of pop anthropology that claimed Black people are inherently inferior, and which southern states were using to promote segregation.* Coon attempted what he called an "OSS-type scheme," telling the janitor that if he saw Coon lift his hand, he should turn off all the lights, forcing the session to an abrupt end as everyone fumbled out of the darkness. But the session in question had far more attendees than he'd anticipated, including some of his friends—so he had to abstain from the dirty trick he'd planned for what he thought would be a gathering of just a few "minorities." After listening to the discussion of the proposed resolution and realizing that the tide of opinion was vastly against him, he grew so enraged that he quit the presidency on the spot and stormed out of the event.[38]

---

* The part of the anticipated resolution to which Coon especially objected was the assertion "All races are of equal intelligence." Carleton Coon, *Adventures and Discoveries: The Autobiography of Carleton S. Coon* (Englewood Cliffs, NJ: Prentice-Hall, 1981), 335.

"Instead of giving the hand signal to my friends lurking in the doorway," he wrote, "I told my fellow members that I would no longer preside over such a craven lot, and resigned the presidency. I would leave them to vote whatever resolution they wished, but not in my name."[39]

He lived for another two decades. He saw the world change, and he was unhappy. That will have to be enough for us.

THE AMERICAN CENTURY

The ethnic and political purge of German universities before the war marked the end of Germany's reign as the global capital of the sciences—and the corresponding rise of America's scientific reputation. Germany's proportion of Nobel Prize winners plummeted; at the same time, America's share skyrocketed, with immigrants comprising a growing portion of its twentieth-century laureates. As the historian Michael Gordin wrote, between 1880 and the 1930s, a large segment of scientific books and journals were written in German: "During that era a scientist would have had excellent grounds to conclude that German was well poised to dominate scientific conversation." Starting in the 1930s, however, Germany declined as a language of science and has never recovered. This is not merely due to the flight of scientists or the horrible reputation Germany acquired during these years, Gordin says; it is also due to "the rupture of the graduate-student and postdoctoral exchange networks." Foreign students stopped studying at German universities, previously a most desirable destination.[40]

"I heard of a scientist, the best in his specialized field," said the refugee physicist Leopold Infeld, "who had two appointments: He spent half the academic year in Germany and half in America. When Hitler came to power the professor resigned from his position in Germany. He finished his letter of resignation ironically by expressing the hope that the German minister of education might succeed in raising the level of German universities during his whole future life as much as he had raised the level of American universities during the first three months of his term of office."[41]

American universities, meanwhile, were flourishing. And in the decades after the war, "the number of colleges and universities in the U.S. doubled," writes the literary historian Mark McGurl. In part, this was because of growing enrollment due to the G.I. Bill and coeducation, then the Baby Boom: "In the 1940s, fewer than 10 percent of traditional college-age Americans were attending college of some kind; by the 1980s, more than half of them were doing so."[42]

Many of the veterans who attended college on the G.I. Bill chose to major in physics, which Smyth's book had helped to make unimaginably glamorous.[43] Others were drawn to the booming fields of American Studies and area studies (the study of specific regions), which came directly out of the new kinds of research that the OSS pioneered.[44]

Unimagined new fields of science and technology also arose out of wartime research. In fact, the war jump-started the information age. Claude Shannon, who worked as a cryptanalyst during the war, used the concepts he developed as a codebreaker to invent information science in the late 1940s. John von Neumann, the Hungarian mathematician who came to the United States from Berlin, pioneered digital computing—work that arose from his military ordnance projects during the war.[45] Historically, modern computers should have been invented in Berlin. Instead, they were invented in Princeton and Pennsylvania. (And Cambridge, in the United Kingdom.) If not for Germany's path of destruction, today we would spell the word *computer* with a *K*.

THE MILITARY-INDUSTRIAL-ACADEMIC COMPLEX

In fact, no department in American universities was untouched by the events of the war and the postwar university boom. In literature departments, professors embraced a new approach known as "close reading," or the close study of a text without relying unduly on historical sources. Many of the newly built universities lacked strong research libraries, and professors at those universities found it useful to tell students that a text's own language is the best guide to its meaning—that all you need to understand a poem is the poem itself.[46]

And a new field arose in both literature and history departments called book history, the study of the material history of texts.[47] It is a discipline saturated with mourning—with a moral urgency to recover lost worlds from the documents those worlds left behind.

Economics departments also changed dramatically after the war. Nobody predicted that economists would make such powerful contributions to R&A. But when they returned to campus, former OSS analysts remembered what economists had achieved. Hiring in economics departments soared after the war; and perhaps it was no coincidence that a dominant form of research and pedagogy in economics departments after the war resembled what economists did in the war—namely, make clever and surprising inferences from unlikely data sets.[48]

Inevitably, many of the students of these former intelligence agents became intelligence agents in turn. For decades, college students followed tunnels that led straight from the seminar room to the CIA. Among intelligence agencies like the CIA, the phrase "the P source"—short for *professor* source—used to be code for the professors and university administrators who recruited on their behalf. For a time, Ivy League schools supplied "a disproportionate amount" of the new employees to the CIA, according to the CIA's in-house journal, *Studies in Intelligence.* For much of the second half of the twentieth century, intelligence agencies recruited in large numbers from departments of English, history, and the social sciences—and they still relied on professors in those departments to help turn data into usable intelligence. Humanities scholars moved in the hidden world of spies, and spies, in turn, shaped major institutions in the humanities.[49]

Reading as a historian entails looking for information about how people put together the information you're looking at. Allen Dulles, the first civilian director of the CIA, was a history major at Princeton. Throughout his career in the Agency, he sought insights from humanities scholarship. During the 1960s, he met several times a year on Princeton's campus with a group of humanities professors, whom he called the "Princeton Consultants," who helped to produce the "blue books" of intelligence analysis that the CIA sent to the White House.

Dulles often gave public talks in which he stressed the value of studying history. He discussed the craft of writing well in documents like the President's Daily Brief. ("How do you get a policymaker's attention?" he asked. "Just as you get the *Princetonian* [Princeton's student newspaper] sold. Make it readable, clear, and pertinent to daily problems."[50]) He noted that reading a text's plain language is not enough to assess its meaning: For example, "many Soviet formal documents—constitutions, laws, codes, statutes, etc.—sound quite harmless, but in execution prove very different than they read."[51] (A politician might say he wants a conflict to end in peace, but omit that he plans to *get* peace by wiping out one of the disputing parties.) Here, he suggested why the innovation of recruiting humanities scholars changed spycraft—and why his CIA recruited so heavily from departments of English and history. Cryptography is not the only way to make codes. Irony, implicature, politesse, euphemism, ambiguity, hyperbole, allusion, and deflection are also codes: They are ways of saying one thing and meaning another.

Today, these may be the last types of codes to resist high-tech "crypto cracking" and digital trawling techniques like keyword searches. Twitter users have perfected subtweets, or tweets written about someone who goes unnamed so that a search won't find the post. Or consider another form of covert meaning-making: weaponized irony. On some extremist websites, writers use irony to convince new readers that they mean their threats as jokes—indeed, to *attract* new readers who find the jokes daring—while longtime readers know they are deadly serious. (The style guide for the neo-Nazi website the Daily Stormer, which was leaked in 2017, advised, "The unindoctrinated should not be able to tell if we are joking or not."[52]) Or again, consider the Chinese government's censorship of certain puns online—the reason being that internet users in China have had great success in using wordplay (the kind that uses *kiss the sky* to mean *kiss this guy*) to discuss forbidden subjects without getting caught in internet filters. Such games with language command the attention of students of history and literature, who know that we toil mightily to make words mean what we choose them to mean.

ART AS A WEAPON

The American alliance between secret intelligence and universities, including humanities departments, didn't just change universities and three-letter agencies. It also changed institutions like galleries and museums—so profoundly, in fact, that one could say that American art in the twentieth century was shaped largely by CIA imperatives.

Alfred Barr, the first director of the Museum of Modern Art in New York City—he left that job during the war, but remained with the museum in an advisory role afterward—developed the museum's vision of modern art in conversation with the museum's quiet relationship with the CIA; for instance, endorsing Abstract Expressionism as a manifestation of the "artistic free enterprise" of the United States—which had the best art, Barr implied, because it had the best system of government.[53] C. D. Jackson moved between the world of intelligence and the media giant Time Inc., eventually presiding, as the publisher of *Life* magazine, over suites of images that celebrated the riches of "The American Century": ingenue actresses, charity fashion shows, White House parties, and handkerchief-waving crowds at Ivy League football games. Freedom and capitalism, American values, all.

The CIA helped to fund and shape the institution of the MFA program in creative writing. In the mid-twentieth century, as the literary historian Eric Bennett writes in *Workshops of Empire,* the CIA, together with other government entities such as the State Department and the United States Information Agency (USIA), began a program of investment in the Iowa Writers' Workshop, which had been founded in 1936 to build an American home for the world's literati. The workshop's director, Paul Engle (who spent the war teaching, though he tried to get a job with the Office of War Information), argued in fundraising campaigns that the Workshop could tame restless intellectuals from the United States and abroad by nurturing them in the heartland. Engle, who celebrated midwestern wholesomeness in magazine articles with titles like "Iowa: the Heart of America's Heartland," boasted about the Workshop's diplomatic value: "In the last few years, we have had students from Ireland, Japan, Formosa, South Korea, the Philippines, Canada, England, Sweden, all of whom go back to their native lands with their view of the United States greatly enhanced because they have found a place for their talent in the University of Iowa, in the heart of the Midwest. It is important that these most articulate of their generation should write and study far from both coasts, where foreign students have tended to concentrate. Here they learn the essential America."[54]

By the late 1960s, intelligence agencies were supporting literary and intellectual journals such as *Daedalus, Partisan Review, Poetry, Kenyon Review,* and *Sewanee Review.* The Congress for Cultural Freedom (CCF), which the CIA founded as an anti-communist front, bought thousands of subscriptions to these magazines and distributed the issues abroad. Many alumni and affiliates of the Iowa Writers' Workshop became affiliates (with or without knowledge of what they were getting into) of the CCF, including Robert Lowell, Norman Holmes Pearson, John Crowe Ransom, and Allen Tate. By controlling the means of intellectual production, the CCF sought to promote, in the intelligentsia, values that the CIA and the U.S. government approved of.[55]

In short, the importance of storytelling was so obvious to the CIA that it went to great lengths to mold storytellers and their platforms.

THE CAMPUS

For a time postwar, William Donovan and his staff continued to work in the temporary buildings and repurposed hospitals and barracks that had served as their offices throughout the war. Even after President Truman created the CIA in 1947, Agency employees were scattered in office buildings around downtown Washington. In 1959, President Dwight Eisenhower dedicated a new headquarters for the agency in Langley, Virginia, a few miles away from the White House and across the Potomac River. (At the dedication ceremony, Dulles sealed a time capsule in the cornerstone of the building. When reporters asked Dulles what the capsule's contents were, he replied, "It's a secret."[56])

In 1956, Dulles appointed Walter Pforzheimer, the man who set up the Yale Library cover for Joseph Curtiss's intelligence work in

Istanbul, to put together a library for the young intelligence agency. The achievements of the OSS during the war had demonstrated the value of wide and careful reading for spycraft. Pforzheimer, who now worked as a lawyer for the CIA, was an avid book collector who was building his own library of rare intelligence books, so he seemed like the right man for the job. The collection started in the ragged little group of buildings on E Street that had served as OSS headquarters; today, it resides on the CIA's ultrasecure, well-groomed campus in Langley.[57]

The CIA's library now holds more than 125,000 books, of which some 25,000 are the kind of odd historical texts that rare-books archives specialize in. A 1683 pamphlet that revealed the methods of Turkish spies in Vienna. A 1699 memoir by Matthew Smith, an English spy who published the secrets of his profession because he was flat broke and preferred the chance of death by hanging to the certainty of death by starving. Color photograph albums of Pearl Harbor. Books on (and by) the legendary Chinese strategist Sun Tzu; books on the New York spies who won the American Revolution; books on the African American spies who won the Civil War. A 1907 book by Allen Dulles, age eight, whose parents privately printed a little history he'd written of the Boer War. ("He directed, at the time, that all royalties go to a fund to help the victims of that war.") It even holds novels, on the principle that novelists often work with real facts.[58]

The CIA has debated from time to time whether to dissolve the historical collection in its library. In 1980, while the Agency was reviewing ways to reduce its budget, a proposal came down to get rid of the collection on the grounds that modern spies don't regularly need to take notes from George Washington's spy ring. The library's curators managed to defend it—though for how long is a question that future generations must answer.[59]

A DAMN DIM CANDLE OVER A DAMN DARK ABYSS

The historian W. S. Holt, a professor at the University of Washington who worked in the OSS during World War II, described history as "a damn dim candle over a damn dark abyss."[60] Even with our best efforts, our knowledge of the past will always be frustratingly limited. Most of the people who have ever lived were illiterate. Most of our knowledge about the past comes from writing. You can do the math yourself.

But—to use a phrase from Shakespeare—how far that little candle throws its beams! And how little we can do without it.

The world was incredibly fortunate that the United States was able to turn its greatest disadvantage at the start of the war, its lack of a standing intelligence service, into its greatest advantage. That advantage came from innovation: because they weren't tied down by established ways of doing things, the professors and librarians of the OSS, and the refugees who joined them, were able to create something new. They became the scholars who invented modern spycraft.

They could do so only because they were experts, themselves, in unsuspected disciplines that turned out to be supremely useful for intelligence work. Disciplines that taught them how to work with messy data. How to sift through paper evidence like newspapers, leaflets, and novels. How to gather clues from unlikely sources like advertisements and society columns. How to read *a lot* in just a little time. How to look at a pile of cracked and curling pages and see a treasure hunt. How to evaluate claims. How to tell stories. How to come up with audacious methods of solving problems using unlikely data: figuring out military secrets, say, by tracking ball bearings, or railroad rates, or the serial numbers of tank components. How to make arguments that aren't merely summaries of what has been said, but that say something new. How to understand another country—because the past, too, is another country—on its own terms. If you're going to fight a war, you can't just put boots on the ground; you also have to put ground under the boots, in the form of maps, blueprints, local knowledge.

Ignorance isn't an actual prerequisite for innovation. Yes, the world was fortunate that the library rats of the OSS were able to make an advantage out of their country's lack of an established intelligence tradition. Unblinkered by convention, they envisioned new possibilities. But the United States could have had institutions and innovation both, had it preserved the lessons of its own adventures in intelligence during previous wars.

Consider what we lost in institutional memory after the Civil War. During that war, Allan Pinkerton, the private eye who founded the Pinkerton National Detective Agency, worked as a spymaster for the Union. He wasn't good at the kind of analytical problem-solving that the OSS later excelled at (which led to some major intelligence failures). But his background made him very good at trapping enemy agents (that is, counterintelligence) and working with confidential sources. Throughout the war, Pinkerton collaborated extensively with Black people who worked as spies and informants for the Union, taking advantage of the social invisibility that came with Blackness: freedmen, runaways from slavery, still-enslaved people, and others.[61]

After the Civil War, the insights of that generation of spies were largely lost to the United States. American politicians and historians simply didn't ask the former spies to share their knowledge, in part because they didn't take that much interest in the experiences of Black people.

There's no reason that America's intelligence service during World War II couldn't have innovated while *also* knowing this lost history. Certainly, the Allies' victory in the war relied on the help of people who were socially invisible: women, children, Jewish people in the ghettoes. And scholars and librarians and booksellers, although *their* invisibility was merely occupational.

So, let's remember how a group of seemingly unlikely people, though novices to spycraft, created new ways of doing intelligence that won a war, revolutionized spycraft, and changed the world.

The task of intelligence—trying to find out secrets the enemy is giving away without realizing it—turned out to be what these professors had been training at all their lives. The French playwright Molière created a character who is astonished to discover that he has been speaking prose all his life without knowing it. So it was with the professors of the OSS. They'd been spies, detectives, heroes all their lives without knowing it. And when they answered the call of a global crisis, they discovered new aspects of their own potential.

Today, we are the heirs to their legacy. The Allies won the war, and in the process saved as much as they could of the archives, artworks, and other cultural heritage artifacts that would have been destroyed, together with the communities that created them, had Hitler won. The effort to do right by those remnants, to cope with the enormous losses of the Holocaust and the war, shaped much of the world of universities, libraries, and museums in the second half of the twentieth century.

And yet we also belong, in the twenty-first century, to a time of profound disdain for the humanities that is prompting us to turn away from the very fields that this book has shown are so important. Research shows, for instance, that declining enrollments in university humanities departments (estimates of the rate of that decline differ, but most people agree that it's steep) are happening not because a humanities degree is a bad bet in the job market—it's not—but because students *think* a humanities degree is a bad bet in the job market.[62] Here as elsewhere, stories matter. And what's most concerning is the fact that we've chosen to tell ourselves a story about the worthlessness of the humanities that doesn't reflect reality, and yet shapes all kinds of decisions we make about our world: cutting library budgets; telling archives to digitize, then throw out, their records; telling young people that some things aren't worth learning.[63]

The forces that shape that story rely on our neglect of history. The excitements of computing, for instance, which Silicon Valley likes to present as a world *without* history, have given thought leaders cause to proclaim that we no longer need that messy paper knowledge. *You don't need to read that whole book; we have an app that will auto-generate a summary of it. You don't need foreign language departments; we have an online translation tool. You don't need to study history if you study coding. You don't need to think about the open society as long as your software is open source. We should close libraries and open maker spaces. Those old disciplines are irrelevant.*[64]

We can decide, ourselves, whether to let that candle go out.

It's a decision that we make together. With the shape of our institutions: our libraries, our museums, our education system. It's also a decision that we make individually. When we read, when we write. When we decide whether to work in those embattled disciplines, and why.

The work is worth doing. The call may come at any time.

ACKNOWLEDGMENTS

This book is the product of the immense generosity of my colleagues and friends with their time and expertise. Sarah Levitt, my agent, has forgotten more than I will ever learn about the book business, and she has the artist's gifts together with the businesswoman's guile. Sarah Murphy has been an astute and insightful editor. Marilyn Marks, development editor extraordinaire, was with this book since before it was an idea for a book. I also owe an immeasurable debt to the editorial expertise of Peter Barzilai, Emily Graff, and Gail Winston.

Kathy Peiss, the author of *Information Hunters*, and Jonathan Petropoulos, the author of *Göering's Man in Paris*, provided invaluable historical insights, as did the intelligence experts Cliff Karchmer and Robert Hutchings.

Kelly Burton and Shannon Morelli helped me find my way through the archives of the National Gallery of Art, and Vincent Turpin did the same in the National Archives. Susan Tomkins answered my questions about Beaulieu and gave me a behind-the-scenes tour. Ahmet Memis, my guide in Istanbul, shared fascinating details about the city's history, as did Frances Gallart Marques, and Tonya Gruber gave me a tour of the salt mine at Alt Aussee.

Lou Cain and Nathaniel Grotte generously provided access to unpublished interviews about the history of the OSS, and the archivists at the University of Chicago Library provided access to unlisted material concerning the same.

Martha Nicholls and Anette Nielsen did heroic work as biographical researchers. Kevin Chesley, Karen Lloyd, Margaret Hanley, and Mike Rubenstein helped with jokes.

Ann Blair, Robert Darnton, Maria DiBattista, John V. Fleming, David Kastan, Catherine Nicholson, James Paradis, Leah Price, Jeffrey Ravel, and David Thorburn provided models for how to do history and book history that I've continued to learn from in the years since studying with them.

Sherman Tecumseh Kent gave me permission to quote from Sherman Kent's unpublished memoir, for which he has my profound gratitude.

Peter Reilly made a cover for the audiobook of "Boo-Boo, Baby, I'm a Spy" that makes me wish I could put it on vinyl on repeat. Fran Perdomo Klukosky, the best lawyer in New York, helped with licenses and legal questions.

Finally, thanks go to my parents for support, Mark Aronoff for wisdom, Robert Crease for expertise, and Mr. W. H., for insight and inspiration.

NOTES

INTRODUCTION

1.   William Donovan, "Intelligence: Key to Defense," *Life*, September 30, 1946, 110. This quotation has been slightly shortened for space.
2.   Cabell Phillips, "The Shadow Army That Fought in Silence," *New York Times*, October 7, 1945.
3.   See, for example, Jacob Soll, *The Information Master: Jean-Baptiste Colbert's Secret State Intelligence System* (Ann Arbor: University of Michigan Press, 2009); Robert Hutchinson, *Elizabeth's Spymaster: Francis Walsingham and the Secret War* (New York: St. Martin's Press, 2006); and John Man, *Ninja* (London: Corgi Books, 2012).
4.   *The Fighting 69th*, directed by William Keighley (1940; Los Angeles: Warner Brothers). See also Louis Menand, "Wild Thing," *New Yorker*, March 14, 2011, 70.
5.   "The R&A branch was the first branch to get going," Sherman Kent later said, "and I suppose I was about the thirtieth member of the R&A branch to receive an appointment." Sherman Kent, unpublished memoir, Yale University archives.
6.   Walter Pforzheimer, comments on Robin Wink's manuscript for *Cloak and Gown*, Yale University archives.
7.   Richard Dunlop, *Donovan: America's Master Spy* (New York: Skyhorse Publishing, 2014), 309.
8.   Kathy Peiss, *Information Hunters: When Librarians, Soldiers, and Spies Banded Together in World War II Europe* (Oxford: Oxford University Press, 2020), 37.
9.   Richard Ovenden, *Burning the Books: A History of the Deliberate Destruction of Knowledge* (Cambridge, MA: Harvard University Press, 2020), 119.
10. Ovenden, *Burning the Books*, 119.
11. Mark Glickman, *Stolen Words: The Nazi Plunder of Jewish Books* (Lincoln: University of Nebraska Press, 2016), 78–81.
12. Ovenden, *Burning the Books*, 120–21.
13. Guenter Lewy, *Harmful and Undesirable: Book Censorship in Nazi Germany* (Oxford: Oxford University Press, 2016), 8.
14. Ovenden, *Burning the Books*, 121–22; Lewy, *Harmful and Undesirable*, 112–28.

15. Ovenden, *Burning the Books*, 122–30.

16. Ovenden, *Burning the Books*, 120–30.

1: THE SPY WHO CAME IN FROM THE CARREL

1. On American journalism during the lead-up to World War II, see, for example, Deborah Cohen, *Last Call at the Imperial Hotel: The Reporters Who Took On a World at War* (New York: Random House, 2022).

2. Michael Lee Lanning, *Senseless Secrets: The Failures of U.S. Military Intelligence from George Washington to the Present* (New York: Birch Lane Press, 1996), 165.

3. Robin Winks, *Cloak & Gown: Scholars in the Secret War, 1939–1961* (New York: William Morrow, 1987), 128.

4. Winks, *Cloak & Gown*, 128.

5. Jim Maclear, "List of Best Study Spots on Campus," *The Daily Maroon*, October 10, 1941, 3. See also "The Gray City Along the Midway," *Chicago Maroon*, September 23, 1946, 3; Ray Poplett, "Maroon Survey Reveals Library Lighting Is Generally Inadequate," *Daily Maroon*, October 29, 1941, 1; and "Return to the Old Days," *Daily Maroon*, November 30, 1945, 5.

6. Loren Flint, "Faddy Clothes Tabooed for Campus Wear," *Daily Maroon*, September 11, 1940, 3. Then as now, college women liked to wear pieces "stolen from the men." Beverly Ward, "Maroon Consultant Gives Fashion Tips," *Daily Maroon*, September 11, 1940, 3.

7. Sergel, "Help," *Daily Maroon*, February 24, 1937, 2.

8. See Eugene Power, *Edition of One: The Autobiography of Eugene B. Power, Founder of University Microfilms* (Ann Arbor, MI: University Microfilms International, 1990).

9. See Harvey Williams Cushing papers, Yale University archives.

10. Power, *Edition of One*, 105. On Adele Kibre, see also Kathy Peiss's indispensable book *Information Hunters*.

11. Ed Ainsworth, "Along El Camine Real with Ed Ainsworth," *Los Angeles Times*, April 20, 1940, 8.

12. Ainsworth, "Along El Camine Real with Ed Ainsworth," 8.

13. Power, *Edition of One*, 137–39; Philip Power, "Eugene Barnum Power (4 June 1905–6 December 1993)," *Proceedings of the American Philosophical Society* 139, 3 (September 1995), 300–304.

14. Power, *Edition of One*, 138.

15. See, for example, John Markland, "All Highways Now Lead to King Football's Big Empire," *New York Times*, October 1, 1939; and "Special Train Arranged for Yale-Harvard Game," *Yale Daily News*, November 17, 1941.

16. Carleton Coon, *A North Africa Story: The Anthropologist as OSS Agent, 1941–1943* (Ipswich, MA: Gambit, 1980), 3.

17. See, for example, Richard Usborne, introduction to *Bulldog Drummond* by Sapper (London: J. M. Dent and Sons, 1920), vii. On the reading habits of lower-class and upper-class English boys during the period of Coon's youth,

see George Orwell, "Boys'Weeklies," *Inside the Whale and Other Essays* (London: Victor Gollancz, 1940), 42.

18. Carleton Coon, *Adventures and Discoveries: The Autobiography of Carleton S. Coon* (Englewood Cliffs, NJ: Prentice-Hall, 1981), 21.

19. The adviser was Earnest Hooton, and he kept the jar on display in his lab, Coon, *Adventures and Discoveries*, 22–25.

20. Carleton Coon, author blurb, *Atlantic Monthly* 156, July 1935, 384.

21. Gretchen Schafft, *From Racism to Genocide: Anthropology in the Third Reich* (Urbana: University of Illinois Press, 2004), 16, 73–74.

22. He eventually mentioned her help in his autobiography, but he didn't thank her for it, Coon, *Adventures and Discoveries*, 56.

23. Coon, *Adventures and Discoveries*, 160–62.

24. Coon, *Adventures and Discoveries*, 162.

25. Winks, *Cloak & Gown*, 449–50; Richard Helms, *A Look Over My Shoulder: My Life in the Central Intelligence Agency* (New York: Random House, 2003), 73.

26. "One Hundred Yale Faculty Members Engaged in National Defense Program," *Yale Daily News*, September 23, 1941. In June 1942, President Roosevelt created a separate civilian agency called the Office of War Information, which became something of a competitor to the OSS.

27. "Library Displays War Documents," *Yale Daily News*, February 22, 1941.

28. Kent, unpublished memoir.

29. Winks, *Cloak & Gown*, and S. Peter Karlow, *Targeted by the CIA: An Intelligence Professional Speaks Out on the Scandal That Turned the CIA Upside Down* (Nashville, TN: Turner Publishing, 2001), 10. See also, for example, Russell Jack Smith, *The Unknown CIA: My Three Decades with the Agency* (New York: Macmillan, 1989), 66 and Robert W. Smith, *Martial Musings: A Portrayal of Martial Arts in the 20th Century* (Eerie, Pennsylvania: Via Media, 1999), 153.

30. Kent, unpublished memoir.

31. Winks, *Cloak & Gown*, 42.

32. Smith, *Martial Musings*, 153.

33. Here's how to do it: grab a section of the newspaper and lay it out flat so it closes at the center crease. Then roll diagonally—and tightly—up from the lower-right corner until you have a weapon that looks a bit like a baton and that tapers to a nasty point. Grip the weapon so the point juts out between your thumb and your pointer finger; use the point to hit him in the gut and then, right afterward, up under the chin, putting all your weight into the blows. As an alternative, if you're sitting beside him, grab three or four sections of the newspaper, fold them in half from the top, roll them into a tight baton, and then swing the weapon, like a police baton, in an arc to hit the side of his head. "Anywhere between the chin and temple will knock him unconscious." Rex Applegate, a weapons instructor at Area B, explains the newspaper attack in Rex Applegate and Chuck Melson, *The Close-Combat Files of Colonel Rex Applegate* (Boulder, CO: Paladin Press, 1998), 58.

34. Kent, unpublished memoir.

35. Kent, unpublished memoir.

36. Kent, unpublished memoir.

37. Winks, *Cloak & Gown*, 42.

38. Lyman Kirkpatrick, Jr., *Captains Without Eyes* (London: Macmillan Company, 1969), 75–157.

39. OSS Assessment Staff, *Assessment of Men: Selection of Personnel for the Office of Strategic Services* (New York: Rinehart & Company, 1969), 12. Hereafter cited as Assessment 1948, with page numbers.

40. Roger Hall, *You're Stepping on My Cloak and Dagger* (New York: Bantam Books, 1964), 34. I'm assuming Curtiss was at Area B based on his testimony that the camp was an hour northwest of Baltimore. But he would have gone through much the same training as a novice regardless of the specific site of his camp.

41. The source of the cover name could differ, as the staffers at one camp noted in a speech to their trainees: "Each of you has come here under the cover of a student name. That name may be your first name, or middle name, or nickname, or a name that has been arbitrarily assigned to you. We don't know which it is, and we don't care. The important thing is that during your stay here you will be known to your associates and to the staff alike only by your student name. There are many things which we on the staff will want to know about you, but we do not need to know and do not want to know your real name or true identity," Assessment 1948, 65.

42. Winks, *Cloak & Gown*, 128.

43. Assessment 1948, 21–22.

44. Assessment 1948, 92.

45. Donald Downes, *Orders to Kill* (New York: Rinehart & Company, 1958), 67–69. I have altered and shortened this passage from the novel for clarity and conciseness.

46. Downes, *Orders to Kill*, 73.

47. See, for example, Elyse Graham, "The Power of Small Numbers," *Princeton Alumni Weekly*, May 16, 2018.

48. Assessment 1948, 137–38.

49. Downes, *Orders to Kill*, 73; Assessment 1948, 138–40.

50. Winks, *Cloak & Gown*, 1987, 128–29.

51. Richard Dunlop, *Behind Japanese Lines* (New York: Rand McNally, 1979), 84.

52. Rex Applegate, introduction to *Commando Dagger: The Complete Illustrated History of the Fairbairn-Sykes Fighting Knife* by Leroy Thompson (Boulder, CO: Paladin Press, 1985), vii.

53. Jerry Sage, *Sage* (n.p.: Miles Standish Press, 1985), 14, 19–20; Applegate and Melson, *The Close-Combat Files of Colonel Rex Applegate*, 46.

54. Applegate and Melson, *The Close-Combat Files of Colonel Rex Applegate*, 46–47; Sage, *Sage*, 24.

55. Applegate and Melson, *The Close-Combat Files of Colonel Rex Applegate*, 46–47; John Ranelagh, *The Agency* (London: Weidenfeld and Nicolson, 1986), 66–67.

56. Dunlop, *Behind Japanese Lines*, 84; Applegate and Melson, *The Close-Combat Files of Colonel Rex Applegate*, 43.

57. W. E. Fairbairn, *All-In Fighting* (Uckfield, UK: Naval and Military Press Ltd, 2020). Italics are in the original.

58. Bruce Wexler, *The Mysterious World of Sherlock Holmes* (New York: Skyhorse Publishing, 2007), 42.

59. Quoted in Denis Rigden, introduction to *SOE Syllabus: Lessons in Ungentlemanly Warfare*, National Archives, 2004, 1. Hereafter cited as Syllabus 2004, with page numbers.

60. Gordon Thomas and Greg Lewis, *Shadow Warriors of World War II: The Daring Women of the OSS and the SOE* (Chicago: Chicago Review Press, 2017), 7–9. Jepsen was only one of several recruiting officers.

61. M. R. D. Foot, *SOE: The Special Operations Executive, 1940–46* (Bury St. Edmunds, Suffolk, UK: St. Edmundsbury Press, 1984), 58.

62. Jepsen discusses meeting candidates in his office in the War Office building in Russell Miller, *Behind the Lines: The Oral History of Special Operations in World War II* (New York: Random House, 2002), 11.

63. Miller, *Behind the Lines*, 10.

64. Jepson cultivated this look on purpose. Foot, *SOE: The Special Operations Executive*, 58.

65. The advice to be inconspicuous is from Syllabus 2004, 38–39.

66. Jepson told candidates that they would have a one in two chance of survival in France, which was the SOE's best estimate at the time. After the war, the SOE calculated that the actual chance of survival for an undercover agent in France was three in four. Foot, *SOE: The Special Operations Executive*, 59.

67. British intelligence did sometimes misname the OSS the "Office of Strategic Studies." See, for example, "Office of Strategic Studies (OSS)," Manuscript HS 7/283, National Archives.

2: A GIRL'S GUIDE TO BURGLARY

1. Virgil, *Aeneid*, 7.312; trans. in Peter Iseley, "The 'Madness of Barbara Blaine,'" *National Catholic Reporter*, October 12, 2017.

2. Applegate and Melson, *The Close-Combat Files of Colonel Rex Applegate*, 51.

3. For a description of the weapons in the students' kits, see Applegate and Melson, *The Close-Combat Files of Colonel Rex Applegate*, 43–46.

4. Keith Melton and Robert Wallace, *Spy Sites of Washington, DC: A Guide to the Capital Region's Secret History* (Washington, DC: Georgetown University Press, 2017), 81.

5. Applegate and Melson, *The Close-Combat Files of Colonel Rex Applegate*, 46.

6. Syllabus 2004, 17–18.

7.   Syllabus 2004, 366; W. E. Fairbairn, *Get Tough!: How to Win in Hand-to-Hand Fighting as Taught to the British Commandos and the U.S. Armed Forces* (London: Naval & Military Press, n.d.), 96.

8.   Quote is from Syllabus 2004, 366.

9.   Syllabus 2004, 366; Rex Applegate, *Combat Use of the Double-Edged Fighting Knife* (Boulder, CO: Paladin Press, 1993), 17–19.

10.   Rex Applegate, introduction to *Commando Dagger*, vii; Applegate and Melson, *The Close-Combat Files of Colonel Rex Applegate*, 47.

11.   Rex Applegate, *Kill—Or Get Killed* (Harrisburg, PA: Military Service Publishing, 1943), 79–82.

12.   Applegate, *Kill—Or Get Killed*, 79–82.

13.   Applegate, *Kill—Or Get Killed*, 82–83.

14.   Applegate, *Kill—Or Get Killed*, 82–83.

15.   Applegate, *Kill—Or Get Killed*, 224–25.

16.   Hall, *You're Stepping on My Cloak and Dagger*, 41–43.

17.   "SOE course at Beaulieu 1945 [actually 1941]," The Security Service, manuscript number KV 4/172, National Archives (1941), Kew, UK. Hereafter cited as KV 4/172, with page numbers. I am working with the assumption that the British shared with the Americans their training materials on cover stories and the like, just as they shared their training materials on fighting.

18.   KV 4/172, 16.

19.   KV 4/172, 17–18.

20.   KV 4/172, 18.

21.   KV 4/172, 18.

22.   KV 4/172, 16.

23.   KV 4/172, 18.

24.   KV 4/172, 18–36.

25.   KV 4/172, 30–36.

26.   KV 4/172, 18.

27.   Donald Downes, Curtiss's recruiter at the Yale Club, was one of the sponsors of this program. Winks, *Cloak & Gown*, 175–76.

28.   KV 4/172, 18.

29.   KV 4/172, 25–30.

30.   KV 4/172, 25–30; Carl Müller Frøland, *Understanding Nazi Ideology: The Genesis and Impact of Political Faith*, trans. John Irons (Jefferson, NC: McFarland & Company, 2020), 204.

31.   Cyril Cunningham, *Beaulieu: The Finishing School for Secret Agents* (Barnsley, South Yorkshire: Pen & Sword, 2005), 128; Carsten Dams, *Gestapo: Power and Terror in the Third Reich*, trans. Charlotte Ryland (Oxford, UK: Oxford University Press, 2014), 59.

32.   KV 4/172, 26.

33.   KV 4/172, 25–30.

34. Power, *Edition of One*, 138–39.

35. Noreen Riols, *The Secret Ministry of Ag. & Fish: My Life in Churchill's School for Spies* (London: Macmillan, 2013), 28.

36. "Training Section 1940–45; Industrial Sabotage Training 1941–44," Special Operations Executive, manuscript number HS 7/51, National Archives (1945), 77. Hereafter cited as HS 7/51, with page numbers.

37. On the transportation of students and staffers to the school, see, for example, Riols, *The Secret Ministry of Ag. & Fish*, 130–32; Stella King, *"Jacqueline": Pioneer Heroine of the Resistance* (London: Arms and Armour Press, 1989), 124; Ralph Vibert, *Memoirs of a Jerseyman* (Jersey: Le Haule Books, 1991), 55; and Cunningham, *Beaulieu*, 5–6. These accounts vary slightly in their details.

38. The two houses that most often housed women students were Boarmans (STS 36) and Blackbridge (STS 32c), Cunningham, *Beaulieu*, 26–30. I am basing the description on Boarmans.

39. Personal communication, Susan Tomkins, June 24, 2022; David Littlejohn, *The Fate of the English Country House* (Oxford, UK: Oxford University Press, 1995), 85.

40. Cunningham, *Beaulieu*, 33.

41. Riols, *The Secret Ministry of Ag. & Fish*, 35.

42. Cunningham, *Beaulieu*, 18–19.

43. Personal communication, Susan Tomkins, June 24, 2022; King, *"Jacqueline,"* 46; Vibert, *Memoirs of a Jerseyman*, 58.

44. Cunningham, *Beaulieu*, vii.

45. Vibert, *Memoirs of a Jerseyman*, 55.

46. These details of life in an OSS camp are from Hall, *You're Stepping on My Cloak and Dagger*, 12–14.

47. This was in addition to security personnel, instructors, interpreters in the case of dormitories with foreign students, and various "general dutymen." Cunningham, *Beaulieu*, 28–29.

48. During World War I, Britain had an Intelligence Corps, but when the war ended, that corps broke up—because, as an English historian later said, sweetly reciting his nation's party line, "the British Establishment abhorred underhanded diplomatic and military practices." Cunningham, *Beaulieu*, 9–12.

49. Cunningham, *Beaulieu*, 11–12.

50. King, *"Jacqueline,"* 49.

51. Cunningham, *Beaulieu*, 49–50; King, *"Jacqueline,"* 45.

52. "SOE group B training syllabus," Special Operations Executive, manuscript number HS 7/52, National Archives (1943–1944), 3–4. Hereafter cited as HS 7/52, with page numbers.

53. Vibert, *Memoirs of a Jerseyman*, 55; Cunningham, *Beaulieu*, 87; HS 7/52, A.1.2–3.

54. HS 7/52, A.1.2–3.

55. One method for doing this was to enter a phone booth, make a call, and slip a letter into the telephone directory in the booth; the receiving agent would be waiting outside the booth to make his own call. Another method was to leave a newspaper on a park bench with the message written in the crossword; the receiving agent would simply pass by the bench and pick up the newspaper to read. As much as the newspaper method might sound like something from a bad spy movie, it genuinely didn't look suspicious, as a Beaulieu staffer, Noreen Riols, later explained: "Newspapers were in very short supply, and everyone wanted to read them, so whenever one was abandoned it was immediately spotted and grabbed. Every newspaper must have been read by at least twelve people," Riols, *The Secret Ministry of Ag. & Fish*, 146–52; Cunningham, *Beaulieu*, 87; Vibert, *Memoirs of a Jerseyman*, 55.

56. Whisperers worked in solitude and followed the instructions of a chief whisperer whom they knew only via intermediaries. Yet together, they composed a secret army: in Turkey, for example, some three hundred whisperers worked for the Allies. KV 4/172, 82–83.

57. Riols, *The Secret Ministry of Ag. & Fish*, 133; Cunningham, *Beaulieu*, viii.

58. Cunningham, *Beaulieu*, 41; Fitzroy Maclean, *Eastern Approaches* (London: Jonathan Cape, 1974), 195–96.

59. Ralph Vibert, *Memoirs of a Jerseyman*, 56–77.

60. Cunningham, *Beaulieu*, 72; Bernard O'Connor, *RAF Tempsford: Churchill's Most Secret Airfield* (Amberley Publishing, 2012), 27–34.

61. Cunningham, *Beaulieu*, 73–74.

62. King "*Jacqueline*," 101–2.

63. Sarah Helm, *A Life in Secrets: Vera Atkins and the Missing Agents of WWII* (New York: Anchor Books, 2005), 286–87; Jean Overton Fuller, *Born for Sacrifice* (London: Pan Books, 1957), 122–29.

64. Vibert, *Memoirs of a Jerseyman*, 52–54; Rita Kramer, *Flames in the Field: The Story of Four SOE Agents in Occupied France* (London: Michael Joseph, 1995), 61.

65. Riols, *The Secret Ministry of Ag. & Fish*, 106–7. One historian estimates that SOE agents had a 30 percent death rate overall, Cunningham, *Beaulieu*, 81.

66. KV 4/172, 51.

67. Here is the matchbox trick, as Fairbairn describes it. Suppose that you are riding in a train car beside a man who is pointing a gun at you. Take out the matchbox and hold it openly ("Do you have a cigarette, please? I have matches."), with your fingers curled around the matchbox, your thumb resting so that your thumb pad is atop the upper joint of your forefinger, and your right arm held near your body. Then, with your right arm still near your body, turn from your hip and punch upward with your right fist, aiming for your opponent's jaw. At the same time, use your left arm to push the gun away from you. "The odds of knocking your opponent unconscious by this method are at least two to one. The fact that this can be accomplished with a matchbox

is not well-known, and for this reason is not likely to raise your opponent's suspicion of your movements," Fairbairn, *All-In Fighting*, 70.

68. KV 4/172, 38.
69. KV 4/172, 16–17; HS 7/52, 24–25.
70. KV 4/172, 16–17.
71. For instance: Which people in town are Nazi collaborators and narks? What methods are the Gestapo, the Abwehr, the local police using to surveil and control the local population, and what new rules—curfew, identity papers, ration cards, restricted zones, travel permits—have they imposed to that end? Among the Gestapo, which officers in town have the most power? KV 4/172, 16–17.
72. KV 4/172, 53.
73. Riols, *The Secret Ministry of Ag. & Fish*, 38–39.
74. You should write the invisible message perpendicular to the words of the Innocent Letter. HS 7/52, 59, 90–91.
75. Cunningham, *Beaulieu*, 53–54.
76. KV 4/172, 39–40, 84–89.
77. One could scramble the indicator number even more by increasing it by a set agreed-upon number. If the indicator number was 37016, for example, adding 11746, without carrying any numbers during the addition, would produce 48752. KV 4/172, 39–40, 84–89. An excellent breakdown of the "poem code" appears in David Hebditch, *Covert Radio Agents, 1939–1945: Signals from Behind Enemy Lines* (London: Pen & Sword Military, 2021), 261–66.
78. Ronald Lewin, *Ultra Goes to War: The Secret History* (London: Hutchinson & Co., 1978), 44–47.
79. HS 7/52, 50.
80. HS 7/52, 24–25.
81. Ramensky taught at Beaulieu sometime in 1943–44. Cunningham, *Beaulieu*, 72–73; Robert Jeffrey, *Gentle Johnny Ramensky: The Extraordinary True Story of the Safe Blower Who Became a War Hero* (Edinburgh: Black & White Publishing, 2010), 59.
82. HS 7/52, X.3a.
83. HS 7/52, 245.
84. HS 7/52, X.3a.
85. HS 7/52, X.3b.
86. HS 7/52, X.3b.
87. The instructor also assigned a "duty officer" to watch the burglary unobtrusively and make observations to critique the students later. The students knew he was there and were told to ignore him. HS 7/52, X.3a–3b.
88. Cunningham, *Beaulieu*, 30–31; King *"Jacqueline,"* 121–22.
89. Ib Jørgen Melchior, a Danish refugee, trained at Area B as well as Camp Ritchie, a now famous intelligence training camp that many Jewish refugees attended. He later recalled his first day at Area B, when a U.S. Army officer

walked his cohort to an imitation graveyard of wooden headstones, which bore inscriptions meant to impress on the students the dangers of carelessness with firearms. ("Emery Wise, bastard son. He closed his eyes to fire a gun." "Here at last lies Bob McQueen. He had a gun, but no magazine.") The officer took out a .45 automatic, and then, after pointing out the component parts of the gun, "suddenly opened fire. The live bullets whizzed through our group, zinging across our ears to slam with a deadened thud into the dirt mound behind us." The students jumped; some fled. "The whole crazy performance was witnessed by . . . two grim-faced civilians, who took notes in little black books," Melchior said. Ib Melchior, *Case by Case* (Novato, CA: Presidio Press, 1993), 8–9. The inscriptions on the gravestones are recorded in Applegate, *Kill—Or Get Killed*, 151–55.

90. Eugene Cunningham, *Triggernometry: A Gallery of Gunfighters* (Caldwell, ID: Caxton Printers, 1947). Applegate consulted this book while studying the methods of Old West shooting, Applegate and Melson, *The Close-Combat Files of Colonel Rex Applegate*, 2.

91. Applegate and Melson, *The Close-Combat Files of Colonel Rex Applegate*, 2; Applegate, *Kill—Or Get Killed*, 106–13.

92. Applegate, *Kill—Or Get Killed*, 104–13.

93. This advice is paraphrased from Applegate, *Kill—Or Get Killed*, 6–7.

94. Applegate, *Kill—Or Get Killed*, 194–98.

95. "Report of Physical Examination," November 10, 1944, Carleton Coon file, CIA archives.

96. Some of the students, like Joseph Curtiss, went to other training schools for additional training.

97. KV 4/172, 51–52.

98. KV 4/172, 51–52.

99. Alice-Leone Moats, *No Passport for Paris* (New York: G. P. Putnam's Sons, 1945), 164.

100. KV 4/172, 51.

101. KV 4/172, 51.

102. KV 4/172, 51.

103. Noreen Riols, an employee at Beaulieu, says in her memoir that the SOE would bid farewell to agents going into the field with the word *Merde*, after the fashion of French actors before a show, Riols, *The Secret Ministry of Ag. & Fish*, 28.

3: THROUGH THE LOOKING GLASS

1. Orhan Veli Kanik, "I Am Listening to Istanbul," in *I Am Listening to Istanbul: Selected Poems of Orhan Veli Kanik*, translated and with an introduction by Talat Sait Halman (New York: Corinth Books, 1971), 25–26.

2. Winks, *Cloak & Gown*, 130.

3. Both Turkey and Sweden made other concessions to maintain their neutrality. See C. G. McKay, *From Information to Intrigue: Studies in Secret Service Based on the Swedish Experience, 1939–1945* (London: Routledge, 2019); and "Stockholm Mission 1940–1945," Special Operations Executive, manuscript number HS 7/190, National Archives (1945), 6–20. Hereafter cited as HS 7/190, with page numbers.

4. Douglas Waller, *Wild Bill Donovan: The Spymaster Who Created the OSS and Modern American Espionage* (New York: Free Press, 2011), 155.

5. "The Abwehr's Use of Deception Material," Security Service, manuscript number KV 3/116, National Archives (ca. 1944–1946), 489. Hereafter cited as KV 3/116, with page numbers. Rakim Ziyaoğlu, Hayreddin Lokmanoğlu, and Emin Raşid Erer, *Tourist's Guide to Istanbul*, trans. Malcolm Burr (Istanbul: Halk, 1951), 241.

6. See, for example, "Istanbul Prepares for Record Tourist Visits," *Oakland Tribune*, July 4, 1954; Burton Yost Berry, *Out of the Past: The Istanbul Grand Bazaar* (New York: Arco Publishing, 1977).

7. Joseph Williams, "Istanbul Incorporated: Minorities and the Market in the Grand Bazaar and İstiklâl Street" (diss., Princeton University, 2016), 1, 48. The examples of what shopkeepers say at the bazaars of Istanbul while hailing customers or bargaining come from Williams, "Istanbul Incorporated," and Berry, *Out of the Past*. I am working under the assumption that they would have said similar things in the 1940s.

8. Berry, *Out of the Past*, 52, 106; Williams, "Istanbul Incorporated," 1, 48; Clifford Geertz, "The Bazaar Economy: Information and Search in Peasant Marketing," *American Economic Review* 68, no. 2 (May 1978): 29.

9. Frank Gervasi, "Let's Talk Turkey," *Collier's*, January 8, 1944, 59.

10. Winks, *Cloak & Gown*, 130–31.

11. Daniel Goffman, *The Ottoman Empire and Early Modern Europe* (Cambridge: Cambridge University Press, 2002), 24; Murat Umut Inan, "Ottomans Reading Persian Classics: Readers and Reading in the Ottoman Empire, 1500–1700," ed. Mary Hammond (Edinburgh: Edinburgh University Press, 2020), 160–81.

12. Winks, *Cloak & Gown*, 131–33.

13. Joseph Toy Curtiss, "The Life and Times of William Lilly: A Study in the Literary Importance of Astrology during the Seventeenth Century" (diss., Yale University, 1926). Modern graduate students might envy how broad a thesis statement Curtiss was allowed to make in the dissertation's introduction: "For the first time a not inconsiderable amount of information concerning astrology and astrologers has been brought together, a prerequisite for further study in this field."

14. Curtiss, "The Life and Times of William Lilly," 145–47.

15. Curtiss, "The Life and Times of William Lilly," 145–47.

16. Curtiss, "The Life and Times of William Lilly," 163.

17. Curtiss, "The Life and Times of William Lilly," 148–51.

18. Curtiss, "The Life and Times of William Lilly," 145–47.

19. Curtiss, "The Life and Times of William Lilly," 145.

20. In one episode that Curtiss recounts with relish, Lilly cozied up to a man named John Musgrave, who had gotten hold of a warrant that proved one of Lilly's friends was a royalist—a dangerous secret during the English Civil War—and offered to give Musgrave even more evidence to damn his friend if they held a private meeting to compare their documents. Musgrave, who planned to take a share of the victim's estate once the republican government sequestered it, accepted. When they met at a hotel in London, Lilly waited for Musgrave to bring out his papers, then "accidentally" upset a candle; while the other man lit it again at the fireplace, Lilly slipped the offending warrant into his boot. Musgrave didn't discover its absence until later. Lilly sent the warrant to his friend with a note reading, "Sin no more." Curtiss, "The Life and Times of William Lilly," 154–58.

21. Curtiss, "The Life and Times of William Lilly," 163.

22. Richard Deacon, *John Dee: Scientist, Geographer, Astrologer, and Secret Agent to Elizabeth I* (London: Frederick Muller, 1968), 4–10.

23. As an aside, in the same way Curtiss was fashioning Lilly as a looking-glass model for himself, Lilly was using as his own model the figure of Merlin, the magician from the King Arthur stories, from Thomas Heywood's *Life of Merlin*, Curtiss, "The Life and Times of William Lilly," 176–77.

24. See, for example, John Barley, "Dee and Trithemius's Steganography," *Notes and Queries* 5, no. 40 (May 24, 1879): 401–2, 422–23.

25. Curtiss, "The Life and Times of William Lilly," 145–46.

26. See, for example, this interview with the Turkish author Jale Parla: "Literature Excites Me the Most in Life," Bilgi Mag, November 19, 2020.

27. Samuel Butler, *Hudibras* (New York: D. Appleton & Company, 1864), 261.

28. Robert Hayden Alcorn, *No Bugles for Spies: Tales of the OSS* (n.p.: Arcole Publishing, 2017), 153.

29. Winks, *Cloak & Gown*, 132–38.

30. Winks, *Cloak & Gown*, 132–34.

31. Winks, *Cloak & Gown*, 132–34.

32. John Maxson, "Report on Organization and Operation of X-2, Turkey" (1944): 3–4. Maxson and Winks give somewhat conflicting accounts of this period.

33. Letter from Joseph Curtiss to Robin Winks, April 23, 1985.

34. See, for example, John Cecil Masterman, *The Double-Cross System, 1939–1945* (New York: Random House, 1995).

35. Winks, *Cloak & Gown*, 131–39.

36. Letter from Joseph Curtiss to Robin Winks, April 23, 1985.

37. Winks, *Cloak & Gown*, 138–39; John Maxson, "Report on Organization and Operation of X-2, Turkey," 11–12.

38. Clifford Geertz, "Suq: The Bazaar Economy in Sefrou," in *Suq: Geertz on the Market* (Chicago: University of Chicago Press, 2022), 87.
39. Maxson, "Report on Organization and Operation of X-2, Turkey," 3.
40. KV 4/172, 83.
41. Gervasi, "Let's Talk Turkey," 59.
42. Curtiss got hold of "the Istanbul notebook" not through the Turkish police, but through a functionary in the U.S. military attaché's office, Winks, *Cloak & Gown*, 142.
43. What makes horse racing thrilling, Scott says, is that every single one of the participants—from the trainers to the jockeys, from the grooms to the bookies, from the syndicate men to the reporters—is trying to get information, hide information, or spread misinformation, often all three at the same time. "The information game is a game of *strategy*," Scott writes. What he means is that everyone who plays the game chooses what to do based on what they think others are choosing to do, and that their interactions with each other are defined by the fact that they are (mostly) not sharing information with each other. The game has winners and losers. The best way to win is to get the most information from others while concealing the most information yourself. The trick is that you're doing this while moving about as an active player on the scene: talking with others, watching others, and performing for the others who watch you. Marvin B. Scott, *The Racing Game* (New York: Routledge, 2017), 4.
44. George Cristian Maior, *America's First Spy: The Tragic Heroism of Frank Wisner* (Washington, DC: Academica Press, 2018), 53.
45. Winks, *Cloak & Gown*, 413.
46. Berry, *Out of the Past*.
47. See Berry, *Out of the Past*. Berry, an American who served as a diplomat in Istanbul during the war years, said that when he first arrived in the city, he learned that the city's diplomatic corps had a shared hobby: everyone kept a collection of something, *anything*, for which they treasure-hunted in the Grand Bazaar.
48. Masterman, *The Double-Cross System*, 7.
49. Scott, *The Racing Game*, 158.
50. Masterman, *The Double-Cross System*, 7–9.
51. Masterman, *The Double-Cross System*, 7–9.
52. Masterman, *The Double-Cross System*, 8–9.
53. Masterman, *The Double-Cross System*, 8–9.
54. In Scott's terms, covering devices include *concealment*, or using subterfuge to mislead other players; *open privacy*, or carrying out secret moves in a place that other players know is secret (say, the paddock in horse racing); and *postponement*, or waiting to make a necessary disclosure until the last possible moment. Scott, *The Racing Game*, 158–65.
55. Masterman, *The Double-Cross System*, 9–10.

56. John Rayner became the head of the Rumor Factory in 1942. "Propaganda: PWE (Political Warfare Executive)/ SOE co-ordination," manuscript number HS 8/310, National Archives, 187. Hereafter cited as HS 8/310, with page numbers.

57. "In class 1, the agents included an M.P., several students, a professor, and a pensioned officer. Class 2 included businessmen, civil servants, journalists, and junior officers. Class 3, hairdressers, waiters, shop assistants, news vendors, merchant-seamen, tailors, etc.," HS 8/310, 228–30.

58. HS 8/310, 228–30

59. HS 8/310, 228–29.

60. HS 8/310, 229–30.

61. HS 8/310, 230.

62. HS 8/310, 229–30.

63. HS 8/310, 229–30.

64. HS 8/310, 229–30.

65. KV 4/172, 82–83.

66. KV 4/172, 82–83.

67. KV 4/172, 82–83.

68. "Propaganda Jan 1944–1945," Security Service, manuscript number HS 7/285, National Archives (ca. 1944–1946), 10–13. Hereafter cited as HS 7/285, with page numbers.

69. HS 7/285, 10–13.

70. HS 7/285, 10–13.

71. Maior, *America's First Spy*, 57–60.

72. Maior, *America's First Spy*, 66–67.

73. Maior, *America's First Spy*, 66–67; Winks, *Cloak & Gown*, 138–39.

74. Maxson, "Report on Organization and Operation of X-2, Turkey," 3–4, 20; B. W. Beebe and George R. Downs, "John Haviland Maxson (1906–1966)," *American Association of Petroleum Geologists Bulletin* 50, no. 11 (November 1966): 2483.

75. Winks, *Cloak & Gown*, 143–44.

76. Winks, *Cloak & Gown*, 139.

4: TOO CLEVER TO BE TRAPPED BY A WOMAN

1. HS 7/190, 20.

2. See, for example, "Ball at American Legation in Sweden," *New York Times*, January 16, 1902.

3. HS 7/190, 120.

4. Pat DiGeorge, *Liberty Lady: A True Story of Love and Espionage in WWII Sweden* (Vero Beach, FL: Beaver's Spur Publishing, 2016), loc. 2987–3023, Kindle.

5. Julien Bryan, *Siege* (New York: Doubleday, Doran & Co., 1940), 27; Polish Ministry of Information, *The Black Book of Poland* (New York: G.P. Putnam's

Sons, 1942), 20–27; Guri Hjeltnes, "Supplies Under Pressure: Survival in a Fully Rationed Society: Experiences, Cases, and Innovation in Rural and Urban Regions in Occupied Norway," in Tatjana Tönsmeyer, Peter Haslinger, and Agnes Laba, eds., *Coping with Hunger and Shortage Under German Occupation in World War II* (New York: Palgrave Macmillan, 2018), 63.

6. Political Warfare Executive, Central Directive, Annexe III, Everyday Life in Poland, February 24, 1944.

7. Political Warfare Executive, Central Directive, Annexe IV, Everyday Life in Norway, May 27, 1943.

8. "Stop Press: Guidance Notes," Political Warfare Executive, 1942.

9. Claire Zalc, *Denaturalized: How Thousands Lost Their Citizenship and Lives in Vichy France*, trans. Catherine Porter (Cambridge, MA: Harvard University Press, 2020), 4–20.

10. "Stop Press: Guidance Notes," Political Warfare Executive, 1942.

11. Meitner had a preexisting Austrian passport, but the Nazi government had designated that passport invalid on the grounds that she was Jewish. Rachel Stiffler Barron, *Lise Meitner: Discoverer of Nuclear Fission* (Greensboro, NC: Morgan Reynolds, 2000), 9–11, 64.

12. Laura Fermi, *Atoms in the Family: My Life with Enrico Fermi* (Chicago: University of Chicago Press, 1961), 120. In 1933, an American professor visiting Germany wrote to a colleague, "In Munich everyone says not to speak too loudly or one will land in Dachau (the nearest concentration camp)," Charles Weiner, "A New Site for the Seminar: The Refugees and American Physics in the Thirties," in *The Intellectual Migration: Europe and America, 1930–1960*, ed. Donald Fleming and Bernard Bailyn (Cambridge, MA: Harvard University Press, 1969), 204–5.

13. Walter Laqueur and Richard Breitman, *Breaking the Silence* (New York: Simon and Schuster, 1986), 14.

14. Albert Breton and Ronald Wintrobe, "The Bureaucracy of Murder Revisited," *Journal of Political Economy* 94, no 5 (1986): 907; Franklin Mixon, Jr., *A Terrible Efficiency: Entrepreneurial Bureaucrats and the Nazi Holocaust* (New York: Palgrave Macmillan, 2019), 6; Harold Rosenberg, "The Trial and Eichmann," *Commentary* 32, no. 5 (November 1961): 380.

15. Hannah Arendt, *Eichmann in Jerusalem: A Report on the Banality of Evil* (New York: Viking Press, 1963), 46. Arendt is giving words to the sentiment of the Jewish officials whom Eichmann invited to inspect his forced emigration system. Breton and Wintrobe, "The Bureaucracy of Murder Revisited," 916; Mixon, *A Terrible Efficiency*, 51.

16. Tom Moon, *Loyal and Lethal Ladies of Espionage* (New York: iUniverse, 2000), 117–18.

17. Thomas Powers, *The Man Who Kept the Secrets: Richard Helms and the CIA* (New York: Washington Square Press, 1979), 36.

18. Laqueur and Breitman, *Breaking the Silence*, 131.

19. In July 1942, a German businessman named Eduard Schulte learned by accident of the Nazis' plans to murder the millions of Jewish people they had in detention—Schulte worked in mining, and the village of Auschwitz had a zinc mine—and he passed that information to the leaders of the Jewish community in neutral Switzerland, where he often traveled for work. (He believed the little group had more power to influence events and speak to world leaders than it did. One historical account comments drily, "Schulte, like many non-Jews, tended to overrate the influence of 'World Jewry.'") Gerhard Riegner in Geneva and Rabbi Stephen Wise in New York City believed the intel, hearsay though it was, and kept slugging away until the New York press and the U.S. State Department heard it too—although some time would pass before U.S. politicians gave it the credence it deserved. When Riegner first heard the report, he wrote to a colleague, "At first sight the affair sounds totally fantastic. But one cannot exclude the consideration that these measures are rooted in the inner logic of the regime and that these people have no scruples whatsoever." Unfortunately, the report turned out to be all too true. Laqueur and Breitman, *Breaking the Silence*, 120–57.

20. Joachim Joesten, *Stalwart Sweden* (New York: Doubleday, Doran and Company, 1943), 78–80.

21. Joesten, *Stalwart Sweden*, 78–80.

22. Joesten, *Stalwart Sweden*, 78–80.

23. R. Taylor Cole, *The Recollections of R. Taylor Cole: Educator, Emissary, Development Planner* (Durham, NC: Duke University Press, 1983), 92.

24. Joesten, *Stalwart Sweden*, 185–87.

25. Joesten, *Stalwart Sweden*, 52–53, 123–24, 185–87. Joesten is referring specifically to "Swedish press policy" during the years 1940 to 1942.

26. Joesten, *Stalwart Sweden*, 65–68, 175.

27. Joesten, *Stalwart Sweden*, 24–38, 169–76.

28. HS 7/190, 20–21.

29. Kibre arrived in Stockholm after spending six weeks in Scotland waiting for the weather to clear for the flight. (She spent nine weeks in Britain as a whole, which gave her three weeks for training in England. She did some of her training at the British Museum, which ran a special course on microfilm photography for agents-in-training. A young employee of the museum, David Wilson, accompanied her to Stockholm to help her set up shop; he wound up remaining in Stockholm, working as a photographer in Kibre's growing OSS unit, for the duration of the war.) Peiss, *Information Hunters*, 43; letter from Adele Kibre to Allan Evans, American embassy, London, September 2, 1942.

30. She also used a Leica camera, Peiss, *Information Hunters*, 42.

31. Letter to Dr. Adele Kibre, c/o American Legation, Stockholm, Sweden, from Frederick Kilgour, May 31, 1943.

32. HS 7/190, 20–21.

33. Cole, *The Recollections of R. Taylor Cole*, 76; DiGeorge, *Liberty Lady*, loc. 2959–89, Kindle.

34. DiGeorge, *Liberty Lady*, 2959–89, Kindle; Joesten, *Stalwart Sweden*, 10; Traveler's Illustrated Guides, *Stockholm, and the Principal Pleasure-Routes in the Interior* (Stockholm: Albert Bonnier, 1875), 8; John Scott, "U.S. Miscellany," *Time*, March 13, 1944.

35. DiGeorge, *Liberty Lady*, loc. 2959–89, Kindle.

36. DiGeorge, *Liberty Lady*, loc. 2959–89, Kindle.

37. See, for example, letter from Adele Kibre to Franz Satow, Henrik Lindståhls Bokhandel, June 9, 1945.

38. Sometimes a press attaché with nothing to lose would push the edges of the rules. Cecil Parrott, who ran the Press Reading Bureau for the British Legation, where Britain's press corps worked, later recalled that Jens Schive, the press attaché for the Norwegian Legation, who of necessity sent his abstracts to the Norwegian government-in-exile in England, since Hitler's forces were occupying Norway, sometimes included in the abstracts interpretations of news stories that technically counted as intelligence. Parrott signed Schive's telegrams, so that they came from the British rather than the Norwegian Legation, and the Swedish government, out of respect for Britain, allowed them to go out. Cecil Parrott, *The Tightrope* (London: Faber and Faber, 1975), 165–67.

39. Memo from Frederick Kilgour to the Interdepartmental Committee, April 4, 1944.

40. Letter to Dr. Adele Kibre, c/o American Legation, Stockholm, Sweden, from Frederick Kilgour, September 20, 1943.

41. Letter via courier to Dr. Adele J. Kibre, c/o Miss Nancy Chappelear, 270 Madison Avenue, Coordinator of Information, New York, New York, May 23, 1942. She must have been working at the New York Public Library at the time.

42. Letter to Adele Kibre from Frederick Kilgour, September 19, 1942.

43. Peiss, *Information Hunters*, gives a wonderful account of her work in the field.

44. Ove Hagelin, ed., *Rare and Important Medical Books in the Library of the Karolinska Institute: An Illustrated and Annotated Catalogue* (Stockholm: Karolinska Institutets Bibliotek, 1992); Anonymous, "Karolinska Institutet Flyttar," *Veckojournalen* 7 (1937), 36.

45. Anonymous, "Karolinska Institutet Flyttar," *Veckojournalen* 7 (1937), 22–23, 36, 43.

46. See, for example, Peiss, *Information Hunters*; letter from Adele Kibre to Sveriges Allmänna Exportförening, Biblioteket, March 14, 1945; letter from Adele Kibre to Sveriges Allmänna Exportförening, Biblioteket, March 16, 1945.

47. In the 1960s, the Swedes adopted the word *mysig* to describe coziness, and the concept that the word describes has continued to evolve to the present day. See Helene Brembeck, "Cozy Friday: An Analysis of Family Togetherness

and Ritual Overconsumption," in *Managing Overflow in Affluent Societies*, ed. Barbara Czarniawska and Orvar Löfgren (New York: Taylor & Francis, 2012), 125–40.

48. Letter from Kibre to Sveriges Allmänna Exportförening, Biblioteket, March 14, 1945.

49. Letter from Adele Kibre to Nordiska Bokhandeln, June 4, 1945.

50. She also found a local company that sold subscriptions to newspapers and magazines, the Wennergren-Williams information service, from which she ordered fourteen subscriptions in a single letter in September 1944; see letter from Adele Kibre to Miss Gunhild Karlsson of the Wennergren-Williams information service, September 9, 1944.

51. Letter from Pontus Soldén of Rönnells Antikvariat to Elyse Graham, October 11, 2022.

52. Letter from Aaron Pratt of the University of Texas at Austin to Elyse Graham, September 26, 2022; letter from Carmel White Eitt to Thomas Staley of the University of Texas at Austin, October 11, 1988; letter from Carmel White Eitt to Don Carleton of the University of Texas at Austin, September 14, 1988.

53. "German Expenditures in Propaganda," in United States Congress, National Agencies War Appropriation Bill for 1945: Hearings (Washington, DC: U.S. Congress, 1945), 30–35.

54. "German Expenditures in Propaganda," 30–35.

55. Laurie Barber, "Hitler Was No Fan of Being Called a 'Nazi,'" *Courier Mail*, My Say, September 5, 2017.

56. Åke Daun, *Swedish Mentality*, trans. Jan Teeland (University Park, PA: Pennsylvania State University Press, 1996), 4.

57. Daun, *Swedish Mentality*, 18, 32–49, 130; Jean Phillips-Martinsson, *Swedes as Others See Them: Facts, Myths, or a Communication Complex?* (Lund: Utbildningshuset Studentlitteratur, 1985), 18. Phillips-Martinsson is referring to the diplomatic world of the early 1950s, well within the time frame of this book.

58. Daun, *Swedish Mentality*, 129.

59. See, for example, letter to Franz Satow, Henrik Lindståhls Bokhandel from Adele Kibre, September 21, 1945; and letter to Sandbergs Bokhandel from Adele Kibre, April 6, 1945.

60. Letter to Axel Boëthius from Adele Kibre, February 26, 1944.

61. The chief of the American Press Section was Walter Washington; the chief of the Special Reporting and Press Reading Section was Harry Carlson.

62. "Ditlef, K.," *Papæsken* (April 1948), 10; David Lampe, *Hitler's Savage Canary: A History of the Danish Resistance in World War II* (New York: Arcade Publishing, 2014), 47.

63. "Ditlef, K.," *Papæsken* (April 1948), 10.

64. Dov Schidorsky, "Confiscation of Libraries and Assignments to Forced Labor: Two Documents of the Holocaust," *Libraries & Culture* 33, no. 4 (Fall 1998): 348–50.

65. André Simone, *Men of Europe* (New York: Modern Age Books, 1941), 108; Richard Bonney, *Confronting the Nazi War on Christianity: The Kulturkampf Newsletters, 1936–1939* (New York: Peter Lang, 2009), 127; Robert Cecil, *The Myth of the Master Race: Alfred Rosenberg and Nazi Ideology* (New York: Dodd Mead & Company, 1972), 17.

66. Glickman, *Stolen Words*, 102–5.

67. Cecil, *The Myth of the Master Race*, 15; Glickman, *Stolen Words*, 12–14, 102–5.

68. Rosemary Lévy Zumwalt, *Franz Boas: Shaping Anthropology and Fostering Social Justice* (Lincoln: Nebraska University Press, 2022), 371; Heather Pringle, *The Master Plan: Himmler's Scholars and the Holocaust* (New York: Hyperion, 2006),106.

69. Glickman, *Stolen Words*, 102–8.

70. Glickman, *Stolen Words*, 111; James Rorimer, *Survival: The Salvage and Protection of Art in War* (New York: Abelard Press, 1950), 159.

71. Glickman, *Stolen Words*, 111–12.

72. Glickman, *Stolen Words*, 112–23; Dov Schidorsky, "Library of the Reich Security Main Office and Its Looted Jewish Book Collections," *Libraries & the Cultural Record* 42, no. 1 (2007), 21.

73. Glickman, *Stolen Words*, 112–18; Schidorsky, "Library of the Reich Security Main Office and Its Looted Jewish Book Collections," 23–27, 30–31; Schidorsky, "Confiscation of Libraries and Assignments to Forced Labor," 347–88.

74. Glickman, *Stolen Words*, 112–18; Schidorsky, "Confiscation of Libraries and Assignments to Forced Labor," 347–88, 367–69; Schidorsky, "Library of the Reich Security Main Office and Its Looted Jewish Book Collections," 27–29.

75. Schidorsky, "Confiscation of Libraries and Assignments to Forced Labor," 352–69.

76. Glickman, *Stolen Words*, 132–36.

77. Bryan, *Siege*, 19, 31.

78. Glickman, *Stolen Words*, 137–40.

79. Glickman, *Stolen Words*, 147–48.

80. Glickman, *Stolen Words*, 147–48.

81. Glickman, *Stolen Words*, 141–43; Solly Ganor, *Light One Candle: A Survivor's Tale from Lithuania to Jerusalem* (New York: Kodansha, 2003), 207.

82. Ganor, *Light One Candle*, 207.

83. Ganor, *Light One Candle*, 207–9.

84. Ganor, *Light One Candle*, 210.

85. Ganor, *Light One Candle*, 210.

5: BREAKING CODES AND READING TRASH

1. Winks, *Cloak & Gown*, 63.

2. Corey Ford and Alastair MacBain, *Cloak and Dagger: The Secret Story of OSS* (New York: Random House, 1945), 3–5; Garrett Peck, *Prohibition in Washington, D.C.: How Dry We Weren't* (Cheltenham, UK: The History Press, 2011), 55.

3.   Ford and MacBain, *Cloak and Dagger*, 3–5.

4.   Ford and MacBain, *Cloak and Dagger*, 3–5.

5.   Ray Cline, *Spies, Secrets, and Scholars: Blueprint of the Essential CIA* (Washington, DC: Acropolis Books, 1976), 41; Russell Jack Smith, *The Unknown CIA: My Three Decades with the Agency* (New York: Pergamon-Brassey's, 1989), 31.

6.   Cline, *Spies, Secrets, and Scholars*, 41.

7.   Herbert Lyons Jr., "Front-Line Librarian," *New York Times*, June 29, 1941.

8.   The annex, which opened in 1939, looked like a prison; it was doubtless more comfortable than the plywood palaces of the E Street Complex, but it was meant to hold books, not people.

9.   Winks, *Cloak & Gown*, 450.

10.   Smith, *The Unknown CIA*, 52, 134.

11.   At that time, the OSS was still called the Office of the Coordinator of Information; it changed its name to the OSS in June 1942, Sherman Kent, unpublished memoir, Yale University Archives, Series II, Tape 5, pages 1–4.

12.   Kent memoir, Series II, Tape 5, 1–4.

13.   "During World War II," the historian Michael Warner writes, "American academics and experts in the Office of Strategic Services . . . had virtually invented the discipline of intelligence analysis—one of America's few unique contributions to the craft of intelligence," foreword, Woodrow Kuhns, *Assessing the Soviet Threat: The Early Cold Wars* (Washington, DC: Center for the Study of Intelligence, 1997), 1.

14.   Cline, *Spies, Secrets, and Scholars*, 42.

15.   Cline, *Spies, Secrets, and Scholars*, 12–13.

16.   Cline, *Spies, Secrets, and Scholars*, 13–14; David Rudgers, *Creating the Secret State: The Origins of the Central Intelligence Agency, 1943–1947* (Lawrence: University Press of Kansas, 2000), 47.

17.   Dean Acheson, quoted in "Beautiful Blondes and Whiskered Spies Are Barred from the Intelligence Service," *New York Times*, November 27, 1945. Cited in Cline, *Spies, Secrets, and Scholars*, 12–13, and Rudgers, *Creating the Secret State*, 47. After Pearl Harbor, a British military officer serving in D.C. wrote to his superior about the United States: "This country [the United States] is more highly organized for peace than you can imagine. At present this country has not—repeat not—the slightest conception of what the war means, and their armed forces are more unready for war than it is possible to imagine. The whole organization belongs to the days of George Washington." William Breuer, *Operation Torch: The Allied Gamble to Invade North Africa* (New York: St. Martin's, 1985), x.

18.   See, for example, Brett Woods, ed., *Letters from France: The Private Diplomatic Correspondence of Benjamin Franklin, 1776–1785* (New York: Algora Publishing, 2006), and David Schoenbrun, *Triumph in Paris: The Exploits of Benjamin Franklin* (New York: Harper & Row, 1976), 58.

19. In 1940, the State Department added a small "intelligence" unit, with fewer than twenty employees, to gather information from aliens entering the United States. Cline, *Spies, Secrets, and Scholars*, 12–13, 42; Dean Acheson, *Present at the Creation: My Years in the State Department* (New York: W. W. Norton, 1969), 16.

20. Corey Ford and Alastair MacBain, *The Last Time I Saw Them* (New York: Charles Scribner's Son, 1946), 9–10.

21. Kent memoir, Series II, Tape 5, 1–5.

22. Kent memoir, Series II, Tape 4, 20–22.

23. Kent memoir, Series II, Tape 5, 1–5.

24. Alfred McCormack, interviewed in "A National Intelligence Program," radio broadcast, December 22, 1945, transcript in *Department of State Bulletin*, December 23, 1945, 988.

25. On their cover pages and in the archives, these estimates are labeled "report," as in "R&A Report No. 1172." However, the term of art in U.S intelligence for the reports of intelligence analysts was, and remains, "estimates."

26. On intelligence estimates, see, for example, Sherman Kent, *Strategic Intelligence for American World Policy* (Princeton, NJ: Princeton University Press, 1966); Thomas Fingar, *Reducing Uncertainty: Intelligence Analysis and National Security* (Stanford, CA: Stanford University Press, 2011); and Stephen Marrin, *Improving Intelligence Analysis: Bridging the Gap Between Scholarship and Practice* (London: Routledge, 2011).

27. Breuer, *Operation Torch*, 6–7.

28. Cline, *Spies, Secrets, and Scholars*, 121.

29. The use of Morocco telephone directories in planning the invasion of North Africa is well attested; see, for example, "New York Library Helped Army in Planning Its Successful Invasion of North Africa," *New York Times*, December 10, 1942; and Inez Robb, "Missionaries Make Contribution to Victory in Second World War," *Daily Courier* (Pennsylvania), October 2, 1945. The details in this conversation are from *Annuaire général du Maroc* (Paris: Presse Marocaine associée, 1917). We don't know which edition of the Morocco directory R&A took from the NYPL, but it would have had substantially the same information as this edition.

30. Breuer, *Operation Torch*, ix.

31. Breuer, *Operation Torch*, x.

32. Breuer, *Operation Torch*, xiii.

33. Breuer, *Operation Torch*, 6–7.

34. Breuer, *Operation Torch*, xiv, 6–7.

35. Breuer, *Operation Torch*, xiv.

36. Breuer, *Operation Torch*, 6–7, 36–37; Harry Butcher, *My Three Years with Eisenhower: The Personal Diary of Captain Harry C. Butcher, USNR, Naval Aide to General Eisenhower, 1942 to 1945* (New York: Simon and Schuster, 1946), 83. Butcher appears to use this phrase while taking notes from Eisenhower.

37. Butcher, *My Three Years with Eisenhower*, 82.

38. Breuer, *Operation Torch*, 36–37.

39. Breuer, *Operation Torch*, 31–32.

40. Breuer, *Operation Torch*, 17; Butcher, *My Three Years with Eisenhower*, 53.

41. Kent memoir, Series II, Tape 5, 1–4.

42. Sherman Kent et al., "Railroads of Northwest Africa: The Railroads of Algeria," Research and Analysis, Office of Strategic Services, February 3, 1942.

43. Kent memoir, Series II, Tape 5, 1–4.

44. Kent memoir, Series II, Tape 5, 1–15.

45. Kent memoir, Series II, Tape 5, 15–17.

46. Kent memoir, Series II, Tape 5, 15–17.

47. Kent memoir, Series II, Tape 5, 15–17.

48. See, for example, "New York Library Helped Army in Planning Its Successful Invasion of North Africa"; "Invasion via the Library," *New York Times*, December 13, 1942; Keir Sterling, "American Geographers and the OSS During World War II," in *The U.S. Army and World War II: Selected Papers from the Army's Commemorative Conferences*, ed. Judith Bellafaire (Washington, DC: Center of Military History, 1998), 217–33; Carlos Hagen, "Map Libraries and the Armed Services: A Story of Uneven Relationships," *Information Bulletin* 11, no. 1 (November 1979), 3; and Alice Hudson, "The Library's Map Division Goes to War, 1941–1945," *Biblion: The Bulletin of the New York Public Library* 3, no. 2 (1995), 127–28.

49. Sterling, "American Geographers and the OSS During World War II," 218–24.

50. Sterling, "American Geographers and the OSS During World War II," 224–25.

51. Often, these maps were produced in punishing time frames. "One morning in London in 1944," one historian writes, "the late Felix Gilbert, for many years a leading authority on European history, together with a geographer attached to R&A London . . . and a British colleague, received instructions to sit down and come up with a plan for the projected Allied occupation zones of Berlin for the Joint Chiefs. They began work at nine in the morning, and were to complete it within three hours. They met the deadline, and with one modification, their recommendations were followed by the four Allied powers." Sterling, "American Geographers and the OSS During World War II," 227–28.

52. Sterling, "American Geographers and the OSS During World War II," 223–28.

53. "City Library Found Inadequate by 30%," *New York Times*, January 17, 1943; "Invasion via the Library."

54. Hudson, "The Library's Map Division Goes to War, 1941–1945," 128–34.

55. Hudson, "The Library's Map Division Goes to War, 1941–1945," 127; Lloyd A. Brown, *The Story of Maps* (Boston: Little, Brown, 1949), 308–9.

56. Barbara Keating, "Contributions of the 1839–1842 U.S. Exploring Expedition," in *Geology and Offshore Mineral Resources*, ed., Barbara Keating and Barrie R. Bolton (New York: Circum-Pacific Council for Energy and Mineral Resources, 1992), 5.

57. Geoffrey J. Martin, *American Geography and Geographers: Toward Geographical Science* (Oxford: Oxford University Press, 2015), 980.

58. Jack Wilson, "War's End Deals Death Blow to OSS, Super Espionage Unit," *Star Tribune* (Minneapolis), December 18, 1946.

59. Breuer, *Operation Torch*, 44, 63–64.

60. Breuer, *Operation Torch*, 34.

61. Stanislaw Ulam, *Adventures of a Mathematician* (New York: Scribner's, 1976), 144.

62. Ulam, *Adventures of a Mathematician*, 144.

63. David Hawkins, *Project Y: The Los Alamos Story* (Los Angeles: Tomash Publishers, 1983), 51.

64. Ulam, *Adventures of a Mathematician*, 169.

65. See, for example, the *Hartford Courant*, February 26, 1945.

66. Breuer, *Operation Torch*, 17–18, 60–61.

67. Breuer, *Operation Torch*, 55.

68. Breuer, *Operation Torch*, 55.

69. Breuer, *Operation Torch*, 55.

70. Breuer, *Operation Torch*, 54–55.

71. Breuer, *Operation Torch*, 54–55.

72. Breuer, *Operation Torch*, 54–55; William Breuer, *The Spy Who Spent the War in Bed: And Other Bizarre Tales from World War II* (Hoboken, NJ: John Wiley & Sons, 2003), 76–77.

73. Breuer, *Operation Torch*, 63–64.

74. W. B. Smith, "Security Classification Lists and Cover Plan," October 11, 1942.

75. Allied Force Headquarters, "Outline Plan: Operation Torch," October 8, 1942.

76. Kent memoir, Series II, Tape 5, 11–13.

77. Kent memoir, Series II, Tape 5, 13.

78. Ernest Harmon, *Combat Commander: Autobiography of a Soldier* (Englewood Cliffs, NJ: Prentice-Hall, 1970), 79–81; Breuer, *Operation Torch*, 84–5.

79. Blaine Browne, *Mighty Endeavor: The American Nation and World War II* (Lanham, MD: Rowman & Littlefield, 2019), 65.

80. The estimate of sixty thousand Allied casualties was for the case of the French fighting back rather than welcoming the Allies as liberators. Julius Holmes, "Eisenhower's African Gamble," *Collier's*, January 12, 1946, 14.

81. This set of arguments is laid out in Research and Analysis Branch, Office of Strategic Services, R&A No. 933, "German Morale After Tunisia," June 25, 1943. The belief that the Allied victories in Stalingrad and North Africa would collapse German morale and therefore Germany was widespread. See, for example, Holmes, "Eisenhower's African Gamble," and a letter that J. Edgar Hoover wrote on June 24, 1942, to Adolf A. Berle, Jr., an assistant secretary of state, which said that intelligence he'd received from a diplomat for a neutral country in Berlin attested that public morale in Germany was even lower than outsiders believed: "According to the indicated source, the morale of the people is expected to break down the Nazi regime during the winter of

1942. In this connection, surprise has been expressed for not continuing the large bombing raid on German cities, since these have done more to break down German morale than anything yet undertaken by the Allies."

6: THE DIRTIEST WORK THAT CAN POSSIBLY BE IMAGINED

1. Fermi, *Atoms in the Family*, 222.
2. Leo Szilard's colleague, Eugene Wigner, described his hair as usually "poorly combed." Eugene Wigner and Andrew Szanton, *The Recollections of Eugene Wigner as Told to Andrew Szanton* (New York: Springer, 2012), 93.
3. George Marx, *The Voice of the Martians* (Budapest: Hungarian Academy Press, 1997), 23.
4. Quoted in William Lanouette, *Genius in the Shadows: A Biography of Leo Szilard, the Man Behind the Bomb* (New York: Charles Scribner's Sons, 1992), 202.
5. Marx, *The Voice of the Martians*, 23.
6. President Roosevelt read the letter that bore Einstein's name and took it seriously. In October 1939, he sent Einstein a reply letter that said, in part, "I found this data of such import that I have convened a Board consisting of the Bureau of Standards and a chosen representative of the Army and Navy to thoroughly investigate the possibilities of your suggestion regarding the element of uranium." This was the start of the Manhattan Project. Cynthia Kelley, ed., *The Manhattan Project: The Birth of the Atomic Bomb in the Words of Its Creators, Eyewitnesses, and Historians* (New York: Black Dog & Leventhal, 2020), 30–31.
7. Knut Haukelid, *Skis Against the Atom* (Minot, ND: North American Heritage Press, 1989), 74–75.
8. HS 7/51, 42, 225.
9. HS 7/52, O.A.2.
10. M. R. D. Foot, *Resistance* (London: Eyre Methuen, 1977), 46; Foot, *SOE: The Special Operations Executive*, 69–70; Syllabus 2004, 7–9. In 1943, Rheam received a promotion from major to lieutenant-colonel, which is the title under which he usually appears in histories of the SOE.
11. "Evaluations: Counter-scorch in France and Belgium," Special Operations Executive, manuscript number HS 8/416, National Archives (1944), 2.
12. Foot, *SOE: The Special Operations Executive*, 69–70.
13. HS 7/51, 41. The Allies saw saboteurs and guerrilla fighters as complementary groups who should take leading roles in the same "Secret Army," in the phrase that the SOE used for the underground resistance, at different stages of the war: saboteurs would work in secret early on, and later, as the enemy withdrew, guerrilla fighters would fight in the open, HS 7/51, 225. See also "Norwegian Section 1940–1945," Special Operations Executive, manuscript number HS 7/174, National Archives (1945), 22–23. Hereafter cited as HS 7/174, with page numbers.

14. Foot, *SOE: The Special Operations Executive*, 69–70.

15. HS 7/174, 11–12.

16. HS 7/174, 12–13.

17. HS 7/174, 11–12.

18. Haukelid, *Skis Against the Atom*, 32–44.

19. Neal Bascomb, *The Winter Fortress: The Epic Mission to Sabotage Hitler's Atomic Bomb* (New York: Houghton Mifflin Harcourt, 2016), 26.

20. Bascomb, *The Winter Fortress*, 6.

21. Bascomb, *The Winter Fortress*, 6.

22. Bascomb, *The Winter Fortress*, 26.

23. "Department of Industrial and Scientific Research: Intelligence; Norway; Heavy Water," Special Operations Executive, manuscript number HS 8/955, National Archives (1941–1944), 50. Hereafter cited as HS 8/955, with page numbers.

24. Barron, *Lise Meitner*, 60. The isotopes that Fermi created emitted not just electrons (beta particles), but alpha and gamma particles as well. Fermi would win the Nobel Prize for his discovery in 1938.

25. One of Meitner's and Hahn's notable feats was the discovery of a new element, which they named protactinium. One of Meitner's biographers notes of this discovery, "Although Lise had done nearly all the work, she allowed Otto's name to appear as the 'senior author' of their papers," Barron, *Lise Meitner*, 44–45.

26. Meitner was Protestant by conversion, but the German authorities didn't care about that. Colleagues in Denmark and Switzerland sent Meitner "letters inviting her to 'conferences' or to be a 'guest lecturer'"—a delicate way of proposing that she use the invitation as an excuse to visit them, then overstay her visa. In May 1938, she tried to take up an invitation from a colleague in Denmark, only for Denmark's embassy to deny her a visa. Because she was Jewish, and because German laws now applied to her as an Austrian, her passport wasn't valid anymore. This is how it happens: the papers that have always worked stop working. After she escaped—not through paperwork and proper procedures, but through subterfuge and pure dumb luck—she learned that the German authorities had been about to arrest her because one of her neighbors had tipped them off that she planned to leave the country. Barron, *Lise Meitner*, 9–11, 74–5; Ruth Lewin Sime, *Lisa Meitner: A Life in Physics* (Berkeley: University of California Press, 1996), 205.

27. Barron, *Lise Meitner*, 11–12.

28. Finn Aaserud, *Redirecting Science: Niels Bohr, Philanthropy, and the Rise of Nuclear Physics* (Cambridge: Cambridge University Press, 1990), 265; Barron, *Lise Meitner*, 11–12, 76–78.

29. Barron, *Lise Meitner*, 76–78.

30. Fermi, *Atoms in the Family*, 155–56; Lise Meitner and O. R. Frisch, "Products of the Fission of the Uranium Nucleus," *Nature* 143 (March 18, 1939): 471–72.

31. Richard Muller, *Physics for Future Presidents: The Science Behind the Headlines* (New York: W.W. Norton & Company, 2008), 125.

32. Marx, *The Voice of the Martians*, 16–17; Fermi, *Atoms in the Family*, 155–56.

33. The room where Bohr gave this talk now bears a plaque that reads: "IN THIS ROOM, JANUARY 26, 1939 NIELS BOHR MADE THE FIRST PUBLIC ANNOUNCEMENT OF THE SUCCESSFUL DISINTEGRATION OF URANIUM INTO BARIUM WITH THE ATTENDANT RELEASE OF APPROXIMATELY TWO HUNDRED MILLION ELECTRON VOLTS OF ENERGY PER DISINTEGRATION," Marx, *The Voice of the Martians*, 16.

34. Marx, *The Voice of the Martians*, 23–24.

35. In Washington, D.C., in 1939, Enrico Fermi's wife, Laura, wondered—while watching her husband, who had just arrived with her from Europe, attempt to persuade naval officers to invest in nuclear research—why only refugees seemed to care about developing atomic weapons: "Why were the persons acting this drama all foreign-born? I asked myself," Fermi, *Atoms in the Family*, 166. A simple explanation may be that refugees felt the urgency of solving wartime problems before most others in the United States did. In 1939, the difference between refugees and ordinary Americans was that refugees were already at war, whereas ordinary Americans were not.

36. See, for example, Ronald Clark, *The Greatest Power on Earth: The International Race for Nuclear Supremacy from Earliest Theory to Three Mile Island* (New York: Harper & Row, 1980), 52; and Richard Rhodes, *The Making of the Atomic Bomb* (New York: Simon & Schuster, 2012), 28–29.

37. Marx, *The Voice of the Martians*, 18–19. The journal's editor, Ernest Merritt of Cornell University, deserves praise for his discretion.

38. Hans von Halban, Frederic Joliot, and Lew Kowarski, "Liberation of Neutrons in the Nuclear Explosion of Uranium," *Nature* 143 (March 18, 1939): 470–74. Joliot-Curie, the son-in-law of Marie Curie, performed the experiment with his colleagues on March 8, Marx, *The Voice of the Martians*, 18–19.

39. Marx, *The Voice of the Martians*, 18–19; Leo Szilard and Walter Zinn, "Instantaneous Emission of Fast Neutrons in the Interaction of Slow Neutrons with Uranium," *Physical Review* 55 (April 15, 1939, originally dated March 16, 1939): 799–800; H. L. Anderson, Enrico Fermi, and H. B. Hanstein, "Production of Neutrons in Uranium Bombarded by Neutrons," *Physical Review* 55 (April 15, 1939, originally dated March 16, 1939): 797–98; Walter Zinn and Leo Szilard, "Emission of Neutrons by Uranium," *Physical Review* 56 (1939): 426–50.

40. HS 8/955, 84.

41. The same report confirms that the shipment was destined for Joliot—at least according to the Germans, for whom Joliot was by then working.

42. HS 8/955, 50.

43. HS 8/955, 100. Specifically, the plant delivered 300 kilograms to Germany between January 1 and March 6, 1942.

44. Another message from Stockholm, relayed in London on July 7, 1943, would report that the Vemork plant produced some 950 kilograms of heavy water "in 1942/1943." The Germans took almost all of it. HS 8/955, 77.

45. He didn't dare stop production, but he said he would slow it down as much as he could, if only to frustrate the German invaders. HS 8/955, 77–84.

46. "Norwegian Section 1940–1945: Appendices," Special Operations Executive, manuscript number HS 7/175, National Archives (1945), 73–74. Hereafter cited as HS 7/175, with page numbers.

47. Haukelid, *Skis Against the Atom*, 15.

48. Haukelid, *Skis Against the Atom*, 15.

49. Haukelid, *Skis Against the Atom*, 81.

50. Haukelid, *Skis Against the Atom*, 7.

51. Haukelid, *Skis Against the Atom*, 20–21.

52. Haukelid did a quick operation back in Norway after fleeing to Stockholm and before arriving in the UK to train, Haukelid, *Skis Against the Atom*, 32–34.

53. On the brownies of Rothiemurchus Forest, see, for example, Hugh MacMillan, *Rothiemurchus* (London: J. M. Dent & Company, 1907), 62.

54. This "Holding School" for Norwegians in the Scottish Highlands was established in late 1941, HS 7/175, 26.

55. HS 7/175, 34.

56. HS 7/175, 32.

57. HS 7/175, 37–38.

58. Haukelid, *Skis Against the Atom*, 31.

59. HS 7/175, 71–74; Bascomb, *The Winter Fortress*, 26–28.

60. HS 7/175, 75–76.

61. HS 7/175, 73.

62. Haukelid, *Skis Against the Atom*, 84–85.

63. Haukelid, *Skis Against the Atom*, 84–85.

64. Haukelid, *Skis Against the Atom*, 85–86.

65. Haukelid, *Skis Against the Atom*, 87–88.

66. HS 7/175, 75; Haukelid, *Skis Against the Atom*, 86–87.

67. HS 7/175, 75; Haukelid, *Skis Against the Atom*, 86–87.

68. HS 7/175, 30–31.

69. HS 7/175, 75.

70. HS 7/175, 73; Haukelid, *Skis Against the Atom*, 89–90.

71. Haukelid, *Skis Against the Atom*, 87.

72. Haukelid, *Skis Against the Atom*, 89–96.

73. Haukelid, *Skis Against the Atom*, 88–89; HS 7/175, 76–77.

74. HS 8/955, 46–48. These maps, which are dated "13.9.43," were used for one of the later sabotage attacks on the plant, but the plant's layout remained the same.

75. HS 8/955, 46–48; HS 7/175, 76.

76. HS 7/175, 76–77.

77. Haukelid, *Skis Against the Atom*, 75.

78. "Operational Reports to Cabinet," Special Operations Executive, manuscript number HS 8/242, National Archives (1941–1944), 154. Hereafter cited as HS 8/242, with page numbers.

79. Haukelid, *Skis Against the Atom*, 102–4.

80. Haukelid, *Skis Against the Atom*, 98–100; HS 7/174, 154; Damien Lewis, *Hunting the Nazi Bomb: The Special Forces Mission to Sabotage Hitler's Deadliest Weapon* (New York: Open Road, 2016), 66.

81. Haukelid, *Skis Against the Atom*, 74, 100–102.

82. Haukelid, *Skis Against the Atom*, 74; HS 7/175, 76–77.

83. Haukelid, *Skis Against the Atom*, 100–102; HS 7/175, 76–77.

84. HS 7/175, 76–77.

85. HS 7/175, 76–77.

86. HS 7/175, 76–77; Haukelid, *Skis Against the Atom*, 100–102.

87. "Norway: Gunnerside and Swallow," Special Operations Executive, manuscript number HS 7/181, National Archives (1945), 19. Hereafter cited as HS 7/181, with page numbers; HS 7/175, 76–77; HS 8/955, 47; Haukelid, *Skis Against the Atom*, 1954, 100–102.

88. HS 7/175, 76–77; HS 7/181, 20; Haukelid, *Skis Against the Atom*, 100–102.

89. HS 7/175, 76–77.

90. HS 7/175, 76–77; Haukelid, *Skis Against the Atom*, 109–10.

91. HS 7/175, 76–77.

92. Haukelid, *Skis Against the Atom*, 109–10.

93. HS 7/175, 76–77; Haukelid, *Skis Against the Atom*, 109–10.

94. Haukelid, *Skis Against the Atom*, 109–10. Rønneberg describes the guard in the lab as a Norwegian, HS 7/175, 76–77.

95. HS 7/175, 76–77; Haukelid, *Skis Against the Atom*, 110.

96. Haukelid, *Skis Against the Atom*, 74, 112–15; HS 7/175, 77–78.

97. Haukelid, *Skis Against the Atom*, 74, 113; HS 7/175, 77–78.

98. HS 7/175, 77–78; Haukelid, *Skis Against the Atom*, 102–4.

99. Haukelid, *Skis Against the Atom*, 74, 102–14.

100. Haukelid, *Skis Against the Atom*, 113–15.

101. Haukelid, *Skis Against the Atom*, 114.

102. HS 7/174, 97–98; HS 8/955, 50–51.

103. HS 7/174, 97.

104. HS 7/174, 97–98.

105. HS 8/242, 154. This report gets some details of the operation wrong—for instance, giving the height of the building as five stories rather than seven, and the number of men who entered the basement of the building as six rather than four.

106. HS 8/242, 154.

107. HS 8/955, 50.

108. Rhodes, *The Making of the Atomic Bomb*, 513.

109. HS 8/955, 71–73.

110. Haukelid, *Skis Against the Atom*, 181; Rhodes, *The Making of the Atomic Bomb*, 513.

111. Haukelid, *Skis Against the Atom*, 181.

112. Haukelid, *Skis Against the Atom*, 191–98.

113. Haukelid, *Skis Against the Atom*, 194.

114. Haukelid, *Skis Against the Atom*, 190–94; Tony Insall, *Secret Alliances: Special Operations and Intelligence in Norway, 1940–1945* (London: Biteback Publishing, 2021), 363.

115. Bascomb, *The Winter Fortress*, 306.

116. Jean-Paul Sartre, *Existentialism and Humanism*, trans. Philip Mairet (London: Methuen, 1973), 35–50.

117. John Craig, *Peculiar Liaisons: In War, Espionage, and Terrorism in the Twentieth Century* (New York: Algora Publishing, 2005), 119.

118. Bascomb, *The Winter Fortress*, 313–14.

119. Bascomb, *The Winter Fortress*, 313–14.

120. Bascomb, *The Winter Fortress*, 255–56.

7: SURRENDER ON DEMAND

1. Quoted in Laura Fermi, *Illustrious Immigrants* (Chicago: University of Chicago Press, 1968), 92.

2. The Emergency Rescue Committee drew the list of names it gave to Varian Fry from a government body called the President's Advisory Committee on Political Refugees, Cynthia Jaffee McCabe, *The Golden Door: Artist-Immigrants of America, 1876–1976* (Washington, DC: Smithsonian Institution Press, 1976), 36–77. For the tangled politics surrounding these and other rescue committees during the war, see David Wyman, *Paper Walls: America and the Refugee Crisis, 1938–1941* (New York: Pantheon Books, 1985).

3. Darryl Lyman, *Holocaust Rescuers: Ten Stories of Courage* (Berkeley Heights, NJ: Enslow Publishers, Inc., 1998), 25–28.

4. Lyman, *Holocaust Rescuers*, 26–28.

5. Varian Fry, *Assignment: Rescue* (New York: Scholastic, 1945), 3.

6. Hans Sahl, *The Few and the Many*, trans. Richard and Clara Winston (New York: Harcourt, Brace & World, 1962), 305–7.

7. Fry, *Assignment: Rescue*, 4. Fry wrote of his first night in Marseille, "I made sure the door was locked. Then I unpacked and settled in. After washing off the dust and grime from the train trip, I took my lists and laid them down on the small night table. Over two hundred names of people I was to save. But how was I to do it? How was I to get in touch with them? What could I do for them once I had found them? Now that I was in Marseille, I suddenly realized that I had no idea how to begin—or where" (Fry, *Assignment: Rescue*, 8).

8. Lyman, *Holocaust Rescuers*, 27–28.

9. Fry, *Assignment: Rescue*, 13.

10. Fry, *Assignment: Rescue*, 21.

11. Fry, *Assignment: Rescue*, 27–30; Lyman, *Holocaust Rescuers*, 27.

12. Fry, *Assignment: Rescue*, 30–37. The American Relief Center eventually grew to a staff of ten; but Fry did not disclose to employees who joined later that they were actually working for a human trafficking operation. Fewer secret keepers meant less risk.

13. Fry, *Assignment: Rescue*, 83–94; Lyman, *Holocaust Rescuers*, 29–30.

14. Fry, *Assignment: Rescue*, 31–32.

15. Fry, *Assignment: Rescue*, 39–43.

16. Fry, *Assignment: Rescue*, 97–98.

17. Fry, *Assignment: Rescue*, 161.

18. Fry, *Assignment: Rescue*, 26.

19. Fry, *Assignment: Rescue*, 41–42.

20. Fry, *Assignment: Rescue*, 166–68.

21. Fry, *Assignment: Rescue*, 161; Fermi, *Illustrious Immigrants*, 91–92.

22. Klaus Fischer, *Hitler and America* (Philadelphia: University of Pennsylvania Press, 2011), 10.

23. Shulamit Volkov, *Germans, Jews, and Antisemites: Trials in Emancipation* (Cambridge: Cambridge University Press, 2006), 154.

24. Personal communication, Robert Hutchings, May 23, 2023. See also Robert Hutchings, "America at War: 2003–2005," in *Truth to Power: A History of the U.S. National Intelligence Council*, ed. Robert Hutchings and Gregory Treverton (Oxford: Oxford University Press, 2019), 106–7; and Irving Janis, *Groupthink: Psychological Studies of Policy Decisions and Fiascoes* (Boston: Houghton Mifflin, 1982).

25. Volkov, *Germans, Jews, and Antisemites*, 154. Volkov is citing Hitler's use of the term in *Mein Kampf*.

26. Weiner, *"A New Site for the Seminar: The Refugees and American Physics in the Thirties,"* 216. For more information on rescue committees for scholars, like Oswald Veblen's, see Elyse Graham, "Adventures in Fine Hall," *Princeton Alumni Weekly*, January 10, 2018; Elyse Graham, "The Power of Small Numbers," *Princeton Alumni Weekly*, May 16, 2018; and a book by the Princeton alumna Laurel Leff, *Well Worth Saving: American Universities' Life-or-Death Decisions on Refugees from Nazi Europe* (New Haven, CT: Yale University Press, 2019).

27. The success of Fry's operation depended on the quiet help of Eleanor Roosevelt. When Germany invaded France in 1940, President Roosevelt asked the State Department to compile the names of refugees in France who were important artists, writers, or thinkers. These worthies would be offered visitor's visas to the United States. (Ultimately, the State Department printed some thirty-two hundred of these visas.) The State Department agreed, but immigration matters tend to get mired in bureaucracy; Eleanor Roosevelt lobbied officials daily to speed up the process and helped to obtain visas for especially

difficult cases. Of course, the government had to pretend not to know that an underground operation in France was finding would-be refugees to use these visas. Fermi, *Illustrious Immigrants*, 88; Roger Daniels, "Changes in Immigration Law and Nativism Since 1924," in *The History and Immigration of Asian Americans*, ed. Franklin Ng (New York: Garland Publishing, 1998), 65–86; Lyman, *Holocaust Rescuers*, 25–27.

28. R&A's other three divisions were the Far East division, the Latin America division, and the Soviet Union division.

29. Sherman Kent, "Early Aspects of the Struggle for Electoral Reform in France Under Louis Philippe, 1830–1837," dissertation, Yale University (1933), 478–507. The historian (and former journalist) Robert Darnton writes insightfully about why, as Darnton says, "newspapers should be read for information about how contemporaries construed events, rather than for reliable knowledge of events themselves." Robert Darnton, *The Case for Books: Past, Present, and Future* (New York: PublicAffairs, 2009), 23–27. See also Robert Darnton, "Writing News and Telling Stories," *Daedalus* 104, no. 2 (1975): 175–94.

30. Kent, "Early Aspects of the Struggle for Electoral Reform in France Under Louis Philippe, 1830–1837," 478–81.

31. Kent, "Early Aspects of the Struggle for Electoral Reform in France Under Louis Philippe, 1830–1837," 494–95; John Stuart Mill, review of *Armand Carrel: His Life and Character*, in *London and Westminster Review* 28 (October 1837–January 1838), 66–111.

32. Kent, "Early Aspects of the Struggle for Electoral Reform in France Under Louis Philippe, 1830–1837," 494–95.

33. Robert Fogles, interview with Richard Ruggles, unpublished manuscript.

34. William Donovan, "Intelligence: Key to Defense," *Life*, September 30, 1946, 108–20.

35. Donovan, "Intelligence: Key to Defense," 110.

36. Jefferson Adams, "Editor's Foreword," in *A Historical Dictionary of German Intelligence*, ed. Jefferson Adams (Lanham, MD: Scarecrow Press, 2009), vii.

37. Donovan, "Intelligence: Key to Defense," 110.

38. Elizabeth McIntosh, *The Role of Women in Intelligence* (McLean, Virginia: Association of Former Intelligence Officers, 1989), 1.

39. Mark Guglielmo, "The Contribution of Economists to Military Intelligence During World War II," *The Journal of Economic History* 68, no. 1 (March 2008), 120–23.

40. Telephone directory, Sherman Kent papers, National Archives.

41. David Hyndman and Scott Flower, *The Crisis of Cultural Intelligence* (Hackensack, NJ: World Scientific Publishing, 2019), 63.

42. See, for example, Danielle DeSimone, "Why Marlene Dietrich Was One of the Most Patriotic Women in World War II," United Service Organizations website, March 5, 2020; and Claudia Roth Pierpont, "Bombshells: How

Marlene Dietrich and Leni Riefenstahl Divided a World Between Them," *New Yorker*, October 12, 2015.

43. Robert Leonard, "War as a 'Simple Problem': The Rise of an Economics of Defense," in Craufurd Goodwin, ed., *Economics and National Security: A History of Their Interaction* (Durham: Duke University Press, 1991), 265–66.

44. Guglielmo, "The Contribution of Economists to Military Intelligence During World War II," 119–34; Walt W. Rostow, "Recollections of the Bombing," in *Discovery: Research and Scholarship at the University of Texas at Austin* 14, no. 2 (Austin: University of Texas, 1997), 45–46.

45. Guglielmo, "The Contribution of Economists to Military Intelligence During World War II," 112–13.

46. Andrew Roberts, *Churchill: Walking with Destiny* (New York: Penguin, 2018), 226; Christopher Andrew and Julius Green, *Stars and Spies: Intelligence Operations and the Entertainment Business* (London: Bodley Head, 2021), 263–65.

47. A CIA historian called Kent's language "unprintable." Harold P. Ford, "A Tribute to Sherman Kent," in *Sherman Kent and the Board of National Estimates: Collected Essays*, ed. Donald P. Steury (Washington, DC: Center for the Study of Intelligence, 1994), 7–9.

48. Ford, "A Tribute to Sherman Kent," 2–3.

49. Quoted in Ford, "A Tribute to Sherman Kent," 2–3.

50. Quoted in introduction, Sherman Kent, *Sherman Kent and the Board of National Estimates: Collected Essays*, ed. Donald P. Steury (Washington, DC: Center for the Study of Intelligence, 1994), xx.

51. Steury, *Sherman Kent and the Board of National Estimates*, xiii.

52. Steury, *Sherman Kent and the Board of National Estimates*, xvi–xxi.

53. Steury, *Sherman Kent and the Board of National Estimates*, xii–xvi; Ford, "A Tribute to Sherman Kent," 10.

54. Quoted in Ford, "A Tribute to Sherman Kent," 1.

55. Donovan, "Intelligence: Key to Defense," 114; Guglielmo, "The Contribution of Economists to Military Intelligence During World War II," 124–25.

56. Guglielmo, "The Contribution of Economists to Military Intelligence During World War II," 124–25.

57. Donovan, "Intelligence: Key to Defense," 114; Office of Strategic Services, Report No. 0–11121, "German Tank Production" (September 12, 1943).

58. Guglielmo, "The Contribution of Economists to Military Intelligence During World War II," 123–25.

59. Guglielmo, "The Contribution of Economists to Military Intelligence During World War II," 116–17; Adam Tooze, *The Wages of Destruction: The Making and Breaking of the Nazi Economy* (New York: Viking, 2006).

60. Office of Strategic Services, War Report. The situation would change as a result of the Allied bombing campaign and the liberation of territories previously captured by the Germans.

61. Guglielmo, "The Contribution of Economists to Military Intelligence During World War II," 117–18.

62. Barry Katz, *Foreign Intelligence: Research and Analysis in the Office of Strategic Services, 1942–1945* (Cambridge, MA: Harvard University Press, 1989), 12–13.

63. Jordan Ellenberg, *How Not to Be Wrong: The Power of Mathematical Thinking* (New York: Penguin Books, 2014), 4–20; "Death of Dr. Wald in India Confirmed," *New York Times*, December 20, 1950.

64. Ellenberg, *How Not to Be Wrong*, 4–20; Robert Leonard, *Von Neumann, Morgenstern, and the Creation of Game Theory: From Chess to Social Science, 1900–1960* (Cambridge: Cambridge University Press, 2010), 178–81.

65. Ellenberg, *How Not to Be Wrong*, 4–20. Wald's memoranda on the subject were later republished as Abraham Wald, "A Reprint of 'A Method of Estimating Plane Vulnerability Based on Damage of Survivors' by Abraham Wald" (Alexandria: Center for Naval Analyses, 1980).

66. Ellenberg, *How Not to Be Wrong*, 4–20; Wald, "A Reprint of 'A Method of Estimating Plane Vulnerability Based on Damage of Survivors.'"

67. Ellenberg, *How Not to Be Wrong*, 4–20; Howard Wainer, *Visual Revelations: Graphical Tales of Fate and Deception from Napoleon Bonaparte to Ross Perot* (Mahwah, NJ: Lawrence Erlbaum Associates, 1997), 58–60.

68. Ellenberg, *How Not to Be Wrong*, 4–20; Wald, "A Reprint of 'A Method of Estimating Plane Vulnerability Based on Damage of Survivors.'"

69. W. Allen Wallis, "The Statistical Research Group, 1942–1945," *Journal of the American Statistical Association* 75, no. 370 (June 1980): 324–25. Of course, women did play other roles in the Nazi war effort and the Holocaust. See, for example, Wendy Lower, *Hitler's Furies: German Women in the Nazi Killing Fields* (New York: Houghton Mifflin, 2013).

70. Ellenberg, *How Not to Be Wrong*, 4–20.

71. Lanouette, *Genius in the Shadows*, 236–56.

72. Ellenberg, *How Not to Be Wrong*, 4–20; Wallis, "The Statistical Research Group," 322–23.

73. Donald Downes, *The Scarlet Thread* (London: Deriek Verschoyle, 1953), 87–88. Douglas Waller gives a slightly different version of this story in *Wild Bill Donovan*, 124–28.

74. Downes, *The Scarlet Thread*, 88–93.

75. Downes, *The Scarlet Thread*, 88–93.

76. Downes, *The Scarlet Thread*, 88–93.

77. "Die Eisenbahn in der Wehrwirtschaft," in Deutschland auf Schienen, supplement 26, 1939, 11, quoted in "German Government Transportation Policy," U.S. Military Intelligence Reports—Germany, 1941–1944.

78. Quoted in "German Government Transportation Policy."

79. Donovan, "Intelligence: Key to Defense," 114; Coordinator of Information, Research and Analysis Branch, East European Section, "Gains of Germany

(and her Allies) through the Occupation of Soviet Territory," March 14, 1942, 71, 120–30; "German Government Transportation Policy."

80. Guglielmo, "The Contribution of Economists to Military Intelligence During World War II," 132–34.

81. One of the champions of the British doctrine of area bombing was an Oxford man named Solly Zuckerman. One R&A economist said drily, "There are Americans, and some British, who to the end of their days regarded the last year of the struggle in Europe as a war against Solly Zuckerman rather than Adolf Hitler," Rostow, "Recollections of the Bombing," 44–51; Guglielmo, "The Contribution of Economists to Military Intelligence During World War II," 132–37; Richard Overy, "Allied Bombing and the Destruction of German Cities," in *A World at Total War: Global Conflict and the Politics of Destruction, 1937–1945*, ed. Roger Chickering, Stig Förster, and Bernd Greiner (Cambridge, UK: Cambridge University Press, 2005), 291.

82. Guglielmo, "The Contribution of Economists to Military Intelligence During World War II," 132–40.

83. On the history of precision bombing in World War II, see, for example, Malcolm Gladwell, *The Bomber Mafia: A Dream, a Temptation, and the Longest Night of the Second World War* (New York: Little, Brown, 2021).

84. "Ball-Bearing Factories in German-Europe," Central Branch, MID, April 28, 1944.

85. See, for example, Gladwell, *The Bomber Mafia*, 37; Overy, "Allied Bombing and the Destruction of German Cities," 277–96; Philip Russell, "Bomb Sight," in *100 Military Inventions That Changed the World* (London: Constable & Robinson, 2013); and W. Hays Parks, "'Precision' and 'Area' Bombing: Who Did Which, and When?," *Journal of Strategic Studies* 18, no. 1 (1995): 145–74.

86. Guglielmo, "The Contribution of Economists to Military Intelligence During World War II," 132–34.

87. Parks, "'Precision' and 'Area' Bombing," 147–55.

88. R&A agents wrote a number of reports detailing the best methods and targets for sabotage operations. See, for example, Office of Strategic Services, Research & Analysis Branch, "Special Operations in Southern France," R&A 1268, June 23, 1943.

89. See, for example, Office of Strategic Services, *Simple Sabotage Field Manual: Strategic Services, No. 3* (1944); "SOE Group B Training Syllabus: Sabotage Handbook, Part I," Special Operations Executive, manuscript number HS 7/53, National Archives, hereafter cited as HS 7/53, with page numbers; "SOE Group B Training Syllabus: Sabotage Handbook, Part II," Special Operations Executive, manuscript number HS 7/54, National Archives; Stephen Bull, ed., *Special Ops 1939–1945: A Manual of Covert Warfare and Training* (Minneapolis, MN: Zenith Press, 2009), 93–131.

90. Riols, *The Secret Ministry of Ag. & Fish*, 29–31.

91. See, for example, HS 7/53, 1–2, and *Simple Sabotage Field Manual*, 1.

92. The handbooks also give instructions to the organizers in *réseaux* who helped to coordinate the work of these slow saboteurs. The advice would still be relevant today for organizers in social movements. For example, the handbooks told the organizers not to talk in terms of large, floating abstractions like freedom, which in practice turned out to be demoralizing. Instead, they should describe the results of resistance in the most concrete terms possible: "Simple sabotage will hasten the day when Commissioner X and his deputies Y and Z will be thrown out, when particularly obnoxious decrees and restrictions will be abolished, when food will arrive, and so on." The organizers must also remind the workers often that, although their individual actions would not seem like much, they belonged to a mighty, though invisible, army that was achieving constant victories against the Reich. *Simple Sabotage Field Manual*, 3–6.

93. Coon, *A North Africa Story*, 3.

94. Winks, *Cloak & Gown*, 180–85; Rick Atkinson, *An Army at Dawn: The War in North Africa* (New York: Henry Holt, 2002), 276; Coon, *A North Africa Story*, 31–32, 60–62.

95. Coon, *A North Africa Story*, 68; Atkinson, *An Army at Dawn*, 276.

96. Carleton Coon, *The Story of Man: From the First Human to Primitive Culture and Beyond* (New York: Alfred A. Knopf, 1962), 181–82. This book is based on his postwar lectures at Harvard.

97. Winks, *Cloak & Gown*, 180–85.

98. Coon, *A North Africa Story*, 79.

99. Elyse Graham, "A Ritchie Boy," *Princeton Alumni Weekly*, November 2021.

100. Atkinson, *An Army at Dawn*, 276–77.

101. Robert Dallek, *Franklin D. Roosevelt and American Foreign Policy, 1932–1945* (Oxford: Oxford University Press, 1995), 363–64; Winston Churchill, *Secret Session Speeches*, ed. Charles Eade (London: Cassell and Company, 1946), 76–96.

102. Winks, *Cloak & Gown*, 180–85; Coon, *A North Africa Story*, 60–62.

103. Winks, *Cloak & Gown*, 180–85.

104. Coon, *A North Africa Story*, 48–49; Winks, *Cloak & Gown*, 180–85.

105. Coon, *A North Africa Story*, 48–49.

106. George F. Howe, *The Battle History of the 1st Armored Division* (Washington: Combat Forces Press, 1954), 167–76; Atkinson, *An Army at Dawn*, 361–65.

107. Howe, *The Battle History of the 1st Armored Division*, 174–75.

108. Atkinson, *An Army at Dawn* 361–65.

109. Atkinson, *An Army at Dawn* 361–65.

110. Donovan, "Intelligence: Key to Defense," 114.

111. Donovan, "Intelligence: Key to Defense," 117–18.

112. Peter Lax, "The Bomb, Sputnik, Computers, and European Mathematics," in Tarwater Dalton, ed., *Bicentennial Tribute to American Mathematics, 1776–1976* (Washington, DC: Mathematical Association of America, 1977), 130–31.

8: THE LONGEST DAY

1. I once read a letter by a former soldier who described having lived this experience. Unfortunately, I haven't been able to track down the original text.

2. Ewen Montagu, *The Man Who Never Was* (New York: J. B. Lippincott and Company, 1954), 74–76.

3. Anthony Cave Brown, *Bodyguard of Lies* (Guilford, CT: The Lyons Press, 1975), 682.

4. Peter Doyle, *World War II in Numbers: An Infographic Guide to the Conflict, Its Conduct, and Its Casualties* (Buffalo, NY: Firefly Books, 2013), 84–85.

5. Doyle, *World War II in Numbers*, 84–87.

6. Doyle, *World War II in Numbers*, 88–89.

7. Charles Klein, quoted in D. M. Giangreco and Kathryn Moore, *Eyewitness D-Day: Firsthand Accounts from the Landing at Normandy to the Liberation of Paris* (New York: Union Square Press, 2005), 105–7.

8. Doyle, *World War II in Numbers*, 86–87. However, in keeping with the principle that secrets aren't secure, these code names did get out, and, for a time, the Allies worried that the plans they protected did too. In May 1944, as D-Day drew close, officials high up in Britain's intelligence services realized that the cryptic crossword in the London *Daily Telegraph* was giving clues that corresponded to secret D-Day code words. On May 22, the clue "Red Indian on the Missouri" yielded the answer "Omaha," the code word for a crucial Normandy beach. On May 27, the clue "(common) . . . but some bigwig like this has stolen some of it at times" yielded the answer "Overlord," the code word for the Normandy invasion. On May 30, the clue "This bush is a center of nursery revolutions" yielded the answer "Mulberry," the term for the ingenious portable harbors that the Allies had built to make up for the fact that the Normandy coast didn't have natural harbors that could handle the Allied ships. On June 1, the clue "Britannia and he hold to the same thing" yielded the answer "Neptune," the code word for the seafaring aspects of Operation Overlord. At some point, frantic intelligence staffers paged through back issues of the *Telegraph* to see how long this leak—this *secret transmission to the Germans*—had been happening. The news was bad. On May 2, the clue "One of the U.S." yielded the answer "Utah," another crucial D-Day beach. In March and April, clues had pointed to the code names for still more D-Day beaches: "Gold," "Juno," "Sword." Panicking, MI5 officials arrested the crossword editor for the *Daily Telegraph*—Leonard Dawe, the headmaster of a boy's school in Surrey—and searched his office and house for evidence that he was spying for the Germans. After spending days on end interrogating the headmaster, who desperately protested his innocence—"They turned me inside out," he later said—they finally figured out what was happening. The grounds of Dawe's school shared a boundary with a military camp, and the schoolboys took great pleasure in listening to whatever they could overhear from the glamorous fighters nearby.

Dawe, in the meanwhile, who after editing the crossword for some twenty years had run his own store of words dry, liked to ask the boys who came into his office to give him words. They did—and those words were the code words they overheard from the soldiers. In a 1958 interview with the BBC, Dawe said he was just happy that British intelligence hadn't shot him: "Had D-Day failed, I suppose they might have changed their minds." Val Gilbert, *The Daily Telegraph: Eighty Years of Cryptic Crosswords* (New York: Macmillan, 2004), 44–46; Dejan Milivojevic, "Crossword Alarm: The Puzzle That Nearly Stopped D-Day," War History Online, March 11, 2019.

9.   Michael Emery, Edwin Emery, and Nancy Roberts, *The Press and America: An Interpretive History of the Mass Media*, 9th ed. (Boston: Allyn and Bacon, 2000), 345.

10. See, for example, Desmond Tighe, Reuters correspondent for the Combined Allied Press, "Invaders Rush Up Norman Shore in Storm of Steel from Sea and Air," *New York Times*, June 7, 1944; "The Invasion," *New York Times*, June 17, 1944; and Jared Frederick, *Dispatches of D-Day: A People's History of the Normandy Invasion* (Centennial, CO: Valor Publishers, 2019).

11. Barton Whaley, *Stratagem: Deception and Surprise in War* (Norwood, MA: Artech House, 2007), 1.

12. Whaley, *Stratagem*, 2–3.

13. Whaley, *Stratagem*, 135.

14. Whaley, *Stratagem*, 5–16. On this front, Whaley also cites the sociologist A. George Gitter's study of hypocrisy, "Concerning the Believed and the Professed Images of Reality as Factors Influencing Behavior" (diss., American University, 1964).

15. Ray Monk, *Robert Oppenheimer: A Life Inside the Center* (New York: Knopf, 2014), 358.

16. "Many of the most successful practitioners" of deception during the war, Whaley says, "had a pragmatic flair for the art rather than a theoretical understanding of it," Whaley, *Stratagem*, 126.

17. Matthew Crowley, "A Distinguished Career: Abbott Henderson Thayer Exhibit to Open at the Hyde," *Post-Star* (New York), February 1, 1996.

18. Roy Behrens, *Camoupedia: A Compendium of Research on Art, Architecture, and Camouflage* (Dysart, IA: Bobolink Books, 2009), 7–8. The book's authors take pains to emphasize that artists, no less than biologists, have expertise that applies to the study of nature: "The entire matter has been in the hands of the wrong custodians. Appertaining solely to animals, it has naturally been considered part of the zoologists' province. But it properly belongs to the realm of *pictorial art*, and can be interpreted only by painters. For it deals wholly in optical illusion, and this is the very gist of a painter's life." Abbott Henderson Thayer and Gerald Handerson Thayer, *Concealing-Coloration in the Animal Kingdom* (New York: Macmillan, 1918), 9.

19. Behrens, *Camoupedia*, 7–8; Theodore Roosevelt, "Revealing and Concealing Coloration in Birds and Mammals," *Bulletin of the American Museum of Natural History* 30 (1911): 123.

20. Gerald Handerson Thayer, preface, in Thayer and Thayer, *Concealing-Coloration in the Animal Kingdom*, 2.

21. Behrens, *Camoupedia*, 8; Thayer and Thayer, *Concealing-Coloration in the Animal Kingdom*, 2. See also Elizabeth Kahn, *The Neglected Majority: Les Camoufleurs, Art History, and World War I* (Lanham, MD: University Press of America, 1984).

22. During World War I, Thayer's cousin, the painter Barry Faulkner, enlisted along with his artist friends and formed, together, a new American Camouflage Corps. The army's agreement to accept such a corps came only after tremendous effort, together with the support of a major who was also an architect. Early in the war, Thayer himself had tried to persuade the British War Office to invest in camouflage, but they wrote him off as an eccentric. Behrens, *Camoupedia*, 8; Barry Faulkner, *Sketches from an Artist's Life* (Dublin, NH: William L. Bauhan, 1973), 85–106.

23. Behrens, *Camoupedia*, 7–9.

24. Quoted in Behrens, *Camoupedia*, 8. Gertrude Stein, *The Autobiography of Alice B. Toklas* (New York: Vintage Books, 1960), 90. I'm using Stein's translation.

25. Cynthia Grabo, *A Handbook of Warning Intelligence, Volume II* (Washington: Department of Defense, Defense Intelligence Agency, 1972), 29, 4–5; Elizabeth Kolbert, "That's What You Think," *New Yorker*, February 27, 2017, 66–71.

26. Brown, *Bodyguard of Lies*, 619–20; Seymour Reit, *Masquerade: The Amazing Camouflage Deceptions of World War II* (New York: Hawthorn Books, 1978), 131–32.

27. Ben Macintyre, *Double Cross* (New York: Bloomsbury, 2012), 3–4; Peter Margaritis, *Countdown to D-Day: The German Perspective* (London: Casemate Publishers, 2019), 41–42.

28. Brown, *Bodyguard of Lies*, 462; Wolfgang Wegner, *The Naval Strategy of the World War*, trans. Holger Herwig (Annapolis, MD: Naval Institute Press, 1989).

29. Brown, *Bodyguard of Lies*, 462.

30. Reit, *Masquerade*, 23.

31. Brown, *Bodyguard of Lies*, 619–20.

32. The camouflage training school was originally at Hamilton Field near San Francisco, and moved to March Field, the site near Los Angeles, in 1943. An Engineer Camouflage Battalion was also on site: a unit of engineers tasked with building and testing new kinds of camouflage to trick the enemy. The film industry illusionists and the engineers worked together. Reit, *Masquerade*, 84–86.

33. Reit, *Masquerade*, 84–86.

34. Peter Rodenkyo, "Camouflage," *Life*, January 13, 1941, 39–40.

35. Peter Rodenkyo, *"Camouflage,"* 39; Fred Basten, *Max Factor: The Man Who Changed the Faces of the World* (New York: Arcade Publishing, 2016), 41–42.

36. Rodenkyo, "Camouflage," 39.

37. Camouflage also called for tricks of perception that only connoisseurs of fabrics, textures, and patterns knew. A military camoufleur with a background in interior design explained one such trick using a silk top hat as an example. If you brush the hat in the direction of the nap (or the lay of the fibers), then the nap will be smooth and therefore shiny. If you brush the hat against the direction of the nap, the nap will be rough and therefore opaque. The same material will reflect or absorb light, depending on how you treat it. So, too, different materials in nature, such as foliage and soil and sand, will appear light or dark in photographs, depending on how you treat their surfaces and how they reflect light. A camoufleur must know how to bend them, and the light, to his will. Rodenkyo, "Camouflage,"40–41.

38. Rodenkyo, "Camouflage," 40.

39. Rodenkyo, "Camouflage," 41.

40. Montagu, *The Man Who Never Was*, 18–20, 28–29.

41. Elyse Graham, "They Called Him 'Mr. Princeton': Frederic Fox '39," *Princeton Alumni Weekly*, July 10, 2019. See also Philip Gerard, *Secret Soldiers: How a Troupe of American Artists, Designers, and Sonic Wizards Won World War II's Battles of Deception Against the Germans* (New York: Plume, 2002).

42. Reit, *Masquerade*, 85–86.

43. "Historical Record of Deception in War Against Germany and Italy," Ministry of Defense, manuscript number DEFE 28/49, National Archives (1939–1945), 55. Hereafter cited as DEFE 28/49, with page numbers.

44. DEFE 28/49, 44.

45. DEFE 28/49, 56.

46. DEFE 28/49, 44.

47. M. E. Clifton James, *I Was Monty's Double* (London: Rider and Company, 1954), 11–13.

48. During his training period, James later recalled, MI5 sent at least one agent to test his ability to keep secrets:

> I remember going into a bar in Shaftesbury Avenue one evening on my way home to Hampstead. A young man standing nearby turned and stared at me.
>
> "Hullo, James, fancy running across you! I don't know if you remember me? We met at a party just before the war—at Mrs. Guy Nicholl's house in Southsea."
>
> I looked him up and down but couldn't place him at all. Certainly I had been playing at Southsea in 1939 and a Mrs. Guy Nicholl had thrown a party to which some of us actors had been invited. But I had no memory at all of this young fellow.

"What's yours?" he asked affably, and when I rather hesitantly accepted his offer he asked, "Are you on a spot of leave?"

I remembered Colonel Lester's warning not to drink or talk with strangers and I knew that my cue was to make some excuse and escape. But a spirit of perversity prompted me to stay and allow this young man to try his hand at pumping me while plying me with drinks.

At length I said: "I believe I do remember you now. At that party you were flirting with the youngest Nicholl daughter, Pat."

"I might have been," he admitted gaily.

"Smashing girl, wasn't she? Do you know where she is now?"

"I believe she's in the Wrens."

"No," I said, "You're wrong. She's in your imagination. The Nicholls never had any children." And with that I left him.

I feel pretty sure that MI5 had put him on my track to see if he could persuade me to talk.

James, *I Was Monty's Double*, 127, 33–34.

49. James, *I Was Monty's Double*, 33, 118.

50. James, *I Was Monty's Double*, 136.

51. James, *I Was Monty's Double*, 51–61, 88, 97–103.

52. On the aims of the double-cross system, see Masterman, *The Double-Cross System*, 8–9.

53. Agostino von Hassell and Sigrid MacRae, *Alliance of Enemies: The Untold Story of the Secret American and German Collaboration to End World War II* (New York: St. Martin's Press, 2006), 181.

54. Von Hassell and MacRae, *Alliance of Enemies*, 178; Tom Dunkell, *White Knights in the Black Orchestra: The Extraordinary Story of the Germans Who Resisted Hitler* (New York: Hachette, 2022), 315–17.

55. See, for example, "Nazi Brutality a Spur," *Kansas City Star*, February 9, 1944.

56. Von Hassell and MacRae, *Alliance of Enemies*, 178; Dunkell, *White Knights in the Black Orchestra*, 319.

57. Von Hassell and MacRae, *Alliance of Enemies*, 178–79, 347.

58. The Abwehr and the SD were both plagued by intelligence failures, but for very different reasons. The Abwehr lacked the kind of analysis unit the OSS had in R&A, as the Abwehr's purpose was not to analyze or evaluate information, but rather to collect it and prevent enemies from doing so. Ultimately, however, its failures were rooted in corruption. The Abwehr attracted a mixture of old military officers past their prime and young businessmen seeking to exploit their positions for personal gain. This culture of corruption, and the lack of loyalty that it inspired, likely played a role in the Abwehr's vulnerability to being infiltrated by double agents. The SD, on the other hand, tended to attract policemen. They were dangerous to *résistants* and spies, since their methods of interrogation were more brutal than the Abwehr's, and they delighted

in atrocities against the populations they were supposed to police. They were also famously loyal, in large part *because* of those atrocities. ("If he survives a German defeat," an SOE document said of SD agents, "his occupation will be gone; the profession in which he was trained and even his own country will be closed to him; and he himself will have joined the fugitives. . . . Whether they like it or not, their future subsists in their past actions. They are bound to their masters as much by a feeling of collective guilt as by any doctrinal attachment or sense of benefits received.") But they weren't unusually dangerous to intelligence *planners*, as they weren't inclined to scholarly intelligence analysis. For a contemporary analysis of the agents who went into the Abwehr and the SD, see, for example, "The German Secret Service," Security Service, manuscript number KV 3/5, National Archives (July 1–31, 1944), 10–22.

59. Maurice Buckmaster, *They Fought Alone: The True Story of SOE's Agents in Wartime France* (London: Biteback Publishing, 1958).

60. Derek Vaillant, *Across the Waves: How the United States and France Shaped the International Age of Radio* (Urbana: University of Illinois Press, 2017), 1326–31.

61. Cunningham, *Beaulieu*, 105; Buckmaster, *They Fought Alone*, 239. These aren't actual examples of *messages personnels*, just an illustration of their format.

62. Buckmaster, *They Fought Alone*, 239.

63. Brown, *Bodyguard of Lies*, 521–22.

64. Brown, *Bodyguard of Lies*, 517–19.

65. Brown, *Bodyguard of Lies*, 519.

66. Allied leadership outlined this strategy in a 1944 memo, "Cover and Deception in Air Force Operations, European Theater of Operations," Brown, *Bodyguard of Lies*, 522–23.

67. Brown, *Bodyguard of Lies*, 521–23.

68. Montagu, *The Man Who Never Was*, 20–23.

69. Montagu, *The Man Who Never Was*, 50–56.

70. Montagu, *The Man Who Never Was*, 52–54.

71. Buckmaster, *They Fought Alone*, 239.

72. Montagu, *The Man Who Never Was*, 41–42, 57–58.

73. Montagu, *The Man Who Never Was*, 81.

74. Buckmaster, *They Fought Alone*, 239–40.

75. Brown, *Bodyguard of Lies*, 459.

76. Griffis was also an executive at Madison Square Garden and a chain of bookstores, Brentano's, two holdings in a veritable media kingdom. In his later career as a diplomat, he once commented to King Farouk of Egypt that he had tried everything "except preach the Gospel and be a whore." The king replied, "I have never preached the Gospel myself." Stanton Griffis, *Lying in State* (New York: Doubleday, 1952), 9–10. See also Brown, *Bodyguard of Lies*, 469–70.

77. Griffis, *Lying in State*, 117.

78. Brown, *Bodyguard of Lies*, 469–70; Griffis, *Lying in State*, 115–21; William Breuer, *Hoodwinking Hitler: The Normandy Deception* (Westport, CT: Praeger, 1993), 134.

79. Brown, *Bodyguard of Lies*, 467–68.

80. Brown, *Bodyguard of Lies*, 467–68.

81. Buckmaster, *They Fought Alone*, 239.

82. Riols, *The Secret Ministry of Ag. & Fish*, 147.

83. Buckmaster, *They Fought Alone*, 240–41.

84. It was actually 960 sections of railroad, Riols, *The Secret Ministry of Ag. & Fish*, 147.

85. Brown, *Bodyguard of Lies*, 648–49.

86. Cunningham, *Beaulieu*, 77–79; Riols, *The Secret Ministry of Ag. & Fish*, 29–31.

87. Vibert, *Memoirs of a Jerseyman*, 52–54; R. J. Minney, *Carve Her Name with Pride* (London: George Newnes, 1956), 132–40.

88. Riols, *The Secret Ministry of Ag. & Fish*, 145–46.

89. Indeed, for each kind of fighting—by air, land, and sea—a different kind of weather was ideal, as the military historian Philip Flammer writes. The navy needed coastal winds of no more than 12 miles per hour and low waves, the air force needed scattered clouds or thick clouds at a height of at least 11,000 feet, and the army needed coastal winds of no more than 20 miles per hour and dry soil for heavy trucks. Philip Flammer, "Weather and the Normandy Invasion," *Military Review* (June 1961), 21; National Weather Service, "Estimating Wind Speed."

90. The tidal range along the Normandy coast is 19 feet. The landing couldn't happen at low tide, or the soldiers would be crossing a beach so wide as to be simply a killing floor; but it also couldn't happen at high tide, since the tide should still be rising as the landing ships came and went, so they wouldn't get grounded, Flammer, "Weather and the Normandy Invasion," 22.

91. Flammer, "Weather and the Normandy Invasion," 22–23.

92. Reit, *Masquerade*, 44–45; Giangreco and Moore, *Eyewitness D-Day*, 105–6.

93. Flammer, "Weather and the Normandy Invasion," 26.

94. Reit, *Masquerade*, 44–45; Brown, *Bodyguard of Lies*, 639.

95. Quoted in Grabo, *A Handbook of Warning Intelligence, Volume II*, 29, 27–28.

96. Flammer, "Weather and the Normandy Invasion," 27–28.

97. Giangreco and Moore, *Eyewitness D-Day*, 111; Brian Betham Schofield, *Operation Neptune: The Inside Story of Naval Operations for the Normandy Landings 1944* (Barnsley: Pen & Sword, 2008), 62–64.

98. Schofield, *Operation Neptune*, 64.

99. Gail Lumet Buckley, *American Patriots: The Story of Blacks in the Military from the Revolution to Desert Storm* (New York: Random House, 2002), 324.

100. Giangreco and Moore, *Eyewitness D-Day*, 105–7.

101. Reit, *Masquerade*, 44–45; Anthony Hall, *Operation Overlord: Day by Day* (Kent, UK: Grange Books, 2003), 113.

102. Brown, *Bodyguard of Lies*, 439.

103. Brown, *Bodyguard of Lies*, 647–48.

104. Brown, *Bodyguard of Lies*, 647–48.

105. Reit, *Masquerade*, 24–25; *Bodyguard of Lies*, 460; Edwin Hoyt, *The Invasion Before Normandy: The Secret Battle of Slapton Sands* (Lanham, MD: Scarborough House, 1999), 71–76.

106. Reit, *Masquerade*, 24–25.

107. Reit, *Masquerade*, 24–25.

108. Reit, *Masquerade*, 24–25.

109. Brown, *Bodyguard of Lies*, 683.

110. Brown, *Bodyguard of Lies*, 685–87.

111. Reit, *Masquerade*, 59.

112. Brown, *Bodyguard of Lies*, 460, 685–87.

113. Reit, *Masquerade*, 129–32.

114. Reit, *Masquerade*, 129–32.

115. Michael Nieberg, *The Blood of Free Men: The Liberation of Paris, 1944* (New York: Basic Books, 2012), 1–2.

116. Nieberg, *The Blood of Free Men*, 3.

117. Nieberg, *The Blood of Free Men*, 4.

118. Nieberg, *The Blood of Free Men*, 8.

119. Nieberg, *The Blood of Free Men*, 199.

120. HS 8/955, 90.

121. Nieberg, *The Blood of Free Men*, 199.

122. Andrew Molnar et al., *Undergrounds in Insurgent, Revolutionary, and Resistance Warfare* (Washington, DC: Special Operations Research Office, American University, 1963), 110. See also Buckmaster, *They Fought Alone*, 239–42.

123. Buckmaster, *They Fought Alone*, 239–42.

124. Buckmaster, *They Fought Alone*, 239–42. The identification of Hervé as Robert Hanote appears in "France: DF Symbols; Codes for Escape Lines," Special Operations Executive, manuscript number HS 8/1003, National Archives (1940–1945), 29, and "Circuits and Missions: PIERRE/JACQUES/HENRI. With French Documents," Special Operations Executive, manuscript number HS 8/161, National Archives (1944–1945), 2. The latter has the biographical information I use here. Other stories and identities of Hervé appear in the SIS archives; it was a code name used for several people.

125. Buckmaster, *They Fought Alone*, 239–42.

126. Nieberg, *The Blood of Free Men*, 199.

127. Victor Brombert, *Trains of Thought: Memories of a Stateless Youth* (New York: W.W. Norton & Company, 2002), 286–87.

9: LIES AND DAMNED LIES

1. James Sachs Plaut, "Activity of the Einsatzstab Reichsleiter Rosenberg in France: C.I.R. No. 1" Art Looting Investigation Unit, National Archives, Maryland (August 1945), 17–18; T. R. Brooke, Monuments, Fine Arts &

Archives Division, A.M.G. Rome Region, "Memorandum on Archives in Rome During the First Four Weeks of Occupation," July 2, 1944.

2.   William L. M. Burke was an art historian who later became the director of the Princeton Index of Christian Art and then a professor at the University of Iowa. Letter to William B. Dinsmoor from William L. M. Burke of the American Commission for the Protection and Salvage of Artistic and Historic Monuments in War Areas, National Gallery of Art, Washington, D.C., June 10, 1944. He did the reading at the Library of Congress, but his office was in the National Gallery of Art.

3.   On the melting of bronze statues, see, for example, Rorimer, *Survival*, 69.

4.   Lane Faison's draft card.

5.   Sanka Knox, "Curator, 36, Named by Metropolitan," *New York Times*, May 27, 1948; Mary Jane Brooks, "Curator Tells of Recovering Art Works Stolen by Nazis," *Nashville Banner*, April 28, 1951.

6.   "Old and New Art Mixed in Exhibit," *New York Times*, August 13, 1948.

7.   "Oral History Interview with Lane Faison Jr., 14 December 1981," Archives of American Art, Smithsonian Institution, Washington, DC; Reinhold Heller, "The Expressionist Challenge: James Plaut and the Institute of Contemporary Art," in The Institute of Contemporary Art, *Dissent: The Issue of Modern Art in Boston* (Boston: Institute of Contemporary Art, 1985), 36.

8.   Christine Temin, "Foreign Exchange," *Boston Globe*, January 3, 1933.

9.   Jonathan Petropoulos, *Göring's Man in Paris: The Story of a Nazi Art Plunderer and His World* (New Haven: Yale University Press, 1990), 4–5.

10.   See, for example, the statements of MFA&A officer Fred Shipman in "Damage to Italian Records Held Light," *Evening Sun*, May 17, 1944, and Helen Myers, "Shipman Gives First Aid to Archives," *Poughkeepsie Journal*, July 23, 1944.

11.   "Rare Documents as Wrapping Paper," *Liverpool Daily Post*, April 19, 1944.

12.   Brooke, "Memorandum on Archives in Rome During the First Four Weeks of Occupation," 3.

13.   After a bombing, a lawyer had searched for the records in the rubble of a municipal building and carted them out in a wheelbarrow. Myers, "Shipman Gives First Aid to Archives."

14.   "Florence's Art Treasures Dispersed in Country," *The Guardian*, August 9, 1944; J. H. Hilldring, "Excerpt for Civil Affairs Summary Re: Arts and Monuments," August 28, 1944.

15.   From this, they learned about the movement of library collections, the names of art dealers and other insiders who should be captured for interrogation, the addresses of archives, the contents of those archives, and more. Letter to William B. Dinsmoor from William L. M. Burk, June 10, 1944.

16.   Owen J. Roberts et al., American Commission for the Protection and Salvage of Artistic and Historic Monuments in War Areas, *Report of the American Commission for the Protection and Salvage of Artistic and Historic Monuments*

in War Areas (Washington: United States Government Historical Reports on War Administration, 1946), 38–40. The number of Art Unit members is variously reported as either six or ten, which probably just reflects personnel changes over the course of the Art Unit's existence. See, for example, Art Looting Investigation Unit Final Report, May 1, 1946, 1. Hereafter cited as Art Unit Final Report 1946, with page numbers.

17. Art Unit Final Report 1946, 1–2.

18. Brooks, "Curator Tells of Recovering Art Works Stolen by Nazis."

19. Art Unit Final Report 1946, 3; Miedl Report, Monuments, Fine Arts, and Archives Section, Ardelia Hall Collection, National Archives, December 13, 1945, 1–17.

20. Art Unit Final Report 1946, 3–4; Interrogation Report on Wilhelm Jakob Mohnen, April 30, 1945.

21. Winks, *Cloak & Gown*, 304. See also Theodore Sizer, "John Marshall Phillips," *Bulletin of the Associates in Fine Arts at Yale University* 21, no. 1 (October 1953): 2–3.

22. On the Vermeer forgeries, see, for example, P. B. Coremans, *Van Meegeren's Faked Vermeers and De Hooghs* (London: Cassell & Co., 1949); Jonathan Lopez, *The Man Who Made Vermeers: Unvarnishing the Legend of Master Forger Han van Meegeren* (New York: Harcourt, 2008); and Edward Dolnick, *The Forger's Spell: A True Story of Vermeer, Nazis, and the Greatest Art Hoax of the Twentieth Century* (New York: HarperCollins, 2008).

23. Art Unit Final Report 1946, 4.

24. "Search for Art," *Kansas City Times*, May 21, 1945.

25. Richard Rubenstein describes, in this vein, the self-understanding of the corporate professionals at I. G. Farben, a chemical company that had manufacturing facilities at Auschwitz: "The business of mass murder was both a highly complex and a successful corporate venture. The men who carried out the business part of the venture were not uniformed thugs or hoodlums. They were highly competent, respectable corporate executives who were doing what they had been trained to do—run large corporations successfully. As long as their institutions functioned efficiently, they had no qualms whatsoever concerning the uses to which they were put." Richard Rubenstein, *The Cunning of History: The Holocaust and the American Future* (New York: Harper & Row, 1978), 62–63. See also Stuart Hills, "Epilogue: Corporate Violence and the Banality of Evil," in Stuart Hills, ed., *Corporate Violence: Injury and Death for Profit* (Totowa, NJ: Rowman and Littlefield, 1987), 187–206.

26. Walter Farmer, *The Safekeepers: A Memoir of the Arts at the End of World War II* (New York: Walter de Gruyter, 2000), 44.

27. Lincoln Kirstein, "Arts & Monuments," in *The Poems of Lincoln Kirstein* (New York: Atheneum, 1987), 264.

28. Lincoln Kirstein, "The Quest of the Golden Lamb," *Town & Country*, September 1945, 182–83.

29. Kirstein, "The Quest of the Golden Lamb," 182. See also Noah Charney, *Stealing the Mystic Lamb: The True Story of the World's Most Coveted Masterpiece* (New York: PublicAffairs, 2010): i–xiii, 237–38.

30. "Semi-Monthly Report on Monuments, Fine Arts and Archives, for period ending 31 March 1945," 47, National Archives catalog ID 1561462.

31. Kirstein, "The Quest of the Golden Lamb," 182–83.

32. Sumner Crosby, "'Venus Fixers' Won Their War, Too," *New York Times Magazine*, January 20, 1946, 14, 44; "German Disposal of Works of Art," memo to Sumner Crosby, Roberts Commission (October 30, 1944).

33. Then again, although the French state understood itself to be the owner of the art, the art had been looted from an art dealership, Wildenstein & Co., that had Jewish owners. Sumner Crosby, "Report No. 3," American Commission for the Protection and Salvage of Artistic and Historic Monuments in War Areas," *American Commission for the Protection and Salvage of Artistic and Historic Monuments in War Areas*, November 6, 1944..

34. "German Disposal of Works of Art," 1–3.

35. "German Disposal of Works of Art," 1–2.

36. "German Disposal of Works of Art," 1–2.

37. "German Disposal of Works of Art," 5–7.

38. "German Disposal of Works of Art," 5–7.

39. "German Disposal of Works of Art," 2–5.

40. Thomas D. Bazley, *Crimes of the Art World* (Santa Barbara: Praeger, 2010), 87.

41. Gladys Hamlin, "European Art Collections and the War," *College Art Journal* 4, no. 3 (March 1945): 157–58; "German Disposal of Works of Art," 1–6.

42. "German Disposal of Works of Art," 5–6.

43. Philip Morgan, *Hitler's Collaborators: Choosing Between Bad and Worse in Nazi-Occupied Western Europe* (Oxford: Oxford University Press, 2018), 2–3.

44. Kenneth Alford, *Hermann Göring and the Nazi Art Collection: The Looting of Europe's Art Treasures and Their Dispersal After World War II* (Jefferson, NC: McFarland & Company, 2012), 459.

45. Alford, *Hermann Göring and the Nazi Art Collection*, 556–66.

46. "German Disposal of Works of Art," 5.

47. Alford, *Hermann Göring and the Nazi Art Collection*, 408–24, 468–77.

48. "French Works of Art Obtained by Reichsmarshall Hermann Goering," Seventh Army Interrogation Center, May 19, 1945, National Archives catalog ID 1537311.

49. Robert Edsel, *The Monuments Men: Allied Heroes, Nazi Treasure, and the Greatest Treasure Hunt in History* (New York: Little, Brown, 2009), 12–13; Volker Ullrich, *Hitler: Ascent, 1889–1939*, trans. Jefferson Chase (New York: Alfred A. Knopf, 2016), 27.

50. Rorimer, *Survival*, 204.

51. Their rationale for setting the fire in Naples was to punish civilians for a German soldier's death. "Looting," 7–8; Rebecca Knuth, *Libricide: The Regime-*

Sponsored Destruction of Books and Libraries in the Twentieth Century (Westport, CT: Praeger, 2003), 53; Peter Harclerode, *The Lost Masters: The Looting of Europe's Treasurehouses* (London: Orion, 1999), 90–91.

52. Letter from Leonard Woolley to Lord Harold Macmillan, November 2, 1944, National Archives ID: 1518822.

53. Letter from Leonard Woolley.

54. Tonya Gruber, personal communication, July 31, 2022; Charney, *Stealing the Mystic Lamb*, 250; Thomas Carr Howe, *Salt Mines and Castles: The Discovery and Restitution of Looted European Art* (New York: Bobbs-Merrill, 1946): 154–56. Howe is also the source of the translated phrase.

55. Howe, *Salt Mines and Castles*, 154–56; Charney, *Stealing the Mystic Lamb*, 257–59.

56. The details of this chase differ from one contemporary account to another. See, for example, Crosby, "'Venus Fixers' Won Their War, Too," 14, 44; Howe, *Salt Mines and Castles*, 24–25; Roberts et al., *Report of the American Commission for the Protection and Salvage of Artistic and Historic Monuments in War Areas*, 141–42; and Rorimer, *Survival*, 149–51.

57. Howe, *Salt Mines and Castles*, 134–35.

58. Howe, *Salt Mines and Castles*, 141, 148–51; Edsel, *The Monuments Men*, 381.

59. Howe, *Salt Mines and Castles*, 136, 148–51.

60. Howe, *Salt Mines and Castles*, 148–51.

61. Howe, *Salt Mines and Castles*, 148–51.

62. Howe, *Salt Mines and Castles*, 148–51; personal communication, Tonya Gruber.

63. Howe, *Salt Mines and Castles*, 148–57.

64. Howe, *Salt Mines and Castles*, 151–52.

65. The mine has a little chapel inside the tunnels where the miners hang decorative boughs of pine. Down there, a bough will stay green and pungent for five years. Personal communication, Tonya Gruber.

66. The building held about fifteen Nazi officials and collaborators, those whom the Art Unit identified as the key figures in the Reich's art looting. Petropoulos, *Göring's Man in Paris*, 107, 190; Howe, *Salt Mines and Castles*, 128.

67. Petropoulos, *Göring's Man in Paris*, 1–4.

68. Personal communication, Jonathan Petropoulos, November 29, 2021.

69. "Handbook: Interrogation of Refugees," Special Operations Executive, manuscript number HS 8/850, National Archives (1943), 5.

70. "Interrogation of Prisoners: Funding," Cabinet Office, manuscript number CAB 301/41, National Archives (1942).

71. "Handbook: Interrogation of Refugees," 5.

72. Petropoulos, *Göring's Man in Paris*, 1–2.

73. Petropoulos, *Göring's Man in Paris*, 1–2.

74. Petropoulos, *Göring's Man in Paris*, 3.

75. Petropoulos, *Göring's Man in Paris*, 107.

76. Petropoulos, *Göring's Man in Paris*, 107; James Sachs Plaut, "Interrogation Report No. 6, Bruno Lohse," August 15, 1945, 1. Hereafter cited as Plaut-Lohse 1945, with page numbers.

77. James Sachs Plaut, "Interrogation report of Karl Kress," August 15, 1945, 1. Hereafter cited as Plaut-Kress 1945, with page numbers.

78. James Sachs Plaut, "Gustav Rochlitz, Detailed Interrogation Report No. 4," August 1945, 11–12. Hereafter cited as Plaut-Rochlitz 1945, with page numbers.

79. James Sachs Plaut, "Detailed Interrogation Report No. 3: Robert Scholz," August 1945, 1, 3–4. Hereafter cited as Plaut-Scholz 1945, with page numbers.

80. Plaut-Rochlitz 1945, 1–12.

81. Lane Faison, "Interrogation report of Hermann Voss," September 15, 1945, 9–10. Hereafter cited as Faison-Voss 1945, with page numbers.

82. Faison-Voss 1945, 22. Scholz protested often to his interrogators that the Rosenberg Task Force worked under complete "legality." Plaut-Scholz 1945, 3–4.

83. Coremans, *Van Meegeren's Faked Vermeers and De Hooghs*, 32–33. I'm using the phrase "He was a Nazi" in the sense that he was a supporter and sympathizer of the Nazis; he wasn't a literal member of the Nazi party. On Van Meegeren's politics, see, for example, Lopez, *The Man Who Made Vermeers*.

84. Farmer, *The Safekeepers*, 68.

85. Farmer, *The Safekeepers*, 68–72.

86. Charles Kuhn, "German Paintings in the National Gallery: A Protest," *College Art Journal* 5, no. 2 (January 1946): 78.

87. Farmer, *The Safekeepers*, 56–57, 66.

88. Minutes, "Special Meeting of the American Commission for the Protection and Salvage of Artistic and Historic Monuments in War Areas," Philadelphia, Pennsylvania (September 25, 1945); George Stout, letter, to Tom Howe, January 6, 1946, quoted in Farmer, *The Safekeepers*, 70.

89. Wayne Sandholtz, *Prohibiting Plunder: How Norms Change* (Oxford: Oxford University Press, 2007), 161; Farmer, *The Safekeepers*, 142, 158–60; Konstantin Akinsha and Grigorii Kozlov, "Spoils of War: The Soviet Union's Hidden Art Treasures," *ARTnews* 90, April 1991, 130–41; Konstantin Akinsha and Grigorii Kozlov, *Beautiful Loot: The Soviet Plunder of Europe's Art Treasures* (New York: Random House, 1995), 50, 204–30.

90. Oral history interview with Charles Parkhurst, conducted by Buck Pennington, Archives of American Art, October 27, 1982. Hereafter cited as Parkhurst 1982.

91. Farmer, *The Safekeepers*, 65.

92. Farmer, *The Safekeepers*, 55–56.

93. Parkhurst 1982.

94. Wiesbaden Manifesto, November 7, 1945, reprinted in Farmer, *The Safekeepers*, 147–52.

95. Farmer, *The Safekeepers*, 58–59.

96. Letter from Edith Standen to David Finley, August 9, 1946, Edith Standen Papers, National Gallery.

97. Walter Farmer, "Will Anything Survive?," undated manuscript, 16–17, Edith Standen papers.

98. Farmer, *The Safekeepers*, 72.

99. Oral history interview with S. Lane Faison, Smithsonian Archives of American Art, December 14, 1981.

100. For these and other examples, see *Art Crime: Terrorists, Tomb Raiders, Forgers, and Thieves*, ed. Noah Charney (London: Palgrave Macmillan, 2016).

101. Walter Schellenberg, *Invasion 1940: The Nazi Invasion Plan for Britain* (London: St. Ermin's Press, 2000), 29–30.

102. Schellenberg, *Invasion 1940*, 29–30.

103. Roberts et al., *Report of the American Commission for the Protection and Salvage of Artistic and Historic Monuments in War Areas*, 1946, 39–40.

104. Jonathan Petropoulos, "Five Uncomfortable and Difficult Topics Relating to the Restitution of Nazi-Looted Art," in *New German Critique* 130, no. 44, 1 (February 2017): 128; Petropoulos, *Göring's Man in Paris*, 285–86.

105. Petropoulos, "Five Uncomfortable and Difficult Topics Relating to the Restitution of Nazi-Looted Art," 128; Petropoulos, *Göring's Man in Paris*, 285–86.

106. Jean Zimmerman, MFA&A, memorandum to "Director, Office of Military Government for Bavaria (Attn: MFA&A Officer) APO 170, Munich," subject, "Julius Streicher Art Collection," April 16, 1946.

107. You can view pictures of Streicher's surviving work as a watercolorist on auction sites online.

108. Petropoulos, "Five Uncomfortable and Difficult Topics Relating to the Restitution of Nazi-Looted Art," 128; Petropoulos, *Göring's Man in Paris*, 286.

109. See, for example, Harry Mitchell, Acting Chief, Legal Advice Branch, United States Office of Military Government for Germany, memorandum, "Confiscation of Paintings, Berlin, Germany," December 7, 1948.

110. Faison collaborated in this supervision with one of his coworkers, the art historian Theodore Heinrich. Some of the art was burned at the Weisbaden Collecting Point. Petropoulos, "Five Uncomfortable and Difficult Topics Relating to the Restitution of Nazi-Looted Art," 128.

10: SEARCHING FOR A NEW PLOT

1. Johann von Goethe, *Faust: A Tragedy*, trans. Martin Greenberg (New Haven, CT: Yale University Press, 2014), 69.

2. Rebecca Schwartz, "The Making of the History of the Atomic Bomb: Henry DeWolf Smyth and the Historiography of the Manhattan Project" (diss., Princeton University, 2008), 57–63.

3. Schwartz, "The Making of the History of the Atomic Bomb," 57–64; "The Talk of the Town," *New Yorker*, January 19, 1946, 14–15.

4.   One problem along the way: Princeton University Press wanted to start publishing the book right away, but didn't have enough paper to print it. Even after the end of the war, the paper scarcity that made British leaders propose using the holdings of the nation's archives for paper scraps persisted. Smyth later wrote, "Almost everyone in publishing at the time used the hyperbole that anyone might find a few sheets of gold lying around but only the super-lucky could find a spare sheet of paper." Eventually, Princeton managed to scrounge up two freight cars of paper, enough to print a first edition. Schwartz, "The Making of the History of the Atomic Bomb," 92–97.

5.   Henry DeWolf Smyth, *Atomic Energy for Military Purposes: The Official Report on the Development of the Atomic Bomb Under the Auspices of the United States Government, 1940–1945* (Princeton, NJ: Princeton University Press, 1945). The government distributed copies of the report before Princeton University Press published it for the book marketplace. "People Who Read and Write," *New York Times*, September 9, 1945. "The Talk of the Town," *New Yorker*, 14–15.

6.   Schwartz, "The Making of the History of the Atomic Bomb," iii; Smyth, *Atomic Energy for Military Purposes*.

7.   Schwartz, "The Making of the History of the Atomic Bomb," iii. As an example of the funding that immediately flowed to physics departments after the war: in August 1946, Princeton University announced that it had started a partnership with the Navy, worth $120,000 per year—about $1.8 million per year today—for a program researching nuclear physics, which Henry DeWolf Smyth would supervise. "Princeton Gets Project," *New York Times*, August 20, 1946.

8.   Donovan issued the executive order that disbanded the OSS in late September; the OSS disbanded on October 1.

9.   Selwyn Jepson, *Outrun the Constable* (New York: Doubleday & Company, 1948), 47.

10.   Winks, *Cloak & Gown*, 149–50; "Kuhn Appointed JE Dean; To Succeed Curtiss in July," *Yale Daily News*, April 19, 1965.

11.   The reprint publisher Hawley Publications was also part of this partnership. "Books—Authors," *New York Times*, August 24, 1945; "People Who Read and Write," *New York Times*, September 9, 1945.

12.   Sherman Kent, *Strategic Intelligence for American World Policy* (Princeton, NJ: Princeton University Press, 1966).

13.   Ford, "A Tribute to Sherman Kent," 4.

14.   Ford, "A Tribute to Sherman Kent," 3; William Jackson, "Military Intelligence," *New York Times*, May 1, 1949.

15.   Ford, "A Tribute to Sherman Kent," 4.

16.   Ford, "A Tribute to Sherman Kent," 4.

17.   Ford, "A Tribute to Sherman Kent," 4–5.

18.   Quoted in Ford, "A Tribute to Sherman Kent," 6.

19. "Over the years, Sherm has himself contributed some nine articles, eleven book reviews, and one other review (of the worst book he said he had ever reviewed), which was so steaming it was not published—although a copy remains in the *Studies* files and in the Historical Intelligence Collection," Ford, "A Tribute to Sherman Kent," 7.

20. Winks, *Cloak & Gown*, 457–61.

21. Winks, *Cloak & Gown*, 457–61; The White House, transcript, "The President's News Conference," October 4, 1951, Truman Library.

22. Winks, *Cloak & Gown*, 457–61; Gary Thoenen, "Secret Yale Survey Spots Security Leak," *Yale Daily News*, October 5, 1951. See also "Dunham Confirms Part in Yale Security Probe," *Yale Daily News*, October 6, 1951.

23. Winks, *Cloak & Gown*, 457–61. As the historian Robin Winks, who gives an entertaining account of this episode, points out, the scholars drew the most secret information in their report not from the newspapers and magazines that Truman sought to censor with his executive order, but from the *Congressional Record*, which is *also* public information.

24. Winks, *Cloak & Gown*, 457–61.

25. Winks, *Cloak & Gown*, 457–61.

26. Coon wrote the letter in 1945. He returned to Harvard in the spring of 1946.

27. Some years later, he grumbled about a "competitor" to his anthropology textbook: a "Statement on Human Rights" that the American Anthropological Association had submitted to the United Nations. The part of the statement that offended him, in particular, was "Respect for differences between cultures is validated by the scientific fact that no technique of qualitatively evaluating cultures has been discovered." Coon objected that, obviously, *his* techniques qualitatively proved the superiority of some cultures to others: "This statement is a logical fallacy. It is like saying that before it had been proven that the earth is a globe it had to have been flat." Coon, *Adventures and Discoveries*, 200–201.

28. Quoted in Anthony Cave Brown, *The Last Hero: Wild Bill Donovan* (New York: Random House, 1982), 269–70. A full reproduction of the letter appears in David Price, *Anthropological Intelligence: The Deployment and Neglect of American Anthropology in the Second World War* (Durham, NC: Duke University Press, 2008), 255–59.

29. Coon, *Adventures and Discoveries*, 192.

30. Derek Davis, "Carleton Coon, Chronicler of Man," *Daily Pennsylvanian*, 71, 92, March 6, 1958; Coon, *Adventures and Discoveries*, 202–5.

31. Price, *Anthropological Intelligence*, 272–74.

32. The Nuremberg Code, which the war crimes tribunal at Nuremberg released in 1947, provided directions for physicians conducting research on human subjects, stressing the importance of avoiding unnecessary pain and obtaining voluntary, informed consent from the subject. Although it was intended for physicians, it had a far-reaching impact on all the human sciences. David H. Price, "A Short History of American Anthropological Ethics, Codes,

Principles, and Responsibilities—Professional and Otherwise" in *Anthropological Ethics in Context: An Ongoing Dialogue*, ed. Dena Plemmons and Alex Barker (New York: Routledge, 2016), 25.

33. Price, "A Short History of American Anthropological Ethics, Codes, Principles, and Responsibilities," 24–25.

34. Price, "A Short History of American Anthropological Ethics, Codes, Principles, and Responsibilities," 24–25.

35. John P. Jackson, Jr., "In Ways Unacademical: The Reception of Carleton S. Coon's 'The Origin of Races,'" *Journal of the History of Biology* 34, no. 2 (Summer 2001), 247.

36. Pat Shipman, *The Evolution of Racism: Human Differences and the Use and Abuse of Science* (New York: Simon & Schuster, 1994), 210–12, quoted in Jackson, "In Ways Unacademical," 249.

37. Coon, *Adventures and Discoveries*, 334–35.

38. Just to give a sense of *how far* the tide of his discipline had turned against him, the previous year, a different professional body of anthropologists, the American Anthropological Association, had passed its own resolution against the book, with a decisive vote of 192 in favor and 0 against: "The American Anthropological Association repudiates statements now appearing in the United States that Negroes are biologically and in innate mental ability inferior to whites, and reaffirms the fact that there is no scientifically established evidence to justify the exclusion of any race from the rights guaranteed by the Constitution of the United States. The basic principles of equality of opportunity and equality before the law are compatible with all that is known about human biology. All races possess the abilities needed to participate fully in the democratic way of life and in modern technological civilization." Jackson, "In Ways Unacademical," 263–66; Coon, *Adventures and Discoveries*, 34–55.

39. Coon didn't say this at the meeting or in his memoir, but he'd exchanged frequent letters with the author of the book while the latter was writing it. The author was a businessman, not an anthropologist, and Coon, who was his relative, suggested ways to launder the racist arguments in the book so that they might look more scientifically respectable. In other words, he knew the scholarship was irresponsible, he tried to help the author hide the fact that it was irresponsible, and he concealed that he'd done so in an attempt to look like his support for the book was scientifically objective. Coon, *Adventures and Discoveries*, 34–35; Ronald Ladouceur, "'All with Stories to Sell': Carleton S. Coon, Bentley Glass, Marston Bates, and the Struggle by Life Scientists in the United States to Construct a Social Mission after World War II" (master's thesis, Empire State College, 2008), 30–31.

40. Michael Gordin, *Scientific Babel: How Science Was Done Before and After Global English* (Chicago: University of Chicago Press, 2015), 192.

41. Leopold Infeld, *Quest: The Evolution of a Scientist* (New York: Doubleday, Doran & Co, Inc., 1941), 323.

42. Mark McGurl, *The Program Era: Postwar Fiction and the Rise of Creative Writing* (Cambridge, MA: Harvard University Press, 2009), 281–82.

43. Peter Galison, *Image and Logic: A Material Culture of Microphysics* (Chicago: University of Chicago Press, 1997), 259–60.

44. Guglielmo, "The Contribution of Economists to Military Intelligence During World War II," 144–45.

45. Alan Turing, in England, helped to lead the wartime use of early digital computers for codebreaking, and after the war, he became an important theorist of computing. Today, we describe a computer as a *Turing machine* with a *von Neumann architecture*. Claude E. Shannon, "Communication Theory of Secrecy Systems," *Bell System Technical Journal* 28, no. 4 (October 1949): 656–715; Jimmy Soni and Rob Goodman, *A Mind at Play: How Claude Shannon Invented the Information Age* (New York: Simon & Schuster, 2017), 131–33, 142; William Aspray, *John von Neumann and the Origins of Modern Computing* (Cambridge, MA: MIT Press, 1990), 25–27. Also see, for example, Mar Hicks, *Programmed Inequality: How Britain Discarded Women Technologists and Lost Its Edge in Computing* (Cambridge, MA: MIT Press, 2018).

46. To be sure, close reading had famous champions at Yale, which had a very well-stocked library. But Yale's English Department abounded with former intelligence agents—not just Curtiss, but also Norman Holmes Pearson, Frederick Hilles, Eugene Waith, and Brad Welles, among others. Winks, *Cloak & Gown*, 257–58.

47. The history of the book isn't the same thing as the bibliographical study of the provenance of books for the purpose of selling or acquiring them.

48. Economists also found surprising food for thought in fictions about spycraft, many of them written by scholars who had once been spies. The Yale economist Thomas Schelling, who worked on behalf of the Marshall Plan in Europe while taking his PhD from Harvard, built a career on the economics of covert and overt warfare. Schelling said he developed his theories of bargaining and negotiation by reading, among other things, spy novels: "I read a lot of espionage stories. John le Carré used to spend a lot of time discussing, in his novels, 'If the West has a Soviet spy and the East has an American spy and they want to trade, how do you trade? How do you make sure that, when it's time to deliver the spy, they bring forth the spy they agreed to trade with you?'" Thomas Schelling, conversation with Richard Swedborg, Institute for Futures Studies, published June 11, 2013.

49. Elyse Graham, "The P Source," *Princeton Alumni Weekly*, December 2020.

50. Allen Dulles, speech at Princeton University, February 6, 1962, Allen Dulles papers, Princeton University. Quoted in Graham, "The P Source."

51. Allen Dulles, letter dated January 12, 1967, Allen Dulles Papers, Princeton University.

52. See, for example, Andrew Marantz, "Inside the Daily Stormer's Style Guide," *New Yorker*, January 15, 2018.

53. Frances Stonor Saunders, *The Cultural Cold War: The CIA and the World of Arts and Letters* (New York: New Press, 2000), 267.

54. Eric Bennett, *Workshops of Empire: Stegner, Engle, and American Creative Writing During the Cold War* (Iowa City: University of Iowa Press, 2015), 87–99.

55. Bennett, *Workshops of Empire*, 87–99. See also, for example, Saunders, *The Cultural Cold War*; and Louis Menand, *The Free World: Art and Thought in the Cold War* (New York: Farrar, Straus and Giroux, 2021).

56. F. Clifton Berry, Jr., *Inside the CIA: The Architecture, Art, & Atmosphere of America's Premier Intelligence Agency* (Montgomery, AL: Community Communications, 1997), 10–38.

57. Ward Warren and Emma Sullivan, "The Historical Intelligence Collection," *Studies in Intelligence* 37, no. 5 (1994): 91.

58. Warren and Sullivan, "The Historical Intelligence Collection," 91–93.

59. Warren and Sullivan, "The Historical Intelligence Collection," 91–93.

60. Winks, *Cloak & Gown*, 482–83. For an account of Holt's World War II exploits, see Jim Kahn, "A UW History Professor's Little-Known Story of Heroism at War," *University of Washington Magazine*, March 2013.

61. Pinkerton caused a famous intelligence failure when he told his superiors that the Confederate army was much larger than it actually was, setting off a domino effect of military miscalculations that gravely imperiled the Union. The problem, the CIA historian Harold Ford has suggested, lay in Pinkerton's very specialized background as a downtown gumshoe. He was used to shadowing suspected thieves, forgers, and confidence men: searching their belongings, questioning their servants, sending female undercover agents to befriend their wives and pry loose details of their crimes. He had no idea how to approximate the size of a military force. Harold P. Ford, *Estimative Intelligence* (McLean, VA: The Association of Former Intelligence Officers, 1993), 11–12. On Pinkerton's training as a private eye, see, for example, James A. MacKay, *Allan Pinkerton: The First Private Eye* (New York: J. Wiley & Sons, 1996). On Black intelligence agents during the Civil War, see, for example, P. K. Rose, "The Civil War: Black American Contributions to Union Intelligence," *Studies in Intelligence* 42, no. 5 (Winter 1998–1999): 1–7.

62. Benjamin Schmidt, "The Humanities Are in Crisis," *The Atlantic*, August 23, 2018.

63. In 2023, Britain's Ministry of Justice proposed a plan to digitize around one hundred million wills and then get rid of the originals. This is a bad idea for many reasons, one of which is that digital copies are lost remarkably easily. See, for example, Robert Booth, "Ministry of Justice Plan to Destroy Historical Wills Is 'Insane,' Say Experts," *The Guardian*, December 18, 2023.

64. See, for example, Adrian Daub, *What Tech Calls Thinking: An Inquiry into the Intellectual Bedrock of Silicon Valley* (New York: Farrar, Straus and Giroux, 2020).

INDEX